Hospitality Marketing

Hospitality Marketing

An introduction

David Bowie and Francis Buttle

ELSEVIER
BUTTERWORTH
HEINEMANN

AMSTERDAM   BOSTON   HEIDELBERG   LONDON   NEW YORK   OXFORD
PARIS   SAN DIEGO   SAN FRANCISCO   SINGAPORE   SYDNEY   TOKYO

Elsevier Butterworth-Heinemann
Linacre House, Jordan Hill, Oxford OX2 8DP
200 Wheeler Road, Burlington, MA 01803

First published 2004

British Library Cataloguing in Publication Data
A catalogue record for this book is available from the British Library

Library of Congress Cataloguing in Publication Data
A catalogue record for this book is available from the Library of Congress

ISBN 0 7506 5245 4

For information on all Elsevier Butterworth-Heinemann
publications visit our website at http://books.elsevier.com

Typeset by Newgen Imaging Systems (P) Ltd., Chennai, India
Printed and bound in Italy

For Julie, Olive, James
and Rowan, Cherry and James
DB

For my parents Bill and Mary, and Dale and Nick
FB

Contents

Preface

Most readers of this textbook will be university undergraduate or college students studying hospitality and/or tourism marketing for the first time. Our main objective in writing the book has been to provide you with an easy-to-read text, which presents a review of modern marketing theory in the context of marketing the hospitality industry. Examples from the industry are provided to illustrate real-life practice and give you a better understanding of hospitality marketing.

The book has the following special features:

- A unique structure, which divides marketing activities into before, during and after the customers' experience of the hospitality encounter. This helps you to understand what has to be done to attract customers, provide them with an experience that meets their expectations, and motivate them to return.
- Fifteen chapters, one for each of the key elements you need to understand about marketing.
- Each chapter contains learning activities, which include Internet searches of relevant company websites and visits to hospitality units as a customer to collect information – you will then need to analyze and evaluate your findings.
- Its own website (http://books.elsevier.com/companions/0750652454), which contains a student section with further information, case studies and hospitality contact details. For tutors, there is a separate section, which provides additional teaching materials.

Structure

The structure of the book is divided into the following sections:

- *Part A: Introduction.* A single chapter, which introduces the key concepts of marketing in the hospitality industry, including market demand, the marketing concept, the special characteristics of service industries, the PESTE environment and the hospitality marketing mix.
- *Part B: Pre-encounter marketing.* This part of the text consists of eight chapters and discusses all the marketing activities which companies have to carry out to attract customers to experience the hospitality offer. Chapters include marketing research; understanding and segmenting customers; competitive strategies; developing, locating, pricing, distributing and communicating the offer.
- *Part C: Encounter marketing.* This section comprises three chapters, which are concerned with managing the customer experience, while consuming the hospitality offer. They include managing the physical environment, managing the service process and managing customer contact employees.
- *Part D: Post-encounter marketing.* These two chapters discuss post-encounter marketing and explain the importance of customer satisfaction and developing mutually beneficial relationships with key customers.
- *Part E: The marketing plan.* The final chapter builds on the previous chapters, and explains how to write a marketing plan for a hospitality business.

Learning features

Each chapter contains the following features to aid understanding:

- *Chapter Objectives:* Each chapter begins with bullet points highlighting the main features and learning to be covered in the proceeding chapter.
- *Activities:* Short practical activities located at appropriate 'break' points throughout the chapter, which enable the reader to assess their understanding and marketing experience.
- *Headlines:* Highlights, appearing in blue type, throughout the chapter, which bring important points to the attention of the reader.
- *Marketing Insights:* Marketing anecdotes and observations to contextualize learning.
- *Case Studies:* International companies and scenarios are used to illustrate how the theories work in real world situations.
- *Conclusion:* Condenses the main themes of the chapter enabling the reader to check learning and understanding.
- *Review Questions:* Appear at the end of each chapter allowing readers to test their knowledge, understanding and to put the theory into practice.

Acknowledgements

We would like to thank the following people who have provided advice, materials and support throughout the writing of this book:

Colleagues from the Department of Hospitality, Leisure and Tourism Management at Oxford Brookes University: Ian Baldwin, Nina Becket, Dr David Bowen, Maureen Brookes, Dr Jackie Clark, Grant Clendining, Dr Liz Doherty, Phil Harpley, Professor Peter Harris, Professor Victor Middleton, Kathy and Ian Mitchell, Alex Paraskevas, Mike Rimmington, Clive Robertson, Dr Angela Roper, and Donald Sloan.

Hospitality industry practitioners: Rowan Aragues, Pauline and David Baldwin, James Bowie, Pamela Carvell, Francesca Castelli, Julia Clarke, John Clifford, Richard Coates, Thierry Douin, Cherry Fleet, Louise Flemming, Chris Grant, John Griffin, Stuart Harrison, David Hayes, Erik Marsh, Alasdair McNee, Nicky Michellietti, Sophie Mogford, Philip Pickering, Rupert Power, Nick Read, Paul Simmons, Cris Tarrant, Gerard Tempest, and Gary Yates.

Part A
Introduction

Chapter 1
Introduction to hospitality marketing

Chapter Objectives

After working through this chapter, you should be able to:

- Define key marketing terms and understand the 'marketing concept'
- Describe major environmental influences which impact on hospitality customers and organizations
- Explain the special characteristics of service businesses to which marketers need to respond
- Identify the eight elements of the hospitality marketing mix.

Introduction

In this chapter, you will be introduced to the key concepts of marketing. We will start by explaining what a market is, and reviewing different definitions of marketing. We will then discuss the macro- and micro-environments in which hospitality companies operate, the special characteristics of services marketing, and the hospitality marketing mix.

Whether we recognize it or not, we are all involved, willingly or unwillingly, in marketing. We come into contact with marketing practice every day as customers making buying decisions and at work, even if we do not have a job in marketing. Although marketing has a powerful influence in modern life, it is often misrepresented and misunderstood.

Students learning about marketing for the first time can be confused, because academic definitions of marketing differ from the everyday use of the term. Students can also be confused about the role of marketing, since marketing is both a business philosophy and a management function.

Activity 1.1

- Write down what you think 'marketing' means, before reading the chapter

- Write down what you think marketers do

- List the jobs that you think marketers are responsible for.

We will review your ideas at the end of this chapter and see whether they have changed!

What is a market?

Originally a market was a meeting place where people could buy and sell produce, and of course this type of market still exists today. In modern societies a 'market' is much more complex, but retains the core principles of bringing together buyers and sellers with common interests. This modern concept of the market is based on groups of people who have similar needs and wants (actual and potential buyers or consumers), and companies that aim to satisfy the consumers' needs and wants better than their competitors (an industry). *Needs* can range from the basic requirements for survival – food, shelter, safety – to much more complex social needs, such as belonging and recognition.

Wants are how different people choose to satisfy their needs, and are shaped by culture and personality. Hence people with similar needs, for example the need to travel for a family event and stay overnight, can have different wants – some may stay with relatives while others book their own hotel accommodation. Obviously, a major limitation on how people can satisfy their wants is the amount they can afford to pay.

Consumers have to make buying choices based on their own resources or buying power. Consumers will often buy the best bundle of benefits provided by a product, for the price that can be afforded. The combined purchase decisions of *all* the individuals buying a product (or service) is described as *market demand*. Market demand is normally measured using two criteria:

1 The number of units sold, which is a reflection of the number of people buying the product or service; this is called the volume
2 How much people have paid for the product; this is called the value.

Individuals can choose different ways to satisfy similar needs. Not everyone wants the same bundle of benefits, and this creates sub-markets, or market segments, within the overall market. In hospitality markets, luxury, mid-market and budget market segments represent different bundles of benefits sought by different groups of customers. Over a period of time the volume and the value of market segments can increase or fall, depending upon a wide range of factors.

Market supply can also be measured, and this is called the *industry capacity*. In the hotel market, the number of hotels and bedrooms in an area is called the *market capacity*. If the number of hotels and bedrooms is increasing, because new hotels or bedroom extensions have been built, then the market capacity increases. In the hospitality industry, market supply is often categorized under the same headings as market demand segments; so the luxury, mid-market and budget classifications are used to describe the different types of operations serving those market segments. Other ways of categorizing hospitality market supply include:

- Tourist board, motoring, or other, organization ratings for hotels and restaurants (e.g. star rating classification)
- Purpose of travel (leisure or business)
- Niche markets (youth action adventure holidays, conferences or gourmet food).

The level of market demand and the amount of industry capacity is a crucial factor underpinning the profitability of hospitality markets:

- When market demand is consistently high and industry capacity low, the hospitality business should be operating at high capacity and be profitable
- When market demand fluctuates and industry capacity is high, the hospitality business will be operating in a highly competitive environment and profitability will rise and fall.

Categories of demand

One way to think about marketing is to view it as the art and science of managing customer demand. Because demand states vary, so does the task of marketing.

Table 1.1 provides a list of eight categories of demand and the marketing response. Where demand states 1–4 occur, actual demand is lower than the desired level of demand and the hospitality marketer is primarily interested in facilitating and stimulating more consumption. Negative demand exists where consumers positively dislike a product – e.g. an unpopular food or drink product. The marketing response is to encourage demand by educating consumers about the positive

Table 1.1 Demand Management (source: taken from Philip Kotler, Marketing Management, 11th edn, 2003, p. 6)

	Category of demand	*Marketing task*
1	Negative demand	Encourage demand
2	No demand	Create demand
3	Latent demand	Develop demand
4	Falling demand	Revitalize demand
5	Irregular demand	Synchronize demand
6	Full demand	Maintain demand
7	Overfull demand	Reduce demand
8	Unwholesome demand	Destroy demand

features of, or benefits from, the product. You can often witness free tastings of food and drink products in supermarkets and wine shops, which enable potential customers to see, taste and buy the product.

Where there is no demand, the marketing task is to create demand. Raising awareness by advertising and public relations activity to demonstrate a product's positive attributes will help to educate consumers, and encourage them to sample the product.

Latent demand means that demand would exist if there were a product/service available to meet consumer needs. The development of domestic short breaks as a hotel product was originally based on consumers' increasing affluence and available leisure time.

Where demand is falling, the task is to revitalize demand. This situation can occur when a product/service is beginning to lose its appeal. Marketers need to research the reasons why the product no longer meets consumers' needs, reformulate the offer and re-launch the product to stimulate consumer interests and revitalize demand.

Irregular demand can be described in hospitality markets as the seasonality of demand. In these situations, companies strive to develop marketing strategies to synchronize demand over the high and low seasons, often using price-led promotions.

Full demand occurs when actual demand matches the desired demand, and the marketing task is to maintain current demand. In hospitality markets full demand rarely occurs, since competitors are likely to enter attractive markets and disturb the equilibrium.

If there is too much (or overfull) demand, the service operation will not be able to cope and there is likely to be considerable customer dissatisfaction. The hospitality marketer will aim to reduce demand either by increasing prices or by managing the booking/queuing process to prevent overfull demand. A long-term solution to overfull demand is to increase capacity by building more bedrooms or extending the seating area in a restaurant, but managers need to be confident that overfull demand will be sustained.

Unwholesome demand can occur when illegal activities such as drug taking, gambling or prostitution are taking place on the hospitality premises. Management clearly has a legal and ethical duty to try and inhibit or destroy unwholesome demand; however, this can be a difficult situation when customers are willingly involved.

Table 1.2 Categories of Demand in Hospitality

	Domestic	*International*
Business	Domestic business demand	International business demand
Leisure	Domestic leisure demand	International leisure demand

Market demand in hospitality

Market demand in hospitality can be broadly described under four key headings:

1 Business travel demand includes all those journeys business people make to meet customers and suppliers, and attend conferences, exhibitions and seminars. Business travel does not include the daily journeys people make when commuting to work.
2 Leisure travel demand includes journeys where people travel away from home for amusement, entertainment or relaxation – for example, holidays, weekend breaks, or same-day visits.
3 Domestic travel demand includes all the travel generated within a country by people living in that country – so, for example, the domestic demand for business travel in Australia is all business journeys taken in Australia by people living in Australia.
4 International travel demand includes all the journeys generated to a country from people living in other countries. France is one of the most popular tourist destinations, and attracts international visitors from all over the world.

Some types of travel do not fit easily into these broad categories. People often combine business and holidays in the same trip. However, these are convenient descriptions which tourist and hospitality organizations use. Table 1.2 summarizes these descriptors of market demand in hospitality.

What is marketing?

The philosophy of marketing

One set of marketing definitions suggests that marketing is primarily a business philosophy that puts the customer first. From this perspective, the primary goal of hospitality businesses should be to create and retain satisfied customers. This concept proposes that satisfying customers' needs and wants should be at the center of an organization's decision-making process. Professional marketers believe that this customer focus is the responsibility of everybody in the organization. Adopting this philosophy requires a total management commitment to the customer, and companies that pursue this approach can be described as having a *customer orientation*.

Definitions of marketing

Early definitions of marketing centered on the exchange/transaction process. Kotler (2000) proposes that in order to satisfy people's needs and wants, products and services are exchanged in mutually rewarding transactions generally, but not exclusively, using the monetary system. Kotler originally suggested that this exchange process, now known as transaction marketing, is a core concept in marketing, and is a 'value-creating process which leaves both parties better off than before the exchange took place'.

Another set of definitions suggests that marketing is a management process aimed at delivering customer satisfaction. Examples of this approach include the definitions offered by the Chartered Institute of Marketing, and the American Marketing Association. These definitions introduce a crucial aspect of marketing management – planning, which is discussed in greater detail later but is implicit in all of an organization's marketing activities.

These earlier definitions of marketing have been criticized on the grounds that the transactional focus is on generating first-time sales only. Relationship marketing evolved as a response to that criticism, and has become more fashionable as academics and practitioners recognize that the lifetime value of a customer can be high, even if the value of each transaction is relatively low. Relationship marketing is the development of mutually beneficial long-term relationships between suppliers and customers. In hospitality markets, a 'relationship marketing' approach has seen the major hotel groups focus their marketing activities upon frequent travelers in an attempt at encouraging repeat and recommended business.

Marketing insight

Different Perspectives of Marketing

'Marketing is the management process responsible for identifying, anticipating and satisfying customer requirements profitably.'

(Chartered Institute of Marketing, UK)

'Marketing is the process of planning and executing the conception, pricing, promotion, and distribution of ideas, goods and services to create exchanges that satisfy individual and organizational objectives.'

(American Marketing Association)

'In services, every contact between customers and employees includes an element of marketing.'

(Jan Carlzon, 1987)

Relationship marketing aims to 'identify and establish, maintain and enhance, and where necessary, terminate relationships with customers and other stakeholders, at a profit so that the objectives of all parties involved are met; and this is done by mutual exchange and fulfillment of promises.'

(Christian Grönroos, 1994)

'Marketing's central purpose is demand management … and marketers … need to manage the level, timing and composition of demand.'

(Philip Kotler, 1999)

Delighting the customer

Another view of marketing proposes that satisfying customers is no longer enough in a competitive environment. Companies, striving to develop sustainable competitive advantage, compete by 'delighting their customers' to ensure repeat and recommended business. Albrecht (1992) suggests that there are four product levels that companies can offer (see Figure 1.1):

1 At the basic level, a company provides essential core attributes (e.g. a clean bed) that customers need. If this basic level is not provided, customers will not buy the product – if the bed is not clean, customers will not be satisfied and might check out of the hotel. A hospitality firm that only offers a basic level of value is not competitive, and is unlikely to generate significant repeat and recommended business.

2 At the expected level, a company provides attributes that customers expect and take for granted – for example, efficient check in, a clean bed and availability of a bar/restaurant might be examples of the attributes expected from a mid-scale hotel. A hospitality company providing attributes at the expected level is only providing an average standard service; there is nothing better about the service offer compared to the competition. Customers may only be moderately satisfied, and there is no incentive to return or recommend this company.

3 At the desirable level, a company provides attributes that customers know of but do not generally expect. The friendliness of the staff, the quality of the food and the efficiency of the service are examples of attributes that customers know, but do not always expect. Companies providing the desirable offer are competing more effectively than most of their competitors.

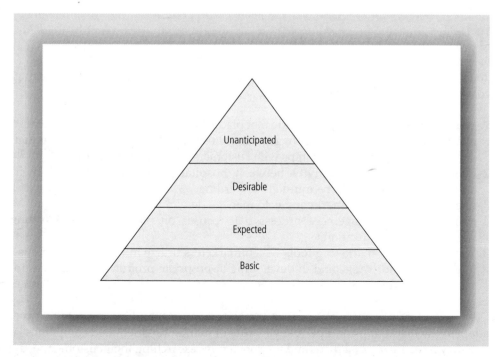

Figure 1.1 The hierarchy of customer value (adapted from Albrecht, 1992)

4 At the unanticipated level, hospitality operators offer customers 'delightful and surprising' attributes that demonstrate outstanding service quality. Examples might include imaginative decor and fittings, staff who perform exceptional service, or cuisine with unforgettable taste sensations. Companies operating at the unanticipated level can be said to *delight* their customers with memorable experiences, and are achieving a significant advantage over their competitors.

The difficulty with providing unanticipated levels of service all the time is that customers begin to *expect* these delightful surprises, and competitors copy them.

Managing demand

All these different definitions must seem quite confusing, particularly when many people who work in marketing are actually involved with increasing sales via promotional activity. Most hospitality marketers are employees in sales, sales promotion, print and publicity, direct mail, advertising, public relations, customer relations and marketing research jobs.

So how can we bridge the gap between the various philosophies and definitions of marketing with the jobs which marketers do?

The key concept that underpins marketing theory and practice is *the management of demand*. After a lifetime devoted to developing marketing theory and promoting the benefits of marketing, Philip Kotler (1999) stated that 'marketing's central purpose is demand management' and marketers need 'to manage the level, timing and the composition of demand'. This definition of marketing seems to explain most accurately what marketers do, and why they do it.

The marketing concept

To summarize the various approaches and definitions of marketing, the following core principles can be put forward:

1 Marketing is the business philosophy that places the customer at the center of a hospitality organization's purpose. Increasingly, hospitality companies recognize that developing long-term relationships with customers is mutually beneficial.
2 There is an exchange activity between hospitality organizations and their customers, which should be mutually rewarding.
3 The central purpose of marketing is to manage demand.
4 Marketing is a management process that focuses on planning for the future success of the organization.
5 There are a set of marketing tools which marketers utilize in understanding customer needs and wants, and in developing appropriate products and services to satisfy or delight customers.

Companies that place the customer at the center of their thinking are said to have adopted the marketing concept. A key feature of marketing orientated companies is that they have an external focus and are constantly researching their customer needs and wants, their competitors, and the environment in which they operate.

Postmodern marketing

Postmodern marketers (Brown, 2001) have criticized formal academic definitions of marketing and the marketing concept, which are predicated on a rational planning and decision-making process. Most modern marketing theories were developed in a period of stable economic and social conditions in the USA between the end of the Second World War and the mid-1980s. The impact of postmodern thinking in the arts, architecture, history, literature and sociology has created considerable interest in marketing practice. Although postmodern criticisms of marketing do not put forward a set of alternative theories, they do challenge the over-reliance on quantitative marketing research, simple geo-demographic segmentation criteria, the concept of a dominant culture being more important than other cultures, and a formulaic approach to marketing planning. Postmodernism in marketing implies recognition of consumers as individuals and the rejection of a coherent marketing theoretical framework. Postmodern marketers suggest that marketing should be more inspirational in connecting with consumers. Whilst these criticisms may be valid, it is important to understand the core principles and practice of marketing. This is our goal.

Management orientations

Five different competing management philosophies have been identified in free market economies (see Figure 1.2). Called 'orientations', some of these generic philosophies have been linked to specific economic conditions, and to certain periods in economic history. It should be noted that a hospitality organization could adopt any one of the following orientations, regardless of the economic circumstances.

Operations or production orientation (mass marketing)

Originally developed by Henry Ford, the production concept is appropriate when there is a rising demand for strong, innovative products. If demand exceeds supply, management concentrates on generating volume to satisfy the growing demand. Improved technologies generate economies of scale, which allows management to reduce prices further and grow the market.

The production orientation is based on conditions of mass production and limited consumer choice. This leads to an inward-looking focus as management strives to control costs, improve quality and efficiency, and increase volume. Critically, from a marketing concept perspective, the needs and wants of customers can be forgotten in the interests of organizational efficiency. Providing customers are satisfied with the low-cost, mass-produced product, then a production orientation is appropriate.

There are many examples of product innovation generating strong demand in the fast-food industry. When American fast-food operations entered the major cities of countries like China and Russia, they generated high demand for what was considered an innovative foreign food product. This meant that McDonald's adopted a production orientation. The McDonald's management's main focus was on achieving operational efficiency by improving their food supply chain and

Starting point	Focus	Means	End
Production orientation			
Innovative, strong, hospitality products	Satisfying high demand	New technology generating mass production at low prices	Profit through mass sales
Product orientation			
Existing hospitality product/service	Maintain and improve existing product concept	Minor improvements and adaptations of existing marketing mix	Profit dependent upon stable market conditions
Selling orientation			
Existing hospitality product/service	Existing and new facilities	Aggressive selling and promotional tactics	Profit through sales volume
Marketing orientation			
Business and leisure markets	Business and leisure customer needs and wants	Integrated marketing (including marketing research)	Profit through customer satisfaction
Societal-marketing orientation			
Business and leisure markets AND the needs and wants of the community and environment	Socially concerned hospitality business activities	Integrated marketing which takes into account the needs and wants of consumers and society	Profit through enhanced image and customer satisfaction

Figure 1.2 Marketing orientations (adapted from Kotler, Bowen and Makens, 2003)

training staff to service the high demand. Airline, contract and welfare food service operations also have a production focus because of the mass markets they serve, with varying degrees of success.

There are also examples of hospitality organizations using a production orientation ineffectively. Holiday Inn used to provide managers with mega-size standard operational manuals detailing the rules and procedures for every aspect of the hotel operation, but such a bureaucratic approach can end up stifling innovation, making hospitality managers focus on the systems and paperwork instead of on customer care. Smaller companies can also neglect customers by adopting an operations focus. Simplifying the production process for operational convenience can lead to limited customer choice – for example, small sandwich shops can easily fall into the trap of limiting the choice of fillings to reduce waste, and thereby losing customers.

Product or service orientation

The product or service orientation is not linked to any specific economic era or to specific market conditions. Companies adopting a product orientation believe that their customers can *only* be satisfied with a particular type of product. Management concentrates on developing better versions of the *existing* product, but fails to recognize that customers could be satisfied better by different *types* of products. For example, hospitality companies with a product orientation include the famous restaurants with celebrity chefs, who serve what they think customers should eat regardless of what the customers actually want! Chefs like this may lose touch with the question of whether customers actually want to buy the product; they become overly focused on the product.

Theodore Levitt's famous article 'Marketing myopia' (Levitt, 1960) warned companies that a product orientation could lead to failure. The product management focus is again inward looking. Whilst a company can prosper with a product orientation, changes in consumer tastes and fashion can quickly undermine a product-led company.

Selling orientation

The selling orientation was developed in the 1920s, when American companies developed efficient production systems and needed to generate more sales to maintain profitability. Companies adopt the selling orientation when their products are competing in markets where supply exceeds demand, and growth is low or declining. A critical issue for management is surplus capacity combined with a high fixed capital investment in the building and plant. This combination can force management to focus on high sales volume and aggressive sales generation to strive to make a profitable return on investment. Despite this external focus on sales generation the management is still inward looking, since it is concentrating on selling the product to potential customers and is not focusing on satisfying customer needs and wants.

Companies with the selling orientation tend to accept every possible sale or booking, regardless of its suitability for the business or other customers. By mixing incompatible customer segments hospitality companies can fail to deliver customer satisfaction, which is ultimately self-defeating. Longer-term, profitable relationships with existing customers can be damaged in the pursuit of short-term sales generation.

A sales orientation is endemic in the hospitality industry, as many marketing programs are really only sales promotions aimed at filling bedrooms, bars and restaurants – regardless of customers' needs and wants.

Whilst selling is a vital element of hospitality marketing, sales strategies should be integrated into the marketing plan and be consistent with a marketing orientation.

The Sales and Marketing Function in Hotels (Source: Hotel Marketing Association and BDRC, 2000)

Marketing insight

The Hotel Marketing Association carries out regular marketing research into the opinions of senior UK hotel marketing executives who work for the top hospitality brands. The 2000 survey discovered that 70 percent of hotel groups combine the sales and marketing function in the same department, with 'sales' dominating 'marketing'. However, seven of the top twenty hotel chains do separate marketing from the sales department. Marketing is not recognized at the main board level – only one in eight heads of marketing actually sits on the main board, and only one in three has a seat on a subsidiary board. Although 57 percent of the senior marketers recognized that the role of marketing should focus on 'the customer and their needs', many leading hospitality marketers still have a strong tactical bias focusing on advertising, public relations and sales.

Marketing orientation

The marketing orientation is considered by some authors to be the same as the marketing concept. It is an alternative strategy to the selling orientation, to cope with similar economic conditions (i.e. surplus capacity leading to a fiercely competitive environment). Companies adopting the marketing orientation recognize that customers have considerable choice in the marketplace. Companies aiming to maintain long-term profitability need to understand and serve customers better than their competitors.

To achieve superior business performance companies therefore need to identify what customer needs and wants are, and to satisfy them better than competitors. This means that companies need to carry out marketing research and to develop an integrated approach to marketing, to ensure that all marketing activities are coordinated and help to deliver customer satisfaction. A marketing orientation is an outward-looking management philosophy, which responds to changes in the environment and considers the business from a customer perspective. As customers' needs and wants change, so the business adapts accordingly.

The advantage of a marketing orientation is that the business focus is on developing long-term relationships with customers, and avoids price competition. The adoption of a marketing orientation suggests that companies are seeking longer-term profits, as opposed to increasing profits in the short term at the expense of longer-term customer satisfaction.

At its most advanced level, a marketing orientation becomes focused on the satisfaction of individual customers, whether organizations or people. Companies that tailor their offer to meet the needs of individual customers are said to be practicing one-to-one marketing. In hospitality, the ability of computers to store and retrieve guest history increasingly enables hotel companies to record customer likes and dislikes, and to personalize services and communications to the needs of individual customers. This one-to-one style of marketing is predicted to become more important in the future.

Societal marketing orientation

In the 1980s, the marketing orientation was criticized for its narrow focus and lack of concern for environmental and social issues. The original marketing orientation ignored the potential conflict between consumers' wants, and societies' needs. The societal marketing orientation was a response to these criticisms, and recognizes that commercial organizations have a wider responsibility than simply looking after customers and staff. A societal marketing orientation suggests that companies should become proactive in the community, adopting a 'good neighbor' policy in their company's best interest.

A number of hospitality organizations have genuinely adopted a societal marketing approach. One example is Prêt à Manger (see Case study 1.1). Other organizations claim to adopt a societal marketing approach, but are really only carrying out public relations activity to gain positive publicity. The distinction between a genuine societal marketing approach and a superficial approach lies in the core values of the organization. If the entire organizational culture is clearly committed to an environmental and social awareness in its philosophy, and demonstrates this in all its activities, then it has adopted a societal marketing approach.

Case study

1.1 Prêt à Manger

Prêt à Manger, a sandwich shop founded by Julian Metcalfe and Sinclair Beecham as a single unit in south London, is now a major brand in the UK and is rapidly expanding in the USA. The company's success is rooted in the values of its owners, who are 'passionate about food'. Prêt's mission statement explains their business proposition: 'to create handmade, natural food, avoiding the obscure chemicals, additives and preservatives common to so much of the "prepared" and "fast" food on the market today'. The mission, website and packaging materials consistently promote examples of their suppliers, who are named along with details of their free-range farms and organic husbandry, and staff, who work in interesting jobs ensuring the natural quality of the produce.

All sandwiches are freshly made on each shop premises; and unsold sandwiches are offered to the homeless. At Christmas, a special festive sandwich is sold with a 10p donation to a homeless charity included in the price. Prêt's human resource management practices are better than most in their sector, including competitive pay and very good promotion prospects.

McDonald's bought a minority shareholding in this privately owned company, so it will be interesting to see how Prêt develops in the future. Prêt's management orientation is based on a societal marketing approach, and continued expansion in the UK, USA, Hong Kong and Japan suggests that its mission works.

(Source: Prêt à Manger)

Summary

A company's orientation may be:

● Formally adopted in a written planning statement
● Informally agreed by the management team
● Simply implied by the company's operating procedures.

Many hospitality companies may not even be aware of their business orientation. Clearly recognizing which orientation a company is using will enable managers to understand their operation more effectively. Opinions differ on whether a specific orientation is appropriate for a given economic situation. Some experts maintain that a marketing orientation is the only appropriate orientation, whilst others suggest that the economic situation should determine which orientation to adopt. Growing companies can adopt different orientations at different stages of their growth, while global companies can adopt different orientations depending upon which country they are operating in.

Environmental influences on hospitality organizations

Since marketing is an outward-looking business philosophy, marketers in hospitality companies need to understand and adapt to changes in the business environment. Both macro- and micro-environmental factors influence the marketing of a hospitality business.

The macro-environment

The macro-environment includes political, economic, socio-cultural, technological and environmental forces, and is therefore known as the PESTE environment. Hospitality companies have limited, if any, control over PESTE influences; but major changes in any one PESTE factor can significantly impact on the business. PESTE factors are constantly changing. These changes affect consumers, drive market demand, and influence the competitive environment. Figure 1.3 provides an overview of the environmental influences on hospitality organizations.

Political

The political direction of a country determines how consumers and commercial organizations can act. The political philosophy of government can either stimulate

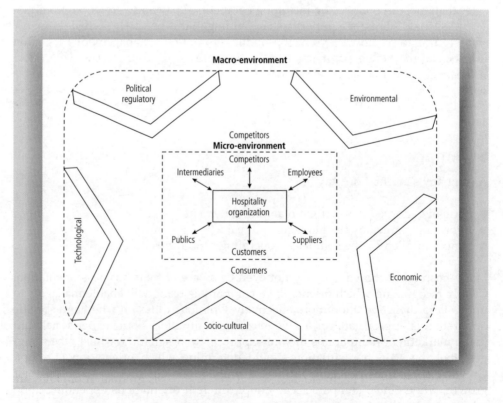

Figure 1.3 Macro- and micro-environmental influences on hospitality organizations

or stifle economic, social and technological development. While the USA fosters an open economy, encouraging tourism and creating a positive climate for hospitality businesses, Burma restricts international access and inhibits the development of tourism and hospitality businesses. Political and governmental decisions are constantly changing the environment in which we live and work and the impact on hospitality marketing activity in a variety of ways.

For Europeans, the political environment includes the European Union as well as their own national governments. Decisions about the Single Market and the euro currency are examples of European political regulation.

The political environment includes the legal/regulatory environment, and covers any legislation that influences the marketplace. Examples include:

● Planning regulations (permission for building hotel, restaurant and leisure extensions or developing new properties), which alter the industry capacity
● Licensing laws, which regulate the opening times of licensed premises
● Local, regional or national government taxes, which impact on prices (Value Added Tax and General Sales Tax rates, and excise duty on alcoholic drinks) and therefore influence the demand for hospitality products
● Regulation of marketing communications (different European countries have different regulations concerning advertising, direct mail and the use of databases for marketing purposes).

Economic

The economic environment includes all those activities that influence the wealth and income of the population. Examples of economic influences are:

● The state of the economy
● The structure of employment and the level of unemployment
● The rate of inflation
● The exchange rate.

These factors combine to influence business confidence, consumers' disposable income and consumer confidence, which play a significant role in changing demand for hospitality markets. When business and consumer confidence is high, hospitality markets thrive; when business and consumer confidence is low, hospitality markets decline and firms are prone to failure.

A key economic factor is the business cycle, which influences demand. Hospitality firms need to respond to the stages in the business cycle. Whilst hospitality businesses all trade at the same stage of the business cycle, firms will respond differently according to their financial and marketing strengths, and their leadership. The stages of the hospitality business cycle (see Figure 1.4) are:

● *Growth*. Occupancy and room rates increase in response to growing demand, there is a strong positive cash flow (which means that capital is available for further investment), property values increase, and hoteliers have high business confidence.
● *Peak*. Occupancy and room rates remain strong, and funds are still available for investment; however, growth tends to slow.
● *Decline*. Occupancy begins to decrease. If the decrease is gradual, room rates are increased in line with inflation. Investors sense the higher risk in declining occupancy and seek increased returns before agreeing to invest in hotel

businesses, property values begin to fall, the rate of decline becomes more rapid as occupancy falls, price competition becomes more intense and achieved room rates fall, and the rate of decline can become faster as the industry moves toward recession.

● *Trough*. There is a large imbalance of supply and demand during a recession; low occupancy, low room rates and a slump in property values means that highly geared (over-borrowed) companies are put into receivership. There is a bottoming out period as demand gradually stabilizes and then slowly begins to increase.

● *Resurgence*. There is a gradual resurgence, and the cycle starts all over again.

A major recurring problem for the hospitality industry is that hotel development projects are funded in the growth and peak stages of the business cycle but, because of the time lag between gaining investment funds and planning permission, many hotels open for business just as the cycle peaks. Hence additional new build capacity is added to the stock just as demand falls, creating further problems for the industry. Capacity does not really diminish during periods of declining and low demand. From a hospitality marketing perspective, companies' response to the business cycle during a downturn period and a recession is problematic. Companies engage in major cost-cutting activities; marketing employees and expenditure are often significantly reduced, and financially weaker brands are vulnerable to take-over. During resurgent and growth periods marketing activity increases as companies respond to the growth in hospitality demand. Whilst nobody can accurately predict the precise timing of a stage in the business cycle, it is vital for hospitality managers and owners to understand the implications of each stage.

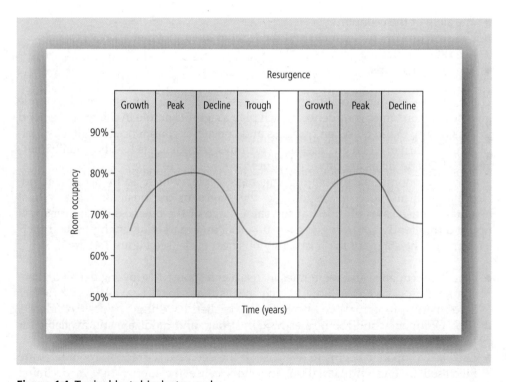

Figure 1.4 Typical hotel industry cycle

Socio-cultural

The socio-cultural environment influences consumers' purchase and consumption behavior. A country's socio-cultural environment is a complex mix of its geography, climate, history, religion, and ethnic make-up. We are all influenced by the values of our own culture, even though we are not aware of this all the time. Indeed, cultural differences between countries provide hospitality marketers with some of the greatest challenges when developing global brands.

One of the key aspects of a country's hospitality industry, which is heavily influenced by national culture, is eating and drinking habits. Each country and region has developed its own cooking based on factors like the climate, which dictates the produce available. The growth of international travel for business and leisure purposes has widened people's cultural knowledge and encouraged the development of new food and beverage concepts.

Demographic changes (changes in the make-up of a population) also make a significant impact on market demand in hospitality. Examples include the following:

● The increase in the number of older people living in Western countries is changing the demand characteristics for holidays
● The increase in the number of single people (caused by people marrying later, and more people getting divorced) is changing the demand characteristics for eating out.

Hospitality marketers need to be aware of socio-cultural and demographic trends to ensure their companies understand changes in markets in order to remain competitive.

Technological

The technological environment in hospitality is closely associated with innovation and developments in information communications technology (ICT). The rapid development of ICT in the late 1990s and during the current decade has had a major influence in the industry. Improvements in the technological environment include:

● The growing sophistication of computerized reservation services
● The development of global distribution networks
● Increasing consumer and commercial use of the Internet
● Improvements in kitchen equipment, which has changed food production techniques
● The development of in-hotel computerized systems, which has improved in-room comfort and security for guests.

The current rate of technological change is fast, and new developments are constantly altering the technological environment.

Environmental

Environmental factors have become more important in all parts of the world as people recognize the impact tourists have on the planet. In particular, mass tourism has become much more controversial. Tourism:

● Encourages new hotel and leisure developments
● Impinges on natural habitats

- Uses up scarce resources
- Generates air and noise pollution
- Creates waste disposal problems.

Although the concept of sustainable tourism is much publicized, and 'green' pressure groups lobby government and hospitality companies to improve the industry's environmental policies, the hotel and restaurant industry does not have a good reputation in this area.

Interaction of PESTE factors

Some factors in the macro-environment will affect all of the PESTE variables, and each individual element of the PESTE can influence other elements. This means that analyzing the macro-environment can be confusing, since it is difficult to separate the impact of each influence.

For example, demographic changes are forecast to become a major influence on economic, social and political factors in the twenty-first century. National population changes affect a country's economy. Global and national changes in population affect socio-cultural forces, and influence the composition and character of travel markets. Countries react politically to migration pressures; and demographic changes can also stimulate the creation of pressure groups, which lobby government on behalf of their interests. Thus one driver of change influences several PESTE factors, and each of the PESTE factors interacts with the others.

The micro-environment

The micro-environment includes internal company factors (customers, employees, suppliers and intermediaries) and external factors (the direct competitors operating in the same locations, and the various 'publics' with which a company interacts). Unlike the PESTE framework for the macro-environment, there is no recognized formula or mnemonic to describe the micro-environment. Hospitality companies have more influence over the micro-environment than over the macro-environment.

Customers

Hospitality companies typically target a broad mix of customers, including business and leisure hotel residents, non-resident diners and drinkers. Managing the customer mix to ensure that all the different types of customers are satisfied or delighted is one of the major roles for marketing. Over time customers can change their needs and wants, so companies have to monitor and respond to these changes.

Employees

For most hospitality organizations, the local labor market is a key resource. The availability and quality of skilled employees who have been educated and can be easily trained is an important factor in delivering a quality service. Because employees interact with customers, they can have a major influence on the level of customer satisfaction.

Suppliers

The hospitality company's performance is dependent upon its suppliers. Although marketers are not directly involved in operational purchase decisions, marketing should have an input into setting quality standards and specifications. The hospitality marketer will certainly be responsible for handling relationships with external marketing communication and marketing research agencies.

Intermediaries

Intermediaries are those companies who advise, influence and make bookings for customers. They include travel agents, tour operators, conference placement agencies and incentive agencies. Intermediaries are important links in the distribution channel from the customer to the hospitality outlets. Marketing managers needed to cultivate good relationships with actual and potential intermediaries.

Competitors

The competitive environment includes different kinds of competitors:

- Direct competitors – these are businesses offering a similar product or service, which is aimed at the same customer group. Direct competitors operate in the same geographic location and in the same (or adjacent) product category. For hotels, a three-star provincial business hotel could have a local competitor set including all three-star hotels, and possibly some two- and four-star hotels, within a 10-mile radius or 15 minutes' travel time. Watching, knowing and anticipating what your competitors are doing is a vital part of knowing your market.
- Competitors offering substitute products – these are offers that potential consumers can choose instead of a hospitality product and which satisfies the same need (e.g. staying at home and cooking a meal instead of going out to a restaurant).
- Indirect competition – this includes all those companies and non-profit organizations that are competing for consumers' disposable income (e.g. choosing between buying a new car or going on an exotic holiday).

The competitive environment in many hospitality markets has become more intense in recent years. The actions and reactions of competitors has radically changed market structure, influenced consumer behavior, and altered market demand.

Publics

The location of a hospitality premises and the size/scale of the company will determine the character of the organizations (also called publics) with which the organization interacts. These publics will include:

- Local government authorities (who enforce health and safety, hygiene and planning regulations)
- Other businesses and people who live in the neighborhood (some of whom may also be customers)
- Community, educational, religious, social and voluntary institutions
- Leisure, sporting and tourism attractions
- The local media.

Local publics can exert considerable influence on a hospitality business. Developing effective public relations activities and fostering good relationships with local publics is part of the marketing task.

Special characteristics of services marketing

The special characteristics faced by services marketers (including of course hospitality marketers) are seasonality, intangibility, perishability, inseparability, variability, interdependence, supply exceeding demand, and high fixed costs. You can use the mnemonic *SIPIVISH* to remember the characteristics.

Seasonality and demand fluctuation

Seasonality refers to the fluctuations and demand in any given period. In hospitality operations, seasonality can occur at:

- Different seasons of the year
- Different months of the year
- Different times of the week
- Different times of the day.

The demand for business accommodation is highest during the middle of the week, outside the peak holiday periods of Easter, summer and Christmas/New Year. Country hotels can have a poor midweek winter business but achieve high occupancies at the weekends, when city hotels can be quiet. Restaurants can be full with customers on a busy Saturday night and empty on a Monday evening.

Case study 1.2 illustrates a seasonal business.

Case study

1.2 Ski Olympic – a seasonal business

Ski Olympic, a British tour operator with a single product – skiing in the French Alps – owns chalet hotels like Les Avals in Courcheval. The chalet hotels are open during the skiing season from mid-December to the end of April, and they are closed for seven months from May to November. Revenue generated in the short twenty-week opening period has to cover the operational costs of running the hotels during the ski season, as well as the annual administrative, marketing and financial costs.

(Source: Ski Olympic)

The under- or over-utilization of capacity creates operational difficulties. Sudden unexpected increases in customers can lead to production problems, unacceptable waiting times and dissatisfied customers. The profitability of hospitality companies suffers during low season periods, so one of the challenging roles for marketing is to increase demand in low season periods and to deflect over-demand from peak periods to other times.

Intangibility

Services are described as intangible products, meaning that they cannot be experienced – heard, seen, smelt, tasted or touched – prior to being purchased. Unlike shopping for a personal stereo or buying a motorcar, hospitality consumers cannot really examine competing hotel, restaurant or leisure products without entering into a purchase contract and buying the product. For example, they cannot stay overnight in a hotel and test out the rooms without being expected to pay first.

Marketing intangibles create difficulties for the service provider. Customers often sense a higher level of risk, and also find it difficult to assess quality. Customers need to be provided with information to help them to choose an appropriate hospitality outlet to satisfy their particular needs and wants. The challenge for marketers is how to provide such information in a way that will encourage customers to choose *their* offer without raising customer expectations too high, and then failing to deliver customer satisfaction. The role of marketing communications in designing effective promotional material to generate appropriate bookings is crucial.

Perishability

Everyone working in hospitality knows that you cannot sell last night's bedroom tonight. Hotels and restaurants have a fixed number of rooms and seats available each day or night. Unlike manufactured products, which can be stored in warehouses, services cannot be stored; this feature of service industries is called 'perishability'. The difficulty for hospitality companies is how to manage their capacity (the inventory) with a fluctuating demand pattern.

Hospitality managers recognize that managing the inventory is a critical issue in optimizing customer satisfaction, sales and profitability. The key marketing principle is to ensure that the price at peak demand times is set to deliver the maximum return to the company, providing it is compatible with customer satisfaction. In low season periods, the aim is to generate additional sales by developing attractive promotions. Managing the booking process to ensure that the business achieves this balance is essential.

Inseparability

Customers have to be present to consume the hospitality product. The simultaneous production and consumption of services means that hospitality employees are an important part of the hospitality product. Equally, customers themselves play a significant part in the hospitality product by enhancing or spoiling the atmosphere for other customers. These factors mean that customer interaction with hospitality staff and other hospitality guests provides a variety of opportunities to influence customer satisfaction positively or negatively.

Ways to manage the problems of inseparability include:

- Ensuring that customer segments are compatible
- Ensuring that the operations system is suitable for the projected market demand
- Adopting appropriate booking policies
- Organizing effective queuing systems
- Training staff effectively.

Variability

Partly as a result of inseparability, hospitality operations suffer from considerable fluctuations in the standards of delivery of the service. This is called variability, and is influenced by human factors. Services comprise a high element of interaction between customers and staff; indeed, every service performance is a unique event.

Human interaction cannot be standardized, and consequently it is impossible for service companies to deliver a totally non-variable experience.

The difficulties arising out of variability are considerable:

- Imagine that the same customers order the same meal, which is cooked by the same chef and served by the same staff, in the same restaurant, at the same time of the week. The resulting meal experience can be very different from one week (possibly perfect) to the next (possibly disastrous)!
- Again, two different sets of customers could be served the same meal, at the same time, in the same restaurant and by the same staff, but because of their different knowledge, experience, personal character and feelings, could have very different experiences.

Some customers may be highly knowledgeable about food and wine. These 'expert' customers, with their different understanding of service and quality, may be highly critical of the meal experience compared to less knowledgeable customers, who may have really enjoyed the occasion. Companies respond to this problem of variability by trying to standardize their operations and training their staff to perform according to the company's standard operating procedures, but with varying degrees of success.

Interdependence

Tourists make a variety of travel purchase decisions in one trip, and their overall satisfaction with a visit is based upon a complex set of evaluations of different elements – including the travel arrangements, accommodation, attractions and facilities of a destination.

The choice of hospitality products is only one element on which the consumer needs to decide. Hotel accommodation sales in particular are influenced by the consumer's choice of other tourism products. First and foremost is the tourist's choice of destination. Visitors may base their decision to travel to a particular destination on the range of attractions, the ease and accessibility of transport to and from the area, the image of the destination, the price, and 'word of mouth' comments made by family, friends and the media. This means that the generation of demand for some hospitality operations is directly connected to the demand for complementary tourism products – i.e. the demand is interdependent.

The response to interdependency is that individual businesses, regardless of the tourism sector they operate in, their size or ownership, have to cooperate in the promotion of their destination. Destination marketing organizations work closely together with local government and tourism authorities to promote demand for tourism in their own particular area.

Supply exceeds demand

The hospitality industry is frequently described as a fragmented industry with low barriers to entry. It is relatively easy to obtain finance and buy or build a hospitality company. Indeed, many of today's great brands (Hilton, Marriott, and McDonald's) were originally small companies developed by visionary entrepreneurs.

Although regulations obviously vary in different countries, government planners have generally welcomed the development of sustainable tourism. The last ten years have witnessed a dynamic building period, with massive investment in new resorts, hotels, restaurants, cruise ships, leisure facilities and casino operations culminating in excess capacity in most sectors of the industry and in many parts of the world. Despite record numbers of people traveling for business and leisure purposes, the growth in hospitality capacity has not always been matched by a sufficient growth in demand. When supply exceeds demand the competitive environment becomes more intense, and price competition can affect all firms' profitability.

High fixed costs

The cost structure of hospitality firms influences marketing activity. Hospitality businesses are capital, labor and energy intensive. Typical hospitality firms have high property costs and also employ large numbers of staff, many of whom are full-time, permanent employees. These costs do not change; they are 'fixed' regardless of the number of customers using the premises. During periods of low demand, high fixed costs erode the profitability of the business. Companies need to generate sales to help make a contribution towards the fixed costs. The marketing response to seasonality and high fixed costs is to design attractively priced promotions to stimulate sales in the low season.

The role of marketing management in hospitality

The main task of the hospitality marketing manager is to *influence demand* for the organization's products and services.

Marketing insight

Marketers aim to:

● Understand the drivers of demand
● Understand consumers and customers
● Increase the *volume* of transactions – bed nights, covers served, number of passengers
● Increase the *value* of transactions – improving the average achieved room rates, the average spend per head, the average price for holiday
● Increase both the *volume* and the *value* of transactions (but normally there is a trade-off between increasing the volume sales and increasing the achieved spend)
● Shift demand from periods where there is too much demand (high season) to periods where there is too little demand (low season or the shoulders).

The marketing manager's tasks include:

1 Research and analysis into
   ● the needs and wants of customers and target markets
   ● changes in the PESTE environment
   ● the actions of competitors

2 Planning marketing strategies to achieve agreed marketing objectives in
  - customer service and satisfaction
  - sales and profits
  - bringing new products to the market
3 Implementing marketing strategies by
  - designing, developing and rolling out new product concepts
  - setting brand standards
  - designing and executing marketing communication campaigns
4 Monitoring and control of marketing campaigns by
  - ensuring that marketing objectives are being achieved during a campaign
  - ensuring that marketing activities are carried out within the agreed budget
  - understanding the reasons why there are any variances between targeted performance and actual performance
  - commissioning marketing research to evaluate marketing performance
5 Influencing other departments to become more focused on the customer – for example
  - operations needs to make or buy what customers want to experience
  - human resources needs to recruit the right type of people to interact with customers.

Some of these marketing activities will be carried out in-house by the company's own marketing personnel; other activities will be delegated to specialist marketing and publicity agencies.

The hospitality marketing mix

The term *marketing mix* is used to describe the tools that the marketer uses to influence demand. The marketing mix is a core concept in marketing. The hospitality marketing mix adopted in this text is based on the eight marketing activities shown in Figure 1.5.

Product/service offer

Hospitality products and services are primarily designed to satisfy the needs and wants of business and leisure travelers. Examples include:

- Accommodation – a bed, bedroom, cabin or suite, in a hotel, inn, chalet, apartment, time-share, cruise ship, hospital
- Food and beverage – a drink, sandwich, fast food, family meal, gourmet dinner, in a café, cafeteria, restaurant, bar or pub, aeroplane, motorway service station or ship, at an attraction or leisure center
- Business services – a meeting, conference, communication bureau, in a hotel or conference center
- Leisure – a short break, domestic holiday or international holiday, in a hotel, resort, self-catering accommodation, camping and caravan site, or a cruise.

Marketing, working with operations, should play a role in developing the product and service offers to ensure that the needs of customers are the focus of planning and product development.

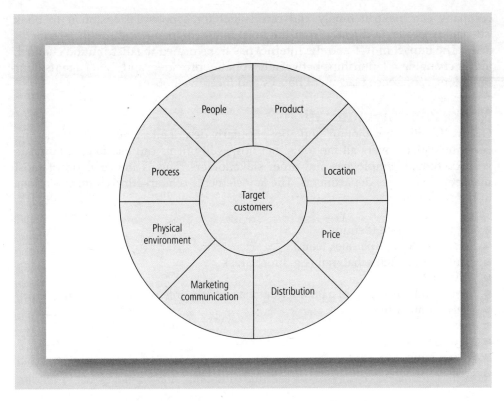

Figure 1.5 The hospitality marketing mix

Location

Location decisions are incorporated with distribution under the heading 'Place' in the generic marketing mix. Because the choice of location is the first and crucial marketing decision for hospitality companies, this text includes location as one of the main elements of the marketing mix. Location decisions focus on where the hospitality business should build, buy, franchise or rent the site(s) from which it operates.

Price

The pricing decisions a hospitality organization makes include:

● Setting the tariff, or rack rates
● Agreeing the level of discounts for key accounts
● Pricing all-inclusive packages (conferences, functions and leisure breaks)
● Developing special priced promotions to increase sales during low season periods.

Pricing decisions influence demand, are crucial in driving profitability, and play an important role in presenting the 'image' the hospitality firms wants to project to customers and stakeholders.

Distribution

In most textbooks, distribution decisions are generally discussed with location under the heading 'Place'. Distribution in hospitality is concerned with how a company can make it timely and convenient for a potential customer to book hospitality products directly from the hospitality company or through intermediaries. The impact of ICT and the Internet has transformed the distribution channel, and is changing relationships between hospitality providers and travel agents, tour operators, conference placement houses and incentive houses.

Marketing communications

Originally called 'promotion' and now popularly described as 'marcom', marketing communication covers all the tools that hospitality firms can use to communicate with customers, employees and other stakeholders. This is the function of most marketing and sales departments. The key elements of marketing communications in hospitality are:

- Brand/corporate identity
- Personal selling (the sales team)
- Print and publicity material (e.g. brochures)
- Advertising
- Direct mail (often part of a broader database marketing or direct marketing effort)
- Sales promotion
- Public relations
- Merchandising
- Sponsorship
- Website design.

Physical environment

The physical environment (or physical evidence) consists of the tangible features of the hospitality offer – the external appearance of the premises (the landscaping, lighting and signage) and the internal layout (appropriate decor, furniture and furnishings). Intangible factors are intimately linked to physical evidence – the ambience or atmosphere – and clearly the success of a hospitality product is dependent upon the appeal of the physical environment to the customers.

Process

Because of the simultaneous production and consumption prevalent in hospitality services, the processes through which customers buy and consume hospitality products are crucial to marketers. Important processes include booking, checking in and checking out, queuing systems and service operations. Marketers need to ensure that the organization's service delivery processes are efficient, customer friendly and competitive.

People

In the services marketing mix, 'people' includes both customers and employees. We have already discussed how hospitality customers interact with each other whilst on the premises – indeed, in certain hotel and holiday environments a good rapport between customers is an essential ingredient of the successful product. Managing the customer mix and ensuring that target markets are compatible plays a key role in delivering customer satisfaction.

Hospitality is a service where the interaction between customers and employees is also a critical element of the customer experience. Marketing therefore needs to have an input into human resources aspects of the operation, and this is called *internal marketing*.

Hospitality brands and integrating the marketing mix

Brands are central to the marketing of multi-unit hospitality businesses. Hospitality companies develop branded concepts, and then blend the elements of the marketing mix to provide target customers with a better brand offer than their competitors (see Case study 1.3). It is crucial that each element of the marketing mix is consistent with all the other elements. For example a luxury hotel brand cannot be successfully located in a 'down market' area, and a cheap and cheerful restaurant cannot successfully promote gourmet cooking.

Those hospitality companies that do not provide a consistent marketing offer confuse customers by sending out mixed messages.

Breaking down each element of the marketing mix helps you to understand the complexity of the marketing offer. However, it should be remembered that customers form opinions based on their overall impression of the offer, and this can be influenced by minor items – for example, the price of a drink – as well as by more obvious factors like the quality of service.

If you reflect upon all the different elements of the marketing mix, it becomes clear that marketers need to work closely with operations (on product, process and physical environment decisions), with finance (on pricing and marcom budget decisions), and with human resources (on employment strategies). In smaller, single-unit operations, where the owner/management is close to the business and is responsible for all these decisions, the integration of marketing with other departments is easier. In large-scale, multi-unit, national and international operations, such cooperation is much more difficult to achieve. Effective marketing is dependent upon all the departments in a hospitality business working closely together.

Case study

1.3 Travel Inn – an integrated approach to marketing

In the 1980s, market demand for better quality low-cost accommodation in the UK grew significantly and Travelodge (the original developer of the concept) expanded rapidly. In 1987, Whitbread developed a competitor concept, called Travel Inn, which imitated the market leader in most aspects. Whitbread franchised the new brand to five of their company-owned restaurant/pub chains, such as Beefeater. Despite intense competition from Days Inn, Express by Holiday Inn, and Accor, Travel Inn overtook Travelodge after ten years. With a marketing objective 'to be the customer's first choice' in the budget market, the Travel Inn brand team – who had complete control of all elements of the marketing mix – focused on setting and maintaining consistent brand standards. Properties that failed the brand standard's inspections were de-branded. The marketing mix comprised:

● *Product* – low-cost, mid-market accommodation standards, with factory-built standardized bedrooms, which are easy to install on site. Each room is refurbished on a regular cycle depending upon occupancy rates – the objective is that old rooms look as good as new rooms, and the product offer is consistent throughout the chain.

● *Location* – there are three types of location. The core product units, called Travel Inns, are located on major roads and motorways; then there are units located in provincial cities and towns called Travel Inn Metro, and finally units located in London called Travel Inn Capital. All units are located adjacent to Whitbread-owned restaurants and inns.

● *Price* – each brand has one single price structure, and there are no discounts.

● *Distribution* – Travel Inn operates a computerized reservation system, with links from its website and a telesales call center. Although intermediaries like travel agents can book rooms, they do not receive any commission.

● *Marketing communication* – a major investment in branding, with standardized material, a new logo, and a £20 million television and radio advertising campaign over four years, promoted the key message 'a good night's sleep'.

● *Physical evidence* – the external signage was changed to incorporate the new logo, and the internal maintenance program is designed to keep product standards consistent.

● *Process* – Travel Inn is a simple product, with minimum service levels (only reception and housekeeping); customers who want to eat visit the Whitbread restaurant or pub next door. The focus is on easy-to-use operating systems.

● *People* – The manager of the Whitbread unit next door aims to recruit local, friendly staff who know the area, rather than 'professional hotel staff' for the Travel Inn. The company has an 'Investors in People' UK government training award.

Investment in the Travel Inn brand has been rewarded by continued growth. The aim is to double the number of properties every five years. The introduction of a 100 percent satisfaction guarantee for comfortable surroundings, quality rooms and friendly staff was a first in the UK market. Travel Inn's integration of all the elements of the marketing mix provides a consistent marketing offer, which is customer focused and financially successful.

(Sources: Travel Inn presentation to the HMA, travelinn.co.uk website, and Middleton and Clarke, 2000)

Activity 1.2

Look back to Activity 1.1.

● Compare what you wrote about the meaning of 'marketing' with the definitions we have presented in this chapter. How different are the academic definitions to popular ideas about marketing?

● Reflect upon the 'marketing concept' and the eight elements of the marketing mix. Write down a new list of all the activities involved in marketing.

● Have you changed your ideas about the role of marketing?

The three marketing mixes

Because of the perishability and inseparability of hospitality products, marketers need to give consideration to producing three marketing mixes, each aimed to influence demand at different times.

Before the customer comes to the property to experience the meal or the accommodation, the marketer is faced with identifying and influencing customer expectations, and trying to generate a first-time purchase. The first marketing mix is therefore called the *pre-encounter marketing mix*, because it happens before the customer has the encounter with the service provider.

The second marketing mix occurs at the point of sale and consumption, and is therefore called the *encounter marketing mix*. The task of this marketing mix is to produce a service encounter that meets or exceeds the customer's expectations, to avoid producing customer dissatisfaction and negative word-of-mouth.

The third marketing mix is known as the *post-encounter marketing mix* because it is designed to influence customers after the service experience, with a view to creating a long-term relationship.

Different parts of the eight-element marketing mix are important at each of the stages – before, during and after the encounter. Before the encounter, marketing communications such as advertising, selling, price lists and brochures influence expectations. Marketers need to understand the product/service expectations of customers, as they design offers for the customers. They also must make products easy to buy by establishing appropriate distribution channels.

During the encounter, customers come in to contact with the people element of the marketing mix (employees and other customers), processes, and physical evidence at locations where the service is produced and consumed.

After the encounter, hospitality marketers will want to communicate with customers to find out what they thought of the experience, to identify and satisfy customer complaints, and to encourage the customer to come back and give positive word-of-mouth. Marketing communications is therefore used to build future demand from existing customers. Table 1.3 summarizes what is important at each stage of the customer relationship with the firm.

Table 1.3 Marketing Before, During and After the Encounter (✓ Indicates which Element is Important in each Particular Marketing Mix)

	Pre-encounter marketing mix	Encounter marketing mix	Post-encounter marketing mix
Product/service offer	✓	✓	
Location	✓	✓	
Price	✓	✓	
Distribution	✓		
Marketing communications	✓	✓	✓
Physical environment	✓	✓	
Process	✓	✓	✓
People		✓	

Conclusion

A popular misconception is that marketing is the same as 'selling and advertising'. This chapter will have shown you that there is much more to marketing than promotional tools. Indeed, effective marketing encompasses virtually every aspect of hospitality organization.

In this chapter, we have explained:

● That marketing is a business philosophy that places the customer at the center of the hospitality organization
● The essential purpose of marketing, which is to manage demand
● How marketing-led companies seek to satisfy customers better than competitors
● Why marketers need to scan the PESTE and micro-environment to understand future changes in the marketplace
● The special characteristics of hospitality (SIPIVISH) and why marketers need to understand them
● The hospitality marketing mix, which comprises eight factors that need to be integrated and consistent to ensure brand integrity
● How marketers work to influence demand before, during and after the service encounter.

Review questions

Now check your understanding of this chapter by answering the following questions:

1 Discuss the advantages and disadvantages of each management orientation. Provide examples of each management orientation from your own experience of the hospitality industry (either as a customer or as an employee).
2 Identify three different definitions of marketing, and explain the differences between them.
3 Discuss the external and internal factors that might influence a hospitality organization you know.
4 Evaluate the special characteristics of hospitality and services marketing.
5 Describe briefly the role of each element of the hospitality marketing mix.

References and further reading

Albrecht, K. (1992). *The Only Thing That Matters*. Harper Business Books.
BDRC (2000). *Hotel Marketing Audit, London*. Hotel Marketing Association.
Brown, S. (2001). *Marketing: The Retro Revolution*. Sage.
Carlzon, J. (1987). *Moments of Truth*. Ballinger Publishing.
Grönroos, C. (1994). From marketing mix to relationship marketing: towards a paradigm shift in marketing. *Management Decision*, **32(2)**, 4–20.
Hotel Marketing Association and BDRC (2000).

Kotler, P. (1999). *Kotler on Marketing*. Simon and Schuster, pp. xiii.

Kotler, P. (2000). *Marketing Management*. Prentice Hall.

Kotler, P., Bowen, J. and Makens, J. (2003). *Marketing for Hospitality and Tourism*, 3rd edn. Prentice Hall.

Levitt, T. (1960). Marketing myopia, *Harvard Business Review*, **38**, 45–56.

Lewis R. C. and Chambers, R. E. (2000). *Marketing Leadership in Hospitality: Foundations and Practice*. John Wiley.

Middleton, V. T. C. and Clarke, J. (2000). *Marketing in Travel and Tourism*. Butterworth-Heinemann.

Part B
Pre-encounter marketing

Chapter 2
Marketing research

Chapter Objectives

After working through this chapter, you should be able to:

■ Explain the role marketing research plays in developing marketing strategies for hospitality organizations
■ Identify sources of information available for marketing research in hospitality organizations
■ Describe secondary and primary research activities
■ Explain the differences between qualitative and quantitative research methods
■ Recognize how bias and sampling errors can distort marketing research findings.

Introduction

This chapter explains how marketing research provides the foundation for taking effective marketing decisions. We will introduce the marketing information system as the starting point for marketing research activity, and will then review the wide range of internal and external information sources available for hospitality managers. Both secondary and primary data collection techniques, and qualitative and quantitative data, are discussed with relevant examples. Finally, we will explain the marketing research process.

You will probably already be aware of marketing research activities in general terms. You may have carried out some primary research, and you will certainly know about surveys and opinion polls in the media. In fact, marketing research is a major industry that impacts on our everyday environment.

Activity 2.1

Before reading the rest of the chapter, try to think about the role of marketing research.

● List as many marketing research activities as you know

● Why do you think hospitality companies carry out research?

When you have completed the chapter, carry out this activity again and then compare your answers.

Marketing information systems

Hospitality managers and marketers need relevant, accurate, current and reliable information to be able to make effective decisions about the future of the business.

Small, single-unit, owner-operated companies normally rely on informal approaches to data collection and interpretation. Owner-managers can easily talk to customers to see how well they are performing, and they can visit and/or discuss what is happening in their own environment with local competitors, suppliers and community leaders. Larger organizations need to develop more sophisticated *marketing information systems* to ensure that corporate executives understand the more complex environments in which they are operating (see Figure 2.1). This is because marketing managers in larger companies are separated geographically, and sometimes culturally, from the markets they serve. This helps marketers to identify trends and plan for the future. A marketing information system utilizes:

● Existing data from company sources (accounts and sales, guest history, customer satisfaction)
● Data collated from external marketing research activities (brand performance, corporate reputation, consumer trends, competitor activity).

The major hospitality companies have invested significant capital in developing computerized databases, linked to guest history, to create systems capable of tracking

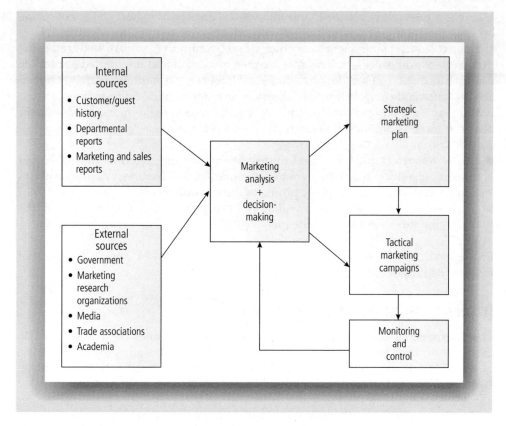

Figure 2.1 The hospitality marketing information system

customer segments and identifying emerging trends. The process of interrogating databases using statistical packages is called *data mining*.

While most of this marketing information will be collected on a routine, regular basis, there are occasions when there is a requirement for specific marketing information. On these occasions, a marketing research project needs to be undertaken. Hospitality managers will use marketing research to help them make decisions regarding such things as:

● Should we increase the number of vegetarian items on the menu? (a review of eating preferences is needed)
● Should we open a new unit near the airport? (a feasibility study will need to be undertaken)
● Should we increase our room rates? (a competitive analysis is needed).

Marketing research

The purpose of marketing research is to inform and improve decision-making by reducing uncertainty. Marketing research can be defined as the systematic gathering and analysis of data to provide relevant information to aid decision-making.

Marketing research is planned, and follows a sequence of logical steps. Following on from the setting of research objectives, information sources are identified. Data are then collected using scientific methods, and quantitative data are analyzed using proven statistical processes. The data are then evaluated and interpreted to provide useful information to aid decision-making. However, marketing research is not an exact science and cannot eliminate all risk in management decision-making.

You may have noticed that throughout this discussion the term *marketing research* has been used – not market research. There is a difference.

- *Market research* is the term used to describe the investigation of consumer and market behavior – the characteristics of a market, its size, the style of consumption patterns, the demographic profile of the consumers
- *Marketing research* has a much wider application including research into all the marketing mix variables and the macro (PESTE) and micro environments.

Professional marketers use the term 'marketing research' to cover all aspects of research activity, including consumer and market behavior.

International marketing research

The international dimensions of major hospitality companies mean they need to carry out research in international markets. This presents unique problems because of the cultural and technological differences between countries (Usunier, 2000). Issues include:

- Translation difficulties (it is usual for English-speaking researchers to compile questionnaires in English, have a native speaker translate it into the local language, then have another English speaker back-translate it into English; this process checks whether translation has changed the meaning of any questions)
- Variations in customer behavior because of different cultural backgrounds
- Variations of customers' product knowledge
- Difficulties in obtaining comparable samples (some countries are unable to provide reliable lists of the population, such as electoral rolls)
- Different cultural responses to market research surveys (in some cultures there can be a reluctance to answer questions, or the answers are biased)
- Differences in the infrastructure – some countries have poor postal systems, and not all consumers have access to telephones.

Companies carrying out international marketing research need to be aware of these difficulties, and should employ specialist local research agencies to provide appropriate advice.

Criticisms of marketing research

Academics and practitioners have criticized modern marketing research for a number of reasons, including the following:

- The focus on collecting data and bureaucratic statistical analysis, which does not provide new insights into the business
- Flawed marketing research methodologies, which provide biased responses
- The emphasis on research stifles creativity in marketing.

Despite these criticisms, major hospitality companies recognize the importance of marketing research and carry out extensive customer and competitor research on a continuous basis.

Sources of information

There are two sources of information in marketing research: internal and external.

Internal

Internal information is held by, and within, the organization. Hotels are fortunate to hold a wealth of information about customers because of legal requirements regarding residents' personal details. Other types of hospitality outlets have less opportunity to collect personal information, but can still utilize internal data effectively. Internal data for accommodation outlets are set out in Table 2.1.

Restaurants and bars do not normally hold such personal details on customers, apart from possibly a mailing list of regulars. Electronic Point of Sale (EPOS) computer systems are used in chain operations to monitor customer food preferences and purchase patterns, which provide essential marketing data. However, one of the problems with internal data is that other departments compile the records for their own use. For example, the accounting department provides analysis in a format that is not always useful to marketers. Other departments need to have a clear understanding of the information needs of marketing managers, and a commitment to providing it.

External

External information can be collected from a large number of sources, including:

● International and national government organizations, e.g. the World Tourism Organization, International Monetary Fund, United Nations and European Union,

Table 2.1 Internal Data Records for Hotels

Customer records	Hotel guest registration details (in most countries it is a legal requirement to record the name, address and length of stay of all residents)
Guest history	Source of booking (direct, travel agent, local company, website); method of reservation (phone, letter, fax, email, Internet, intranet, walk-in); type and number of guests (corporate, private, tour operator); customer feedback; any special requests
Departmental reports	Weekly/monthly accounts recording actual performance, against budget, for sales, occupancy, yield; non-residential sales (food and beverage, banqueting, conference, leisure outlets)
Marketing and sales reports	Customer satisfaction feedback questionnaires and surveys; customers' written compliments and complaints; sales force information from key accounts and intermediaries; monitoring of loyalty club activity; mystery customer surveys; brand conformance audits; brand performance surveys

who publish a wide variety of useful marketing data and analysis; however, you should be aware that direct comparisons of key statistics between different countries are not always accurate due to cultural, sampling or respondent bias

- UK government publications such as the Annual Abstract of Statistics; the National Census, which is carried out every ten years; the Social Trends Survey; the British Tourist Authority (which produces a range of publications that provide relevant market intelligence for the industry)
- Marketing research organizations like Mintel, Keynote and the Economist Intelligence Unit; management consultancies like Deloitte Touche Roche and PKF, which produce commercial market reports on the major sectors of the hospitality industry (e.g. hotels, brewing and holidays)
- Trade associations, such as the Hotel, Catering and International Managers Association, the Hotel Marketing Association (UK) and the American Hotel Sales and Marketing Association, which provide market information and services for members that are also sometimes made available to the public
- Publicly quoted companies, all of which publish annual accounts for shareholders that are also available to the public; annual accounts provide essential information about competitor companies' marketing strengths and strategies, and often the Chairman's report will contain information about the future plans of the business
- The media, which provide useful company market information in the trade press (*Caterer and Hotelkeeper*), the financial press (*Financial Times*), and surveys like the Media Expenditure Analysis Ltd (MEAL), which reports on advertising expenditure in the UK
- Universities and academic publishers, which produce journals reporting on current academic research; the journals discuss academic theory and provide insights into current industry practice (e.g. *International Journal of Contemporary Hospitality Management* and *Journal of Vacation Marketing*).

Increasingly this type of information is becoming available on the Internet. The ABI/Inform Global database, for example, contains full text records of 1,000 business periodicals, and information on over 60,000 companies.

Marketers analyze data collected from the marketing information system, and use the information as a basis for developing the organization's strategic marketing plan.

Secondary and primary data collection

Marketing researchers distinguish between secondary and primary data.

Secondary (or desk) data

Secondary data means information that has already been collected by another source. Most of the external sources listed earlier in this chapter are examples of secondary data. It is relatively easy to obtain secondary data since the information has already been published.

However, there are limitations to secondary data. First, the data have been collected and analyzed by another organization, which will have had its own reasons for carrying out the research and its own research objectives. This means the information may not be completely accurate or relevant. Some organizations, including government bodies and pressure groups, may deliberately manipulate data to present findings to pursue their own agendas. Other organizations may have inadvertently introduced bias into their data collection due to poor methodology, and so present flawed findings.

Another limitation of desk research is that the information is generally available to other organizations, including competitors, the media and pressure groups. Finally, secondary data and analysis can often be 'dated' because of the long time between carrying out the research and publishing the findings. When carrying out secondary research, it is therefore essential to check the date of the research and verify the credibility of the source of the material.

Despite these limitations, secondary research is usually the starting point for a research project and provides useful background information cost-effectively.

Primary data

Primary data consist of original information collected by an organization for a specific purpose. The data have not been published before. The organization conducting or commissioning the research determines the research objectives and research questions. The data are collected directly to provide answers to those questions.

Primary research is more costly than secondary research. The advantages of primary research include the following:

- The ability to frame the research questions to the needs of the organization
- Research is current and not dated
- The research is confidential to the commissioning organization.

This can enable a hospitality company to gain a competitive advantage if its rivals are not carrying out similar primary research.

Closed and Open Questions

There are two types of questions used in research: closed questions and open questions.

Closed questions provide a number of alternative answers from which the respondent chooses one answer. Examples include questions about the respondent's age, sex, employment or income; or about the frequency with which a respondent visits a restaurant, drinks coffee or takes a holiday. Closed questions use a structured format, and this creates a data set that can be efficiently analyzed using quantitative statistical methods. The research findings are described as 'hard' data, and provide numerical information. If the research uses a quantitative approach, then closed questions are essential.

Open-ended questions allow respondents to provide their own answers, without any guidance. Examples of open questions include: 'Why did you choose to stay in this hotel?' and 'How did you feel about the quality of service?' The response to an open question allows the respondent to use their own words

Marketing insight

to describe their experience, feelings and opinions. The research findings provide 'rich' data, which are used in qualitative research.

Researchers usually ask a combination of both closed and open questions, and combine quantitative with qualitative analysis.

Qualitative and quantitative data

Qualitative data

Qualitative research aims to provide a deep understanding of people's contextualized behavior. It aims to explain how and why people behave as they do. As such, it examines beliefs, perceptions, motives, attitudes and opinions. This type of research can provide deep insights into consumers' responses to an organization, its products, services, brands and image. Qualitative research in hospitality uses observation, in-depth interviews, focus groups (also known as group discussions), and qualitative questions in surveys.

Observation is a powerful research tool. Simply sitting in a reception lobby or dining in a restaurant and watching the customer/employee interaction can provide insights into the efficiency of the service operation, the friendliness of the style and the level of customer satisfaction! The Scandinavian airline SAS used video observation of passengers waiting in airport terminals as an effective marketing research technique to improve its customer service.

In-depth interviewing enables a researcher to ask a respondent open-ended questions, often in a semi-structured format. The interviews can take place face-to-face, by telephone or using email. Face-to-face interviews allow the researcher to get close to the interviewee, which helps the researcher to react to the interviewee's body language and to probe with more searching questions in order to obtain more accurate and honest responses. However, face-to-face interviewing is more time-consuming and more expensive to conduct than telephone or email interviews.

Focus group discussions use group dynamics to explore important marketing issues. The researcher invites a number of people (no more than ten) to participate in the discussion, which is normally held in a neutral environment. Depending on the purpose of the discussion, the invitees may be existing customers, potential customers, former customers or employees. A small reward is often offered for participation. A moderator hosts the discussion, which is conducted in a friendly, informal, even 'chatty' way. Focus groups start by discussing broad issues, then begin to focus on the core topic of the research. The researcher often asks the participants' permission to record or video the session, to enable further analysis to be undertaken later. The group dynamics enable a skilled moderator to draw out different perspectives from each member of the group, as well as the group's collective views.

Questionnaires often include both qualitative and quantitative questions. The qualitative questions are open-ended, thus enabling the respondents to give opinions using their own words. We will discuss quantitative questions in the next section.

Whilst qualitative research provides rich, detailed information based on consumers' personal experience and using their own words, there is a methodological limitation to the technique. Respondents who are willing to participate by giving an interview or joining a focus group cannot be considered to be a truly representative sample. Many hospitality customers are too busy, or not sufficiently interested, to give up their valuable time to participate. The inducements to participate – if any – are modest. Although the findings are valuable they cannot be generalized, and other forms of marketing research need to be used to corroborate the qualitative research.

Sometimes, however, qualitative research is performed after quantitative research. This happens when quantitative research has thrown up some interesting information that needs further investigation. For example, a customer satisfaction survey may indicate that a high percentage of customers don't like a hotel's food service. Qualitative research can explore the reasons behind the statistic.

Quantitative data

Quantitative research uses a wide range of statistical methods to measure or quantify data. Quantitative research counts numbers, in terms of either volume or value (for example, the number of customers, passengers, residents, diners, room nights, room occupancy, sales, satisfaction). If results are numeric, then the research and the data are quantitative. Quantitative research techniques are founded upon statistical theory. It is important that the correct statistical method is adopted to reduce possible error and bias. There are four main classes of error in marketing research:

1 Sampling errors. This type of error includes a common problem: sample bias. To be valid, the research has to be based upon a representative sample of the population.
2 Respondent errors. People can change their behavior when asked to participate in marketing research. Some people may give answers which they think are the 'right' answers, rather than being honest and giving their own opinion.
3 Investigator errors. Researchers can accidentally make errors, for example by entering the data inaccurately. This type of recording error can easily happen when inexperienced researchers are not trained thoroughly.
4 Administrative errors. Responses to questionnaires often vary according to the day of week and the weather. For example, on a rainy or oppressively hot day, more hotel guests remain in the property. On a pleasant day, in-hotel surveys will therefore have fewer guests to interview.

In large surveys, computers using statistical software packages process the quantitative research data. Optical scanners read the completed questionnaires and provide detailed data analysis.

There is a variety of survey methods used in quantitative marketing research. The methods commonly used in hospitality organizations include exit surveys, mystery customer audits, telephone surveys and omnibus surveys.

Exit surveys are held by virtually all major hotel chains and many independent hotels, which have questionnaires (often in the bedrooms) available for residents to complete. Questions typically seek customer feedback on the quality of accommodation, food and service, and value for money. These customer satisfaction surveys are important tools for evaluating how a unit is performing, but they suffer from a low response rate and normally attract either the extremely dissatisfied or the highly delighted customer. The example in Figure 2.2 shows the Le Meridien Hotels' exit

Le MERIDIEN
GROSVENOR HOUSE

MOMENT OF TRUTH
L'INSTANT DE VERITE

Dear Guest

Thank you for staying with us at Le Meridien Grosvenor House.

In order to ensure our products and services are of the highest standards available, and that we are best able to meet your requirements, we would be very grateful if you would take a few minutes to let us know how we are doing. We would also greatly appreciate any suggestions you may have to make a stay at Le Meridien Grosvenor House more enjoyable.

Please leave this card with our Front Office Reception upon check-out.

Thank you for your valuable assistance and we look forward to welcoming you back in the near future.

Gregoire Salamin
Hotel Manager

ART + TECH
by Le MERIDIEN

YOUR ARRIVAL

Rating scale: Unacceptable (1) — Average (4–6) — Outstanding (10)

	1	2	3	4	5	6	7	8	9	10
Accuracy of reservation										
Appearance of hotel										
Appearance of lobby										
Speed of check-in process										
Helpfulness of front-desk staff at check-in										
Helpfulness of doorman and bell staff at check-in										
Overall Rating of Arrival										

GUEST ROOM

	1	2	3	4	5	6	7	8	9	10
Cleanliness of guest room										
Decor/furnishing/style of guest room										
Comfort of bed (include mattress, linens...)										
Quietness of guest room										
Availability of amenities (hair dryer, iron etc)										
Ability to work in room										
Lighting for reading or working										
Connection/speed of internet										
Variety of in-room video/TV/music/entertainment										
Cleanliness of bathroom										
Bath/shower water pressure										
Quality of bathroom amenities (soap, shampoo, etc)										
Room Smell										
Overall Rating of Guest Room										

FOOD & BEVERAGE

	1	2	3	4	5	6	7	8	9	10
Menu choices available in restaurant/bar										
Ambience/atmosphere in restaurant/bar										
Accuracy of restaurant/bar service										
Quality of food and beverage in restaurant/bar										
Helpfulness of restaurant/bar staff										
Timeliness of room service										
Quality of room service food and beverage										
Quality of breakfast (taste, variety)										
Overall Rating of Food & Beverage										

HOTEL SERVICES

Rating scale: Unacceptable (1) — Average (4–6) — Outstanding (10) — N/A

	1	2	3	4	5	6	7	8	9	10	N/A
Availability of business facilities/services											
Fitness/Recreation facilities (pool, fitness centre)											
Timeless of voice mail/message/fax											
Helpfulness of front desk staff or concierge staff											
Hotel security/safety											
Overall Rating of Hotel Services											

DEPARTURE/CHECKOUT

	Unacceptable			Average				Outstanding			N/A
	1	2	3	4	5	6	7	8	9	10	
Speed of check-out process at front desk	1	2	3	4	5	6	7	8	9	10	☐
Accuracy of billing	1	2	3	4	5	6	7	8	9	10	☐
Helpfulness of front desk staff at departure	1	2	3	4	5	6	7	8	9	10	☐
Helpfulness of doorman and bell staff at departure	1	2	3	4	5	6	7	8	9	10	☐
Overall Rating of Departure/Check-out	1	2	3	4	5	6	7	8	9	10	☐

Did you experience any significant problems with this hotel? ☐ Yes ☐ No

What type of problem was encountered? Mark all that apply.

☐ Billing ☐ Hotel/Room maintenance ☐ Room cleanliness ☐ Staff attitude
☐ Check-in ☐ Noise ☐ Room location/type ☐ Staff service
☐ Check-out ☐ Reservation accuracy ☐ Room Service ☐ Other
☐ Heating, Ventilation, and/or Air Conditioning ☐ Restaurant/Bar ☐ Small room

Did you report the problem to hotel staff? ☐ Yes ☐ No

If you reported the problem, how would you rate the hotel's resolution of the problem?

Unacceptable			Average				Outstanding		
1	2	3	4	5	6	7	8	9	10

☐ Problem was never solved

Please rate your OVERALL guest experience?

Unacceptable			Average				Outstanding		
1	2	3	4	5	6	7	8	9	10

Considering your entire guest experience, how would you rate the value for money?

Unacceptable			Average				Outstanding		
1	2	3	4	5	6	7	8	9	10

How likely would you be to return to this hotel if in the same area again?
☐ Definitely Will not ☐ Probably Will not ☐ Probably Will ☐ Definitely Will

How likely would you be to recommend this hotel to a friend or colleague?
☐ Definitely Will not ☐ Probably Will not ☐ Probably Will ☐ Definitely Will

How likely would you be to stay at a Le Meridien property again?
☐ Definitely Will not ☐ Probably Will not ☐ Probably Will ☐ Definitely Will

If the hotel you stayed at had NOT been available, which ONE other hotel would you have chosen instead?

☐ Crowne Plaza ☐ Sofitel ☐ Hilton ☐ Ritz Carlton ☐ Sheraton ☐ Four Seasons
☐ Intercontinental Hotels ☐ Other ☐ Hyatt ☐ W ☐ Marriott ☐ Westin

Which of the following best describes the reason for your stay:

☐ Business ☐ Leisure ☐ Both ☐ Conference

How was the reservation made? ☐ Directly through the hotel ☐ Le Meridien reservation centre ☐ Travel Agent ☐ Corporate travel department ☐ Internet ☐ Other

Are you a member of the Le Meridien Moments guest reward programme? Yes ☐ No ☐

Additional Comments and Suggestions

....
....
....
....
....
....
....
....

Thank you for your time and suggestions, please return this questionnaire to front desk.

Mr / Mrs / Ms Last Name................ First Name................

Company................ Position................

Address................

City................ Postcode................ Country................

Your Room No................ Dates of stay................

Figure 2.2 Customer questionnaire (source: Le Meridien Hotels)

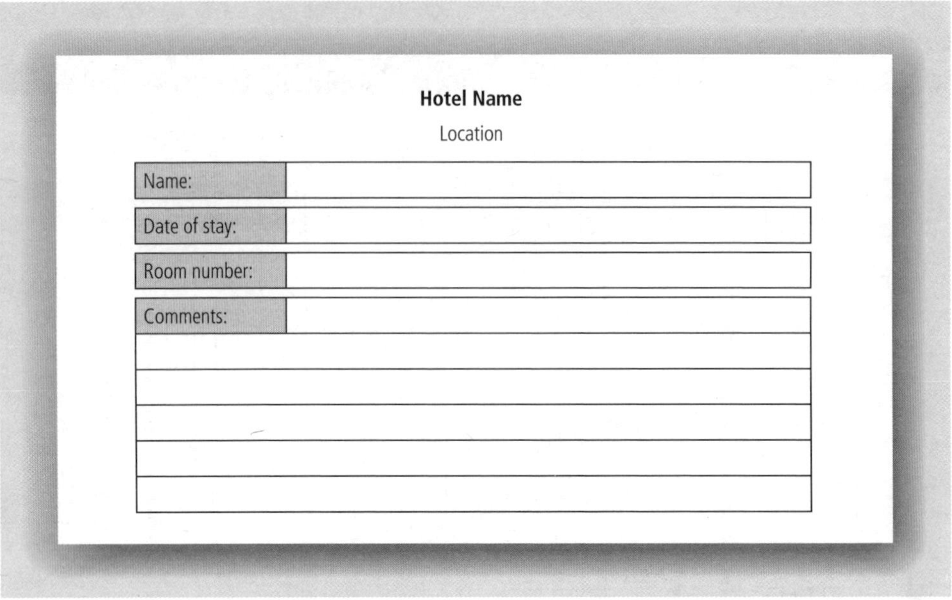

Hotel Name

Location

Name:	
Date of stay:	
Room number:	
Comments:	

Figure 2.3 Open-ended questionnaire

survey, which has both closed and open questions asking customers to comment in detail on every department in the hotel. Companies like Malmaison do not ask any questions but simply allow customers to write what they feel (see Figure 2.3).

Activity 2.2

Compare the two questionnaires.

- What is the main difference between Le Meridien's approach and companies who use an open-ended questionnaire?
- What type of questions are used?
- How will the research findings be analyzed?

Mystery customer audits are used by multiple-unit branded operators to assess how individual units are performing. Researchers posing as customers check whether a unit is conforming to the brand standards, and evaluate the operation from a customer perspective. Each aspect of the operation is marked, and an overall 'score' is recorded. Unit managers and employees do not know who the 'mystery customer' is, but later receive a copy of the report, which highlights brand and operational compliance and deficiencies.

Telephone surveys have been used in consumer research since telephone ownership levels reached saturation point in Western economies. Telephone research is a cost-effective tool to investigate specific segments (e.g. the conference market). Key accounts and conference placement agencies can be contacted to ascertain changes in customer needs and wants. The marketing manager can then introduce adaptations to improve the offer to the customer.

Omnibus surveys are a marketing research method where several companies share the costs of the research. The survey is carried out by an independent marketing research agency. The companies can either come from different industries (e.g. a car manufacturer, an insurance company and a tour operator) or be competitors in the same industry sector. The UK Hotel Brands omnibus survey is carried out each year by BDRC (see Case study 2.1). An omnibus survey, which can also be called syndicated research, is a major research exercise. It is relatively expensive to carry out because of the large sample size, but can be very cost-effective for each individual brand. The cost of participation varies according to the number of questions and types of analysis required.

Case study

2.1 BDRC hotel brands survey

Business Development Research Consultants (BDRC) is an independent marketing research agency founded by Dr Crispian Tarrant and specializing in the service sector. Most of the leading hotel companies, including Accor, Best Western, Copthorne-Millennium, Hilton, InterContinental, Marriott, and Westin participate in the syndicated research. The research benchmarks each brand's performance against competitor brands.

BDRC has carried out qualitative research into hotel guest behavior for over ten years, using in-depth interviews of business and leisure hotel customers. This longitudinal research allows each brand to monitor its own performance year on year. Key performance measures include brand awareness and brand image. BDRC also surveys the meetings, training and conference market by researching the views of corporate event organizers and venue finding agencies, and by extensive mystery shopping to evaluate how enquiries are handled. Whilst elements of the syndicated research are published, each company also receives a confidential report regarding its competitive position. De Vere Hotels made the following comment about BDRC in its annual report: 'the British Hotel Guest Survey is the most comprehensive of its kind … and tracks brand performance across a host of measures such as awareness, preferences and loyalty'.

(Source: BDRC)

Marketing research process

A company can either carry out its own marketing research (this is called in-house) or contract out the marketing research to a specialist agency. Although marketing research agencies can appear to be more expensive, as specialists in their field they will have the expertise, experience, qualified staff, connections and appropriate equipment to carry out the research professionally.

The decision will depend upon the type of research undertaken and the budget available. Observation, customer satisfaction and exit questionnaires, and competitor surveys are normally handled in-house. Focus groups, in-depth interviewing, mystery customer, telephone and omnibus surveys are more often conducted by specialist marketing research agencies.

Effective marketing research follows a number of logical stages, described below.

1 *Formulation of research objectives*. The aims, scope and limitations of the research project need to be established at the start. Clearly identifying the research problem, deciding the desired research outcomes and defining the research objectives at the beginning saves time and money later. Establishing the available budget is essential, since budget constraints will determine what type of marketing research is undertaken and whether the activity is carried out in-house or by an agency. Research objectives are largely determined by the marketing decisions that are to be made. In order to limit the scope of the research, it is helpful to construct empty tables – i.e. tables into which the data will be put once the research is completed. This discipline forces managers to decide precisely what information is needed.

2 *Development of a research plan*. Each stage of the research process needs to be carefully planned, with provisional actions, costs, people, planning and deadlines set out. An evaluation of which research methods (the methodology) are most appropriate needs to be based upon the research objectives and budget.

3 *Data collection*. There are two major components to this phase of the process: first, identifying sources of information (who has the information and where is it?); and second, deciding how to collect the information from the sources (using primary or secondary research methods). Research activity usually starts with a review of secondary sources. This desk research enables the researcher to understand what has been collected in the past, and the data collection methods that have already been used. A good understanding of secondary sources provides the researcher with a solid foundation before embarking on any primary research. Indeed, some research projects can be completed with secondary data alone. If primary research is required, a pilot study to test the research instrument (or method) is essential. Changes can then be made to the research instrument, before the marketing research study is rolled out.

4 *Data analysis*. There is a wide range of statistical tools available to aid marketing data analysis, including:
   - univariate techniques, which analyze single factors such as customer complaints
   - bivariate techniques, which analyze data linking two variables and establish the relationship or correlation between them – for example, the correlation between foreign tourist arrivals and movements in exchange rates
   - multivariate techniques, which analyze three or more variables to establish what, if any, link exists between them – an example might be all the complex factors that influence customer satisfaction on holiday.

5 *Reliability and validity of data*. Responsible researchers recognize that marketing research has limitations, and that it is important to identify any possible statistical error or bias in the findings. Professional marketing researchers are particularly concerned with the issues of reliability and validity. Measures are valid when they measure what they are supposed to measure. If you want to measure customer satisfaction, it would be invalid to use an instrument (questionnaire) designed to measure service quality perceptions. Valid measures are free from the sources of error described earlier: respondent error, investigator error, sampling error and administrative error. A reliable measure is one that is consistent and does not vary over time. Remember that some organizations deliberately manipulate or distort information. In particular, the data from research have to be placed within the context of the PESTE environment at the time of the research,

since research findings into the hospitality industry are obviously influenced by different periods of economic prosperity and recession.

6 *Presentation of findings.* Finally, the researcher has to present the findings. Normally there will be large amounts of data and analysis, which need to be presented in an accessible manner. Key findings should be provided in an executive summary. The main report should contain an explanation of the methodology and detailed discussion of the findings. Any research limitations and possible bias should be explained. The raw data can be presented either in the appendices or in a separate booklet.

Case study 2.2 provides an example of global marketing research.

Case study

2.2 InterContinental Hotels' global marketing research

InterContinental Hotels (ICH) carried out extensive customer and employee research as part of a repositioning strategy. The company conducted 2500 interviews, received 150,000 feedback questionnaires, and organized focus groups in over 50 countries to establish what customers and employees expected from the brand. Six key target markets were identified and described using lifestyle descriptors, such as 'contemporary classics' (successful international business travelers, who have discriminating taste and enjoy modern living).

A proposition was developed for positioning ICH: the thought was 'we know what it takes'. Although this was regarded as an ambitious positioning statement, both customers and employees liked the idea. The research suggested that the proposition was credible because the brand had a strong heritage, appropriate because of the positive service promise inherent in the idea, and relevant because the target market is demanding. The research also revealed that although ICH customers maintained that their rational needs were dominant, they also had strong latent emotional needs. International business travelers are employed to carry out important work, and therefore work is clearly the dominant purpose of their visit. However, these customers also wanted to enjoy their stay and have a pleasurable business trip. This research was used to inform the £25 million re-launch campaign for ICH, which combined effective internal marketing with new advertising and print material.

(Source: Paul Simmons, Vice President Global Marketing, presentation to the HMA 29/4/03)

Conclusion

You now know that marketing research is based upon scientific principles and provides hospitality companies with essential information to help decision-making. Managers use marketing research to confirm or reject their own gut feelings about a project. In the final analysis, marketing research is a tool that managers use in developing, implementing and controlling marketing plans, but no amount of marketing research can actually make decisions for the hospitality manager. It is the manager's task to make decisions based on the information available.

In this chapter, we have explained:

● The role of a marketing information system
● How hospitality organizations can utilize internal information for marketing research purposes
● Where to find external sources of information
● Secondary and primary research techniques
● The difference between qualitative and quantitative data
● The marketing research process.

Review questions

Carry out Activity 2.1 (page 38) again and compare your answers. Now check your understanding of this chapter by answering the following questions:

1 Discuss the components and the role of a marketing information system for a major hospitality organization.
2 Evaluate the relevance of secondary and primary research methods for:
   ● an owner-managed hospitality unit
   ● a branded hospitality unit
   ● a national branded hospitality chain.
3 Describe the differences between qualitative and quantitative data in hospitality marketing.
4 Draw up a marketing research plan for the opening of a new restaurant in your neighborhood.

References and further reading

Finn, M., Elliott-White, M. and Walton, M. (2000). *Tourism & Leisure Research Methods*. Longman.

Kotler, P., Bowen, J. and Makens, J. (2003). *Marketing for Hospitality and Tourism*, 3rd edn. Prentice Hall.

Lewis, R. C. and Chambers, R. E. (2000). *Marketing Leadership in Hospitality: Foundations and Practice*. John Wiley.

Lumsden, T. (1997). *Tourism Marketing, International*. Thomson Business Press.

Middleton, V. T. M. and Clarke, J. (2000). *Marketing in Travel and Tourism*. Butterworth-Heinemann.

Usunier, J. C. (2000). *Marketing Across Cultures*. Prentice Hall.

Chapter 3
Understanding and segmenting customers

Chapter Objectives

After working through this chapter, you should be able to:

■ Understand the core concepts of hospitality consumer, and organizational customers', behavior
■ Discuss the role of customer expectations
■ Identify the factors that influence the hospitality consumer buyer decision-making process
■ Explain the principles of segmenting demand in hospitality markets
■ Describe hospitality segmentation variables
■ Evaluate the characteristics of hospitality target markets.

Introduction

In this chapter we will review the complex topics of consumer behavior and customer expectations, and then explore the principles and practice of market segmentation and target marketing. Segmentation and targeting are based on two simple facts. First, hospitality consumers are enormously varied in their expectations and requirements. Nonetheless, we can identify subsets of hospitality customers who broadly share similar needs and wants. Secondly, by identifying customers with similar needs and wants, we can design and brand our services in a way that will deliver better customer satisfaction to the targeted customers, and compete more effectively against our competitors.

Consumer behavior

In Chapter 1 we established that marketers manage demand. Demand is a form of behavior. So marketers study consumer behavior to try to understand and predict what customers will buy, how, and why. Marketers need to understand the *process* consumers go through in buying and consuming hospitality products. If we can understand who buys which hospitality products where, when and why, then the probability of success in striving to influence that demand will be enhanced. By understanding and meeting customer expectations, companies can better deliver customer satisfaction. Research into this subject area is broadly termed *consumer behavior*. Extensive research has been conducted into consumer behavior in a wide range of social science disciplines, including psychology, social psychology, sociology, anthropology, philosophy, economics and marketing. Each discipline takes a different perspective in seeking to understand consumer behavior.

We will now discuss the influences on consumer behavior and the hospitality buyer decision-making process.

Influences on consumer buyer behavior

The amount of disposable income consumers have to spend varies according to environmental conditions. When countries are at peace, economies are growing and there are many employment opportunities, consumers are more optimistic about the future. These factors create the conditions where consumers can enjoy real increases in disposable income. Consumer confidence is higher, and they are likely to spend more on hospitality products. In developed countries, consumer confidence is tracked on a regular basis to measure the 'feel-good' factor. In market economies, consumers have choice – they can choose to spend their disposable income as they want. In this sense, hospitality competes against other consumer purchases for the consumers' disposable income. A young, newly married couple may have to choose between buying items for their home or going on holiday.

Naturally, individual consumers will choose to buy different products for different reasons at different times. Researchers are very interested in consumer purchase behavior, and carry out research to identify the major influences. These influences on individual consumer buyer behavior can be categorized under three broad headings: socio-cultural influences, individual differences, and contextual circumstances.

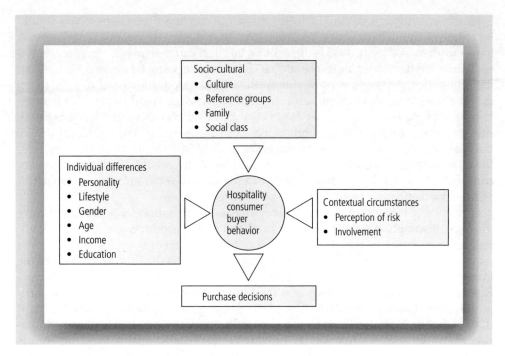

Figure 3.1 Influences on individual hospitality consumers

Socio-cultural influences include culture, reference groups, family and social class. Individual differences include personality, lifestyle, gender, age, income and education. Contextual circumstances include perception of risk and involvement (see Figure 3.1).

Socio-cultural influences

We will now discuss how culture, family, reference groups and social class influence buyer behavior.

Culture   All of us are born into a culture. Culture can be thought of as the shared values and beliefs that help individuals to understand how society functions. These values and beliefs provide us with guidelines for behavior. Our culture is expressed in and reinforced by learnt behaviors such as consumer behavior. Culture is passed from generation to generation as part of the socialization process we undergo when growing up. Some of the factors that make up culture include:

Human needs	Geography	Climate
History	Social Organization	Family and food
Language	(individualism versus collectivism)	Education
Religion	Economics	Customs and habits
Art	Architecture	Attitudes

We can all see that people from different cultures behave differently. When we look after foreign customers, whether they are from America, Australia, Britain, China, France, Germany, Italy or Japan, we notice differences that can clearly be attributed to culture.

However, although culture is deeply rooted, it can and does change. You should be aware of the debate about 'globalization' in today's international marketplace. Some academics (Levitt, 1983) suggest that cultural differences are being eroded as consumer markets become more global. Erosion is caused be several conditions, including the emergence of powerful multinational corporations and of technology that enables companies to communicate identical messages worldwide. This homogenization of global consumer needs and wants, called convergence theory, is predicated on the *similarities* that international consumers share. The rapid growth of international business and leisure travel means that hospitality organizations cater for an increasing number of visitors from all parts of the world. If global hospitality consumers have similar needs and wants, then companies can provide a more standardized marketing offer, which is also more cost-effective.

However, critics of convergence theory suggest that postmodern consumers have diverse consumption patterns mixing local and global products and services. Local culture remains an important dimension, which marketers targeting international markets need to understand and respond to (Usunier, 2000). This recognition of the importance of culture in marketing focuses on the *differences* between consumers from different cultural traditions and their buying preferences. If international hospitality consumers have different needs and wants, then companies should adapt their global products and services to local cultural requirements. This local adaptation of the hospitality offer should provide enhanced customer satisfaction, but is not as cost-effective as standardizing the marketing offer.

An interesting example of international consumer expectations for hotels revealed that the top four choice criteria for selecting a hotel by US and Korean business travelers were the same (McCleary *et al.*, 1998). Customers, regardless of nationality, want clean, safe, comfortable hotels with friendly staff. However the bottom four choice criteria had nothing in common. Americans were more interested in non-smoking rooms and family restaurants, whilst Koreans preferred a convenient location and in-room mini bars. This type of research suggests that the primary choice criteria are common to all consumers, whilst culture has a considerable influence on secondary choice criteria.

Family Families have a huge influence on consumer behavior. Our adult preferences for food, beverage and leisure activities are largely products of the influences of our childhood. The stereotypical Western family unit of a working father, stay-at-home mother and two children is no longer dominant. Today, Western families comprise a wide range of different combinations, including dual-earning couples with no children, single working parents, same sex partners, and traditional family groupings. An interesting trend in Western societies is the growing number of people who live by themselves. In Asian countries the extended family plays a much greater role, and many consumer decisions are discussed collectively. The composition of a household affects the amount of disposable income – and, typically, higher disposable income leads to higher household expenditure on hospitality and tourism services.

Reference groups Individual consumer behavior is also influenced by our identification with or membership of groups. A distinction is made between primary groups and secondary groups. Primary groups are those in which we interact face-to-face with other members – for example, family, friends and classmates. Secondary groups, being larger or dispersed, do not experience that face-to-face interaction; they include cultural and nationality groupings, business associations and alumni. Reference groups can be classified in three useful ways:

1 *Membership groups*. These are groups to which we belong. Your choice of holiday destination is influenced by your membership groups of classmates and family.
2 *Aspirational groups*. We want to be (seen to be) associated with these groups. If you want to be thought of as a gourmet, you might choose to dine or work at high-priced restaurants.
3 *Disassociative groups*. We want not to be (seen to be) associated with these groups. If you do not want to be thought of as a student, you may choose to wear business clothes to functions.

Reference groups perform two functions: they set and enforce standards, and they act as points of reference for individuals to compare their behaviors. Within peer groups and communities, individuals whose opinions are most respected influence others. These people are described as 'opinion leaders'. In hospitality and tourism, travel writers and food critics are critical opinion leaders whose positive or negative comments in local and national media can boost or destroy demand for individual hotels and restaurants.

Socio-economic class   All countries have social class systems (also known as social grading or socio-economic classifications), though some are more formal than others. Class systems are important influences on consumer behavior. Social class is linked to education, occupation and income, and provides a broad segmentation base for market segmentation. In the UK the socio-economic classification system JICNARS (see Table 3.1) is widely used as a descriptor of consumer groups in marketing research, marketing planning, new product development, and advertising media audience profile. However, social class is not strictly homogeneous and there are wide differences in the attitudes, interests, opinions and therefore purchase behavior of individuals within the same social class category.

Table 3.1 Social Class Classifications in Britain (Source: JICNARS)

Social grade	Social class status	Characteristics
A	Upper middle (3%)	Higher managerial, administrative, or professional
B	Middle (14%)	Intermediate managerial, administrative, or professional
C1	Lower middle (22%)	Supervisory or clerical and junior managerial, administrative or professional
C2	Skilled working (29%)	Skilled manual workers
D	Working (18%)	Semi-skilled and unskilled manual workers
E	Lowest income (14%)	State pensioners, widows, casual and lowest grade workers

Individual differences

Individual differences that influence buyer behavior are discussed under the headings of age and gender, education and income, personality, and lifestyle.

Age and gender   A person's age clearly influences needs and wants. Young adults have very different interests, tastes and income levels compared with people in their sixties and seventies. Older people tend to think of a 'good meal' in traditional terms and as a formal dining occasion, whilst younger people tend to be much more experimental in their food tastes and look for a more informal dining experience. However, many people who grew up in the 1960s think and act much younger than previous older generations. Marketers realize there is a difference between chronological age (reflected in the passage of years) and cognitive age (what we think and how we act).

Women and men can have different needs and wants, and gender can therefore influence an individual's purchase behavior. Often, women feel less safe and secure than men when traveling and staying in hotels. Men have a different approach to consuming food and beverages (in terms of taste and portion size) compared to women. You can clearly identify these gender differences when viewing adverts on the television and cinema – beer advertisements are sometimes overtly masculine and 'laddish', whilst adverts for drinks like Taboo® are designed for a younger, female market.

Education and income   Education influences job opportunities and income, and also shapes our values, beliefs, attitudes, interests, activities and lifestyle. Students who go to university meet a variety of different people, often from foreign countries. They develop their analytical and intellectual competencies and learn a wide range of transferable skills, as well as studying a subject in greater depth. They also gain a broad education, which provides them with enhanced employment prospects. This enables graduates to eventually earn higher salaries in their workplace.

The level of income helps to determine the amount of consumer disposable income available for discretionary purchases. People with higher income levels spend proportionately less on household necessities, and therefore have more disposable income. This has considerable influence on holiday and dining out expenditure patterns.

Personality or psychographic attributes   An individual's personality can influence the type of products purchased. People in the same family can, because of their different personalities, have different purchase and consumption habits – especially in more individualistic societies. Research has identified clusters of consumers with similar personality traits. Personalities are often described in terms of the individual's position on a number of scales, such as:

Sociable	_:_:_:_:_:_	Shy
High self-esteem	_:_:_:_:_:_	Low self-esteem
Assertive	_:_:_:_:_:_	Submissive

Some companies evaluate these psychological attributes when developing new product concepts, as personality is closely linked to lifestyle choices.

Lifestyle   An individual's lifestyle is a powerful influence on the purchase of discretionary products like travel and dining out. Lifestyle is a reflection of an individual's personality and social influences. Researchers have claimed that we can describe a lifestyle in terms of a person's activities, interests and opinions.

These can be summarized as follows:

- Activities include work, shopping, sport and entertainment, hobbies and travel
- Interests include family, the home and garden, watching TV, food and fashion
- Opinions – about our own culture, other cultures, ourselves (and self-belief), social and political issues, business and economics, and even about the future – inform our lifestyle.

Activities, interests and opinions cross cultural, social and demographic divides – for example, there are supporters of Manchester United Football Club of both sexes, from every continent, socio-economic class and age group throughout the world. A person's passion for sport, music or bird watching will influence how that person spends his or her time and money. Lifestyle has become an increasingly important concept in understanding consumer behavior and predicting consumer purchase and consumption activity.

The New Consumer (Source: Middleton and Clark, 2000)

Marketing insight

As society has become more atomized and less collective, Western consumers see themselves as individuals who are 'more diverse, more experienced, more demanding, more quality conscious and generally more sophisticated' than 25 years ago. Today consumers have more wealth, with high levels of disposable income; are more educated and knowledgeable about food, travel and tourism, both from personal experience and via the media; have more leisure time entitlement (although some consumers are described as cash-rich and time-poor, since the heavy demands of their work means they have limited leisure time opportunities); and are becoming more computer and Internet literate. The 50- to 65-year-olds of today experienced the youth revolution of the 1960s, have traveled extensively to visit many different countries over the past 30–40 years, and have encouraged their children to travel as well. These sophisticated modern consumers are less prepared to tolerate mediocre service, and are more likely to complain if the hospitality standards do not meet their high expectations.

Contextual circumstances

Sometimes, socio-cultural influence and individual differences are less important than contextual circumstances in influencing our behaviors. Two concepts that are helpful for understanding the role of context are perception of risk, and involvement.

Perceived risk   A consumers' perception of the risk associated with buying a hospitality product influences the purchase decision. Perceived risk exists when the consumer is uncertain about the consequences of a purchase, or about the decision itself. The perceived risk is higher when a consumer has little experience or knowledge about the product, has low self-confidence about making a purchase decision, or faces significant long-term consequences as a result of buying the product. There are different types of perceived risk, including financial, social and psychological risk:

- *Financial risk* occurs when there is a large amount of money at risk. It is linked to major hospitality purchases – organizing a wedding day or planning a significant holiday. The larger the amount of money involved, the greater is the perceived financial risk.

● *Social risk* is linked to product symbolism, and relates to hospitality products that have a social significance for the consumer. The choice of where to have dinner sends social signals to the other diner(s).

● *Psychological risk* occurs when consumers perceive a threat to their self-image and self-esteem. In Asian societies the concept of 'face' is very important, so consumers are very concerned about making the correct hospitality purchase decisions to avoid losing face in front of their family and friends.

Involvement   Consumers vary regarding the level of involvement they have in purchasing decisions. A highly involved purchase decision is one that is personally significant and relevant for a consumer – for example, most parents consider that their choice of a venue for a child's birthday party is highly involving. On the other hand, the choice of a coffee shop for a quick refreshment may be a low involvement decision. Involvement tends to vary between individuals (some people are highly involved in many decisions), products (some products are more involving than others) and context (the level of involvement can vary across purchasing context). For example, the choice of a restaurant for a lunch break may be low involvement, until a business guest is invited – then it becomes a high involvement decision.

Involvement is an important idea to understand, because the buying process varies according to whether the decision is high or low involvement. High involvement decisions (for example, planning a honeymoon or organizing a conference) are more complex than low involvement decisions (for example, planning where to meet friends for a drink at the weekend). A high involvement decision will involve much more pre-purchase search for information about alternatives and a post-purchase evaluation of whether the decision was successful.

Buyer decision-making process

If marketers are to influence customer demand, they need to understand how customers make buying decisions (see Table 3.2).

The starting point for decision-making is when a consumer recognizes that he or she has a need that is not currently being satisfied. The need may be caused by internal conditions (feeling hungry) or motivated by external stimuli (seeing an advertisement). If the decision involves a low involvement product, the consumer's response is more likely to be a routinized buying decision – feeling hungry at lunchtime and visiting the local sandwich shop. If the decision involves a high involvement product, the consumer will have to search for a solution. This search process can be internal or external. An internal search uses our memory to recall previous experiences (or information) to provide a satisfactory solution. If the internal search does not provide a solution, then the consumer has to engage in an external search.

Consumers evaluate alternative ways of solving the problem, weighing the alternatives against their own set of criteria. In hospitality, some of the criteria used by consumers include location, quality, convenience, reputation, price and availability. After evaluating options, the consumer makes a buying decision – assuming that the price is affordable, and the time to purchase and consume the hospitality product is available. After the transaction has been completed, the consumer assesses whether

Table 3.2 Hospitality Consumer Decision-making Process for a Complex Product

Hospitality consumer decision-making process for a high involvement or high perceived risk product

Process	Example
Perception of need	Engaged couple planning a honeymoon
Information search	Search travel agents and Internet, ask family and friends for advice on alternative honeymoon holidays in various destinations
Evaluation of alternatives	Agree 'decision criteria' – these include the budget, number of days on the honeymoon, where to go (domestic, short-haul, long-haul), what type of holiday (sun and sea or culture; all-inclusive or go-as-you-please), which destinations
Purchase	Make the decision and buy the honeymoon
Post-purchase evaluation	Upon returning home, evaluate the consumption experience, which will inform future anniversary holiday decisions and whether to recommend the destination and accommodation to family and friends

the product actually satisfied the relevant needs, and this post-purchase evaluation influences the consumer's propensity to repeat purchase and to recommend positively (or negatively) the hospitality product. If a customer who is not satisfied complains and the company is able to recover the situation, the customer can repeat purchase and positively recommend the product. However, if the complaint is not handled effectively, the unhappy customer is likely to tell many more people about a bad experience than a good experience (see Chapter 13). Unfortunately most unhappy customers do not complain, so the hospitality company has no chance to recover the situation.

Understanding customer expectations

An important concept for marketers is *customer expectation*. Customers have expectations of hospitality encounters, which marketers must meet if customers are to be satisfied.

Customer beliefs

Customers form beliefs about what a hospitality experience will be like. Customers' beliefs are formed by a combination of different influences, including culture, reference groups, word-of-mouth, previous experience, marketing communication, and individual personal characteristics. Whilst individual customer beliefs can be idiosyncratic (such customers are often called eccentric because of their unusual behavior), different national cultures have a strong influence on customers' belief systems, which in turn influence customer expectations. For example, international tourists who come from high service cultures (like Japan and Taiwan) have higher expectations when traveling abroad and staying in hotels, while the expectations of travelers from countries with the limited service culture (like some of the East European countries) have lower expectations.

There have been a number of attempts to understand and classify expectations. One scheme suggest that there are four different types of expectation:

1 The ideal level – 'what can be'
2 The predicted level – 'what will be'
3 The minimum tolerable – 'what must be'
4 The deserved level – 'what should be' (this is the level that customers think is appropriate given what they have invested in finding and buying the product).

Parasuraman and his colleagues (Zeithaml *et al.*, 1993) have suggested that customer expectations fall within a *zone of tolerance* ranging from 'what must be' (minimum tolerable) to 'what can be' (desired level). It is also suggested that customers are willing to accept a level of performance that falls within a *zone of indifference*. This zone ranges around the customer's judgment of what is a reasonable expectation of the supplier.

Zone of tolerance

During and after service performance, customers compare their expectations to their perceptions of the service they have received. However, the special characteristics of service in the hospitality industry mean that the quality of service delivery fluctuates. Customers who are knowledgeable about the variability in hospitality service can have greater tolerance for the variations in a service performance (i.e. a wider zone of tolerance; see Zeithaml and Bitner, 2003). On the other hand, there are customers who are much less sympathetic and therefore have a lower tolerance to service fluctuations. This range of tolerance represents a customer's propensity to accept variable service standards and still be satisfied with the service offered.

A number of factors influence the customer's level of tolerance, including the customer's personality and current circumstances, the importance of the purchase occasion, and the characteristics of the product and the price paid. The levels of perceived risk and involvement can explain variations in the zone of tolerance. Clearly, customers have different levels of tolerance at different times. As individuals we can all have mood swings, and so sometimes we feel more tolerant and relaxed about service quality whilst on other occasions (for reasons we do not always understand) we can be less tolerant and become more easily upset by service quality failings. Customers who have a time constraint will be intolerant of service failure.

Organizational markets

Whilst individual consumers represent a significant proportion of hospitality customers, especially for smaller hospitality companies, the larger hospitality organizations cater for the needs of organizational markets. These include business companies generating corporate travel and corporate meetings; professional and trade associations; convention, exhibitions and trade fairs; tour groups; aircrew; and other miscellaneous types of volume bookings. In tourism and hospitality, some of these activities are linked under the heading of the MICE market (Meetings, Incentives, Conference and Exhibitions).

Organizations have a different approach to the buying process compared to individual consumers. These differences include the following:

- The number of participants involved in the organization's purchase decisions tends to be greater
- The users are not always the buyers
- The complexity of the arrangements (coordinating hundreds or thousands of people's travel, accommodation, catering and entertainment needs is not a simple task)
- The technical requirements, involving conference and banqueting arrangements, audiovisual and stage facilities, and exhibition stand details, are complex.

Organizational buyer behavior researchers have identified several roles in group purchase decisions: users, influencers, deciders, buyers and gatekeepers. These roles are collectively known as the 'decision-making unit' (DMU):

- *Users* are the guests who actually stay in hotels
- *Influencers* are people who are close to the decision-maker and can influence any part of the decision, such as location, hotel, and food service
- *Deciders* are the people who actually make the decisions – the manager, executive or director
- *Buyers* are the people who make and pay for the booking
- *Gatekeepers* are people who control the flow of information to other members of the DMU – secretaries or personal assistants (PAs) often play a key role as gatekeepers in their organizations.

The buying process in organizations is more formalized, with varying degrees of bureaucratic and/or committee reporting structures. A professional approach is required when discussing or negotiating bookings with these types of organizations. The value and volume of organizational bookings varies, but for many of the major hospitality companies the MICE market represents a key element in their business.

Market segmentation

We have established that understanding individual consumer behavior and organizational market behavior helps us to understand customer expectations. Marketers use this information to identify potential customers having similar needs and wants, and describe these customers as *target markets*. This process of identifying subsets of consumers who have distinct, homogenous demand characteristics is called market segmentation. There is a broad consensus that segmentation is the starting point for developing effective marketing strategies because:

- Trying to target all consumers is not cost-effective (remember, some consumers may never want to buy your hospitality product)
- Identifying the characteristics of target markets enables a company to design and develop the hospitality offer to satisfy customers more effectively

- Concentrating a company's limited marketing resources on key markets leads to a more focused and cost-effective marketing strategy
- Segmentation improves profitability by maximizing customer satisfaction, and generating repeat and recommended sales.

However, there are difficulties for hospitality firms trying to establish effective segmentation strategies, due to:

- The costs of carrying out marketing research
- The lack of flexibility in hospitality products
- The additional costs of developing and communicating separate offers for different target markets
- The complexity of constantly changing consumer behavior
- The problem of targeting different and often incompatible target markets who use the premises at the same time.

The key point is that market segments are inherently unstable. Their membership, size, value and volume change in response to changes in the PESTE environment.

We will now review the segmentation process, followed by a discussion of key hospitality segmentation variables.

The segmentation process

There is a logical sequence that can be followed during market segmentation. The stages of the segmentation process outlined in Table 3.3 are discussed here in more detail.

1 *Specification*. The market to be researched and segmented needs to be clearly identified, taking a broad definition of consumers' needs and wants in the sector.
2 *Establish segmentation criteria*. A set of criteria needs to be developed against which the various segmentation opportunities can be evaluated for market attractiveness. Segmented markets should be:
   - discrete – can the segment be described as having a unique set of shared requirements and expectations requiring a specific marketing program?
   - measurable – can the market size be measured in terms of value and/or volume, growth rates and market share of current players?
   - of a profitable size – does the segment have sufficient profit potential to justify the investment? By careful analysis, companies can often identify smaller, more profitable 'niche' markets within larger market segments. For single-unit hospitality companies, the market will primarily be focused on the company's

Table 3.3 The Segmentation Process

1. Specify the market
2. Establish segmentation criteria
3. Generate segmentation variables
4. Develop and evaluate market segment profiles
5. Evaluate company's competences to serve selected segments effectively

micro-environment and depends upon the local characteristics of demand and existing/potential competitors.

- accessible – can the segment be reached via distribution and marketing communication channels? There is no point in targeting a segment if the company cannot communicate with potential consumers.
- compatible – marketers should ensure that any new target markets are compatible with existing target markets.

3 *Generate segmentation variables*. Segmentation variables provide the basis for classifying consumers into different market segments. Hospitality segmentation variables include purpose of visit; geo-demographics; buyer, user and lifestyle characteristics; price; and time. In hospitality, a wide number of variables are used to build a more detailed profile of the target markets. The more detailed the segmentation data, the greater the understanding of potential customers.

4 *Develop market segment profiles based on segmentation variables*. Detailed market segment profiles include the size of the market in terms of value and volume, customer purchase details (frequency of visit, average room/food/bar spend, number in party), consumer characteristics (benefits sought, price sensitivity), and accessibility/responsiveness to marketing programs.

5 *Evaluate the company's competencies*. The company needs to ensure that it has the competencies and resources to serve and satisfy the segment's needs and wants profitably.

This approach suggests that there is a precision in the analysis of market segments, which is not strictly true. Many hospitality markets are fragmented, and it is difficult to calculate the volume and value of a market segment accurately. Market share can be even more difficult to ascertain accurately. The benefit of using segmentation analysis in hospitality operations is to identify consumer trends to establish which market segments will become attractive in the future and which market segments are becoming less attractive now.

Hospitality segmentation variables

Segmentation variables are the basis for classifying consumers into different market segments. Some of these segmentation variables have already been discussed in the consumer behavior and customer expectations sections of this chapter. The segmentation variables form the building blocks in developing target market profiles of customer expectations.

The primary segmentation variable used by virtually all hotel and lodging companies is *purpose of travel*. The three main categories are business, non-business (variously defined as leisure, holiday, personal, or social) and visiting friends and relatives (VFR). Each of these main categories can be further subdivided in to several distinct market segments, but a key point to remember is that the *same person* can have different customer needs and wants depending upon whether the purpose of travel is business or non-business. Each micro-segment will have its own market demand factors and individual characteristics with implications for hospitality providers. (See Figure 3.2 for a summary of hospitality market segments.)

Hospitality market segments

Tourist accommodation market		Purpose of visit	Segments	Price	Geographic		Demographic & family unit	Party size	User status
Business		FIT Corporate Local company Meeting Conference Exhibition	[Management [Sales [Training [Recruitment [Professional advisors [Board	Luxury Mid-market Budget	Domestic International	Cities Counties States Regions American British Chinese Japanese	Age: 18–24 25–34 35–54 55–65	Single 2–4 Small group Large group	Non-user Potential First-time Light Medium Heavy Lapsed
Leisure		Overnight stopover Family holiday Honeymoon Package holiday Leisure break Exotic holiday Go-as-you-please Fly-drive Incentive	[Destination [Activity [Cultural [Event [Relaxation [Sight-seeing [Sand, sea, sun	Luxury Mid-market Budget	Domestic International	Cities Countries States Regions American British Chinese Japanese	Age: Under 18 18–24 25–34 35–54 55–70 70+ Family cycle: Young single Young couple Couple & children Older couple Old single	Single Couple 2–6 Small group Large group	Non-user Potential First-time Light Medium Heavy Lapsed

Figure 3.2 Hospitality market segments

Business

Business customers tend to:

- Be less price-sensitive, since the employer generally meets hospitality and travel expenses
- Be more likely to stay for one night, or only a few, on each trip
- Be more frequent, or regular, users of hotel accommodation
- Stay at establishments that are within a reasonable (10–30 minutes) travel time of their place of work – hence the higher demand for business accommodation close to commercial, industrial, and retail areas
- Be less seasonal – business travel patterns are less dependent upon weather and holiday schedules.

The business travel segment contains business trips that are unavoidable, like sales meetings with customers and technical visits to factories by engineers. Other trips are more discretionary, for example attending a conference or exhibition.

Leisure

Leisure customers tend to:

- Be much more price-sensitive than business travelers, since they are paying for the accommodation out of their own taxed income
- Be more likely to stay longer on each trip – short breaks are normally at least a couple of days, two-week holidays are common, and longer holiday periods are not unusual
- Be less frequent users of hotel accommodation (unless they are also business travelers)
- Stay at establishments that are close to leisure amenities and tourist attractions – hence the demand for cultural, rural and seaside resort hotels
- Be much more seasonal, both in terms of climate and the time of year.

There are some business and leisure travel markets that overlap. For example, international conferences and exhibitions often include an element of free time, to be enjoyed as a leisure period. The incentive travel sector uses the appeal of free, and often luxurious or adventurous, leisure travel to motivate and reward performance in business markets.

Visiting friends and relatives

From an accommodation demand perspective, this segment does not generate significant volumes of business for hotels since people tend to stay in the homes of their friends and relatives. This market is more important to tourism establishments in the day-visitor leisure and recreation sectors, and to restaurants and bars.

Geographic

A simple segmentation variable is identifiable from a customer's home address and/or country of origin. National governments require hotels to collect passport details from international visitors, and these data provide important marketing information about the types of international markets being served. Geographic segmentation variables within a country's domestic market include cities, counties, states and regions.

The benefits of segmenting consumers using geographic variables include the following:

- Hotel guest registration data makes it easy to identify customers' addresses
- Nationality is a universally recognized method of categorizing visitors in international tourism marketing
- The special needs and wants of consumers from particular regions can be researched and products can be specifically developed to satisfy those needs and wants
- Media channels, which depend upon advertising revenues, provide audience statistics and demographic data that profile potential consumers within their catchment area. This data can be used to target marketing communications campaigns cost-effectively.

ACORN (A Classification Of Residential Neighborhoods) is an example of a geo-demographic (mix of geography and demography) segmentation tool, commercially available in the UK from the company CACI. All UK homes are allocated a postcode (or zip code), and there are approximately 30 homes in each postcode. Each UK postcode has been classified, in conjunction with the government's census data, according to the type and status of the housing and area. Having identified the clusters of housing, representative samples are regularly interviewed with in-depth personal face-to-face interviews. The research provides a wealth of data about the purchasing habits of people who are representative of their area. CACI has classified British consumers into 17 groups and 54 types based upon this research.

Activity 3.1

- Log onto the CACI website at www.caci.co.uk

- Explore the site and review the research into customer profiling and ACORN – how can this information help hospitality marketers?

Demographic

Demographics is the study of population characteristics, and to a large extent relies on data collected by governments during censuses. Market research companies in developed countries utilize the census data to develop sophisticated consumer profiles. One of the key influences in changing the demand for tourism products is the change in birth and survival rates, which alters the age structure of populations. Marketers are keenly interested in the growth of the ratio of older people living in Western populations. This 'grey' market is creating new leisure and tourism opportunities for hospitality companies, while the relative declining youth market creates difficult challenges for companies targeting younger people.

Demographic variables include age, gender, family size and structure, ethnic origin, religion, nationality and socio-economic class.

The Experience Economy (Middleton and Clark, 2000)

The structure of society influences modes of consumption. During the industrial era, the focus of production was on mass standardized goods bought and consumed by mass markets. In hospitality and tourism, this style of consumption was predominant in Western markets during the period 1955–1995. As developed economies shifted from the industrial phase into the service economy, the focus of commercial activity shifted to segmenting markets and delivering a more customized product, based on responding to the benefits that consumers seek. In hospitality and tourism markets, more companies have recently adopted a segmented approach to marketing and strive to customize their offer to niche markets. Pine and Gilmour (1996) postulate that there is an emerging economy, which they have described as the *experience economy*. In the experience economy, companies stage events that offer individual customers memorable and personalized experiences. Innovative hospitality and tourism companies, like Disney and Virgin, focus on the customer experience, and have succeeded in capturing the imagination and loyalty of their target markets.

Age

A comparison of two holiday tour operators, Club 18–30 and SAGA, provides an effective illustration of how companies segment demand, using age as the defining criterion. Club 18–30 only targets young adults interested in holidays abroad in fashionable Mediterranean resorts like Ibiza. The main focus is on a 24-hour, 7 days a week opportunity to party with similar young people. The language of the advertising, brochures and website reflects the young target market, with modern colloquial, 'in-your-face' language. The brochure and website carry endorsements by satisfied customers, who send suggestive messages and rave about the events, gigs and reps; photographs of fleshy, nearly naked young people having lots of fun clearly position the offer to the age group. Customers are encouraged to participate, and can enter a competition to become a model in next year's brochure. Hotels are selected for their proximity to the club scene, bars and beach. The explicit, raunchy messages turn on their young adult target market and turn off family and mature markets.

SAGA targets the over-fifties mature market and originally focused on travel, but now also provides complementary health, insurance and financial services. SAGA offers package holiday and travel services to major tourist destinations in every continent. The holiday product, which is carefully designed for people aged over 50, concentrates on safe traveling. Many of the customers' grateful comments stress how the SAGA staff solved minor travel problems. The focus is on companionship, excursions with cultural/historic sightseeing and shopping, educational trips – one holiday is called 'art treasures in Italy' – and good quality, comfortable hotels. Consumer concerns about help for disabled and elderly people traveling (for example, porters to carry the luggage at airports and hotels) are answered on the frequently asked questions (FAQ) pages on the website. The language in the publicity material and on the Internet is mature and very sympathetic to the needs of older people. Photographs show groups of older people dressed in smart/casual clothes sedately enjoying attractive views of scenic areas. Hotels are selected for comfort and quality, and are unlikely to be very noisy late at night. The message clearly conveys confidence that SAGA has great experience in looking after older people when traveling and on holiday.

Activity 3.2

- Log on to the websites of Club 18-30 and SAGA (www.club18-30.co.uk and www.sagaholidays.co.uk)

- Compare and contrast the language, products and photographs of each website, and identify the differences between the needs and wants of the different age groups targeted by these companies.

Gender

Some hospitality products may be specifically geared to the needs of men or women. Hotel companies have responded to the expectations of women travelers by providing greater security measures in bedrooms, feminizing the bedroom decor, and offering healthier menu options in restaurants. The provision of Nintendo electronic games in the bedrooms of Jarvis Hotels was intended to cater for the needs of younger male business travelers. However, gender segmentation is not always precise – men can notice and prefer greater security measures, more feminine decor and healthy menus, whilst younger women business travelers can also enjoy playing Nintendo.

Some hotels target the gay market, and there are a number of women-only hotels. In London, the New York Hotel in Earls Court is a small award-winning hotel that is exclusively gay, while the Reeves Hotel in Shepherds Bush is a women-only hotel and is lesbian-friendly.

Family size and structure

The hotel facilities that individuals and couples without children find acceptable are often not suitable for families with several children, and *vice versa*. When Mark Chitty founded Mark Warner, he began by targeting his own age group – people in their twenties. Many years later, when Mark started his own family, he developed a family resort product targeting middle-class, middle-aged parents with younger children. The Mediterranean resorts feature a club hotel with all-inclusive facilities, including a wide range of leisure and sporting facilities, English-speaking qualified nannies who look after the children for up to six hours per day, *al fresco* lunches and evening meals with wine. This family resort product caters for the needs of families, and is unlikely to appeal to individuals or couples without children.

The growth in the number of people living alone, especially through divorce, has created a market for singles clubs and organizations that provide opportunities for single people to meet and socialize.

Ethnic origin, religion and nationality

Ethnic origin, religion and nationality are important demographic variables that are closely linked to each other and to culture. One consequence of these cultural influences is our very different attitudes to food, and what constitutes acceptable food items. Kosher cuisine is one of the well-known religious food disciplines for orthodox Jews, whilst fasting during Ramadan is equally important for Muslims. The differences between Eastern and Western style cooking are recognized by international hotels in the Far East, who provide both styles of cooking at breakfast, lunch and dinner. Restaurants are typically segmented according to their ethnicity. In the UK there are traditional British, modern British, French, Italian, American (fast food), Chinese, Indian and Thai restaurants in most cities; while almost every cooking style in the world is offered by the London restaurant industry.

Socio-economic class

Hospitality companies may not state explicitly which socio-economic class they target, but this is implicit in their marketing strategies. Ian Schrager, whose 'hip-hotel' empire includes the Mondrian in Los Angeles, Morgans in New York and the Sanderson in London, targets a new generation of affluent consumers who want exclusivity and the opportunity to mix with celebrities. The hotels have accommodation designed by Philippe Starck (pure white, all white décor and stainless steel bathrooms), fashionable restaurants and attractive staff (aspiring actors and models recruited from adverts in *Variety*). The prices are suitably expensive, and only people in the highest socio-economic class can afford to stay in Schrager's hotels.

Butlins, the famous UK holiday camps founded in 1936, clearly target socio-economic groups C1, C2 and D. The product, revitalized at the end of the 1990s with a £139 million investment, provides an indoor all-weather 'sky-line pavilion' which includes entertainment, fast-food outlets (e.g. Burger King and Harry Ramsden's), a 'Splash Waterworld', and a beach nightclub. Accommodation is family budget standard, with a choice of half-board or self-catering; and prices are competitively low. The marketing communications campaign includes advertising in newspapers like the *Sun, News of the World, Sunday Mirror* and *Sunday People*, whose readership consists primarily of the lower socio-economic groups. Today the three resorts attract over a million guests each year, and in 65 years Butlins, which used to have many more resorts in its heyday, has looked after 105 million customers.

Buyer needs and benefits

The idea of segmenting markets according to the benefits sought from products is well established. Examples of benefits which buyers look for in hospitality products include:

● Convenience – this is often linked to location and speed of service
● Luxury – this is naturally associated with high levels of service and high prices
● Children-friendly accommodation – families traveling have specific needs (like informal, low cost dining facilities)
● Improved health facilities – spa resorts offer exercise and dietary regimens for the benefit of their health-oriented patrons.

A number of different 'benefits' can be combined together to provide the total solution to a customer's set of problems. All-inclusive holiday resort hotels not only provide the accommodation and food elements of holiday, but also all the sporting activities, excursions, leisure and entertainment facilities, and even alcoholic drinks, in a safe environment. This process of creating product/price benefit bundles should be based on a deep understanding of customer needs.

Table 3.4 Typical City Hotel Accommodation – Segmentation by Rate

Hotel accommodation segmentation by rate description	Sales volume (1 = highest volume of sales)	Profit contribution (1 = highest profit contribution)
Rack rate (published in tariff)	6	1
Conference rate	3	2
Corporate rate	5	3
Leisure rate	7	4
Local business discounted rate	1	5
Guests attending a function	10	6
Exhibition	9	7
Walk-in (standby rate)	4	8
Weekend rate	8	9
Group rate	2	10

Price (or rate)

Price sensitivity is a crucial segmentation variable in hospitality markets. Each hospitality market segment has its own specific pricing dynamics, which need to be understood. Research and analysis should determine what consumers can afford to pay and what they are willing to pay. The price consumers are willing to pay plays a key role in determining the design, facilities and amenities, and the standard of décor, fixtures and furniture in planning a new product concept.

In hospitality, the link between price and quality in different product classes is strong. Consumers looking to be pampered in a luxurious environment expect to pay higher prices, while consumers looking for basic products expect to pay lower prices. Whilst the price/quality difference between product class extremes (for example, the expensive, gourmet restaurant versus the cheap and cheerful café) is clearly apparent to consumers, the difference between adjacent product classes (for example, a four-star hotel and a three-star hotel) can be virtually indistinguishable. This can lead to customer confusion, as the relative value for money between competing offers is not transparent.

Many hotel companies describe their segmentation targets in terms of rate. If we look at Table 3.4 and compare the rate segmentation variables for this typical city hotel in terms of volume (ratio of sales generated for each segment) and profit contribution, we can see that the rack rate (which is the highest possible price printed in the tariff) is only the sixth largest in volume terms, whilst the group business (primarily tour operators) delivers the second highest number of customers in volume but generates the lowest profit because of the low prices negotiated to obtain volume sales.

Current user characteristics

Identifying the characteristics of customers who use hospitality products provides marketers with a profile of current users. These customer profiles can then be analyzed to identify attractive market segments for targeting purposes. There are a number of user characteristics that are important to hospitality operators, and these are described here.

Usage status

This characteristic categorizes consumers in to non-users, potential users, first-time users, regular users (who can be either light, medium or heavy users) and lapsed users (see Figure 3.3). Marketing communication campaigns can be developed to target the different user categories, to encourage first-time visits, regular patronage, or repeat visits after lapsed patronage. Understanding the different usage patterns enables marketing communication campaigns to be designed to influence the category of user.

Frequency

In business markets, frequent travelers – people who stay away from home on business travel for five or more trips per annum – are a highly attractive segment because their lifetime value is high. Hotels strive to encourage regular and repeat customers, and over time hoteliers can build strong, long-lasting, special relationships with their 'regulars'. The importance of repeat and regular business customers has long been recognized by hotel groups. Indeed, 2 percent of Travel Inn's revenue is from frequent guests who stay for more than 200 nights per year in Travel Inn

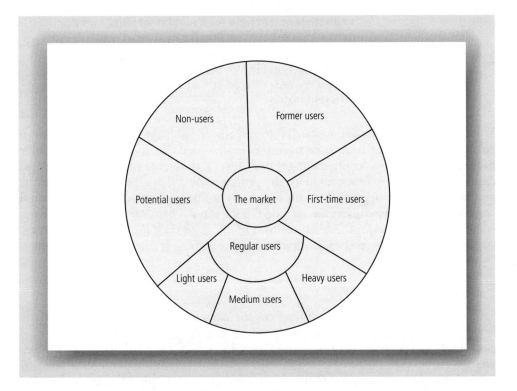

Figure 3.3 Guest usage status (source: Osman, 2001, p. 41)

hotels. Frequent guest promotions, often linked to loyalty programs, have been designed to reward frequent guests for their patronage.

Given the lower frequency of leisure trips, a regular customer might return to a favorite leisure hotel infrequently. A distinction needs to be drawn here between those hotels catering for long stay, long haul holidays and those catering for short leisure breaks within a couple of hours traveling time of the customer's home. The long haul guest might only return once per year, if that – indeed, a highly satisfied customer may only return once every five years – whereas the short break leisure guest might return to a favorite hotel three or four times per year. One consequence of this user factor is that hotels targeting leisure customers need to allocate a higher promotional spend to attract a wider customer base, or distribute their product via tour operators and travel agents.

Brand loyalty

A key objective of frequent guest programs is to build brand loyalty amongst those business travelers who are heavy users of hotel accommodation. Consumers' loyalty to hospitality brands varies. Research suggests that hospitality customers can be categorized in the following way:

Hard-core loyal	Guest only stays at one preferred hotel brand
Split loyal	Guest stays at two or three brands on a regular basis (these customers may have preferred hotels in different locations, which belong to different brands)
Shifting loyal	Guest stays at one brand on a number of visits; then moves to another hotel brand for a number of visits; and then moves to another hotel brand etc.
Switchers	Guest has no loyalty to any brand; these customers may make their hotel choice based on the lowest price available, or best rewards offered at that time, or simply like to stay at different hotels

There has been considerable research into customers' habits in general and loyalty in particular. Customers have become more promiscuous in their shopping habits; indeed, promiscuous consumers might have several different hotel company reward cards. However, the investment in loyalty programs by airlines, hotels, petrol stations and supermarkets suggests that consumers are influenced especially when several complementary service offers are included in the same scheme. In the UK, customers collecting British Airways' Air Miles from multiple sources (hotels, petrol stations, supermarkets) have been shown actively to seek out those retailers offering Air Miles.

Purchase occasion

The type of purchase occasion influences the consumers' needs and wants. Many hospitality banqueting and restaurant products are aimed at the special family occasions that mark every important event in our lives – birth, coming of age parties, weddings, special birthdays, retirement functions, wedding anniversaries and funerals. The honeymoon market is often used as an example of a special holiday purchase occasion.

Size of party

Hospitality managers recognize that party size, which has a considerable influence on the needs and wants of hospitality consumers, can be used as a segmentation variable. Clearly, groups of travelers have different check-in, check-out, dining, drinking, meeting and entertainment requirements compared to individual travelers. Companies that specialize in volume hospitality operations develop the facilities and skills necessary to cater for large-scale events. Sensible smaller outlets should avoid taking bookings from larger parties, which they know they cannot cater for effectively, to avoid alienating their regular customers.

Lifestyle (or psychographics)

Psychographic segmentation is a classification of consumers according to their personality traits and lifestyle. It is based upon detailed marketing research into the activities, interests and opinions (AIO) of consumers, which can be linked to geo-demographic variables to provide consumer profiles. Marketing research analysts combine individual responses to questions about a person's AIO with details about his or her geo-demographic characteristics, and then cluster consumers in to groups with similar responses to form psychographic profiles of market segments. The data collated from each psychographic segment provides a detailed picture of where consumers live; what education, occupation and income they enjoy; what their activities, interests and opinions are; what media they buy; and what products they purchase. There have been numerous studies investigating psychographic consumer profiles, including American visitors to the UK, and the Belgian holiday market (Witt and Moutinho, 1997).

Proponents believe that psychographic segmentation:

● Develops a deeper knowledge and understanding of consumer behavior
● Is a good predictor of consumer behavior
● Enables companies to design products better to meet consumer needs
● Provides the opportunity to develop cost-effective marketing campaigns for selected target markets (see Figure 3.4).

Critics contend that psychographic segmentation:

● Is unable accurately to define lifestyle variables
● Develops lifestyle segments that are not strictly homogeneous
● Is very expensive – research costs are high because of the detailed face-to-face interviewing techniques at home
● Is not effective because people change occupation and move homes frequently.

Time

There are two aspects concerning the role of time as a market segmentation variable. First, from a seasonality perspective, hospitality operators need to understand why consumers patronize hotels in restaurants during quieter periods in order to develop effective marketing campaigns to increase sales during low season periods. Some older people, who do not live with children and have flexible holiday arrangements, enjoy relaxing in a quiet, peaceful environment, and can be considered a potential target market for holiday/hotel organizations in the low season.

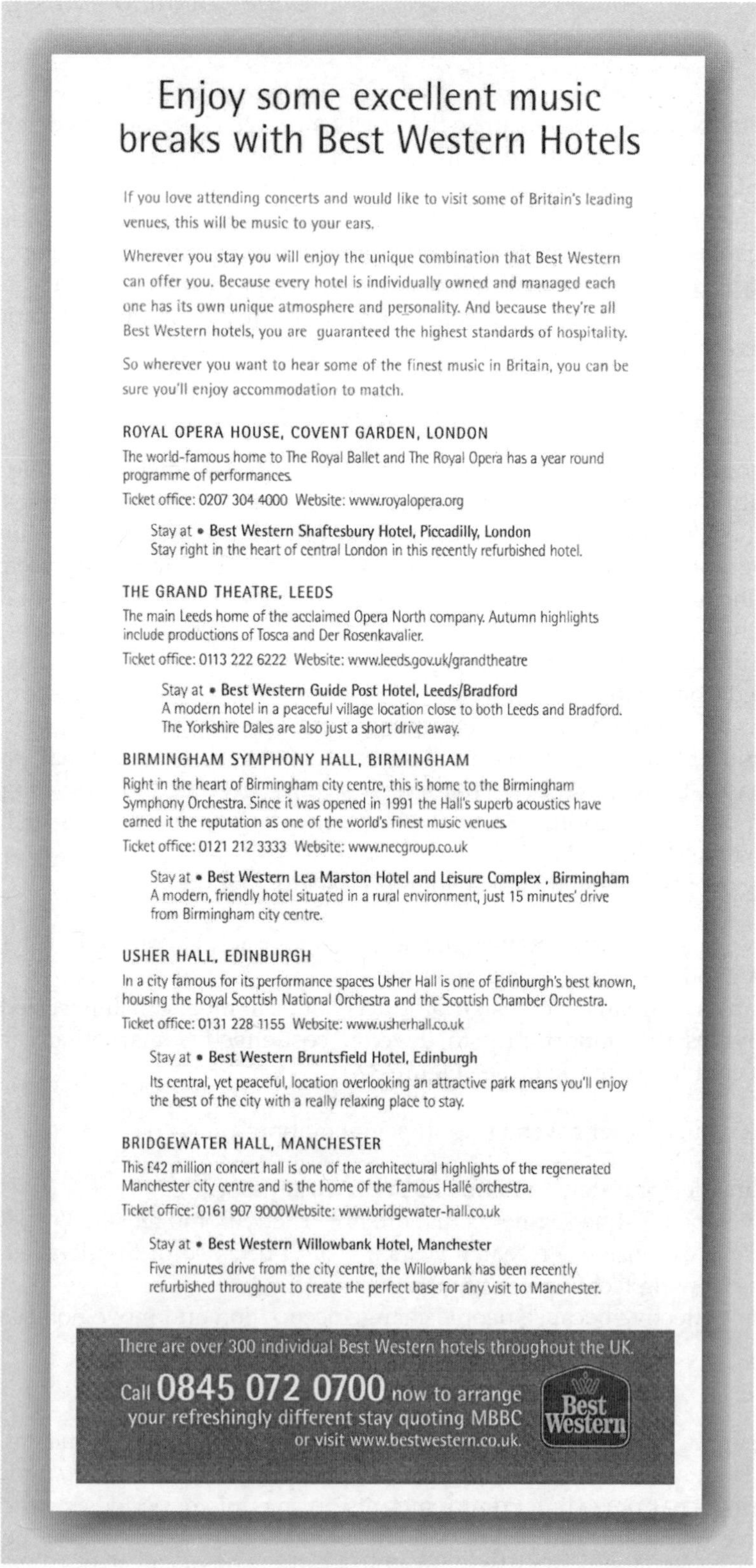

Figure 3.4 Best Western advert targeting classical music lovers (source: Best Western Hotels)

The second aspect of time, in this context, refers to the advance booking period – the time between the customer booking and then actually consuming the hospitality product. This time period is an important segmentation variable, because the length, whether it is a couple of hours in advance or several years away, influences the design of the marketing program aimed at capturing the customer. The marketing program targeting a convention planner who is booking an international conference to be held in three years time will be different to the marketing program targeting an impulse diner who wants to eat out this evening.

Hospitality target markets

Companies need to evaluate the potential of market segments using the following criteria:

1 *Market data* – size, growth, accessibility, consumer needs and wants and benefits sought, customer power.
2 *Competitor analysis* – number of competitors, their market share, capabilities, resources, strengths and weaknesses, differentiators and profitability, and the potential for new entrants.
3 *Internal company audit* – capability of servicing the market segment, compatibility with existing and future segments, compatibility with the company's resources and values.

Major hospitality firms planning to enter a new market segment will invest in detailed marketing research to evaluate fully the attractiveness of competing market segments before deciding which to enter. The smaller operator will adopt a less formal process. Once selected, the market segment is defined as a 'target market' for which the company designs an appropriate marketing program. Target markets are groups of consumers, with similar needs and wants, for whom a marketing program is specifically developed to satisfy those needs and wants.

Hospitality companies target several different market segments at the same time, but each target market should have its own marketing mix program. Hospitality operators generally recognize that the 'Pareto Rule' – the principle that about 20 percent of the users of a product account for about 80 percent of volume sales and profits – works for hotel companies. Heavy users of hotel accommodation represent the highest profit potential target market. However, a hotel company's prime target markets are also going to be the competitor's prime target markets, and the relatively small number of heavy hotel users is therefore highly sought after.

Throughout this chapter, we have provided examples of hospitality organizations targeting market segments. There are two broad classes of target markets; consumer markets and organizational markets. Each requires a different marketing approach, because buyer behavior differs between individuals and organizations.

Consumer target markets

Consumer markets can be defined as travelers who use hotels and restaurants, as individuals, couples, families or small groups of people, for business or leisure purposes. Consumer markets have an influence over their choice of hospitality provider, set their own budget, and pay from their own resources. Examples of consumer markets include FIT ('free independent travelers' or 'foreign independent travelers'), individual woman business travelers, international travelers, older people, single people, the gay market, and celebrities (the new rich).

International markets

Hotels located in English-speaking countries and targeting significant sales from non-English-speaking markets like mainland China and Japan need to provide the following amenities and services:

- Multilingual front desk staff who can speak Chinese or Japanese
- Hotel information and safety notices written in Chinese or Japanese
- Oriental food options, which are essential (either a Chinese or a Japanese restaurant), and in-room food service options.

Although English is the common language for international business, hoteliers should not assume that all their international customers can understand English.

The seniors market

The senior citizen market is often described as the 'grey' market, and includes people in the following age groups:

- Older people aged between 55 and 64
- Elderly people aged between 65 and 74
- Aged people between 74 and 85
- Very old people aged over 85.

Although this division is somewhat arbitrary, it does help when evaluating the different needs and wants of the sub-segments of the grey market. For example, people over 70 are less interested in participating in leisure and sporting activities, whilst people aged between 55 and 70 are still relatively active and interested in participating in leisure and sporting activities.

The disposable income of the over 55s is higher than that of the general population because they have fewer financial outgoings on expenses like raising a family or paying the mortgage. This provides older people with more money to spend on leisure purchases. We have already identified that one of the characteristics of well-off Western older people is that they are more educated, sophisticated and well traveled than previous generations, and they therefore have higher expectations when staying in hotels and dining out. The special needs and wants of older people include quieter rooms with safety features like bath rails and non-slip shower mats, good porterage facilities to help with luggage, early evening dining options, and smaller food portions.

Restaurant and bar target markets

Apart from a small number of high-profile outstanding eating and entertainment establishments (where the reputation is so high that customers are prepared to travel a long distance), customer markets for restaurants and bars are focused on locally defined areas. Market variations occur according to whether the unit is sited in a city center, the suburbs or a countryside location, and are determined by the different geo-demographic characteristics of the neighborhoods. The characteristics of restaurant and bar target markets are also defined using gender, income and stage in the family life cycle, and using benefit segmentation criteria like service/quality, price/value, and time/convenience.

Research consistently demonstrates that diners look for quality of food, quality of service, value for money, friendly staff and cleanliness. Different target markets will rate the importance of these criteria according to their own needs. For example, price/value and time/convenience are rated more highly by the family eating-out segment, because of the costs of taking a family out, and the need to dine quickly to avoid restless children becoming disruptive. Adults dining out without children can afford the time and money to have a more sophisticated eating out experience. Since the geo-demographic characteristics of an area are the prime influence on potential dining-out target markets, restaurateurs and bar owners need to choose the sites of their operations with great care to ensure they target appropriate customer markets.

Singles market

Single people are a growth market for many hospitality products. The singles market can also be subdivided according to age and lifestyle. Single people who are working and still living at the family home enjoy eating out with friends, while older single people take holidays to meet new people.

Organizational markets

Organizational target markets are groups of travelers who use hotels and restaurants for business and leisure purposes. Individual customers who are traveling as part of a group of travelers have less influence (or none) over the choice of hospitality provider, and will sometimes have to pay for the service out of their own resources. If the organization is a corporate business, then the company (not the individual) will pay and will normally set expenditure limits. Examples of hospitality organizational target markets include corporate travel, corporate meetings, association meetings, conventions, exhibitions and trade fairs, tour groups, and a miscellaneous category called SMERF (social, military, educational, religious and fraternal).

Corporate travel

Corporate travel is a major expense item for national and international companies. Corporations regard the purchase of hotel accommodation in the same way as the purchase of any other commodity item. Companies are aware of their own purchasing power and expect discounted rates. Most hotel groups and larger independent hotels offer a standard corporate rate with a minimum 10 percent discount off the accommodation rack rate, and those companies booking larger volumes of nights negotiate higher discounts. However, if the agreed volume of business is not achieved and the contract is not sufficiently specific, there can be problems between hotelier and corporate client.

One independent British hotelier, Alan Morris, of the 60-bedroom Best Western Westminster Hotel in Nottingham, resolved this problem by agreeing to pay a monthly retrospective discount to companies based on the actual number of the nights sold each month. This same contract rate was available to any company using the hotel. Invoices were based on the rack rate, with discounts calculated on the number of rooms actually occupied by the company during the month.

There is an image of business executives enjoying the most luxurious travel and hotel accommodation, dining out in the finest restaurants and conspicuously consuming the best wines with 'no expense spared'. This might be true for some executives, but is certainly not case for all business travelers. Corporate organizations are hierarchical in design, and most companies agree expense limits according to the position of employees within the hierarchy of the company. Business travel allowances depend upon the corporate culture of individual organizations, which will vary immensely.

Corporate meetings

The corporate meetings market includes company management meetings, planning, recruitment and sales meetings, and training events, in locations that are not company-owned. The number of delegates attending a meeting can range from only two to over a hundred. The market is a major source of revenue for hotel operations, and includes both day meetings and meetings requiring overnight accommodation. Delegates attending such meetings do not have any choice about their participation and are obliged to attend. The company organizing (and paying for) the event needs to achieve its own specific organizational goals for the meeting to be a success.

Organizers and delegates who attend corporate meetings have professional standards and high expectations for service standards. Prior to the meeting, the hospitality venue has to work with the meeting organizer to plan the event and ensure that all the details are carefully agreed. In recent years, the major hotel brands have developed guaranteed conference packages to satisfy the needs and wants of meetings organizers and their delegates.

Association meetings

In addition to corporate meetings, there are a large number of professional and trade organizations that hold regular meetings for members. These voluntary meetings are normally held in the evenings, have a variable attendance, and do not generate significant amounts of accommodation, food or beverage revenue. However, most associations will hold functions such as annual dinners, and individuals involved with the associations may be important potential users of hospitality outlets in their places of work. Examples of such organizations include the Lions, Masonic Lodges, Rotary Club and Round Table.

Conventions, exhibitions and trade fairs

The lead (or booking) time for major national and international events involving hundreds or thousands of delegates ranges from two to more than ten years. The number of venues capable of hosting these events is limited by the large scale of such events. Major convention and exhibition centers are often built by government initiatives in recognition of the economic value these venues can generate in a region in terms of employment, revenue and prosperity. Cities like Birmingham (UK), Milan (Italy) and Dallas (USA) have provided dedicated facilities that attract major national and international events.

Key issues for event organizers include:

- An effective transportation infrastructure (for example, good airport and road connections)
- Provision of modern convention and exhibition facilities of sufficient size

- The availability of a wide range of quality hospitality facilities
- Resort, leisure and recreational amenities.

For international events, climate factors and the relative cost and travel distances are additional influences in deciding which venue to book. There is considerable international competition between the different venues, which has led to the emergence of convention or visitor bureaux linked to tourist information centers and funded by local government and business. The role of the visitor bureaux is primarily to promote the area and act as an information provider. Events may last for several days and, apart from a main event, include several ancillary minor functions.

Event organizers will be responsible for coordinating the booking of the venue, the dissemination of publicity for the event, and possibly some of the catering arrangements. Individual companies and visitors are responsible for making their own travel and hotel arrangements. Individual visitors may see the event as an opportunity to combine work activities with some leisure, relaxation, sporting or sightseeing activities, which explains the appeal of more exotic locations for international events. Examples of organizations booking exhibitions and conferences include professional and trade bodies, and political parties.

Aircrew

An unusual market segment that hotels target in 'gateway' locations is that of airline employees, and specifically airline crew. The high volume of intercontinental, regional and international flights, coupled with the need for aircrew to have proper rest periods between flights, has created a demand for group accommodation for hotels within approximately 15–45 minutes travel time of major airports. Aircrew have special needs and wants, including:

- Efficient 24-hour check-in and check-out procedures
- Bedrooms that are available immediately upon arrival and check-in
- Quiet and dark rooms, preferably with blackout blinds, to facilitate sleeping at any time of the day or night
- A 24-hour food and beverage service, at a reasonable charge, since airline crew have limited expense allowances
- Efficient wake-up calls, since the airline crew must meet their flight schedules on time.

Some years ago aircrew had a glamorous image, appearing to mix well with other guests, and upscale hotels regarded them as a compatible and attractive target market. Today, the growth of mass air travel has led to a less glamorous and more workaday image of airline crew, and the more exclusive hotels are less interested in targeting this market. The Arora Group has opened three hotels, two in Heathrow and one in Gatwick, which primarily target airline crew. Facilities in the bedrooms include triple glazing, full blackout curtains, king-sized beds, air conditioning, 24-hour room service, and interactive TV with Internet, games and video; this provision enables aircrew to sleep, eat, connect and relax in their room at any time of the day or night.

Tour groups

The growth of global tourism has increased the demand for international group travel that is organized by intermediaries. These groups of travelers are provided with inclusive travel and accommodation products and, depending upon the location, food service. This is high-volume business, and the hotels interested in this market have to offer low, competitive prices to win the business. Groups need:

● Dedicated, efficient group check-in and check-out procedures and concierge/porters' services
● Good-sized lobby/lounge areas, where members of the tour group can conveniently meet
● Efficient food service, because they are often on a strict schedule and do not want to run late.

Sometimes hotel employees treat tour group customers as the least important of all clients, but in volume terms tour groups represent a significant market, especially in major tourist attractions.

SMERF

SMERF is a North American expression that stands for social, military, educational, religious and fraternal (i.e. family events such as weddings and funerals), and is a convenient heading to discuss all the group market segments not already discussed.

This segment is generally very price sensitive. SMERF organizations are non-profit making, and members/family pay for their event out of post-tax income. Consequently, the organizers of SMERF bookings are inclined to take advantage of low season bargain rates. Although the room rates offered have to be low to attract SMERF bookings, there can be a significant food and beverage spend linked to the event. An exception to these general comments about the SMERF market is the special family occasion, like weddings and wedding anniversaries, which can be less price sensitive.

Intermediaries

The complexity of efficiently arranging group travel has created a role for speciality intermediaries, to act on behalf of organizations in their negotiations with hospitality and travel providers. These intermediaries have become target markets for hospitality companies in their own right. Key intermediaries, who book volume business and expect competitive rates, include:

● Conference and meetings planners
● Travel agents
● Wholesalers and tour operators
● Incentive travel houses.

We will discuss the role of intermediaries in more detail in Chapter 8.

Mixing market segments

A key issue for all hospitality operations is to ensure that the various target markets are compatible. Mixing incompatible market segments leads to customer dissatisfaction, and serious customer complaints. In hotels, the imperative of filling rooms in low and shoulder seasons can motivate reservation managers to accept bookings from customers whose needs and wants are not compatible with prime target markets. Examples of mixing incompatible segments include mixing business and leisure customers, mixing elderly tour groups with families and children, and mixing different levels of employees in the same hotel.

Similar problems can arise when hotels cater for banquets, and residents are disturbed by large, noisy, late-night functions with music and dancing. The principle of separating segments with incompatible needs is the answer to this problem. Therefore, accommodation reservation managers need to be aware of the banqueting diary and banqueting sales executives need to be aware of the rooms situation when they are taking potentially disruptive bookings.

Conclusion

Understanding consumer behavior and customer expectations is essential if hospitality managers are to succeed in delivering customer satisfaction. Segmenting markets is the starting point for effective marketing. Marketers need to identify attractive market segments and then develop appropriate marketing strategies to win customers. We will discuss how to develop the marketing strategies in later chapters, but the process should always start with the needs and wants of target markets.

In this chapter, we have explained:

- The different factors that influence hospitality consumer behavior
- Customer expectations and the 'zone of tolerance'
- The hospitality buyer decision-making process
- The importance of segmentation in developing effective marketing strategies
- The segmentation process
- Key hospitality segmentation variables
- How to evaluate potential hospitality target markets
- The characteristics of hospitality consumer and organizational target markets.

Review questions

Now check your understanding of this chapter by answering the following questions:

1 Discuss the influences that impact on hospitality consumer behavior. Provide examples to illustrate your answer.
2 Evaluate customer expectations and the concept of 'zone of tolerance'. How does this model help explain customer behavior?
3 Discuss the consumer buyer decision-making process for hospitality products.
4 Describe the segmentation variables that hospitality companies can use to categorize potential customers.
5 Evaluate the characteristics of hospitality customer and organizational target markets.

References and further reading

Kotler, P., Bowen, J. and Makens, J. (2003). *Marketing for Hospitality and Tourism*, 3rd edn. Prentice Hall.
Levitt, T. (1983). The globalization of markets. *Harvard Business Review*, **38**, 45–56.
Lewis, R. C. and Chambers, R. E. (2000). *Marketing Leadership in Hospitality: Foundations and Practice*. John Wiley.

McCleary, K., Choi, B. M. and Weaver, P. A. (1998). Comparison of hotel selection between US and Korean business travellers. *Journal of Hospitality and Tourism Research*, **22(1)**, 25–38.

Middleton, V. T. C. and Clark, J. (2000). *Marketing in Travel and Tourism*. Butterworth-Heinemann.

Osman, H. (2001). Practice of Relationship Marketing in Hotels. PhD Thesis, Oxford Brookes University.

Pine, I. J. and Gilmore, J. H. (1996). Welcome to the experience economy. *Harvard Business Review*, July/Aug., 97–105.

Usunier, J. C. (2000). *Marketing Across Cultures*. Prentice Hall.

Witt, S. F. and Moutinho, C. (1997). *Tourism Marketing and Management*. Prentice Hall.

Zeithaml, V. A. and Bitner, M. J. (2003). *Services Marketing*, 3rd edn. McGraw-Hill.

Zeithaml, V. A., Berry, L. L. and Parasuraman, A. (1993). The nature and determinants of customer expectations of service. *Journal of the Academy of Marketing*, **21(1)**, 1–12.

Chapter 4
Competitive strategies

Chapter Objectives

After working through this chapter, you should be able to:

■ Understand how the hospitality industry has developed in different regions of the world
■ Carry out a competitive analysis, using the Five Forces model
■ Explain segmentation, positioning and differentiation strategies in the hospitality industry
■ Understand the role of branding in hospitality organizations.

Introduction

In this chapter, we will examine how the hospitality industry has evolved in different regions of the world, and look at the characteristics of hospitality firms – especially the differences between large-scale companies and smaller independent operators. We will discuss the 'five forces' that influence an industry's competitive environment, and finally we will explain how companies develop their segmentation, positioning, differentiation and branding strategies. The competitive environment for hospitality companies can be described as dynamic, intense and turbulent, since most markets have excess capacity. Competition is fierce, and knowing their competitors is of crucial importance to hospitality marketers.

Development of the hospitality industry

The hospitality industry has evolved with different structures in different parts of the world because each region has experienced economic development during different periods of history. Hotel market demand is strongest in Europe, North America and Asia Pacific. We will now look at how the industry has evolved in these regions (Todd and Mather, 1998).

In Europe the hotel industry has origins dating back more than 500 years, and there are many historic old town hotels and highway inns. The European industry is dominated by independent, family owned and managed small hotels. France, Germany, Italy and the UK are dependent upon domestic markets, while other European countries have a higher proportion of international customers. There is a low penetration of branded hotel chains in Europe. Although the UK has the highest concentration of brands, approximately 70 percent of British hotels still have less than fifteen bedrooms.

In the USA and Canada, hotel development coincided with economic and social development in the nineteenth and twentieth centuries. Since 1945, American hospitality entrepreneurs such as Conrad Hilton, Bill Marriott and Ray Kroc have pioneered the development of branded hotel and restaurant chains, which today dominate both American and international hospitality markets. Over 60 percent of North American hotels with 20-plus bedrooms belong to a branded chain, and there are over 200 such hotel brands in the USA. Demand is dependent upon domestic customers and, despite the relative young age of the industry compared to Europe, the North American market is the most mature and sophisticated in the world. However, European companies have bought leading USA hotel chains – Ladbrook bought Hilton International and later changed the corporate name to Hilton; Accor bought Motel 6 and Red Roof Inns; and Bass (now InterContinental Hotels Group) bought Holiday Inn and InterContinental Hotels.

In Asia Pacific, hotel development, linked to dynamic regional economic development and growth in leisure travel, grew exponentially in the last quarter of the twentieth century. Major hotel building was originally designed to cater for the needs of international business and leisure travelers and focused on the upscale market, with four and five-star international branded hotel products. These hotels include the best elements of American, European and Asian hospitality traditions. Recently Asian chains have targeted a growing mid-market segment, whilst the budget hotels primarily target domestic markets.

International expansion

Another feature of the latter part of the twentieth century was the rapid internationalization of supply in hotel markets. International hotel companies expanded at an exceptional rate. For example:

- Marriott Hotels spread from 29 countries in 1996 to 56 countries in 1999
- Best Western Hotels expanded from 63 countries to 84 countries in the same four-year period
- InterContinental Hotels Group (formerly Bass) and Starwood emerged as major hotel competitors.

In due course, virtually all of the major hotel companies will have a presence in every country where it is politically possible to operate.

The characteristics of a hospitality company's home country play a central role in determining how successful its international expansion is. In particular, the nature of demand and competition in their domestic market shapes the culture of the management team – indeed, the core competences and competitive advantages of international firms are first developed in the home environment. For example, Accor's French origins and Marriott's North American origins clearly influence their different approaches to managing hospitality operations in other parts of the world. A typology of firms' different approaches to managing international operations is frequently used to describe a company's activities (Perlmutter, 1969), and this is described here.

Ethnocentric

Companies taking an ethnocentric approach to their international hospitality operations are adopting a *home country orientation*. Home country operating systems and procedures are set up in their international subsidiaries (the host countries), and a home country 'knows best' culture is implied. This approach is suitable if the domestic marketing strategies are applicable in the foreign countries, or if the company is targeting home country customers. An all-inclusive holiday resort operated by a British home country tour operator (like Mark Warner Holiday Villages) in a host country like Greece, and targeting British customers, could adopt an ethnocentric approach. However, because host country cultures can be very different from the domestic country culture, the ethnocentric approach is not suitable if the target markets comprise large numbers of host country residents.

Polycentric

Companies taking a polycentric approach to their international hospitality operations are adopting a *host country orientation*. The home country management recognizes that managers in the host country know their own culture better than the home country managers, and local operating systems and procedures are retained in foreign markets. This approach is suitable if the host country marketing strategies are targeting host country customers. It is based upon the premise that there are fundamental differences between domestic and foreign marketing, and that local managers understand their customers better than does the international head office. The marketing of Best Western Hotels is typically polycentric; each country has considerable autonomy in devising its own marketing campaigns, which are developed for host country consumers.

Regiocentric

Some hotel operations are geared towards a particular continental region, which has a similar culture and is at a similar stage of economic development. The Scandinavian countries of Denmark, Finland, Norway and Sweden have a strong regional identity. A similar marketing offer can be developed for a hospitality brand operating in Scandinavia, which is culturally suitable for all Scandinavian consumers. Indeed, Scandic Hotels used to operate on this basis before the company was bought by Hilton International. One advantage of a regiocentric approach is the cost and marketing benefits of standardizing the offer. One of the largest regiocentric hotel companies in the world is the Hong Kong-based Shangri-La Hotels in Asia.

Geocentric

A geocentric approach implies a world-wide orientation that does not favor either the home or the host country. This is often called a global approach to management. The company adopts a positive attitude towards other cultures, and borrows what is best from many countries. 'Global consumers', who have similar consumption patterns regardless of where they live, are an attractive target market for companies seeking to adopt a geocentric approach. However, many of the international hospitality companies who claim to be 'global' still retain elements of their ethnocentric origins.

   None of the international hospitality firms operates purely in an ethnocentric or a polycentric or geocentric style, but firms do exhibit ethnocentric, polycentric and geocentric management tendencies.

Characteristics of hospitality firms

We will now discuss the characteristics of hospitality firms that impact on marketing. These include ownership and size, ownership and affiliation, and hotel classification schemes.

Ownership and size

Virtually all hospitality firms started as single-unit enterprises – Americans use the term 'Mom and Pop firms' to describe these small businesses – and most remain single-unit operations throughout their commercial life. The characteristics of small, single-site hospitality firms include the following (Morrison and Thomas, 1999):

● The owner and management roles are combined
● Owners are close to the customer

- Owners can be more entrepreneurial and innovative, responding quickly to changes in the PESTE and micro-environments
- There is a focus on operations and the immediate issues facing the business
- There is a short-term planning timeframe.

Firms have a life cycle, and can develop from a single-site owner/management business operating in a simple environment to multi-site, multiple business units with hierarchical corporate organizations, operating in a complex environment. As organizations grow, decision-making often becomes more remote from the customer and frontline staff. Hotel groups rarely own small hotels, and one- and two-star hotels also tend to be privately owned. Small hotels do not deliver the required revenue and profitability expected from a group-owned hotel.

In hospitality, large firms tend to manage the larger-size units and have a higher proportion of hotel bedrooms and restaurant seats compared to small firms. For example, the top 25 British hotel chains control 33 percent of all room stock with only 4 percent of properties (Jones, 1999). This trend towards concentration of ownership is likely to continue. Whilst the three-star market incorporates both privately owned hotels and mid-market chains, larger upscale and luxury units tend to be owned by large organizations.

The characteristics of larger hospitality firms include the following:

- The separation of ownership and management – typically the general managers and directors of a hospitality corporation will only own a token share holding or share option
- Ownership is normally diffused across a large number of shareholders, although financial investment companies may hold larger stakes in the business
- Multiple-site operations – the largest hospitality corporations comprise thousands of geographically dispersed units, across dozens of countries in all continents, under a complex combination of different brands, targeting a variety of markets, using a range of business formats (ownership, franchising, management contract) and employing hundreds of thousands of staff
- Employment of professionals to manage at both the unit level and at head office – these professionals have developed considerable expertise in hospitality operations management, as well as the functional disciplines of finance, human resources and marketing management.

Large firms enjoy significant advantages in terms of:

- Economies of scale, giving cost savings in purchasing
- Economies of experience (this comprises the accumulated managerial experience that large companies enjoy)
- Access to financial markets, which provide significant financial resources for investment
- Being powerful and popular brands
- Powerful computerized distribution systems
- Access to specialist agencies like financial consultants, design consultants, and advertising and public relations agencies
- The focus on long-term strategic planning

But:

- Management procedures are more formalized and bureaucratic
- Management is much more remote from the customer.

Although smaller, single-site, owner-managed hospitality units can give regular customers a more personalized service, it is more difficult to reassure visiting tourists who do not know the unit that the service quality is good. However, powerful hospitality brands do provide the reassurance that customers are looking for when traveling. These brands dominate the marketplace and the competitive environment.

Hospitality ownership and affiliation

There are at least six forms of hospitality ownership and affiliation, and these are described here.

Owned

A company, partnership or individual can own the freehold property. Ownership enables the organization to develop the property without constraints (subject to planning controls and permission). The organization may borrow funds from lenders to purchase or develop the business. Ownership of freehold property ties up capital within the business.

Leased

A company, partnership or individual can lease the property from a landlord and pay commercial rents. The landlord has to approve structural alterations, and lease contract details can be complex. In recent years, major hospitality companies have sold their freehold properties and then leased them back to continue to operate the hotel business. This has released funds to help fuel the expansion of hospitality corporations.

Management contract, with an equity stake

Specialist hotel management companies take an equity stake in the property, which demonstrates a long-term commitment to the landlord and the business. This type of management contract enables the management company to share in the profits of any property inflation.

Equity-free management contract

Specialist hotel management companies can be responsible for the entire operation of a hotel property on behalf of the owners. This type of management contract is less complex than an equity-stake contract.

Franchise

In franchise operations, the franchisor (the company who owns the franchise) will offer a branded concept to a franchisee, who operates the business according to the standards set by the franchisor. The franchisee buys the franchise and pays a commission on turnover to the franchisor for continued marketing and organizational support. Franchising has been an extremely successful concept for companies like McDonald's, which wish to expand rapidly. It enables the franchisor to grow the business without needing too much capital, since the franchisee pays to buy a franchise and also for the business start-up costs. The rapid increase in the number of outlets in a country or region enables the franchising company to gain a critical mass, which funds heavy investment in advertising and promoting the brands. A frequent cause of tension in franchising is the relationship between the franchisee and franchisor. The franchisor needs to have consistent brand standards, and will monitor each unit to check conformance. Franchisees often expect more investment in advertising and product development from the franchisor, and this can also become a source of conflict.

Activity 4.1 Cendant – the world's largest hotel franchisor

Cendant claims to be the world's largest franchisor of hotels. It owns nine hotel brands – Amerihost Inn, Days Inn, Howard Johnson, Knights Inn, Ramada, Super 8, Travelodge, Villager, and Wingate Inns – with approximately 6400 hotels and nearly 540,000 rooms throughout the world.

● Log onto the Cendant website, www.cendant.com, and read about its hotel brand franchising opportunities.

(Source: Cendant)

Consortium

Independent hotels seeking the benefits that group-owned chains enjoy can affiliate to a hotel consortium. Membership of a hotel consortium enables independent hoteliers to retain their entrepreneurial freedom and to:

● Link to global computerized reservation systems
● Buy into an international or domestic brand
● Participate in the consortium's national and international marketing communication campaigns
● Extend their distribution channels
● Enjoy discounted prices when purchasing, due to the consortium's bulk purchasing power
● Belong to a group of similar independent hoteliers, and share management and marketing information.

Case study 4.1 describes a successful hotel consortium.

Case study

4.1 Best Western Hotels – the largest consortium in the world

Best Western International is the largest hotel company operating under a single brand name, with more than 4000 independently owned and operated hotels. Based in Phoenix, Arizona, Best Western offers over 300,000 bedrooms in 78 countries. Best Western Hotels is a membership organization which gives hoteliers the opportunity to remain independent whilst also providing the benefits of a full-service, international hotel group with a global reservations system, marketing, advertising, purchasing, training and quality standards.

(Source: Best Western Hotels, www.bestwestern.com)

Implications of ownership/affiliation

Independent operators typically own or lease their property. Although many have joined consortia like Best Western Hotels to maximize their marketing efforts, most independent hotel owners remain unaffiliated apart from in the USA. The branded hotel chains utilize all forms of ownership – companies like Hilton, Marriott and InterContinental Hotels Group use a combination of ownership, lease, management contract and franchise to operate properties throughout the world. The fast-food chains like Burger King and McDonald's use franchising as a marketing tool to grow their business.

Hotel classification schemes

The World Tourist Organization and most national tourist boards use the internationally recognized star rating system to classify hotels. The scheme is as follows:

One-star	A budget market hotel with limited facilities, offering bed, breakfast and evening meal, and characterized by informal standards of service to residents
Two-star	An economy market hotel with limited facilities, offering more extensive dining facilities, and characterized by informal standards of service to residents
Three-star	A mid-market hotel with more extensive facilities, offering a full range of dining and bar services, with professional standards of service, to residents and non-residents
Four-star	An upscale hotel offering formal standards of service, with extensive facilities and services to residents and non-residents
Five-star	A luxury hotel offering 'flawless' service standards, with professional multilingual staff, and a full range of facilities of the highest quality

Many motoring organizations also use the star rating system but add their own awards, like the Automobile Association in the UK and the *Michelin Guide* from France. Consumer groups have also developed a variety of classification schemes for hotels and restaurants using their own criteria. From a marketing perspective, schemes like the AA Red Star hotel and Restaurant Rosette Awards provide quality standards which discerning customers understand. These endorsements reinforce the quality image projected in letterheads and brochures, and can be used in public relations campaigns to generate publicity.

Understanding the competition

Although some hoteliers and restaurateurs claim their product is so unique that they 'do not have any competitors', the reality is that all hospitality businesses compete against a variety of different types of competition. A broad distinction can be made between macro-competition and micro-competition.

Macro-competition

Macro-competition comprises all those industries that are competing for the consumers' disposable income, including hospitality. Examples of these indirect competitors include:

● Major household purchases – for example, a new bathroom or motorcar – compete with luxury holidays in exotic hotels and on the cruise ships
● Shopping for clothes and accessories competes with visits to health and sports clubs
● Supermarket outlets, with their pre-prepared, easy-to-cook meals, compete with restaurants and takeaway shops
● Shops that sell alcohol for consumption at home compete against bars and pubs.

Before examining micro-competition, we discuss Porter's Five Forces, and Competitive Environmental Analysis, which are tools used in the analysis of industry competition.

The influence of Michael Porter's generic marketing theory on both practitioners and academics has been significant. Porter (1980) proposed that firms benefit from understanding the forces that drive competition and profitability in their industry, and that firms should explicitly formulate a competitor strategy. To understand the competition, a competitive analysis needs to be undertaken. Porter's model is often referred to as the *five forces competitive analysis*.

The five forces driving industry competition

The external PESTE environment impacts on the general hospitality industry and affects all competitors. Porter identified five macro factors that influence industry competition:

1 *The bargaining power of customers (buyers).* This force reflects the strength of the bargaining position, particularly regarding price, which customers have over suppliers. Customers who purchase larger volumes of bed-nights and seats and who have low switching costs (i.e. it is easy to change the supplier) leverage a strong bargaining force in the competitive environment. For example, tour operators, who book thousands of customers in to hotels, have a strong bargaining position and can demand lower prices from hotels. Customers have a weaker bargaining position if demand is high and capacity low, but when demand is variable and capacity high the customers have a stronger bargaining position. However, individual customers who book and consume hospitality products have limited or no bargaining power.
2 *The bargaining power of suppliers (including employees).* Suppliers, including employees, can influence the attractiveness and profitability of a sector by increasing their prices (or wages) and thereby increasing industry costs and reducing profit margins. Powerful suppliers are those organizations that control the supply of goods and services to the hospitality industry. This varies from country to country. Examples include monopoly suppliers controlling electricity, gas, or water supplies; oligopoly suppliers, which are concentrations of only a few major suppliers (as in the UK brewing industry); and powerful trade unions, which can negotiate improved pay and conditions on behalf of the workforce.
3 *The threat of new entrants.* The threat of new entrants is dependent upon the barriers to entry into an industry. These include the ability to generate economies of scale and experience, the opportunities for product differentiation, the amount of capital required to buy into the industry, and access to distribution channels. In hospitality, there are low barriers to entry in most sectors.

4 *The threat of substitutes*. Substitute industries provide competing product offers that perform the same function. An example is the convenience eating-out market, which competes against substitute convenient eat-at-home products marketed by supermarkets. Continual developments in technology keep changing the potential threat from substitute products. The rapid development of video-conferencing is a substitute product for the hotel meetings market.

5 *The intensity of rivalry between competitors*. Rivalry varies between industries and sectors. The character of rivalry varies, and includes conflict (efforts to destroy competitors), competition (to provide better solutions to customer problems), co-existence (rivals allow each other to operate in different segments), cooperation (rivals cooperate in some activities such as purchasing) or collusion (illegal cooperation to fix prices and produce a managed market). The rivalry is dependent upon the number of dominant players, the level of industry profitability, levels of demand and capacity, and the personalities of competitors. In hospitality markets, whilst competition is intense, most people working in the industry have good personal relationships with rivals working for competitors.

The first step in a competitive analysis is to agree a relevant definition of the market sector, which sets the parameters for analysis – for example, the fast-food market in central London, the budget hotel market in Germany, the luxury hotel market in Europe. Each of the five forces is then evaluated using the information collected in the PESTE analysis. The five forces analysis identifies major opportunities and threats facing the company from the macro-environment. Figure 4.1 illustrates Porter's Five Forces using a full-service hotel example.

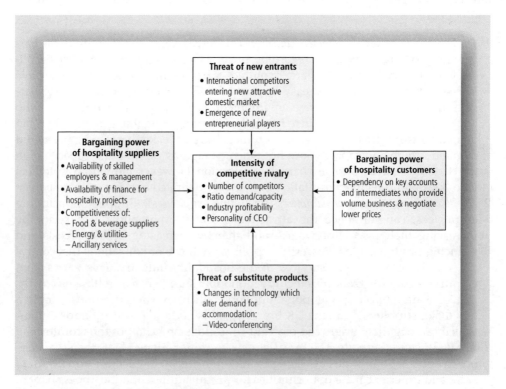

Figure 4.1 Five Forces Analysis (source: Porter, 1980)

Competitive environments

The Five Forces analysis evaluates the nature of the competitive environment in an industry. Another framework developed by Porter for analyzing the competitive environment of an industry identified four generic categories, which are described as fragmented, niche, volume and stalemate. Each of these competitive environments (except stalemate) is common in hospitality, and this language is regularly used to describe the characteristics of hospitality sectors.

Fragmented   In a fragmented competitive environment, no firm has a significant market share. The industry has low entry barriers, with high product differentiation and low economies of scale. Profitability is unrelated to size; this means that large firms are not more profitable than small firms. A fragmented market comprises a large number of small- and medium-sized businesses. In hospitality, examples of a fragmented market include the Italian hotel market (which is dominated by small privately-owned family run hotels) and British ethnic/fast-food restaurants (such as fish and chip shops, and Indian and Chinese restaurants).

Specialized or niche   In a specialized or niche competitive environment, there are many ways of achieving competitive advantage. Companies focus on serving specific market segments and become specialized businesses. The marketing objective is to be best in class, and a price premium is charged. Image, quality and service are important factors in serving customers in a niche market. There are many examples in the hospitality industry – Gleneagles Hotel in Scotland has a niche market in the luxury leisure golfing market.

Volume   The volume competitive environment is characterized by mass players serving mass markets. There is a limited number of ways to achieve competitive advantage, and control of costs is a key factor for success. Economies of scale, experience and technology are used to reduce the cost base. The marketing objective is to be the cost and volume leader. Examples of volume businesses in hospitality include brewing, contract catering and tour operators. In Norway, three companies (SAGA, Star Tours and Ving) dominate the travel industry.

Stalemate   The stalemate competitive environment is characteristic of industries in the mature or declining stages of the life cycle (for example the European steel industry) with a commodity product and limited opportunities for differentiation. This type of competitive environment is characterized by a small number of very large players which dominate their industry. There are few competitive advantages, so the focus is on large-scale production and improving productivity. Stalemate industries suffer from excess capacity, limited innovation and high barriers to entry. There are few examples of a stalemate industry in hospitality.

Micro-competition

Micro-competition comprises the branded and independent hospitality units that compete directly with a similar product and similar price, and target the same customer in the same location. This type of direct competition, which is normally local depending upon the product category, is also described as *product form* competition. First, a company needs to identify the brands/establishments in its competitor set.

Criteria that can be used to define a competitor set include competitors who are:

- Patronized by your target customers
- In the same product class
- Within a specified geographic area
- In a similar price category.

An effective marketing research technique adopted by the Marriott County Hall Hotel, London, is to ask residents where they would be staying tonight if the Marriott were full. The customers' replies help to establish which hotels are in the competitor set. Desk research and local knowledge can establish which businesses compete in the same product, geographic and price set. Examples of direct competition include:

- Five-star international hotels in Shanghai
- Pubs and bars on West Street in Sheffield
- Restaurants clustered around Circular Quay in Sydney Harbour.

Once the competitor set has been established, marketers need to carry out research by visiting their competitors and evaluating their marketing offer. One of the best ways to analyze competitors is actually to use their facilities as a paying customer, staying in the bedrooms, having a drink in the bar and dining in the restaurant. The desk and primary research should include assessment of the following:

- The size, quality, décor and facilities of the bedrooms, public areas
- Food and beverage facilities
- The staff and their approach to customer service
- The price and value offered
- The marketing communications and the service promise in print and advertising
- The image projected by the brand signage and physical appearance.

Although managers should be aware of any competitor developments on an ongoing basis, the preparation of an annual marketing plan provides an obvious opportunity to revisit competitors and monitor their activity.

International competitor sets

There is also strong competition on both macro- and micro-levels between the major global and international hospitality brands. Examples include:

Luxury	Four Seasons against Ritz Carlton
Upscale	Hilton International against Marriott
Mid-market	Best Western against Holiday Inn
Budget	Motel 6 against Super 8

However, competition also depends upon the number and type of brands an international hospitality company owns. Some companies compete in several mass markets on a global scale – Accor, Marriott and the InterContinental Group all own a range of budget, mid-market and luxury brands – and are striving to build global demand. There are a small number of hotel companies that operate on a global scale with a single brand, and these brands can be described as operating in niche markets. Four Seasons is a luxury niche operation, whilst Best Western is a mid-market niche operator. In many countries, the international brands also face domestic competitors.

Table 4.1 International Competitive Strategies

	Mass market	Niche market
Global coverage	Global/regional high market share (InterContinental Hotels Group)	Global/regional niche (Four Seasons Hotels)
National coverage	National high market share (Whitbread–Marriott franchise and Travel Inn)	National niche (Hotel du Vin)

A domestic competitor can own several brands in one country, and therefore competes in mass markets (a UK example is Whitbread), whilst a domestic competitor who focuses on a single market can be described as a domestic niche operator (another UK example is Hotel du Vin). Table 4.1 provides a summary of this scenario. Companies choose the markets in which they want to compete, and in that sense we can say that they choose their competition. Equally, if companies find they are not competing effectively in a marketplace, they can choose to exit and sell their units and/or brands.

Sustainable competitive advantage

Companies are constantly striving to compete more effectively. However, not all factors are equally influential, and some can be regarded as more important in achieving competitor advantage than others. These *critical success factors* (CSFs) – also called *key factors for success* – need to be identified so that a company can ensure that it delivers value that meets and exceeds the expectations of its targeted customers better than competitors. The process of analyzing critical success factors includes:

- Researching customer expectations (e.g. consistent food quality)
- Identifying the key components of the offer that create value for customers
- Identifying four to six potential critical success factors that impact on satisfying these expectations (e.g. close relationships with suppliers of fresh produce, efficient batch production operations)
- Analyzing company competencies that underpin the key factors identified
- Scrutinizing the list of critical factors to ensure that superior performance will deliver a competitive advantage
- Identifying the performance standards that need to be achieved to outperform competitors
- Assessing the ability, competencies and resources of the company to achieve the required performance standards
- Assessing the ability of competitors to imitate improved performance on the critical success factors.

International hospitality companies initially start developing their own unique competences in their domestic market as a response to consumer needs, competitor activities and the environmental situation.

Defining the CSFs in a market enables a company to understand its market position *vis-à-vis* competitors, and helps to build competitive advantages. CSFs need to be identified that deliver the experiences and attributes most valued by customers. Examples of critical success factors in the hospitality sector include:

- Lowest cost base for chain budget hotels
- High brand image and high brand awareness for international hotel luxury chains
- Technical superiority in food production processes for fast-food chain restaurants
- Consistent standards of service in standardized hospitality branded concepts
- Easy to find locations and secure parking facilities for provincial business hotels competing in urban locations
- Superior service, provided by well-trained and highly motivated personnel, in luxury country house hotels.

Whilst the most successful hospitality companies have clearly defined competences and understand the critical success factors in their competitive environment, many hotels and restaurants are not so aware. These companies often fail to understand their own competitive strengths and do not analyze their competitors for weaknesses, and thus they lose an opportunity to develop a competitive advantage.

Competitive advantages that are easily copied have limited value. 'Amenity creep' can become a serious problem for hospitality competitors when striving to gain a competitive advantage. When a company starts to offer customers additional product enhancements in an attempt to gain competitive advantage, this is called amenity creep. For example, if a hotel chain starts to offer customers additional complimentary in-room amenities (chocolates on the pillow, turning the bed down, providing more luxurious bathroom products, increasing the reward benefits on a frequent guest program) to try and increase customer loyalty and repeat business, this is called amenity creep. Since each added amenity is easily copied by competitors, and also significantly increases room costs and prices, chains using this tactic are unable to develop a genuine sustainable competitive advantage. Amenity creep can also inadvertently alter the positioning of the brand and lead to inappropriate pricing policies that erode the original market position.

For hospitality companies the reputation and image of a business is built up over many years, and a distinctive brand can become a focus for sustainable competitive advantage. Hotels like the Savoy in London, the Marriott chain of international hotels, and McDonald's fast-food restaurants have all developed strong and sustainable competitive advantages, based on a deep understanding of key factors for success in their market segments. Success factors change over time. New competitors can seize a sustainable competitive advantage by recognizing – earlier then their established competitors – environmental factors that alter the structural dimensions of the market.

Measuring competitive success

Key measures of competitive success for publicly quoted companies include operating statistics such as sales revenue increases, profit margin increases, room occupancy, achieved room rate, and yield. Market share is another important criterion. Hotels in the same local competitor set (branded chains and independents) sometimes exchange room occupancy and achieved room rates to enable each hotel to bench-mark its performance against competitors. The Leicester Association of Tourist and Conference Hotels carried out a market share analysis, which provided all participating hotels with important market data. To calculate market share, the following information is required for each hotel:

- Number of rooms available for letting
- Rooms sold during the given period.

The fair market share is calculated by dividing the number of bedrooms available in each individual hotel by the total number of bedrooms in the competitor set. For example, Hotel A has 100 rooms available and the total number of rooms in the competitor set is 1000. To calculate the fair market share:

$$\frac{\text{Number of bedrooms available in Hotel A}}{\text{Total number of bedrooms in the competitor set}} = \frac{100}{1000} = 10\%$$

When each hotel provides the actual number of rooms sold in the period, the market share of each hotel can be calculated by dividing the actual number of rooms sold by the total number of rooms sold. Again, using the same example, the actual market share can be calculated as follows:

$$\frac{\text{Number of rooms sold in Hotel A}}{\text{Total number of rooms sold in the set}} = \frac{70}{600} = 11.6\%$$

Finally, the difference between each hotel's actual market share and their fair market share can be calculated by subtracting the actual market share from the fair market share. In this example, Hotel A's actual market share is 11.6 percent and its fair market share should be 10 percent; therefore Hotel A has achieved 1.6 percent above its fair market share. This means that Hotel A has over-performed in occupancy terms compared to its competitors.

Market share analysis provides each hotel with important information concerning its actual performance against competitors, and can be used to monitor the effectiveness of marketing campaigns aimed at increasing market share. However, occupancy can be manipulated by lowering room rates, so managers are also interested in comparing achieved room rates. Increasingly, hotels are interested in using room yield as the benchmarking measurement for accommodation performance. Essentially, yield is a measure of the productivity of a company's assets. In hotels, yield is measured by comparing the actual revenues generated by rooms with the potential revenues that could have been yielded at full occupancy (see Chapter 7 for more details).

Hotel managers track their hotel's statistics month by month (see Table 4.2), and aim to improve their hotel's performance compared to competitors. When all the hotels in the competitor set experience an increase or fall in business the change can be attributed to factors in the external environment, but if one hotel's performance is consistently better (or worse) than its competitors', this indicates that local competitor factors (as opposed to external environmental factors) are responsible for the difference in performance. Thus performance needs to be placed within the context of the micro- and macro-environments, and reasons for inferior or superior performance need to be identified.

Table 4.2 Market Share Analysis

	Rooms available	Fair market share	Rooms let	Actual market share	Achieved room rate
Hotel A					
Hotel B					
Hotel C					
Hotel D					
Total					

Segmentation strategies

In Chapter 3 we discussed hospitality segmentation variables and target markets in detail. There are significant differences between the segmentation strategies of large hospitality organizations with multiple sites and those of independent, single-site operators. For larger organizations there are three alternative strategies: mass marketing, differentiated marketing and focused marketing (see Figure 4.2).

Mass marketing

Companies that adopt a mass marketing (or undifferentiated) strategy are responding to the *similarities* of consumers' needs and wants in large markets. They develop a single product to satisfy those customers. The benefits to the company include a standardized single product operation, leveraging significant savings in purchasing, production, staffing and promotion via massive economies of scale. The most visible example of mass marketing in hospitality is the fast-food market, although even here it is possible to detect marketing responses to segmentation variables. For example, McDonald's has developed special breakfast menus (a time-based market segment) and adapted the ingredients of their burgers in India (an ethnic/religious market segment).

Differentiated marketing

Major hospitality organizations adopting a differentiated segmentation strategy identify the *differences* between the needs and wants of various market segments, and develop individual marketing programs to satisfy the needs and wants of each market segment. An example of an international hospitality company that has successfully differentiated their marketing offer is Accor, which has developed specific international brands each catering for distinct market segments. The advantages of a differentiated approach, compared to mass marketing, include the opportunity to increase sales and market share by providing more bedrooms in several different hotels in the same location, with each hotel serving different market segments. The development of specific marketing programs for each segment should enable hospitality operators to satisfy customers better than a mass marketing approach, and generate higher repeat and recommended sales.

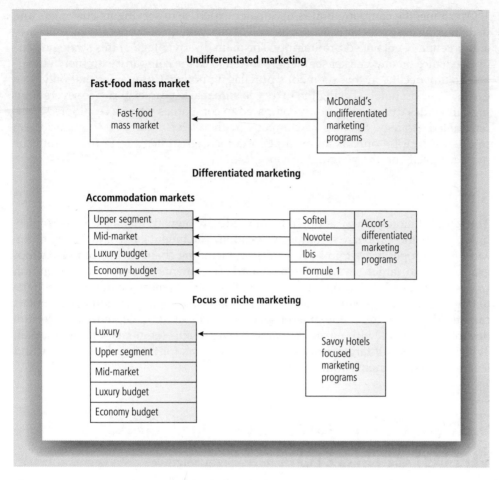

Figure 4.2 Segmentation strategies in hospitality

In the long term, organizations that have developed a portfolio of companies serving different segments of the market are less reliant on any particular segment, thus reducing the financial risk to the group. The disadvantages of a differentiated strategy are mainly cost-based. The cost of developing different marketing programs for separate market segments is higher with separate design and build costs, different purchasing schedules, more specialized staffing and different marketing communication activities.

Focused, concentrated or niche marketing

Hospitality companies that concentrate their marketing programs on a single market segment adopt a concentrated or focused segmentation strategy. This strategy can also be called a niche marketing strategy. Hospitality operators can either focus on a specific market segment, for example the luxury leisure market, or adopt a geographic concentration where all the company's outlets are focused within a specific geographic region. Because of their focus on a single segment, this strategy enables hospitality operators to really understand the needs and wants of their customers in that market segment.

Over time, the company builds up greater expertise in serving its customers and in delivering customer satisfaction, as well as enjoying greater operational efficiency and potentially enhanced profitability. The main disadvantage of this strategy is the over-reliance on one market segment, which makes the company extremely vulnerable to any decline in that segment's purchasing power. Companies that only own exclusive resort hotels serving the luxury leisure market can experience severe trading difficulties during recessions, compared to companies who have adopted a differentiated strategy. Sandals, a company with twelve luxury leisure Caribbean resorts for couples only, is an example of a focused strategy in terms of both the market served and the geographic concentration.

Single-site businesses

The segmentation strategy adopted by individually owned/managed units is interlinked with the property's character, location, catchment area and competition. Most hotel properties within a product class, including chain-owned branded properties, need to target several different market segments to ensure the operation trades profitably. The seasonality of hospitality markets means that operators have to target different segments at different times of the day, week, or month. Few hotels can afford to only target one market segment, and even unique, individual leisure destination hotels will normally target several sub-segments of the market. Typically hotels will target business market segments for midweek occupancy and leisure market segments at the weekends.

Targeting, positioning and differentiation

The selection of target markets provides a focus for the development of positioning and differentiation strategies. It is difficult for companies to compete effectively in today's crowded, media-dominated marketplace, where consumers are bombarded by thousands of messages from hundreds of commercial, non-commercial and government organizations on a daily basis. This intense competitive environment forces hospitality firms to try and create a distinctive marketing offer that will help the company to stand out and be noticed by its target markets. The dilemma for hospitality operators is that there are virtually no real differences between the core product offered by rivals in the same product class. Generic products, which do not have any real differences, are described as commodity products. The original commodity products were items like table salt and drinking water. In hospitality, the tangible elements of a hospitality experience – a bed, a meal, a drink – are so similar that they can be considered commodity products, and this means that it can be extremely difficult to provide a product offer that is genuinely different to that of your competitors. An innovation or improvement which one company introduces is often quickly copied or imitated by the competition.

However, hospitality consumers do recognize that some products and companies have very distinct images compared to their rivals, and those companies have worked hard to cultivate that image. This process, the design and maintenance of a distinctive position in the minds of target markets, is the focus of a positioning strategy.

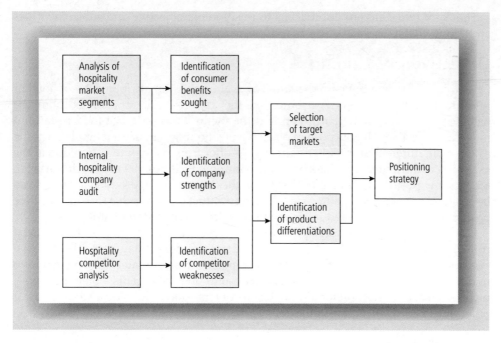

Figure 4.3 The process of segmentation, targeting and positioning in hospitality (adapted from Lovelock, 2002)

Positioning strategy is the process whereby hospitality companies try to develop a distinctive and favorable position in the minds of target markets, compared to competitors. The purpose of positioning is to ensure that target markets clearly understand what the product, service or brand stands for in the marketplace. Figure 4.3 demonstrates the link between segmentation, targeting and positioning.

Marketing research and analysis of the market segments should lead to an understanding of what consumers really want. The internal audit should identify the company's strengths, which can be developed into product or service differentiators. The competition analysis should identify competitors' weaknesses and possibilities for effective product or service differentiation. The marketer then evaluates the three separate analyses, with the aim of establishing a match between the benefits sought by consumers, the strengths of the company, and the weaknesses of competitors. The process culminates in the articulation of the company's desired position in the marketplace, which is designed to produce a competitive advantage.

Product or service differentiators are tools used by hospitality marketers as part of the positioning process. Product or service differentiation helps to distinguish between the tangible (and/or intangible) product characteristics of the service offer from competitors in the same product class. Again, the purpose is to create a competitive advantage attractive to selected target markets. The attributes that hospitality companies seek in order to differentiate themselves from competitors include location, quality, price, range of facilities and services, parking, safety/security, and, for frequent travelers, reward programs. The product or service differentiators may only be minor in nature – they may not even be real – but when articulated effectively over a period of time, they help the brand to stand out from competitors in the mind of the target markets.

There are two different approaches to positioning: objective and subjective (Ries and Trout, 1986).

Objective positioning

Objective positioning refers to the tangible, real or physical attributes that a hotel or restaurant offers customers. Attributes like the size of a budget motel bedroom, the facilities in a luxury hotel bathroom and the menu items on a fast-food restaurant menu are objective. The purpose of objective positioning is to use a tangible attribute as the main differentiator to distinguish your offer from competitors. Looking at the examples of attributes – the bedroom, the bathroom facilities, the menu – it is easy to see that any positioning statement based on these commodity product attributes can be easily imitated by competitors in the same product class. For this reason, objective positioning is not considered to be an effective long-term differentiator.

However, surveys of hospitality advertising reveal that all sectors of the industry, from international luxury hotel chains to local independent restaurants, use objective positioning images in their promotional campaigns. Unfortunately, managers fail to understand that pictures of their empty bedrooms and restaurants – or, even worse, pictures with their staff pretending to be customers – look the same as thousands of other hotel bedrooms and restaurants.

Subjective positioning

Subjective positioning focuses on the intangible aspects of the offer or experience. It is important to note that the perceived image of a hospitality company may not necessarily reflect the true or real state of the product or service offered. What matters is the customer's perception of the service. If the customer believes that a company's hospitality offer is high quality, with exceptional value, then the customer is right – and the offer is high quality, with exceptional value, to that target market. Subjective positioning offers hospitality operators more opportunity to position their company effectively because the basis of the positioning strategy is linked to intangible attributes, which are more difficult for competitors to imitate.

There are two approaches to subjective positioning, and the approach selected depends on whether the product is more tangible-dominant or intangible-dominant. Where hospitality products are tangible-dominant (for example, the hotel bedroom) and there is little if any difference between the competitors' offers, marketers aim to differentiate their product by stressing intangible attributes. This is not an easy task.

Marketing insight	**'Selling The Sizzle'**
	One technique adopted by advertising copywriters to overcome the difficulty of positioning tangible-dominant products is to 'sell the sizzle, not the sausage!' Instead of promoting the tangible facts about a sausage – its ingredients and dimensions – the copywriter strives to conjure up a mental picture of people enjoying the tempting smells of the sausage being cooked, the sound of the sausage crackling under the grill, the sight of a beautifully cooked sausage with appropriate garnishes and relish, the anticipation of a great tasting sausage! Copywriters really do promote intangible benefits by 'selling the sizzle'. McDonald's, for example, has run many advertising campaigns in which the tangible product, the burger, is of secondary importance. One campaign featured the golden arches as a wonderful place to meet and mingle after school; here, the benefit sold was sociability.

The second approach to subjective positioning focuses on intangible-dominant products. The intangible attributes of hospitality are the service, the atmosphere, the reputation, the history, the impressions, the image. Given that these attributes are abstract, how can hospitality marketers position their intangible products positively in the minds of consumers? One answer is to 'tangibilize the intangible' – in other words, to provide tangible evidence that reinforces the position the company is aiming to attain. Hyatt's subjective positioning strategy aims to create an exotic, grand, majestic and distinctive image for its hotels by focusing on innovative modern architecture in the building of their atrium-style hotel lobbies. This relatively minor product differentiator was consistently used in Hyatt's promotional campaigns, and succeeded in positioning Hyatt, in the minds of consumers, as a more exotic hotel than its competitors. Today, many hotels in the Hyatt's product class provide spacious atrium-style lobbies, but Hyatt still maintains its original and distinctive image.

Positioning strategies

Positioning strategies are designed from answers to two basic questions:

1 Against whom should you position? These are usually other brands in the same competitive group – for example, Burger King positions against McDonald's. They will be competitors against whom you can demonstrate competitive advantage.
2 How should you position? This provides the basis for your competitive efforts. Burger King, for example, positions itself as a healthier burger option because its burgers are flame broiled, not fried.

The following positioning strategies in hospitality companies have been identified:

● *Product feature or special attributes*. This strategy focuses on a tangible-dominant feature – for example, the largest function suite in the area might position a company in terms of space, grandeur and style.
● *Price/quality*. This positioning strategy for a luxury property might focus on the high quality, high price, exclusive image; for a budget property, the focus might be a standard quality at a lower price, implying better value for money in the economy product class.
● *Customer benefit*. This type of positioning proposes solutions to solve customers' problems – for example, Seoul's Hotel Shilla advertising campaign emphasizes the quality, choice of menu, convenience and efficiency of their 24-hour room service to international business travelers.
● *Use or usage*. This is a positioning strategy that focuses on the reasons why consumers use a product, and is often targeted at specific markets – for example, a resort hotel with a championship golf course targets executives who enjoy mixing business with sport.
● *User*. This positioning strategy focuses on the class of user – for example, families, younger people, religious people, well-off older people – and emphasizes the product's appeal to the class of users; it will often feature endorsements by celebrities pertinent to the target market.

Positioning new hospitality ventures

In new hospitality ventures there is likely to be a much greater focus on the positioning strategy, in part because financial backers will expect the marketing plan to be well formulated before advancing any loans. A new venture provides the hospitality company with the opportunity to plan the new concept using marketing research methods, and then to position the offer more effectively.

Positioning existing properties

In hospitality, there is a key difference between developing positioning strategies for existing properties and those for new ventures. In existing hotel and restaurant operations, a number of factors are fixed. These include the location, the geo-demographics of the catchment area, the property's current facilities, size and standards, the customer mix, and the property's historic image. These fixed factors are not easily changed, and the positioning strategy must take into account which strategy best fits the needs of the business and potential markets.

Repositioning

It is not unusual for hospitality operations to re-examine their current position in the marketplace and decide to reposition their property. The reason for repositioning may be:

- Falling sales (often a symptom of customer dissatisfaction)
- An opportunity to service an emerging market segment
- The threat of competition eroding market share.

The process for developing a repositioning strategy is similar to that of developing a positioning strategy for a start-up operation, with one caveat. In trying to reposition a hospitality property, there is the danger of sending out confusing signals to existing and potential target markets. This can damage the business by alienating existing customers, who do not like the changes. They might even abandon the property. If the lost customers are not replaced with new customers quickly enough, the business can rapidly lose sales and profitability. Repositioning can involve the company in significant capital expenditure to alter the physical product, and may require changes in the personnel to implement the new strategy. For these reasons, repositioning can be a risky strategy, but the alternatives are either to continue trading in a deteriorating, downward spiral, or to dispose of the property.

Positioning maps

Positioning maps, also called perceptual maps, are tools used by marketers to plot consumer evaluations of competing hospitality products using two or more attributes. The attributes used to map competitors are variables that are important to consumers, and can include price, quality, location, reputation, value for money, quality of food and service, conference and banqueting facilities, and availability of car parking (Dev *et al.*, 1995). Quantitative research using websites, guidebooks, hotel tariffs and brochures provides useful competitor information. Qualitative consumer research can be undertaken using focus groups of hotel users to evaluate the quality of food, personnel and service items amongst competitors.

Sophisticated statistical packages analyze the data and draw up a series of perceptual maps using two or more dimensions as the axes. Positioning maps are used to identify the strengths and weaknesses of hotels and their competitors over a series of measures. Figure 4.4 provides an illustration of a positioning map using hotels' quality and price points from budget to luxury. Note the relationship between quality and

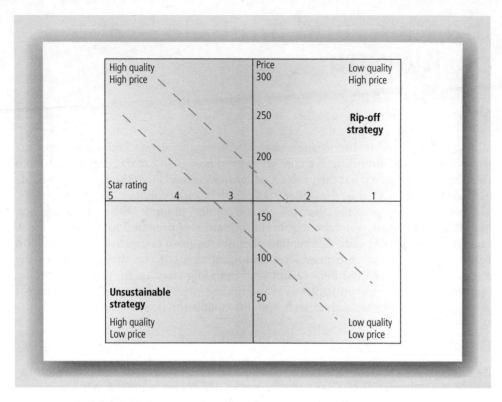

Figure 4.4 Hotel positioning map (adapted from Lovelock, 2002)

price, where luxurious hotels charge higher prices and budget hotels charge lower prices. Normally a unit must stay within its price/quality product class, which is indicated by the dotted lines on the map. If a hotel is charging more than the price/quality norm it could be accused of 'ripping-off' customers, unless there is another factor, for example a convenient location, which compensates for the higher price charge. If a hotel is offering genuinely higher quality at a lower price (five-star quality at three-star prices), this strategy is not sustainable in the long run.

Activity 4.2

Identify five hotels in your local area that represent luxury, upscale, mid-market (full service), mid-market (rooms only) and budget offers.

- Research each hotel's prices for accommodation.
- Draw a positioning map and plot each hotel's price and product quality on your perceptual map.
- Evaluate your findings.

Positioning maps can be used to track changing competitive positions over time. This is useful, because the marketing environment does not remain static and consumers' perceptions will change in response to competitors' actions. Hotels constantly battling for competitive advantage continue to adapt their positioning strategies.

Branding and multiple brand positioning

While the segmentation, targeting and positioning (STP) process identifies target markets, differentiates the product offer and positions the company or offer in the minds of consumers, it is the brand that is the most overt manifestation of STP strategy. A hospitality brand immediately distinguishes one company's product from competitors'. Branding is a core concept in hospitality marketing. Brands help customers to identify what the product or company stands for. There is considerable evidence to support the view that successful brands enhance company profits. When consumers perceive that one brand offers superior value to competing brands, they not only purchase that brand but are also prepared to pay more for it. Successful brands not only differentiate themselves from competitors, but also add value by meeting the consumer's psychological needs. Even though most of the discussion and research into hospitality branding relates to multi-unit chain operations, many of the principles of brand management apply equally to individual properties. In this sense, individual hospitality outlets can be perceived as brands.

Defining the brand

At its simplest, a brand is a specific name, term, sign, symbol, design or a combination of these characteristics applied to a product or organization. Brands function in a number of ways (de Chernatony and Dall'Olmo Riley, 1998), including:

- As a legal instrument – companies value the ownership of the brand name, logo and design, and protection of the brand from imitators leads to the prosecution of companies infringing on the trademark
- As a logo, which differentiates the offer with a visual identity and name, providing customers with quality assurance
- As an integral part of a company image, reflecting the culture, people and personality of the company
- As a shorthand symbol that is easily recognized by consumers
- As a risk reducer, giving consumers confidence that their expectations will be fulfilled – the brand as an unwritten contract
- By adding value to the customer's subjective experience.

Over time, the marketing investment in brands is rewarded by consumer goodwill and loyalty. This investment is sometimes reflected in a company's balance sheet.

Brand awareness and brand image

Two key measures are used to monitor the effectiveness of brands: brand awareness and brand image. Public and target-market awareness of a brand can be measured using marketing research techniques. In brand awareness surveys, respondents are asked to name any brands they know. This is called unprompted awareness. Respondents are then asked if they know the names of specific named brands; this is called prompted awareness. High brand awareness means that the brand is well known and enjoys a high profile; low brand awareness means that consumers do

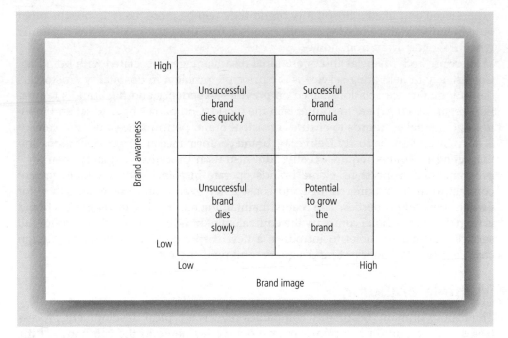

Figure 4.5 Brand awareness and brand image

not know the brand. Brand image is a measure of the brand's reputation – a high brand image means that the brand has a very good reputation, and a low brand image means that the brand has a poor reputation.

In Figure 4.5, brand awareness and brand image are plotted against each other. A brand's position in this matrix is indicative of its future fortune:

- Brands that have low awareness and a poor image are fortunate that their reputation is not well known. They have time to improve their performance. However, if no action is taken then the brand will gradually lose sales and become unprofitable.
- Brands with low awareness and a good image have the potential to grow, if brand awareness is increased.
- Brands with high awareness and good image are successful brands that need to be protected and nurtured.
- Brands with poor image and high awareness are in a difficult situation. If action is not taken quickly to improve the brand image, then the brand will die quickly.

Benefits and disadvantages of branding

It takes a long time to develop a positive brand image in the minds of consumers. Many of the top hospitality brands have been around since the end of the Second World War; and some of the exclusive, grand old European hotels date back for more than a hundred years. Brands provide consumers with quality assurance, and this is especially the case in an industry like hospitality, where consumers are primarily looking for a good night's sleep in safe, comfortable accommodation, and good food and drink efficiently served by friendly staff. Once consumers have experienced and liked a hospitality brand they will be more likely to use the other outlets in the chain, since the brand promises to reduce the risks for the customer when traveling away from home.

There are both financial and operational disadvantages associated with branding. Consistency in delivering service is the principle problem in hospitality. Customers develop quality expectations based on previous experience and the brand's reputation, regardless of where the outlet is in the world. Companies have to set and monitor operational standards to ensure consistent brand performance, but enforcement is not easy and can be costly. Delivering brand conformance in service operations and marketing programs requires costly administration procedures, quality assurance programs and inspections. Some brands operate in franchised and management contract formats, making control and consistency even more problematic than for owner-operated properties. The cost of maintaining and further developing a brand is high. It cost one hotel company the equivalent of building a new 100-bedroom full service, mid-market hotel to introduce a new corporate identity, with the design costs, exterior and interior brand signage, and publicity material.

Multiple branding

The history of many hospitality companies reveals a typical development process based upon a founding entrepreneur who gave his name to the company – Ritz, Hilton, Marriott, Forte. It's interesting to note just how many new chains still use the founder's family name when developing their corporate identity. Starting with one or a few properties, the founder grows the business, often focusing on a specific market segment and offering his or her single 'branded product'. The commercial pressure to continue growth, and to protect the company from relying on a single market segment, eventually leads to the development of multiple branded hospitality companies targeting a wide range of market segments. Multiple branding has become the preferred development strategy for the major hotel groups. Indeed, Best Western is the only single branded company in the top ten global hospitality corporations.

The way in which the hospitality corporations have introduced branding has varied. Some have retained the original name and added brand extensions to distinguish the various branded concepts – Marriott Hotels, Marriott Suites, Courtyard by Marriott; Holiday Inn, Holiday Inn Crowne Plaza, Holiday Inn Garden Court, Express by Holiday Inn. Other hotel groups have ensured that each brand name is completely distinct from the other brands in the group – for example, Accor with their Formule 1, Motel 6, Ibis, Etap, Mercure, Novotel and Sofitel brands.

The advantages of multiple branding include:

● Increased market share
● Less dependency upon the volatility of a single market segment
● Reduction in financial risk.

The main danger of multiple branding is the potential to 'cannibalize' the company's sales by encouraging the company's existing customers to trade down and stay at a cheaper brand of lodging facilities also owned by the same company. This criticism is particularly directed at corporations who have retained one family name for the entire range of lodging brands. This strategy gives lower graded accommodation the badge of approval from a higher graded brand.

Harder or softer hospitality brands

Multi-unit hospitality operations have considerable difficulty in delivering a uniform, consistent standard of product and service because:

- Inconsistent service personnel and erratic customer behavior changes the customer experience
- Refurbishment schedules mean the product varies enormously between the most recently redecorated unit and the most tired unit
- There are differences in the seasonality of demand and in the different locations of the units in the chain
- There are differences in local and regional, planning and building legislative requirements.

Hospitality chains have responded to the inherent inconsistencies in hospitality operations by developing different approaches depending upon the type of product class, and the age, design and style of properties in the portfolio.

A hospitality brand seeking to establish a standardized product/price formula, in similar locations and with a consistent customer experience throughout the chain, is described as a 'harder' brand. A collection of hospitality units being marketed under the same brand name but with limited emphasis on standardization can be described as a 'softer' brand. There is no absolute hard or soft brand, since all chains incorporate elements of standardization and elements of adaptation, and there is nothing inherently better about a harder or a softer brand. However, it is essential that softer brands are not promoted as harder brands, since they will not be able to deliver the standardized offer that customers expect from harder brands. Table 4.3 provides details of 'harder and softer' marketing strategies.

Examples of harder hospitality brands include Burger King and Travel Inn. They have purpose-built properties, using standardized design, décor and food offers. Examples of softer hotel brands, or collections of hotels which have been individually built in different styles during different historical periods and offer an eclectic choice of dining, include Best Western and Relais et Château.

Table 4.3 Harder and Softer Hotel Brands (adapted from Connell, 1992)

Factor/strategy	Harder	Softer
Use of same brand name across hotels	Yes	Yes
Level of physical product consistency	Higher	Lower
Level of service range consistency	Higher	Lower
Consistency in pricing	Higher	Lower
Level of national coverage	Higher	Lower
Consistency in type of locations	Higher	Lower
Emphasis on national advertising & promotion	Higher	Lower
Reliance upon growth through acquisition	Lower	Higher
Emphasis on product planning & development	Higher	Lower
Markets targeted	National/specific segments	Local/range of segments

It should be pointed out that there is nothing inherently better between hard or soft brands. However, problems will be experienced if a soft brand is promoted as a hard brand

Hotel–restaurant co-branding

Co-branding is the pairing of two or more recognized brands in the same space (Boone, 1997). The principle of linking well-known brands in marketing activities has been well established in hospitality. The benefits to both brands include greater exposure to a wider market, and a proportionately greater impact than a single brand's activities. Examples of co-branding include serving branded coffee in restaurants (Starbucks coffee is served in Sheratons); providing quick service food kiosks in hotel lobbies (Pizza Hut in Marriott) and leasing hotel restaurant space to branded restaurants (TGI Friday's in Carlson and Marriott).

The development of co-branding between American hotel chains and American restaurant chains was an appropriate strategic response to one of the endemic problems for hotels – the poor performance of their restaurant operations. Research into the effectiveness of hospitality co-branding demonstrates increased sales not only in the branded hotel restaurant, but also in the hotel accommodation. This suggests that both hotel residents and non-residents accept and patronize branded food concepts that they recognize, thus generating significant increases in restaurant sales. Other advantages included better cost control, improved staff training, and greatly increased operating profits.

There are disadvantages to leasing out restaurant operations to external partners, and these include the following:

● Lack of control, inflexible menus and food concepts
● Restaurant opening hours may not suit hotel guests
● Lack of cooperation between the restaurant management and the hotel management.

Criticisms of branding

Branding, and in particular the proliferation of hospitality brands, has been criticized. One of the criticisms of branding is that hospitality companies have used purely descriptive criteria for segmenting markets. This product-orientated approach has led to inaccurate positioning strategies, resulting in consumer confusion over the lack of perceived differences between competing brands.

The example of Choice Hotels, one of the innovators in multi-brand development, supports the critics' argument. Choice Hotels currently promote thirteen different products under seven brand names, but all are marketed under the Choice corporate name, with similar logos and collateral, and one toll-free call number for reservations. This has led to a confused product offering, where consumers are not clear which Choice brand stands for which lodging offer.

Conclusion

Segmenting markets to identify profitable target markets, developing a differentiated offer to deliver enhanced customer satisfaction, and positioning the hospitality brand against competitors are essential components in the development of marketing strategies to compete effectively.

In this chapter we have explained:

- How the hotel industry has developed in different ways in different regions of the world
- Different forms of ownership and affiliation, including ownership, lease, management contract, franchising and consortia
- The four industry competitive environments – fragmented, niche, volume and stalemate
- The Five Forces competitor analysis
- Three segmentation strategies – undifferentiated, differentiated and niche
- The difficulties of differentiating the hospitality product
- The criteria for successful positioning a hospitality offer
- The benefits and disadvantages of branding in hospitality.

Now check your understanding of this chapter by answering the following questions:

Review questions

1 Analyze a hospitality industry competitive environment using Porter's Five Forces model
2 Discuss differentiation and positioning strategies in the hospitality industry
3 Discuss the advantages and disadvantages of branding in hospitality:
   - from a customer's perspective
   - from a company's perspective.

References and further reading

Boone, J. M. (1997). Hotel–restaurant co-branding: a preliminary study. *Cornell Hotel & Restaurant Quarterly*, **Oct**, 34–43.

Connell, J. (1992). Branding hotel portfolios. *International Journal of Contemporary Hospitality Management*, **4(1)**, 26–32.

de Chernatony, L. and Dall'Olmo Riley, F. (1998). Defining a brand: beyond the literature with expert's interpretations. *Journal of Marketing Management*, **14(5)**, 417–444.

Dev, C. S., Morgan, M. S. and Shoemaker, S. (1995). A positioning analysis of hotel brands. *Cornell Hotel & Restaurant Quarterly*, **Dec**, 48–55.

Jones, P. (1999). Multiunit management in the hospitality industry: a late C20 phenomenon. *Journal of Contemporary Hospitality Management*, **11(4)**, 155–164.

Kotler, P., Bowen, J. and Makens, J. (2003). *Marketing for Hospitality and Tourism*, 3rd edn. Prentice Hall.

Lewis, R. C. and Chambers, R. E. (2000). *Marketing Leadership in Hospitality: Foundations and Practice*. John Wiley.

Lovelock, C. H. (2002). *Principles of Service Marketing and Management*. Prentice Hall.

Morrison, A. and Thomas, R. (1999). The future of small firms in the hospitality industry. *International Journal of Contemporary Hospitality Management*, **11(4)**, 148–154.

Perlmutter, H. V. (1969). The tortuous evolution of the multi-national corporation. *Columbia Journal of World Business*, **4(1)**, 9–18.

Porter, M. E. (1980). *Competitive Strategy; Techniques for Analyzing Industries and Competitors*. The Free Press.

Ries, A. and Trout, J. (1986). *Marketing Warfare*. McGraw-Hill.

Todd, G. and Mather, S. (1998). *Building Global Brands*. Travel Research International.

Chapter 5
Developing the offer

Chapter Objectives

After working through this chapter, you should be able to:

■ Identify the core, tangible and extended product in hospitality operations
■ Describe the function of product/benefit bundles in hospitality markets
■ Explain the characteristics of standardized and customized products in branded hospitality chains
■ Identify all the stages in the product life cycle and explain the marketing implications of each stage.

Introduction

Although authors discuss the product offer using a variety of different approaches, all agree that the product is a complex combination of tangible and intangible elements. The product/service is the starting point in the development of the marketing offer, and without the product concept, we have nothing to sell. Products simply deliver the basic functional solution to consumers' needs and wants, and must be designed to deliver customer satisfaction to specified target markets. However, there is no reason why consumers should choose one commodity product from another, apart from price. In Chapter 4 we discussed commodity products and branding in detail, and explained that successful brands add value for consumers. In this chapter we will explore the components of the hospitality product, product/benefit bundles, the standardization versus adaptation debate, and the product life cycle.

We can look at the product from two perspectives – first from the customer's perspective as a bundle of benefits that will solve their problems, and secondly from the firm's perspective in terms of what we create for and offer to the customer. It is important to note that the product that marketers strive to create and deliver may be quite different from the hospitality product actually experienced by the customer. Especially in service situations, unplanned elements can dramatically distort and disrupt the experience, leading to unplanned customer dissatisfaction, or, for that matter, satisfaction.

Activity 5.1

Reflect upon your own experiences as a customer eating out.

● Can you identify an 'unplanned' element of the product that led to you being dissatisfied?

● Can you explain what aspect of the experience went wrong?

Defining the product

An important distinction can be drawn between the core product, the tangible product, and the augmented or extended product (Kotler, 2000). Figure 5.1 provides an example of each component of the product for a budget hotel (Horner and Swarbrooke, 1996).

Core product

The core product delivers the fundamental functional benefits that the customer is seeking. In hospitality, a hotel offers a place to sleep, and a restaurant offers somewhere to eat. It is the customer, not the company, that defines the core product. If a customer chooses to stay at a resort hotel for 'rest and recuperation', then R&R is the core product for that customer. Normally hospitality organizations do not compete

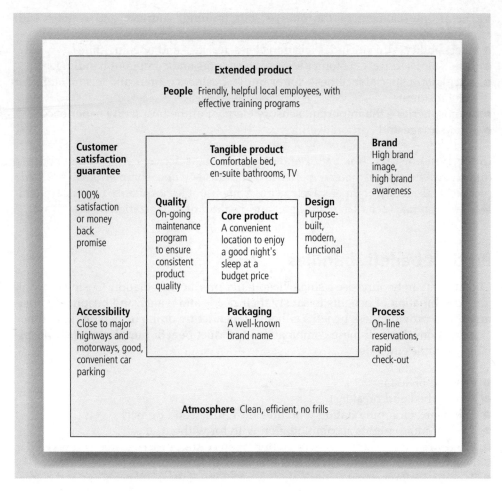

Figure 5.1 Budget hotel example of the core, tangible and extended product

at the core product level; however, companies should ensure that the requisite core capabilities and competencies are in place to deliver the core product effectively.

Tangible product

The tangible product is composed of the physical elements that are necessary for the core product (benefits) to be delivered. The tangible product includes product features (the size and range of facilities), design (external and internal), and quality and service standards. In hospitality, companies can differentiate their offer in the form of the tangible product. Pizza Hut, for example, has introduced an upscale range of 'Gourmet' pizzas to differentiate itself from other operators.

Extended product

The extended product includes intangible elements of the product that can add value, differentiate the offer, and provide customers with additional benefits. The extended product includes:

- The people element of the offer – staff training, courtesy and contact with customers
- Accessibility – this includes location characteristics and opening times
- After sales service – customer billing procedures and complaint handling
- Ancillary or special facilities – for example, business centers and leisure clubs for hotel residents
- Atmospherics – the important sensory element of the hospitality experience
- Brand image and corporate ethics.

In service industries, it is the extended product that delivers what is distinctively different about the customer experience – and this is where competitors in the same product class really compete. Delivering a memorable hospitality experience consistently is a major challenge for hotel and restaurant organizations.

Product benefit bundles

Consumers rarely purchase a single hospitality product in isolation. Customers look for a combination of benefits to satisfy their needs and wants, and hospitality businesses can provide these benefits either independently or in partnership with other organizations. We call these combinations 'product benefit bundles'. *Within* hospitality examples include:

- Bed and breakfast
- Dinner, bed and breakfast
- Full board (accommodation with breakfast, lunch and dinner)
- Two (or more) nights accommodation with (or without) meals
- Fixed-price menus (inclusive of starter, main course, desert, coffee and tax)
- Restaurant, function and wedding menus with drink packages
- 24-hour conference packages including accommodation, all meals, tea and coffee, hire of meeting room.

Activity 5.2

Obtain a conference or wedding brochure from a hotel and review the different product combinations and prices. What are the benefits of product bundles for:

- The customer?

- The hotel?

In addition, hospitality businesses can work with *external* organizations – for example, local leisure and sporting attractions – to offer inclusive product benefit bundles, like theatre weekends or golfing breaks.

The accommodation, food and drink products offered by hospitality businesses form part of the larger tourism product, either formally through a tour operator or informally through the customer experience of visiting the tourist destination. External factors, which are outside the control of hospitality operators, can affect the customers' enjoyment during a trip. Typically, the weather influences our holiday experience as well as the service provided by other retail and tourism outlets. Tour operators combine all the essential elements, such as flights, transfers, rooms and food excursions, and offer a combined product in one inclusive package. Tourists buying a package holiday regard the hospitality product simply as one component of the entire package, not as an independent product, and customer satisfaction with the hospitality product cannot always be easily separated from satisfaction with the other elements of the travel package.

This means that hospitality businesses need to work in collaboration with other organizations to have an effective marketing strategy and to ensure repeat and referral business. This collaboration can take different forms:

- Individual hospitality operations formulate, develop, promote and deliver their product as part of the total tourist offer of the destination
- At the destination, hospitality operators work with official tourist organizations who formulate and develop tourism products based on the destination attributes and promote them to target markets
- Tour operators coordinate the products offered by hospitality operators and other suppliers, and then formulate them into a single offer (package) which is promoted to target markets.

Service delivery concepts and the product

Any consideration of the product in hospitality must be based upon a thorough knowledge and understanding of the needs and wants of target markets. Understanding customer needs, within a given price band, is fundamental to successfully providing products which match customer expectations. One of the most important product decisions facing multiple-unit organizations is how much of the product should be standardized and how much should be customized. When hospitality organizations aim to standardize a product, the objective is to provide an identical standard service for all customers in every unit. A customized hospitality product deliberately offers a modified product, which can be different in each unit.

Standardized products

The international fast-food restaurant chains provide good examples of standardized hospitality products. They offer the following features in all their restaurants:

- The same menu at the same price
- The same kitchen production process
- The same service delivery process
- The same staff recruitment, training and service standards
- The same layout, seating and internal décor
- The same external frontage, signage and brand logo.

There are advantages to both the consumer and the organization with a standardized product. Customers receive a consistent, reliable product that fulfills their brand expectations. Companies gain significant economies of scale and experience through fully preconfigured design concepts, volume purchasing, reduction in stock levels, lower employee skills requirements, and easier staff training procedures. Service processes can also be blueprinted. Essentially, a blueprint is a flowchart that sets out the various tasks that have to be performed for a service to be delivered to a customer. Blueprints can also identify who is to perform the task and the required performance standards. There are also opportunities to maximize brand awareness through marketing communication campaigns based on promoting the same, standardized product formula.

A precondition for developing a genuinely consistent standardized product in hotel operations is to build new developments instead of adapting existing buildings and structures. The budget hotel chains are more likely to have a standardized product because the accommodation is factory built, with prefabricated bedroom units erected on the building site. As we saw in Chapter 4, hospitality brands offering a standardized product can be described as 'harder' brands. However, trying to adapt older buildings to a standardized brand formula inevitably creates some brand inconsistencies.

Companies with successful standardized offers can expand more easily – every time a new unit is proposed, all the product decisions have already been tried, tested and agreed. This has enabled a small number of standardized hospitality branded products to grow rapidly throughout the world. The standardized product concept is either loved or loathed by consumers!

Customized products

The alternative approach to standardization is to adapt or customize the product according to the needs of niche market segments, and even individual customers. Many European hotel chains offer customized products, which include:

● Individually designed hotels in different sites, often built in different historical periods, offering a different range of services and facilities in different locations
● Restaurants with different menu concepts, and different menus reflecting local ingredients and different cultures of cuisine
● Different décor and different types of furniture
● Staff who are trained to unit standards of operation, instead of brand standards of operation.

An adapted approach to hospitality product development implies higher costs, since there are limited opportunities for economies of scale. Hospitality brands offering an adapted product can be described as 'softer' brands. A good example of a global softer brand operating in the mid-market is Best Western Hotels.

International product decisions

The level of standardization or adaptation is a major product decision in international marketing (Usunier, 2000). The international hospitality product needs to take into account local country cultural differences and make suitable adaptations to gain local consumer acceptance. Identifying target markets is crucial when developing the international product.

If the target market is primarily from the home country, then the product can be standardized using the home country culture. The British-based tour operator, Ski Olympic provides a British skiing holiday product for British customers in the French Alps. The product includes British-style food (porridge and cooked English breakfast, Tetley teabags, evening meals using British recipes), British beers, British television (especially sport and TV soaps), British and Commonwealth staff and management, and even British ski instructors. This British product in France delivers customer satisfaction because the customers are all British.

If the target market is primarily people from the host country, the product should be adapted to take into account local cultural values – for example, McDonald's adapts the meat in its burger products to conform to the cultural expectations of customers in Indian countries, and provides rice as an alternative to fries for Asian markets.

If the target market has regional or global characteristics, then a standardized product should be developed. Scandic Hotels, which is part of the Hilton Hotels group, provides a relatively standardized regional hotel product in the Scandinavian countries of Denmark, Finland, Norway and Sweden. Scandic Hotels incorporates a distinctive Scandinavian atmosphere, décor and design in its product offer, which is strongly influenced by environmentally friendly policies.

In reality, most international hospitality groups have varying degrees of standardization and adaptation (Roper and Brookes, 1996). For hotel companies, accommodation, the range of facilities offered and service standards tend to be easier to standardize, whilst décor, design, staff uniforms and some elements of the food and beverage offer tend to be adapted to reflect local country culture and cuisine. Even the most standardized concepts, like McDonald's, adapt elements of their product offer when necessary, whilst Best Western Hotels – which operates the most heterogeneous brand of hotels on the international arena – strives to standardize the product offer through its quality audit for each property. The concept of providing international product standards with local adaptations – sometimes called globalization – combines the best of both approaches effectively.

Product life cycle

All products experience a life cycle, which charts their sales and profit behavior from birth, through various stages, to decline and extinction (see Figure 5.2). The product life cycle (PLC) is one of the most well known concepts in marketing theory (McDonald, 1999), and hospitality managers are aware of its importance when developing marketing strategies for their businesses. PLC concepts can be applied to an item on the menu or in the bar, a sales outlet within a hotel (the accommodation, the restaurant, the banqueting), an individual property or unit, a brand or chain of outlets, a destination, and even an industry. The global hospitality industry comprises hundreds of thousands of 'products', all at different stages of their life cycle.

The PLC includes the following stages, but note that the timescale can vary from a very short period of only a few months to a very long period lasting several generations and even hundreds of years (see Figure 5.3):

● *Product development.* During this period the new product concept is conceived, researched, assessed and, in some cases, test-marketed prior to introduction in the

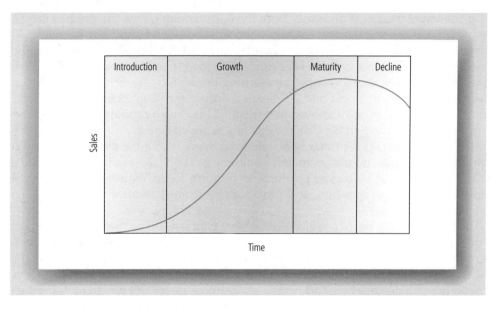

Figure 5.2 The product life cycle

marketplace. Most new product concepts fail at this stage and are never actually launched.

- *Introduction*. This is the launch period, when the new hospitality product is introduced to the market – for example, the opening of a new restaurant.
- *Growth*. This is the period when the new product becomes more widely accepted by consumers, and sales grow as the concept becomes better established.
- *Maturity*. At this stage, the product has reached its potential and growth slows.
- *Decline*. Eventually the product no longer satisfies the needs and wants of its customers, as alternative products/competitors provide better benefits to consumers. Sales fall as the product goes into decline, and the management has to decide whether to retain or dispose of the declining product. However, a product that is in decline for one company can still be highly profitable for a different company. There are many products in declining markets that are still highly profitable – for example, bed-and-breakfast houses in British seaside resorts.

There are a number of criticisms of the PLC. First, it is not always clear where a product is located on the PLC. Secondly, the PLC is not an accurate forecasting tool, and sales may fall due to an economic downturn instead of a change in the stage of the PLC – so if a manager makes a marketing decision based on a faulty analysis of the PLC, then the marketing strategies adopted might be incorrect and damage the business. Whilst accepting these valid criticisms, the simplicity and terminology of the PLC helps us to understand important product development issues, which we will now explore.

New product development concepts

Effective hospitality managers constantly seek to improve customer satisfaction by reviewing their offer. As a result of managers' observations, business performance

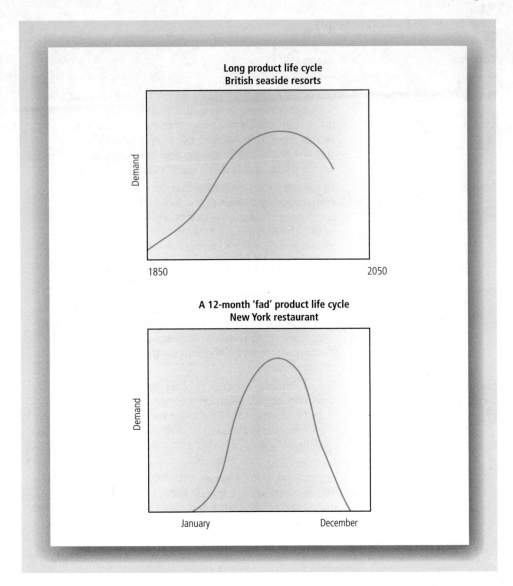

Figure 5.3 Product life cycles for British seaside resorts over 200 years, and for a New York fad restaurant opening and closing in 12 months

and customer/staff feedback, product improvements can be introduced. These can range from minor low-cost enhancements to multi-million pound new-build developments. Clearly many product developments are successful, but the rate of new product failure in hospitality is high – especially in food service. Unfortunately, many independently owned restaurants open and close within twelve months. The reasons for the high failure rate of new products in hospitality include:

- Inexperienced and over-optimistic entrepreneurs
- Poor marketing research
- A flawed product concept

Table 5.1 Hotel Product Concepts

Concept	Examples
Exclusive luxury hotels	Dubai's Burj Al Arab Hotel claims to be the world's first 'seven-star hotel'. Built in the shape of a giant sail and taller than the Eiffel Tower, it combines modern architecture, extravagant décor and furniture with state-of-the-art technology, and provides superior service with a six-to-one staff-to-guest ratio
Boutique hotels	These are exclusive hotels that focus on contemporary design as the key factor in delivering customer satisfaction – examples include Ian Schrager's hotel, The Morgan, in New York; London's Hempel Hotel; and Sweden's Icehotel
Convention complexes	The Venetian, Las Vegas, claims to be the world's largest hotel and convention complex, with 3000 bedroom suites, 120,000 square feet of gaming floors, a massive shopping center called The Grand Canal Shoppes, a luxurious Spa Club, and approximately 500,000 square feet of meeting space. This complex in the middle of the Nevada desert is themed on the old European city of Venice
Mid-market classic contemporary hotels	The Malmaison concept focuses on individually designed, stylish bedrooms complete with modern sound systems, state-of-the-art interconnectivity, and French brasserie cooking at mid-market prices
No-frills budget hotels	Formule 1, Accor's budget European product, focuses on functionality, with small bedrooms (a double bed and upper bunk bed), shower and WCs that are NOT en-suite, and minimal service levels. There is, however, a high use of technology, with self-cleaning showers and toilets, and automatic computer terminals to provide check-in and billing services when reception is closed

- An inappropriate location
- Competitors' responses
- Inconsistent service delivery
- Poor interior and/or exterior design
- Limited market potential
- Higher development costs than planned
- Undercapitalization
- Poor timing (e.g. opening during the decline phase of the business cycle).

Innovation

Major hospitality organizations have a wide range of products at different stages of the product life cycle. Since all products decline, there is a constant requirement to research and find successful new product concepts to ensure continuous profits.

Table 5.2 Restaurant Product Concepts

Restaurant	Concept
Conran	Conran's fashionable restaurants combine innovative and stylish design with fine dining on a mass-market scale in London, Paris and New York
Rainforest Café	An environmental concept café based upon the rainforest, with special effects including mist and regular thunderstorms with thunder and lightening, and a Magic Mushroom Bar, operating in North America, Asia-Pacific and Europe
Futurist Diner	An Australian space exploration restaurant, where customers are transported via a 4D-visual reality turbo space ride to Planet XERTS
Brazilian BBQ	Koiti Aida developed the first Brazilian BBQ concept restaurant in Guangzhou, China

Companies use two different methods to find new concepts: they can either *acquire* products that have been developed by others; or they can *develop* their own new products.

Acquisition   The bureaucracy of larger organizations can inhibit creativity whilst entrepreneurs, who are often closer to customers, can innovate with much more freedom. In hospitality there are many examples of people with limited work experience in the industry, who develop successful new product concepts based on their 'gut' feeling, their intuitive understanding of customer needs and their entrepreneurial flair. Once a successful entrepreneur has proved the viability of the new product concept, larger hospitality organizations can either imitate the concept or buy out the entrepreneur's company.

Development   The alternative route for new product development in larger organizations is to set up a new product in-house development team to generate and evaluate new product concepts formally. The team may be an established part of the organization structure or an *ad hoc* cross-functional group. New product teams need marketing input to ensure that the customer's voice is heard. Most so-called new products are actually product modifications, cost reductions or product line extensions, as opposed to original product concepts.

New product development process

Many companies have a formal new product development process that features some or all of the following stages:

- *Idea generation*. There are several sources for new product ideas, including managers, employees, customers, suppliers, intermediaries and competitors.
- *Idea screening*. Ideas need to be screened to ensure they can be developed further; some ideas lack potential and are immediately discarded; other ideas might be desirable but do not fit the competencies of the company. Screening aims to

eliminate bad ideas quickly so that the costlier stages of new product development (such as concept development) are not required.

- *Concept development and testing.* In this stage the idea is more fully developed into a new product concept with a detailed, workable proposal. Companies then need to test consumers' reaction to the new concept, using marketing research techniques such as focus groups.
- *Marketing strategy.* A marketing strategy statement is developed that describes the innovation's target market, market positioning and marketing mix. Initial costs, sales and profit projections are then formulated.
- *Business analysis.* In this stage the new product is evaluated against company investment and return hurdles. Investment in new product development is a board-level decision when significant capital sums are involved.
- *Product development.* Finally the idea starts to become a reality. Large companies develop a prototype for test marketing. A test market is a limited-scale launch of the product concept to establish the potential for the innovation and the marketing necessary to make it a success. New brand concepts can be experimented in a single unit to gauge customer reactions before rolling out the concept, but smaller businesses cannot afford to test market the concept.
- *Commercialization.* The final decision to proceed is based on the results of the test marketing. Depending upon consumer response and the capital investment/ profit return calculations, a final decision will be given to proceed or halt the new product development.

Whilst larger companies have a more structured approach to new product development, smaller hospitality companies are generally more entrepreneurial. A restaurant proprietor can introduce new menu items for a trial period before making the add-or-drop decision. Failed ideas can be dropped without serious cost consequences.

Adoption and diffusion theory

Some new products become popular very quickly, whilst it can be years before others take off. Some never become viable. Researchers have identified a number of different categories of new product adopters, according to whether the customer is amongst the first or later groups to buy. These categories are as follows:

- *Innovators.* These are the first people to buy a product once it appears. In hospitality, they are the first customers to visit a new restaurant when it opens. They are prepared to experiment and take risks, and are an important influence on the next category.
- *Early adopters.* These people respond to good word-of-mouth reports from innovators, and form the next category to try a new product. They are opinion leaders, whose judgment about a product can determine whether it will succeed or fail. If the early adopters endorse the product, it will become more established.
- *Early majority.* These people follow the early adopters, whose opinion matters to them. This group consists of people who tend to conform to social trends, are well-integrated socially and accept change.
- *Late majority.* This group is very slow to purchase new products. They are less responsive to change, are more skeptical, and prefer products they know rather than experimenting.

- *Laggards*. These people are suspicious of change and are reluctant to alter their purchase patterns. They are cautious and conservative, and continue to buy products even when they are no longer fashionable.

New product launch strategies

The introduction stage for new hospitality products includes new-build openings for hotels, restaurants and bars, new brand launches, and re-launches of tired products that have been refurbished and repositioned in the marketplace. For hotels, the time involved in planning, gaining permission, building and completing a new-build project can take several years and substantial capital investment. For restaurant and bar concepts, the lead-time will be shorter and investment costs lower. A common problem is that hospitality new-build and refurbishment programs are rarely completed on time, and often the new hospitality product has to be opened incomplete. Customers experience a distressingly long list of minor problems, such as incomplete décor finishes, that can take several months to complete.

A typical launch strategy will include a 'soft opening', where invited guests stay and/or dine on a complimentary basis. This provides an opportunity to train staff on the job, and test the service process and the equipment before paying customers arrive. Feedback from invited customers and staff helps to identify problems, which can then be resolved. If problems are not identified and resolved in the soft opening, then (especially with new restaurants) a poor reputation can quickly spread – which is often fatal. The marketing communications challenge during the launch period is to establish the market position, and create awareness and interest in the new hospitality product concept in order to generate trial purchases.

During the launch period sales are low and there can be major fluctuations in demand, causing service problems at crucial times. Start-up costs are high owing to the uncertain patterns of demand, staff training and recruitment costs, and the promotional spend to raise awareness. The unit is unlikely to be profitable during the introduction stage. However, the launch period is vital for the new hospitality product because the business needs to generate:

- Satisfied customers
- Positive word-of-mouth
- Repeat sales.

Smaller companies may never recover from a poor launch, since they may not be able to repair the damage from negative word-of-mouth publicity quickly enough. They may run out of working capital. A successful opening means that sales growth will increase, leading to the growth stage of the PLC.

Growth product strategies

In the growth stage, the hospitality product should be earning a good word-of-mouth reputation, the early adopters return and recommend the product to the early majority, who patronize the establishment in growing numbers. Sales grow, but despite this healthy trend there are pitfalls associated with growth. Successful hospitality products are dependent upon a consistent product/service offer, and as the business grows there can be over-demand at peak periods, resulting in either excessive waiting times or having to turn customers away. Hospitality customers are notoriously fickle, and once they have found another hospitality product that suits them, they may never return. Management can also inadvertently create problems by raising prices on ancillary products to boost profitability (for example on drinks and wines), which might disappoint repeat customers. Arrogant management, thinking that the business is now a success, may start to overlook customers' special requests and even ignore customer complaints.

Marketing strategies that hospitality companies adopt in the growth stage include:

- Relationship marketing to build long-term relationships with customers
- Enhancing the product and service delivery by continuous feedback from customers and staff
- Setting prices to gradually grow the market; this means not raising prices quickly simply because the establishment is becoming popular, and in some cases might involve making minor price adjustments downwards
- Targeting new market segments to grow demand, possibly with minor product modifications
- Continued investment in marketing communications activity, to maintain awareness and build loyalty based on product preference
- Encouraging word-of-mouth recommendation by inviting satisfied customers to refer friends
- Opening additional units in similar geographic and demographic catchment areas
- Building partnerships with other organizations that can generate a stream of customers, such as theaters or hospitals.

The growth stage should be increasingly profitable, since fixed costs are spread over a greater number of customers and, as trading patterns become more established, the management become more experienced at controlling staff rotas to enhance customer satisfaction and reduce wage costs.

Mature product strategies

The majority of hospitality product concepts operate in the mature stage of the life cycle, which can last for a very long period of time. The market for the product is well established, and the product itself is clearly positioned against its competitors. Sales level off, as the business has consistent demand from a loyal customer base. Growth is limited, and is largely dependent upon gaining market share from competitors. The mature hospitality product can suffer from a number of problems, including:

- A dated product concept
- A tired product in need of refurbishment
- Management and staff working in a routinized way and no longer 'wowing' the customers
- More intense competition from newer product concepts, which cater better for customer needs and wants
- Increased segmentation of the market, ultimately with the risk of market fragmentation.

Managers who are aware will recognize these symptoms and take action to avoid the product entering the decline stage prematurely. Mature product strategies in hospitality include:

- Relationship marketing to nurture and sustain loyal customer segments
- Continued investment in product quality to maintain and enhance service
- Product modifications – for example, introducing new menus/new recipes – which can revitalize a tired hospitality product
- Reformulation of the product concept and/or refurbishment of the premises to re-launch the product
- Adaptation of other marketing mix elements – for example, lower prices, increased promotional activity – and targeting new intermediaries to generate additional sales.

By careful management of the marketing mix, the mature stage can remain profitable for a very long time. Gradually profits will begin to decline as increased investment, with heavier promotional costs to maintain market share, coincides with lower prices. Even major international brands suffer from many competitors nibbling at their leading market share. Eventually the mature stage will enter decline, unless the product has been reformulated and re-launched to start another cycle.

Case study 5.1 provides an illustration of the PLC.

Case study

5.1 Beefeater restaurants

Beefeater, a UK family restaurant chain owned by Whitbread since the 1970s, has been in the mature stage of the PLC for many years. New menu items are continually introduced to revitalize the product offer, whilst retaining popular traditional dishes. There is a continuous investment program to maintain high standards of restaurant décor. Whitbread expects a very good return on capital, and under-performing units are sold. There is a constant drive to offer greater consistency across the brand, and management invests in heavy marketing communications activity to maintain market share. However, following poor trading results over a number of years, Whitbread has undertaken a major review of Beefeater Restaurants. This has included selling off dozens of the less profitable units, re-branding other units under alternative Whitbread restaurant brand names, and further investment in remaining sites.

What stage of the PLC is Beefeater operating in? This is a difficult question to answer. Perhaps Beefeater is still in the mature stage, or perhaps it has entered the decline stage – or maybe Beefeater has been in decline for several years, and the company is now rejuvenating its offer and entering an entirely new PLC.

Declining product strategies

There is no precise moment when a product or brand enters the decline stage, and the decline period can take place over a long period of time or be extremely rapid. Once decline really sets in, then the rate of decline accelerates. The decline stage can be caused by changes in consumer tastes, changes in technology, increased competition causing overcapacity, changes in management personnel, or changes in ownership. As sales begin to fall, the typical hospitality operator will:

● Aim to cut costs in every facet of the business
● Reduce staffing levels
● Only invest in essential repairs (there will be limited, if any, investment in redecorating or refurbishment)
● Reduce overall product quality by purchasing cheaper food ingredients, bar and housekeeping products
● Take a longer time to pay suppliers.

Disappointed customers, overworked employees and dissatisfied local suppliers can combine to generate powerful negative word-of-mouth publicity. Returning customers will notice the poorer standards of product quality (for example, tired décor and furniture, worn-out crockery, cheaper quality in-room amenities) and stop patronizing the hotel or restaurant. Customer complaints increase, with little prospect of management being able to encourage the unhappy customers to return. The spiral of decline increases in a deadly no-win situation for all concerned. As sales deteriorate faster, more desperate cost-cutting measures are introduced to try and stem the losses, which in turn reduces customer satisfaction.

For larger firms with several hospitality outlets or brands the problem of a unit in decline is exacerbated by the negative publicity, which can damage the overall brand image of successful units in other stages of the life cycle. In addition, the costs of managing a declining brand are disproportionate to the benefits generated. Owners and managers need to decide whether to keep a declining product and harvest it to maximize profits, or whether to dispose of it. If the product is retained, costs have to be reduced and unprofitable segments eliminated, which further reduces sales.

Disposal or rejuvenation

At any one time there are thousands of hospitality businesses that have reached the end of their product life cycles. A declining business that is for sale has similar problems to the decline stage; but if staff and customers know the business is for sale, the spiral of decline accelerates more quickly. Indeed, if a hotel or restaurant is not sold quickly, the business can go bankrupt. The key point to remember is that when a hospitality product is sold, it normally remains in the sector. The new owners can reformulate the product offer and invest in the re-launch of the business, and a new product life cycle starts. In destinations that are in decline, the hospitality product might be bought and converted into other uses – for example, housing and retail outlets.

Alternatively, the existing owners might decide to rejuvenate the product by closing the existing business, investing in a new product concept, and starting the PLC again.

Conclusion

Throughout this chapter we have explored different perspectives of the hospitality product, and emphasized the importance of matching the product to the needs of target markets. Given the intense competition in the hospitality business, it is essential for marketers to ensure that the product concept is designed to deliver customer satisfaction.

In this chapter, we have explained:

- The complex combination of tangible and intangible elements that comprises the hospitality product
- How products should be designed to cater for the needs and wants of target markets and to deliver customer satisfaction
- That the hospitality product comprises a core product, a tangible component and an extended element
- How hospitality businesses design product-benefit bundles to satisfy a combination of consumer needs and wants
- That multiple chain operations need to decide the degree of standardization and the degree of customization in their branded product
- The product life cycle, which charts the sales and profits during the lifetime of every product
- The five stages in the product life cycle – product development, introduction, growth, maturity and decline
- The high failure rate of new products in hospitality
- The different marketing strategy at each stage of the product life cycle
- That when a product reaches the decline stage of the PLC, management needs to decide whether to dispose of, or rejuvenate, the product.

Now check your understanding of this chapter by answering the following questions:

Review questions

1 Discuss the tangible and intangible elements of the hospitality product
2 Discuss the advantages and disadvantages of standardizing the product offer for a branded hospitality chain
3 Evaluate the effectiveness of the product life cycle in marketing decision-making. Illustrate your answer by providing examples from the hospitality industry.

References and further reading

Bateson, J. E. G. (1999). *Managing Services Marketing: Text and Readings*. Dyrden Press.

Horner, S. and Swarbrooke, J. (1996). *Marketing Tourism, Hospitality and Leisure in Europe*. International Thomson Business Press.

Kotler, P. (2000). *Marketing Management*. Prentice Hall.

Kotler, P., Bowen, J. and Makens, J. (2003). *Marketing for Hospitality and Tourism*, 3rd edn. Prentice Hall.

Lewis, R. C. and Chambers, R. E. (2000). *Marketing Leadership in Hospitality: Foundations and Practice*. John Wiley.

McDonald, M. (1999). *Marketing Plans*. Butterworth-Heinemann.

Roper, A. J. and Brookes, M. E. A. (1996). To standardise or not to standardise? *Marketing International Hotel Groups, CHME Annual Research Conference, Nottingham*.

Usunier, J. C. (2000). *Marketing Across Cultures*. Prentice Hall.

Chapter 6
Locating the offer

Chapter Objectives

After working through this chapter, you should be able to:

■ Understand the importance of location as a prerequisite for developing a profitable hospitality business
■ Identify the main classes of hospitality locations
■ Research the characteristics of potential sites using relevant criteria
■ Recognize the complexity of the destination product
■ Evaluate the components of a destination's image
■ Understand how hospitality companies work with destination marketing organizations.

Introduction

When the target markets have been defined and the product concept has been agreed, the next crucial marketing decision is to find the appropriate location(s) for the development of the hospitality business. The characteristics of a location actually influence potential hospitality target markets and determine the demand potential. Finding suitable locations is a prerequisite for managing a profitable hospitality company. The famous quotation from Conrad Hilton, who defined the three most important factors for success in the hotel business as 'location, location, location', remains valid today.

We will now discuss in more detail why location is important for both a single-site business and for multiple-unit operators, and examine the marketing research task in the search for finding appropriate locations. Finally, we will review destination marketing from the hospitality operators' perspective.

Importance of location

For owners, the location decision is a major capital investment with long-term consequences. When the agreement to buy or rent a site or premises is finalized, it is difficult and costly to change the decision – the location is fixed. So the initial selection of the site is most important. An appropriate site will have the necessary characteristics to ensure strong demand for the business. Although there are many examples of poorly managed hospitality outlets that trade successfully because of an outstanding location, even very good marketing cannot really compensate for a poor location. Clearly, thorough research needs to be undertaken to establish the patterns of demand in potential locations. Companies need to know whether there is a sufficient level of demand from target markets for the product concept to justify the investment in a specific location. Hard Rock Café recognizes the importance of location, and can research a potential location for up to three or four years in advance (Customer Management, 2000). This ensures that a thorough evaluation of the area's future growth and economic potential is undertaken before investing in the acquisition of a site.

For the single-site operator the choice of location is even more important, since the costs of a poor decision cannot be spread amongst the chain of outlets. Unfortunately, too many individual operators have overly optimistic demand projections and underestimate how long it can take to establish a new hospitality business. This is one of the reasons why so many small hospitality businesses fail in the start-up period. There are, of course, examples of successful hospitality businesses located in difficult sites, but this is because of the extraordinary skills of the entrepreneurs involved.

Developing a network of hospitality units

Multiple-site operators, and in particular the leading branded hospitality chains, have dramatically expanded their network of outlets during the past ten years. This expansion is driven by the need to:

- Grow the business (sales and profits) to satisfy shareholders' expectations
- Locate where customers need to stay or dine
- Be where competitors are located.

If your brand is not located where your customer wants to stay or dine, then you might lose that customer forever to one of your competitors.

The theory of location strategy has primarily been developed for multiple retail shopping outlets; however, the principles are applicable to hospitality operations. Academic models concerning optimal site location strategy include sales forecasting and spatial interaction models. Although computerized models have been developed for multi-unit tourism companies, their use in hospitality is limited. Most hospitality companies use a combination of checklists, feasibility studies provided by specialist consultancies, and managerial intuition to make location decisions.

Main classes of hospitality locations

Hospitality locations can be categorized in several ways, and these are described here.

Capital city

Capital cities usually generate strong demand from business, government and leisure markets. Capital cities, like London and Paris, attract both domestic and international visitors, and often have the highest room occupancy, achieved room rate and yields in a country.

Provincial city

Provincial cities are more likely to generate good domestic business demand, with a proportion of international business customers, and limited leisure demand. Provincial cities like Leicester, Lyons and Stuttgart fall into this category.

Gateway locations

Gateway locations are locations based at convenient destination access points, such as major airport terminals, key shipping ports and railway station termini. These sites handle large volumes of travelers, although not all travelers actually stay in the gateway location. For example, Zurich is a major gateway for visitors taking a skiing holiday in the Alps, but few skiers actually stay in Zurich. Heathrow, as a major international airport and gateway to London, England, the UK and Europe, generates one of the highest levels of demand for hotels in any location in the UK.

Highway locations

Highway locations are found on motorways and roads and serve the driving public, whether on business or leisure. Highway stops are normally associated with budget accommodation, and travelers typically stay for one night only.

Resort locations

Resorts primarily focus on leisure markets, but often include conference facilities to attract the corporate business market in shoulder months and low seasons. Many resorts have been developed at coastal and country locations. Resorts offer accommodation with a wide range of leisure and sporting activities, often on an all-inclusive basis.

Rural locations

Country locations also focus on the leisure market and frequently target niche markets, for example walkers in the Lake District or climbers in the Peak District.

Honey-pot destinations

Major tourist destinations are also described as 'honey-pots' because of the large volume of day-trip and overnight visitors. European examples include York and Venice.

Researching hospitality locations

Researching suitable sites for a hospitality operation is time-consuming. One British hotelier looked at over 50 locations, which took six months, before buying a hotel. This experience is typical. For international hospitality groups, there is the added complication of deciding which countries to enter.

There are three levels of spatial analysis in researching locations (Ghosh and McLafferty, 1987). The research starts with market selection, then focuses on the area analysis within a chosen region, and finally the most attractive sites are identified from sub-areas:

- *Market selection* decisions analyze the geo-demographic and socio-economic characteristics of a geographic region or country; this includes looking at the current situation and projecting future developments.
- The *area analysis* focuses on the characteristics of specific local areas within a region.
- *Site evaluation* examines local demographics, traffic flow and accessibility, individual competitors and the attractiveness of specific sites.

We will now review the criteria used by hospitality companies in country, regional and site selection.

Country selection

We have already mentioned the rapid growth of international hotel companies. This growth has been driven by the globalization of travel markets and intense competition by the major players. As one competitor develops operations in a new country, so other competitors feel obliged to follow. A PESTE analysis identifying the advantages and disadvantages of specific countries provides the basis for analysis. Key criteria for evaluating the attractiveness of a country market include political stability, planning risk, development route and market attractiveness.

Political stability

High political stability creates a favorable investment climate. Most Western countries have stable political systems, whilst countries that have considerable political turmoil, like Columbia, Nigeria and Pakistan, are more risky and therefore less attractive to international investors. In countries with high political stability, the option to purchase freehold properties or negotiate long leasehold agreements is likely. In countries with high political instability, the preferred entry option is to franchise the brand to a local company or negotiate an equity-free management contract, because local organizations understand how to manage their own political environment better than foreigners. The USA and British governments provide information for companies planning international investment and advice about political stability in websites such as the American Central Intelligence Agency (www.cia.gov).

Planning risk

Regardless of the stability of a political regime, countries have different approaches to planning control. This can mean there are difficulties in obtaining planning consent for building new developments, converting existing properties into hospitality outlets, or carrying out major refurbishment programs. Knowledge of the local culture and business/governmental customs is essential when negotiating planning permissions. A key aspect of international marketing is to understand the influence of culture on customers and on the way of doing business in a foreign country. It is much easier to conduct business in a familiar cultural climate.

Development route

There are three options for network expansion:

1 *Acquisition* – companies buy a group of hotels, and/or an independent hotel, and re-brand these properties. This is the most convenient, proven and popular approach, especially if a brand wants to grow rapidly. However, there are issues of ensuring brand conformity between the newly acquired properties and the company's international brand standards.
2 *Conversion* – companies buy an existing property (for example, an office block or flats) and convert the property into hotel premises. This is much more time-consuming and expensive. Whilst groups may occasionally convert a suitable property, this is the least preferred option.
3 *New-build development* – companies purchase the land and build their own product to their own design specifications (subject to planning controls). This can be more time-consuming than acquisition, but the advantage is that the brand standards are delivered from the moment the property opens.

The major international hospitality companies use a combination of all three development routes. Which route is preferred depends upon the target location, the form of ownership, and regulatory planning constraints.

Market attractiveness

The evaluation of market attractiveness uses demand analysis and competition analysis. The essential hard data, which help companies to forecast operating performance in a new country, include:

- Visitor arrivals, visitor mix (by country) and visitor spend
- Population and demographic statistics
- Economic statistics
- Hotel industry average occupancies, achieved room rates and yield.

The attractiveness of a country market will depend upon the potential demand from the selected target markets and the intensity of competitor rivalry. An interesting factor for ethnocentric companies is the number of home market visitors traveling to target countries. One North American hotel company used the ratio of American visitors to a city as a criterion for European site selection, because American tourists are likely to stay at brands they know and trust.

Country evaluation

When all the data have been collated, companies draw up a matrix to evaluate the attractiveness of different countries and locations. Table 6.1 provides a typical example of a European Development strategy for a major international hotel group. Each criterion is awarded marks using an internal company grading system. For example, a gateway location might be awarded between three and five marks, whilst a secondary location might be awarded between one and two marks. In the example, London, Paris and Berlin as major capital cities and the airports Heathrow and Charles de Gaulle are all gateway locations, so each might score a maximum five marks, whilst Manchester and Strasbourg are clearly secondary locations, possibly scoring one mark in this system. When all the criteria for all the destinations have been allocated, the accumulated scores for each location are computed and the ranking scheme provides a prioritization of the locations.

Regional selection

Having selected the country, the next decision is to choose which region, area or city to locate in within the country. Many hospitality organizations are domestic companies that only operate in their own country. Compared with international companies, local hospitality operators have one major advantage: they understand the local environment, the culture and markets, and how to conduct business in their own country.

Regional location decisions include the criteria discussed in Table 6.1, as well as the following factors:

- Microclimate – a detailed examination of regional climates, the hours of sunshine, level of rainfall, temperature and seasonal variations is important for companies locating in leisure resorts
- Infrastructure – establishes access for target markets via air, road, rail and sea connections
- Regional demographic characteristics – within a country there are wide differences between regions in terms of employment opportunities, disposable income distribution, cost of living, and living standards, which impact on domestic and local levels of demand
- Competitors – an evaluation of the locations of major competitors is essential; indeed, locating where your competitors are based is a logical entry strategy.

Expanding hospitality companies need to identify the location gaps with their regional network of units to complete their portfolio of properties.

Table 6.1 Location Criteria for a European Hotel Chain Development Strategy

Geographic			Location		Timing	Development route			Attractiveness of market segments		Risk		Mix home tourists	Score	Ranking
Country	City	Population	Gateway	Secondary	Urgency	1	2	3	Business	Leisure	Political	Planning			
UK	London														
	Heathrow														
	Birmingham														
	Manchester														
	Edinburgh														
France	Paris														
	Charles de Gaulle														
	Lyons														
	Bordeaux														
	Strasbourg														
Germany	Berlin														
	Hamburg														
	Munich														

Urgency: Based on company internal development needs
Development route: 1 Acquisition; 2 Conversion; 3 New build
Political risk: Country stability
Planning risk: Ease or difficulty of obtaining hotel planning permission.

Site selection

This decision refers to the process of identifying actual sites that are suitable for purchase, rent and development. Hospitality outlets in good demand areas can fail due to poor site selection. Sites can be categorized as follows:

- *Prime*. These sites are the best locations. They are in high demand and can be difficult to acquire (because most are already in the hands of existing operators), and expensive to maintain. An example is the famous Dorchester Hotel on Park Lane, London.
- *Secondary*. These sites are not prominent, but are still reasonably accessible. Most hospitality units are in this category.
- *Tertiary*. These sites are less accessible, and may have other negative factors – for example, being close to a lorry park or an industrial estate. An example of a hospitality company having successfully developed a low-cost product concept using tertiary sites is Accor, with its Formule 1.

Factors influencing site selection include:

- Local demographics and the characteristics of neighborhoods. De Vere Hotels has explicit site selection criteria for the Village Inns brand to ensure high hotel occupancies and membership of their health and fitness clubs. These clubs target affluent consumers, not families, aged 25–55. To generate a club membership of between 4000 and 5000, De Vere look for sites with over 100,000 ABC1 consumers within 20 minutes' drive time (De Vere Hotels, 2000).
- Accessibility, pedestrian and vehicle traffic flows and car parking. An interesting example of two new UK roadside restaurants illustrates the complexity of site selection. One restaurant opened by a busy roundabout in Humberside with a very high traffic density, and the other opened on a quiet stretch of road on the A11 in Norfolk. The A11 unit was more profitable than the Humberside unit because in the Humberside area most of the car journeys were local people traveling to school, work and shopping. Motorists traveling long distances, who needed a break during their journey, used the A11 site in Norfolk (Jones, 1999).
- Competitors. The number, size, quality, prices, occupancy and seasonality of branded and local competitors provide an insight into the local marketplace. Restaurant operators targeting local consumers often cluster together in prime sites, which is an indicator of the attractiveness of the location.
- Individual site characteristics, which include the size, landscape, adjacent buildings, aspect (south or north facing), and further development potential.

Case study 6.1 illustrates the importance of site selection.

Case study

6.1 Sophie's Steak House and Bar, Fulham Road, London

Sophie Mogford had always wanted to open her own restaurant, and her friend Rupert Powell had always wanted to own his own bar. Both already had very good restaurant and bar operational experience; Sophie worked for the Mezzanine Group, owners of Smolensky's

Restaurants, and had been involved in opening one of their new restaurants, whilst Rupert had worked at Browns and at Quaglino's – a Conran Restaurant. On holiday in New York they ate out in a different type of steak house, which really caught their imagination. The concept of Sophie's Steak House was born, but both knew that getting the right site is crucial if you're going to launch a successful restaurant business.

The search took eighteen months; they looked at hundreds of sales brochures for restaurants on the market. They visited over 50 sites, and actually asked their architect to draw up plans on five sites that were really promising. Originally they looked at the West End of London, but the property prices were too high; however, they eventually found a site in Fulham that fulfilled their criteria. They needed a minimum 90 covers to make the business viable. Rupert wanted a separate bar area, with its own license to attract non-diners, and seating for another twenty customers; and they both thought that the production kitchen should be visible to diners. This meant they needed approximately 2000 square feet of floor space.

Why was the Fulham Road such a good site for Sophie's? Rupert says the restaurant, which had been part of a chain, was situated in the middle of an affluent cosmopolitan neighborhood where house prices are high and the socio-economic profile of residents indicates high disposable income. The Fulham Road has a wide range of quality shopping, professional offices, is close to fashionable Knightsbridge, and has lots of passing traffic. It's a busy place, with several other bars and restaurants in the area. The premises are located opposite a cinema and supermarket, and only half a mile from a major hospital. Sophie and Rupert believed all of these factors would generate strong demand for their mid-market restaurant.

After eighteen months of searching, Sophie and Rupert finally agreed to buy the leasehold, and as soon as they got possession in October they closed for a three-month refurbishment. The kitchen was re-equipped, the ceiling levels altered, the décor and external signage were improved, and finally, two years after starting their search, Sophie's opened for business at the end of January. Twelve months have passed, during one of the worst economic periods for a long time, and Sophie's 90-cover restaurant is serving 2000 meals each week. They are open from midday to midnight, and can re-lay tables three times on a Saturday night, with a good spend. The cinema, hospital staff and visitors generate demand at normally low season periods, like early Saturday evening.

The long search for the right site has paid off, and Sophie's has become a very popular eating house.

(Source: Rupert Powell)

Location decisions

Clearly a considerable amount of research is invested in the location decision, and making a correct decision is fundamental to the success of the hospitality business. However, location decisions involve a trade-off between the different characteristics of potential sites and the capital available for investment. From a marketing perspective the crucial factor is the potential demand of a site, but sites with greater demand potential have more expensive site acquisition costs. Location decision theory assumes a high element of rational decision-making, but, historically, hospitality companies have expanded opportunistically. So despite all the research, many location decisions are based on 'gut feelings' and instinct. As Rupert Powell, of Sophie's Steak House, says: 'You walk into a property and you just know, that gut feeling is really important!'

Activity 6.1

Identify three hospitality units, one in a prime site, one in a secondary site and one in a tertiary site. Carry out some marketing research, both desk research and a site visit if you can, to evaluate the demand characteristics of each site using the following criteria:

- Local demographics and neighborhood characteristics
- Accessibility
- Competition
- Individual site characteristics.

Destination marketing from the hospitality perspective

We have discussed the importance of location, and the criteria that hospitality companies use to evaluate the attractiveness of the destination. Although chain hospitality operators do have the advantage of access to their own branded distribution systems, the activities and effectiveness of the marketing of a destination does impact on most units in the destination. However, destinations are complex products (Middleton and Clark, 2000):

- Destinations exist within a wide spectrum of different geographic levels
- Destinations have layers of administrative bodies responsible for the development and promotion of tourism, and responsibilities can either be confused and/or duplicated
- Destinations comprise physical characteristics (the natural landscape and climate), which obviously cannot be changed, and the built environment
- Destinations comprise deep-rooted cultural and historical heritages, which influence the character of local people and the visitor experience
- Destinations incorporate all the components of the tourism product – hospitality, attractions, transport, travel, intermediaries, and destination marketing organizations
- There is no single owner of the tourism product in a destination.

The confusion of geographic and administrative layers is illustrated by the example of Castleton, a village in the Hope Valley, Derbyshire, which is in the Peak District National Park. Table 6.2 details eight layers of administration, from the local parish council to the European Union. Each administrative body has an interest in tourism. However, there is often conflict within and between the different administrative organizations. This conflict reflects the differing perspectives of companies wanting to develop tourism further for more visitors, and local people and conservationists who want to control and inhibit tourism development.

Table 6.2 Layers of Tourism Administration, Castleton, Derbyshire

Boundary	Destination	Administrative responsibility
Village/town	Castleton	Parish/Town Council
District	High Peak	District Council
County	Derbyshire	County Council
National Park	Peak District	National Parks Board
Region	East Midlands	Regional Tourist Board
Country	England	English Tourist Board
Country	United Kingdom	British Tourist Authority
Continent	Europe	European Union

Destinations also have a polyglot of public and private stakeholders, including:

- National tourist organizations, local tourist organizations, and partnerships between government and private sectors
- Tourism companies (mainly small and a few larger businesses), their owners, management and employees
- Pro- and anti-tourism lobbies
- Local inhabitants and visitors.

No single organization has total control over the tourism product and the destination image. This has implications for tourism development, quality control, and marketing.

Tourist area life cycle

In Chapter 5, we discussed the product life cycle and explained that life cycle theory can be applied to a wide variety of products and brands, including destinations. Butler (1980) introduced the concept of the tourist area life cycle (TALC), which follows the classic stages of the product life cycle. The TALC is a useful tool for understanding the stages of development in a tourist destination, but suffers from similar limitations to the PLC. It is difficult to establish where the tourist area is located during the cycle's evolution. External environmental factors and competitor destination activity is not incorporated into the model, and the TALC is not an effective forecasting tool. The example (see Figures 6.1, 6.2) of the development of Cancun in Mexico between 1972 and 1996 illustrates how a TALC can be modeled, but the model is unable to predict accurately when growth will slow and stagnation/decline will set in.

Destination image

The image of a destination is a crucial component in today's competitive tourism market. A destination's image is a mixture of:

- Inherited physical attributes
- The built environment
- The cultural and historical heritage

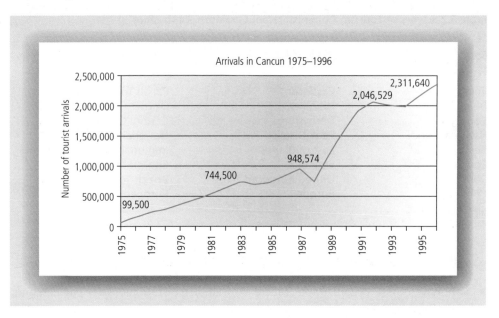

Figure 6.1 Visitor arrivals 1975–1995 at Cancun, Mexico (source: Dessylas, 1997)

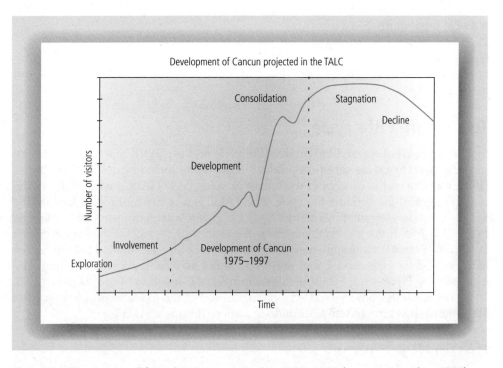

Figure 6.2 Tourist area life cycle, Cancun, Mexico 1975–1995 (source: Dessylas, 1997)

- Myth
- The people.

When we discussed brand image in Chapter 4, we explained that image is a perception in the minds of consumers. We all have images of a tourism destination,

regardless of whether we have visited the place or not. Images that are formed from indirect sources, through the media (news reports, television travel programs, newspapers and advertising) and by word of mouth from friends and/relatives, are *induced images*.

Organic images are formed by actually visiting the destination in person. Our organic perceptions are based upon the actual experiences, enjoyable or otherwise, of visiting the destination. The organic image we form is more fixed and less likely to be influenced by destination marketing activity. When we tell family and friends about our impressions of a destination, we are projecting an induced image.

Activity 6.2

- Identify two tourism destinations, one which you have visited and one that you have not.

- Analyze the 'induced' image you have formed about the destination you have not visited.

- Analyze the 'organic' image of the destination you have visited.

- Compare the image of the destinations – can you identify the differences between an induced and an organic image?

The problem with an induced image is that it may be completely inaccurate, depending upon the reliability of the source. For British tourists, the induced image of a country like Romania is largely negative, because the British tabloid media portray Romania in an entirely negative tone. Interestingly, the organic image of Romania formed by British tourists visiting the country is largely positive (Bota, 2000), but the Romanian tourist organization does not have sufficient resources to counter Romania's negative image in the British media.

The world's major tourist cities have powerful images, which in tourism terms are represented by one or a series of iconic images easily recognizable by international tourists. The iconic images of a red double-decker bus, the Eiffel Tower and the Golden Gate Bridge immediately suggest London, Paris and San Francisco. Iconic images can be manufactured; the Big Apple and 'I Love New York' campaign is a successful example of a manufactured iconic image supported by an effective marketing communications campaign.

Image and personal safety

The overwhelming majority of tourists are concerned about their personal safety when traveling. Political instability, the threat of war, war itself, terrorist incidents and crime have a major negative impact on the tourist destination image, and on visitor arrivals. The hijackings of 11 September 2001 in North America, when aeroplanes were flown into the Pentagon and into the Twin Towers of the World Trade Center in New York, provide the most obvious example of terrorism incidents damaging tourist consumer confidence in the safety of flying. The tourist massacre at Luxor in Egypt, the IRA bombing campaign and Protestant response in Northern Ireland, and the Israeli/Arab conflict have all had serious negative impacts on the image of these destinations.

Destination marketing organizations (DMO)

Destination marketing organizations can be government funded, a private company, or a combination of the public and private sector. Their primary role is to:

- Carry out marketing research and provide market intelligence for stakeholders
- Monitor visitor statistics and trends
- Coordinate marketing campaigns, and in particular Marcom activity
- Build and maintain destination websites and links
- Liaise with intermediaries
- Provide tourist information for visitors before and during visits (this may include booking services)
- Manage the brand image of the destination.

Case study 6.2 illustrates successful destination marketing.

Case study

6.2 Destination marketing at work

The Seychelles Tourism Marketing Authority is responsible for marketing the Seychelles, a collection of 115 unspoilt islands in the Indian Ocean. Tourism is a major source of employment and revenue for the Seychelles. The STMA coordinates promotion for approximately 150 resorts, hotels and guesthouses, most with less than 10 bedrooms and fewer than 6 with over 100 bedrooms. There are tourist offices in the key target countries of France, Spain, South Africa, the UK, Germany and Italy, with tourist representatives working in India, Switzerland, Dubai and Ireland.

The STMA carried out extensive research with European travelers and intermediaries to identify the positive brand attributes for the Seychelles. Francis Savy states: 'travelers have never had so many places to choose from. They're confused. So to make it easier, we're presenting the Seychelles as a brand.' The SMTA developed a marketing communication campaign with a new logo and specially commissioned, evocative black-and-white photography. The focus of the campaign is the Seychelles' untouched beauty and natural perfection. The brand logo uses four circles, which represent the lush green tropical islands, the white beaches, the coral reef, and the Indian Ocean. The positioning statement is 'As Pure As It Gets', and reflects the brand attributes of the natural image of a tropical island. The campaign includes magazine advertising with a minimal amount of copy, emphasizing the natural beauty of the Seychelles.

(Source: Seychelles Tourism Marketing Authority brochures and www.aspureasitgets.com)

We noted earlier that organizations responsible for marketing a destination suffer from limited control of the product, and have to resolve the conflicting demands of stakeholders. Limited resources and unrealistic stakeholder expectations compound these problems. Hospitality companies within a destination work with destination marketing organizations in the following ways:

- Companies join the destination marketing organization, which normally involves paying a membership fee
- Companies provide detailed information for guide entries, and pay for advertising in destination tourist brochures

- Companies participate in tourist information and accommodation booking services
- Companies provide hospitality for familiarization (FAM) visits by travel journalists, conference/exhibition organizers and other key intermediaries visiting the destination.

Proactive hospitality managers join the committees of destination marketing organizations and can leverage a degree of competitive advantage by developing good personal relationships with the personnel and management of the DMO.

Conclusion

Location decisions involve considerable research, and the consequences are significant. Attractive sites with good demand characteristics have to be balanced with the capital available. Once the location decision has been made, hospitality companies work with destination marketing organizations to market the destination.

In this chapter, we have explained:

- Why the location decision is a major investment with long-term consequences
- The thorough research that needs to be undertaken to evaluate the potential demand and competition in a location
- That tourism destinations can be categorized under the headings capital city, provincial city, gateway, highway, resort, rural, and honey-pot
- The three levels of spatial analysis in researching locations – market selection, area analysis and site evaluation
- The wide range of criteria used by hospitality companies to evaluate the market potential of locations
- That destinations are complex products with a polyglot of public and private stakeholders
- That destination image is a crucial component in today's competitive environment, and induced images are formed from indirect sources while organic images are formed by actually visiting the destination
- How hospitality organizations work with destination marketing organizations to market the destination effectively.

Review questions

Now check your understanding of this chapter by answering the following questions:

1 Why is the location decision an important element of the marketing mix?
2 What are the differences between single-site owners and multi-unit hospitality retailers in making location decisions?
3 Discuss the site selection criteria for locating a hospitality product.
4 Explain the characteristics and relevance of destination image in hospitality marketing.
5 How can hospitality managers work with destination marketing organizations?

References and further reading

Butler, R. W. (1980). The concept of a tourist area cycle of evolution: implications for the management of resources. *Canadian Geographer*, **24**, 5–12.

Bota, T. (2000). Romania's Image as a Tourist Destination, Unpublished MSc Dissertation, Oxford Brookes University.

Customer Management (2000). Towards best practice. *Customer Management*, **Jul/Aug**, 6–11.

Dessylas, E. (1997). Development Strategies in Cancun, Mexico. Unpublished MSc Dissertation, Oxford Brookes University.

De Vere Hotels (2000). *Greenalls Sectors Strategy*. De Vere Groups plc.

Ghosh, A. and McLafferty, F. L. (1987). *Location Strategies for Retail and Service Firms*. Lexington Books.

Jones, P. (1999). Multi-unit management in the hospitality industry: a late twentieth century phenomenon. *International Journal of Contemporary Hospitality Management*, **11(4)**, 155–164.

Kotler, P., Bowen, J. and Makens, J. (2003). *Marketing for Hospitality and Tourism*, 3rd edn. Prentice Hall.

Lewis, R. C. and Chambers, R. E. (2000). *Marketing Leadership in Hospitality: Foundations and Practice*. John Wiley.

Middleton, V. T. C. and Clark, J. (2000). *Marketing in Travel & Tourism*. Butterworth-Heinemann.

Chapter 7
Pricing the offer

Chapter Objectives

After working through this chapter, you should be able to:

- Understand the significance of pricing in the pre-encounter mix
- Identify external and internal factors that influence pricing decisions
- Explain quality/pricing strategies in a hospitality context
- Understand pricing methods in hospitality organizations
- Describe the role of price promotions to increase revenue in low season periods
- Recognize the complexity of pricing in an international context.

Introduction

In this chapter, we will review the significance of pricing in the pre-encounter marketing mix and examine how companies set prices. We will then look at the external and internal factors that influence pricing decisions, and explain the pricing techniques that are especially relevant to hospitality organizations.

Pricing is the tool that matches supply and demand. Price influences the demand for a product, which in turn determines volume sales. Therefore, setting an appropriate price is one of the most critical factors in demand management and in generating revenue. Price is the only element of the marketing mix that is not a cost, because price generates revenue. Pricing decisions contribute to product and brand image, and product and pricing decisions are therefore inseparable.

Significance of pricing in the pre-encounter marketing mix

There is a clear link between the price a customer pays and the customer's quality expectations. The higher the price, the greater the expectations of a high quality hospitality experience. Price is an indicator and a measure of quality, particularly in the absence of other cues. If a high quality gourmet restaurant was routinely to offer cheap menus, or a five-star hotel was continually promoting budget holidays, customers would be confused and suspect that the product quality offered was not genuine. Price plays an important part in establishing customers' perceptions of a product and of a company's position in the marketplace. Over time, brands often become associated with particular value propositions, which become fixed in the consumers' perception of that brand. McDonald's brand values are firmly placed in the fast food, family, and lower spend position.

Although price is the easiest variable of the marketing mix to change, it is the most complex and least understood of the variables. In hospitality, short-term tactical price changes are often not consistent with strategic objectives, and can send out strong negative messages to consumers with damaging, long-term consequences. Price is:

the summation of all sacrifices made by a consumer in order to experience the benefits of a product.

This definition includes both financial and other sacrifices, such as time and effort. It is a broad definition, because monetary price is not the only consideration consumers have to think about when making purchase decisions. In many countries, some consumer groups are described as 'money rich and time poor'. These affluent consumers have busy lifestyles with limited time to enjoy discretionary purchases. 'Time is money' is an appropriate expression for these important target markets.

One of the first questions customers ask before booking a hotel or restaurant is 'how much is a room?' or 'how much is the price of a meal?' Although the reply will be given in money terms (and customers quite sensibly want to know if the room or meal is affordable), what they are really interested in is value, not price. Customer value is found in the relationship between costs incurred (cash, time, effort) and benefits enjoyed (food, beverage, service, entertainment, atmosphere, experience). If costs rise without enhanced benefits for the customer, then value falls. If additional benefits can be included for the customer, without increasing price, then the customer enjoys better value.

An important distinction to recognize is that consumers' perception of the value/price of a product is strongly linked to their perception of the product concept. Product concepts are targeted at selected market segments with different needs and wants. Two very different product concepts are those that cater for special occasions and those that provide convenient solutions to consumers' everyday needs.

The price band for dinner at a luxury gourmet restaurant, a special occasion, is at the top end of most consumers' affordability, whilst the price band for a self-service meal, often a convenience purchase, is at a much lower price point. Consumers form expectations of what they will have to pay for a gourmet meal, and compare competing gourmet restaurant price/product offers. Equally, consumers choosing a self-service restaurant have price expectations of what to pay for a self-service meal, and compare competing self-service price/product offers.

Consumers tend not to compare the value/price offer between different product concepts; whereas they do compare the value/price offer within the same and adjacent product classes. In most cases, branded hotels are able to charge a higher price than independently owned, non-chain hotels. Consumers seem to be prepared to pay more to stay in a branded hotel, which guarantees a familiar product standard, rather than risk staying in an unknown, non-branded hotel.

Activity 7.1

- Contact hotels in the same competitor set in a city or town you know, and establish the prices for a room in each hotel for the same night.

- Evaluate the reasons why hotels in the same product class charge different prices. For example, normally the branded hotels will charge a higher rate than similar standard independents – but a prime location carries a price premium.

Stages in setting prices

Kotler (2000) proposed a generic pricing model that recommends eight stages in setting prices:

1 Select pricing objectives
2 Assess the target market's ability to afford the purchase price and consumers' perception of the price/product offer
3 Determine the potential demand, including the price elasticity of demand
4 Analyze the demand, cost, volume, price and profit relationships; businesses need to understand their fixed and variable costs
5 Research competitors' price/product offer
6 Select a pricing strategy

7 Select appropriate pricing methods

8 Set specific prices for rooms, food, beverages, conference and leisure products, and for special product-price bundles.

This approach requires a considerable amount of consumer, competitor and internal company research. Major companies are in a position to adopt this approach. One example is the large tour operators, who monitor their unsold capacity and competitors' prices on-line on a daily basis and alter their pricing schedule up or down accordingly.

The managers of smaller hospitality companies adopt a much simpler approach to setting prices, based upon a combination of historical factors and the current economic situation. The process of setting prices might be as follows:

1 Review last season/year's prices and business performance

2 Review current and potential cost increases.

3 Take into account current and forecast inflation

4 Take into account the general economic situation, and factors likely to influence customers' attitudes to prices

5 Check competitors' current prices

6 Set prices by adding a percentage (for example, 5 percent on the tariff of each room price) or a fixed amount (add £1 to each *à la carte* menu item) onto the current prices.

Marketing-orientated managers will try to find out what competitors are intending to charge next year, before setting their own prices. Although this process is flawed, managers of smaller businesses set prices using the historic price, plus or minus a sum, because it is simple and easy to adopt.

Factors influencing pricing decisions

Factors that influence price decisions can be sorted in to two major categories (Kotler, 2000):

1 External environmental factors, over which companies have little (if any) control

2 Internal factors, over which companies have a considerable amount of control.

External factors

The outer circle of Figure 7.1 illustrates five of the environmental variables that impact on pricing decisions – demand, inflation, industry structure, competition, and legal/regulatory factors.

Demand

We discussed the drivers of demand in detail in Chapter 3. In this section, we will review price elasticity, business and consumer confidence, exchange rates and the micro-environment within the context of pricing.

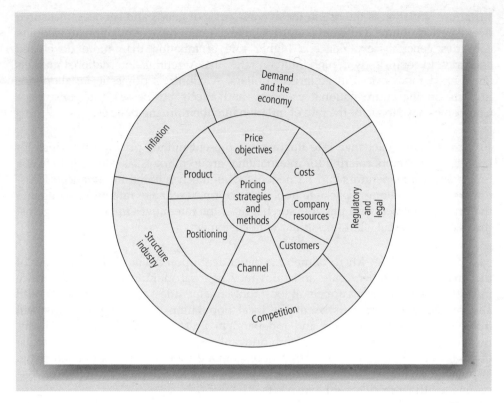

Figure 7.1 Factors that influence pricing decisions

Price elasticity of demand   Understanding the price elasticity of demand is essential to making good pricing decisions. The sales volume of a product that has *inelastic* price demand does not vary significantly when price changes. In hospitality, the business market for accommodation is traditionally considered to be more price-inelastic in its demand schedule. Conversely, the sales volume of a product that has an *elastic* price demand varies significantly when prices change. Traditionally, leisure products are considered to be more price-elastic in their demand schedule because they are discretionary purchases. A simple way to understand the price elasticity of demand is to consider essential purchases as being price-inelastic, and non-essential purchases as being more price-elastic. The price elasticity for generic products can change over the long term, as products that were originally considered to be 'non-essential' become an 'essential' part of consumers' lifestyle. For example, many consumers now regard holidays abroad as an essential purchase.

Business and consumer confidence   We have already discussed the business cycle and its impact on business and consumer confidence. During periods of economic growth, there is rising confidence and less price-sensitivity from business and consumers. This means there is less resistance to price increases. However, during a recession, the loss of business and consumer confidence significantly reduces demand. Both corporate and individual consumers become much more price-sensitive, and there is resistance to price increases – indeed, customers will expect price discounts.

Inflation   Inflation is the rise in the average price of goods and services, measured over a period of time. Different countries have different rates of inflation; developing countries generally experience a higher rate of inflation than more developed countries. In countries with high inflation rates, like Argentina, international markets are quoted room prices in American dollars. A country's domestic inflation rate impacts on the entire national economy and affects businesses and consumers. Companies have to factor the rate of inflation into their pricing policies.

Exchange rates   Exchange rate fluctuations present unique pricing difficulties for hospitality operators catering for international group markets, as contracts between hotels and tour operators can be negotiated eighteen months in advance of customers actually taking a package holiday. Factoring exchange rate movements into the pricing contract, with possible surcharges if the rate moves unfavorably against the hotel, is essential – but unpopular with customers.

Micro-environment   Micro-demand is dependent upon the local characteristics of the area – the number, scale and buoyancy of local manufacturing and service industries; the image and appeal of local tourism amenities; and the density, wealth and purchasing characteristics of the local population. All of these factors will influence both group-owned and independent units within the area. Typically, most of the businesses in an area with buoyant demand will be prospering, whilst businesses in an area suffering from poor demand will generally all be suffering. Popular destinations can charge higher prices, and less popular destinations use pricing to attract price-sensitive markets.

Type and structure of industry

Structural factors that influence the pricing dynamics in hospitality sectors include the cost structure, number of players, and capacity of the industry.

Cost structure   Different hospitality sectors have different cost structures, which impact on pricing policies. A five-star luxury hotel requires a high investment in the building, décor, facilities and staffing ratios compared to budget hotels constructed with pre-fabricated standardized bedrooms, in secondary locations, offering minimal staffing levels and no ancillary facilities. The pricing policies of the five-star hotel sector must reflect the higher investment and operating costs, whilst the pricing policies of the budget sector should reflect the lower investment and operating costs.

   The sourcing of produce in remote destinations increases the cost structure – for example, hotels in the Seychelles have to fly in food produce that is not available locally, increasing food costs significantly.

Number of players   If the sector is highly concentrated and dominated by a small number of very large players, the sector's overall profitability is dependent upon players *not* adopting price competition to gain market share. The impact of genuine price competition results in all players cutting their prices to prevent a loss of market share, thus leading to erosion of the sector's profitability. In this case, competition should be based on product differentiation rather than price. The rivalry between McDonald's and Burger King in the fast-food sector is primarily based on product differentiation, not price.

Where there are a large number of players, and no firms are dominant, the opportunity for players to adopt different pricing strategies is greater.

Capacity   Given sufficient demand, limited capacity will enable firms to charge higher prices; while sectors with lower demand and 'over-capacity' will suffer from intense price competition. Because of the relatively low start-up costs, the restaurant market also suffers from excess capacity and remains intensely price competitive.

Competition

In Chapter 4, we discussed the 'five forces' model driving industry competition. If the competitive environment is benign and the intensity of rivalry gentlemanly, industry pricing policies should enhance profitability. However, if the competitive environment is fierce and the intensity of rivalry bitter; industry pricing policies can adversely affect profitability.

Legal/regulatory

National government taxation policies, like Value Added Tax (VAT), tourist taxes levied by a charge on letting bedrooms and excise duties imposed on alcoholic beverages, impact on the prices charged by the hospitality industry. Since each country sets its own taxation policies, companies operating in countries with lower taxation policies can gain a competitive advantage over companies operating in higher-taxed countries.

Governments can impose regulations on companies, which increase the costs of running a business. For example, the European Union directives on minimum wages, health and safety have forced hospitality companies to introduce new work practices and equipment/maintenance schedules, which has often led to companies having to increase prices to help pay for these regulations.

Internal factors

The inner circle in Figure 7.1 shows seven internal factors that affect the pricing decision: pricing objectives, costs, company resources, positioning, customers, product, and channel.

Pricing objectives

Price objectives are dependent upon marketing objectives, which in turn are dependent upon corporate objectives. Organizations often have long-term strategic price objectives, and short-term tactical price objectives; crucially, pricing objectives need to be consistent with the objectives of the other elements of the marketing mix. Pricing objectives should be SMART – Specific, Measurable, Achievable, Realistic, and within a set Timetable.

Pricing decisions are linked to the financial and marketing planning process of setting sales, cost and profit budgets. In some instances, the corporate objectives very clearly dictate pricing objectives – a corporate objective to maximize profits in the short term leads to a marketing objective of setting prices designed to maximize current cash flow, regardless of the type or suitability of the sales generated. Pricing objectives can be classified into the following categories: marketing-orientated, financial-orientated, and competitor-orientated.

Marketing-orientated pricing objectives   Marketing-orientated organizations try to understand how price influences customers' perception of their product offer, and develop pricing objectives using a customer's perspective.

Market leaders in high quality hospitality markets, such as luxury hotels, gourmet restaurants, first-class travel providers and luxury cruise ships, adopt a 'prestige' or premium pricing objective (that is, to charge the highest prices for the highest quality service), and must ensure that the customer perception of their service matches the premium prices charged.

Hospitality operators adopting the 'best value for money' objective in a given product class monitor customers' perception of their product value, scanning competitors' price activity and ensuring that their offer delivers the best perceived value for money.

Another marketing-orientated pricing objective is to encourage trial or repeat purchases. When launching a new hospitality concept, marketers need to generate interest in the new venture, and one of the tools used is a free sample or discounted trial purchase. Repeat visits can be encouraged using price promotions.

Unfortunately, hospitality companies seldom commission in-depth psychological research regarding customers' perceptions of their product/price offer and are therefore rarely able to set optimum prices that are acceptable to customers whilst delivering the maximum contribution to the company.

Financial-orientated pricing objectives   The majority of for-profit hospitality organizations focus on financial objectives rather than marketing-orientated objectives.

Profit-orientated pricing objectives focus on the company's profit requirements and include survival, target return on investment, skimming, optimal current profit and harvesting. Profit-orientated pricing objectives are effective for setting management performance targets, but typically fail to take in to account the external environment, competitor and customer factors. A typical profit-orientated pricing objective would be: 'to set prices to achieve a 15 percent return on investment, per annum, over a five-year period'.

Marketing insight

Profit-orientated Pricing Objectives (Source: Kotler, 2000)

- *Survival*. A company fighting for survival, e.g. during a recession, adopts short-term low prices, designed to attract value-sensitive customers. These prices are justified on the grounds that even a small contribution to fixed costs is better than none. Generating cash flow is critical to servicing high finance and labor costs. This pricing objective could have serious consequences for competitors, who not only lose market share but could also be forced in to financial difficulties as a result of the price competition.
- *Target Return on Investment (ROI)*. The selected ROI depends upon the type, scale and risk of the investment; the rate of inflation; and the company's internal minimum ROI policy. Prices are calculated to ensure that the ROI is achieved. If the initial investment needs to be repaid within a short time period, the pricing policy must also be set to achieve a rapid payback of the capital invested.
- *Skimming*. The objective of a skimming pricing policy is to charge the highest possible price at the launch of a new product, to maximize the contribution from price-insensitive customers. This objective is quite commonly employed for manufactured goods but is rarely used by hospitality companies, who tend to operate in markets with well-established price bands.

- *Optimal current profit.* In the mature stage of the market/product life cycle, companies generally seek to optimize their profit by setting prices that are consistent with maintaining market share. In mature markets it is difficult to charge higher prices, because customers have well-established price expectations.
- *Harvesting.* In the late maturity or decline stage of the market/product life cycle corporations can 'milk' a product by using the profit generated as a source of cash for investment in an alternative product that has greater growth potential. This requires a pricing policy designed to protect market share whilst maximizing the cash contribution of the product.

Sales-orientated pricing objectives focus on maximizing sales, market share and volume. A typical sales-orientated pricing objective would be: 'to set prices to achieve a 20 percent market share within two years'.

Sales-orientated Pricing Objectives (Source: Kotler, 2000)

Marketing insight

- *Maximizing sales revenues.* Firms with well-defined, highly differentiated market positions may be able to maximize sales revenue by managing prices upwards. For this to be possible, the business must have strong demand. Firms that are not market leaders and suffer from inconsistent demand flex prices with a view to increasing sales revenues.
- *Market share.* Larger corporations measure their performance not simply in terms of capacity filled, but also in terms of market share. Hotels and resorts, and newly opened restaurants/bars, urgently need to develop sales. Unless the location and offer is unique, this is normally achieved by attracting competitors' customers. Pricing objectives to build market share quickly, a strategy known as penetration pricing, include a special offer encouraging potential customers to trial purchase.
- *Volume.* Key intermediaries, such as major tour companies, booking agents and high-volume customers, are able to negotiate large discounts from larger hotel companies for a guaranteed sales volume. This negotiation can be one of the most crucial pricing decisions affecting the hotel's profitability for that period.

Cost-orientated pricing objectives involve setting a target cost/profit margin, and calculating the cost and selling price of each item in order to provide the required margin. This pricing method is typically used in catering operations, where the management will agree the food/bar operating margins. Although cost-orientated objectives are widely used in hospitality operations, they fail to take in to account external competitor and customer factors. A typical cost-orientated pricing objective would be: 'to set restaurant prices to achieve a food operating cost of 30 percent during the financial period from April to September'.

Competitor-orientated pricing objectives   It is easy for hospitality companies to find out competitors' published and quoted prices; and many do. Competitors' prices establish a benchmark and range for players in the same and in neighboring product classes. When competitors' prices change, market followers will simply move their prices up or down in line with them to maintain the same price differential as before. The problem with this 'me-too', follow-the-leader strategy is that the cost base of competitors might be very different, and the policy does not take in to account what customers might be prepared to pay.

Activity 7.2

Compare the menu prices of two fast-food restaurants and two fine-dining restaurants.

● Identify the similarities and differences in pricing between the two fast-food menus.

● Identify the similarities and differences in pricing between the two fine-dining menus.

● Can you find examples of product/price bundling, price-led promotions and prestige pricing?

Costs

A major input into the pricing decision is the cost of producing and marketing the product. Marketers need to understand the nature of the costs in hospitality products (Harris and James, 1999). *Fixed costs* do not vary with sales volume – examples include rent, property taxes, salaries of permanent staff, insurance, and depreciation. In some companies, bank interest and loan repayments are considered to be fixed costs. The key feature of fixed costs, given the seasonality of hospitality products, is that they do not vary and must be paid on a regular monthly or quarterly basis.

Variable costs vary in proportion to sales – examples include food and beverage purchases, and laundry usage. *Semi-fixed costs* vary in sympathy with, but not in proportion to, sales volume – examples include energy costs (light, heat, air-conditioning and cooking) and part-time wages.

In hospitality businesses, a high proportion of costs are fixed or semi-fixed. This is partly due to the high level of capital invested in buildings, equipment and refurbishment. Although the total capital investment is usually smaller in catering establishments, the predominance of fixed assets is similar.

There are several difficulties associated with the incorporation of cost considerations into pricing decisions. Cost-based pricing techniques are essentially retrospective – that is, prices tend to be based on costs that are known because they have already been incurred. Yet companies need to recover future costs, which may be quite different. Most companies do not try to apportion indirect costs, but assess departmental performance on a gross profit or contribution basis.

Whatever prices are set, they must recover the long-term total costs of being in business. In the short term, however, companies can use marginal costs to set prices. The *marginal cost* is the cost to the company of making the last sale – for example, letting the last room. If a room is unoccupied there is no margin earned; if the room is occupied at any rate above the marginal cost, there is a contribution to fixed costs.

Company resources

The size and financial assets of a company influence the pricing decision. International hospitality companies operating with strong brands in many countries have easy access to a variety of capital markets, and develop a strong resource base. They enjoy economies of scale and better purchasing, which reduces operating costs and improves profitability. Larger companies have more business experience, and can afford to experiment with different pricing policies in selected outlets. They can also tolerate short-term losses during the launch of a new product concept and, if the product concept fails, they can afford to write the investment off and learn from the experience.

Single-unit, privately owned operations do not have significant financial resources, and a single pricing error can seriously (perhaps even fatally) damage a smaller business.

Positioning

Prices must accurately reflect the property's desired position, be consistent across the range of products offered, and match the target market's expectation of quality and value. The relationship between the price and the product quality is symbiotic, in that the price charged has to cover costs, generate company profits and reflect the positioning strategy. In planning new hospitality concepts, the price the target markets are prepared to pay is a key determinant in the sales volume/cost/profit relationship, and helps to shape the product format.

Distribution channel

When setting prices, hospitality operators must understand their channels of distribution and factor in the costs of intermediaries. The minimum commission paid to travel agents is 8 percent and the norm is 10 percent, but on certain products (for example, weekend leisure breaks) the commission can rise up to 30 percent. The transaction charges of computerized reservation systems and credit card payments incur additional costs, which the business has to cover. Credit card commission can vary from less than 1 percent for major international companies to over 5 percent for smaller operators.

Customers

Customers' response to pricing, and changes in prices, is complex. Customers not only judge the total bill in determining whether they have enjoyed value for money, but may also focus upon its component parts. High individual drink prices can generate dissatisfaction, even when the overall bill is regarded favorably. As part of an effective positioning strategy, we should emphasize the dangers inherent in mixing incompatible market segments. In attempting to maximize sales, hospitality marketers' use of discounted prices can attract and encourage the 'wrong' type of customers.

Product

Characteristics of the hospitality product that influence pricing policy include the product class, the stage in the product life cycle, the production process, and the level of people-skills involved in producing the product. Different classes of hospitality products are sold within different price brackets, which determine the boundaries for setting prices.

Pricing strategies

Having established the price objectives, hospitality companies need to consider pricing strategies, which must be linked to the quality standards offered by the operation. In hotels, consumers often associate star ratings with quality standards. Alternative pricing strategies include the market leader and market follower options but there are also unsustainable pricing strategies, which are ultimately self-defeating.

Market leader strategies

Well-established hotel companies, with a loyal customer base and a strong brand image, can adopt *market leader strategies* where the prices are aligned with service quality. These strategies are suitable for:

- The most exclusive, luxurious, 5-star hotels in the world; they deliver the highest quality customer experience, and can justify charging premium and prestige prices
- Traditional 3 star, well maintained hotels, in good locations and with a high level of loyal customers and repeat business, offering appropriate value for money and competing effectively with a mid-market pricing strategy
- Budget hotels and motels charging relatively low prices for a product offering fewer facilities and delivering value for money.

Market follower strategies

New entrants and less established hotel brands, seeking to build market share by penetration pricing, adopt a *market follower strategy*. A market follower strategy offers similar quality but pitches prices lower than the market leader in order to be more competitive, attract customers and grow market share. These strategies are suitable for:

- High quality 4/5 star properties, seeking to grow market share by exceptional value pricing
- Mid-market hotels competing against more established properties; or aggressive chains, and individual properties, seeking to increase room occupancy and build market share by offering exceptional value pricing.

Unsustainable strategies

Unfortunately, some hotels implement *over-priced* strategies, which are unsustainable as a long-term proposition. These companies charge rates higher than the quality can justify. Some of these hotels might have myopic management who unknowingly have become over-priced. As customers recognize the poor value for money, the reputation of the business will rightly suffer. Either the company will have to adopt a more appropriate balanced strategy, or be forced in to either selling or liquidating the business.

● Old-established, grand 3/4 star hotels, which are no longer as luxurious as they used to be, and whose facilities no longer match the price charged; these properties are trading on an historic image as they gradually decline; they will eventually either have to re-invest in their facilities or reduce their prices
● Once glorious, now shabby hotels, possibly in good locations, which only generate passing trade and charging high prices; this rip-off value will lead to a poor reputation, and limited – if any – repeat and recommended business
● Mid-market hotels with falling standards but still maintaining a medium pricing strategy, which does not represent value for money
● Budget operations, which have gradually increased prices to pay for 'amenity creep' items, and are no longer competitively priced.

Finally, some hotels can adopt an unsustainable price/quality strategy, where the price offered is too low to support the product/quality offer indefinitely.

● High-quality 4/5 star properties charging unsustainable prices either because of low season or due to a decline in the destination's popularity
● Mid-market hotels operating in highly competitive environments and offering budget hotel prices without reducing quality standards.

Companies need to adopt a pricing strategy, which takes into account their relative quality compared to the competition. Table 7.1 provides several examples of hospitality products combined with price objectives, strategies and tactics.

Pricing methods

The next aspect of pricing is to review how prices are calculated in the hospitality industry. Pricing methods can be classified under similar headings to pricing objectives: cost-led, profit-led, competition-led and marketing-led. Here is a summary of the main features of each pricing method, which is then followed by a more detailed discussion.

● *Market-led* – the highest price that customers are willing to pay; considers the competition, demand and profitability, and sets the ceiling for prices
● *Competitor-led* – prices simply follow competitors; fails to take in to account customers' willingness to pay, return on investment goals, and company costs
● *Profit-led* – return on investment target provides internal goals to motivate managers; fails to take in to account customers and competitors
● *Cost-led* – cost-based is the lowest pricing level that a company can charge to remain viable; fails to take in to account customers' willingness to pay and return on investment goals; sets the floor for prices.

Table 7.1 Examples of Hospitality Price Objectives, Strategies and Tactics

Price objective category	Hospitality product	Price objective	Price strategy	Price method and pricing tactics
Customer – prestige	Five-star international luxury hotel	To charge the premium price for the highest product quality in order to maintain a prestige price positioning offer for the next five years	Monitor customers' perceptions of value for money Monitor local and international competitors' product/service/price offer Introduce innovations and improvements to maintain the product quality, whilst always charging premium prices	Carry out regular customer and consumer marketing research via focus groups to establish price image and value for money Scan international hospitality trade magazines to find out about competitor innovations Visit new-build and recently refurbished competitors; evaluate innovations and develop detailed plans to improve product/service constantly Check competitors' prices regularly
Customer – trial purchase	Health and leisure club	To set a special offer price that will encourage 100 trial purchases of club membership in March	Research existing and potential club members' attitudes to price-sensitivity towards health and leisure clubs to identify price points	Identify most cost-effective method of reaching consumers Draft questionnaire and run pilot study; adapt questionnaire and carry out main study Analyze results and set special price offer; test price offer and promotional material with focus groups Fix price of special offer and launch promotion Monitor results of promotion
Financial – volume	International 500-bedroom four-star gateway hotel	To win a 60-rooms-per-night contract for six months from April to September, from a major airline company, at a rate of $125 per room per night	Research current and potential demand for aircrew room-nights Research existing and potential hotel supply to major airlines	Identify major airline operators and their number of flights requiring overnight stopovers for crew, number of crew per flight, length of stopover Visit competitor hotels to establish which competitors are catering for which airlines

Financial – sales target	60-bedroom provincial mid-market city hotel	To increase room sales revenue by 5 percent above inflation, for the twelve-month period from October to September	Scan environment for potential increases in inflation, consumer demand and hotel room supply during the next eighteen months Review historic and current trading performance Set price increases	Carry out detailed research into local and national economy to evaluate forecast industry and general inflation Identify potential market demand during period, including seasonal variations Research competitor prices and any additional accommodation supply Identify volume (number of bednights) and value (achieved room rate) of each market segment Set room rates to guarantee 5 percent increase across total room revenue
			Evaluate contract aircrew room rates Develop a good rapport with airline	Establish competitor rates and estimate discount offered to airline companies Prepare discount rate and confirm with general manager Contact airline purchasing departments and request opportunity to quote for business Negotiate competitive market-orientated rates
Financial – cost-led	Nightclub bar and restaurant	To achieve a bar cost of 35 percent for the next financial year To achieve a food cost of 30 percent for the next financial year	Utilize a computerized stock-control system to set and monitor bar and food costs and prices to ensure that the target is achieved	Carry out a monthly bar and food computerized stock check on all items' purchase and selling prices Monitor the sales mix and ensure that high-volume food and drinks are achieving their required target profit margin
Competitor – price followership	Three-star resort hotel	To undercut the mid-market price leader by 10 percent on all bedroom rack rates during the high season	Monitor competitor price movements and adjust room prices accordingly	Telephone competitor hotels on a monthly basis to check on current room rates Adapt own hotel's prices accordingly

Cost-led pricing methods

Break-even analysis

The purpose of break-even analysis is to enable management to calculate various cost, volume and profit scenarios to make appropriate pricing decisions. To work out the break-even point (the price at which sales revenues equal total costs and no profit or loss is made) the following information is required: fixed costs (FC) and variable costs (VC). Total costs (TC) are the sum of fixed costs plus total variable costs (variable costs per unit multiplied by the number of units produced). Therefore:

$$TC = FC + VC$$

Break-even analysis is useful in working out profit/loss projections for specific events, weddings, outside catering functions, and corporate hospitality at sporting occasions, when demand is established and fixed and variable costs can be easily calculated.

Cost-plus

Cost-plus pricing sets the selling price of a product based on the cost of production, plus a share of the company's overheads, plus a set percentage profit margin. Most food and beverage outlets utilize a form of cost-based pricing, which is called cost percentage pricing, factor pricing, or mark-up pricing.

The following equation explains cost-based pricing:

$$P = C + f(C)$$

where P = price, C = cost, f = percentage mark up.

For example, the cost of a bottle of wine is £2.00. If the company has a mark-up policy of 300 percent of the cost price, to provide a 25 percent cost margin and a 75 percent profit margin, then the selling price of £8.00 is calculated thus:

$$P = 2.00 + 300\%(2.00) = £8.00$$

Table 7.2 provides a range of possible selling prices for the bottle of wine, depending upon the company's target cost/profit margin. The advantages of using cost-plus pricing are as follows:

● The selling price is based on factual costings
● Management judgment is not required; the calculations are easily computed
● It is the most simple pricing method to implement
● Similar costs for outlets within the same product category should follow similar pricing policies, thus avoiding competition based on price alone

Table 7.2 Cost-plus Pricing

Cost (C) (Purchase price) (£)	Mark-up (f(C)) (%)	Selling price (P) (£)	Cost (% margin)	Profit (% margin)
2.00	50	3.00	66.6	33.4
2.00	100	4.00	50	50
2.00	150	5.00	40	60
2.00	200	6.00	33.4	66.6

- It helps management to forecast costs, and can be used as a control mechanism to monitor performance.

The disadvantages include the following:

- It ignores the price elasticity of demand
- It ignores consumer perceptions of quality and may produce prices that are inconsistent with market positioning and desired company image
- It fails to consider competitors' prices
- When purchase prices increase, selling prices may be increased without taking into account alternative options (changing the supplier or changing the recipe and ingredients), thereby alienating loyal customers.

Fixed mark-up

An unusual pricing feature of some restaurant wine lists is a standard (or fixed) mark-up, regardless of the cost of the wine. For example, a restaurant charges $10 for a house wine that costs $3. Instead of aiming for a 30 percent bar cost, the management aims for a $7 profit per bottle of wine sold. Therefore, a wine costing $10 will be sold for $17 (giving a wine cost of 58 percent), and a wine costing $20 will be sold for $27 (giving a wine cost of 74 percent). The argument in favor of this pricing policy is to encourage repeat and recommended customers by providing exceptional value on more expensive wines. The problem with this pricing method is that it ignores the financial and storage costs of acquiring and keeping high quality wines.

Profit-led pricing method

Rate of return

Historically, American and European hoteliers used to adopt a $- or £-per-thousand pricing method to ensure that the target return on investment was achieved. The target average achieved room rate was calculated on the basis of the total capital invested in the building project – if a 100-bedroom hotel cost $10 million to build, then the total cost per room would be $100,000 and the average achieved room rate required might be $100. Today investors' calculations on the ROI are much more complex, but rate of return (ROR) pricing techniques are still important in helping to determine the feasibility of a project. The goal of ROR pricing is to find a price structure that provides the required return on investment. To apply the ROR method:

- Estimate the capital required for the project
- Set a target rate of return
- Calculate the volume of sales required to generate the profit target.

For example, a company invests $20 million in a resort development. Given a target ROR of 20 percent, the profit required from the venture is $4 million each year. The question now becomes: what volume of sales is needed to produce a net profit of $4 million? If the company operates in a market where a net profit on sales of 10 percent is the norm, then it is evident that sales revenues of $40 million are required ($4,000,000 × 0.10). Now, the task for marketing managers is to select a sales mix (total sales from room yield, meetings, food and beverage, leisure) and pricing policies that can generate the $40 million sales revenue and $4 million profit.

Management produces spreadsheet estimates, based on different sales mixes and sales volumes, taking into account the patterns of fixed and variable costs for each sales mix, and the pricing sensitivity of selected target markets. If a particular sales mix does not achieve the required ROR, there are several options available: adjust the sales mix to emphasize high margin products; seek savings in variable costs; seek savings in fixed costs; adjust the price mix across the product range; or even reduce the target ROR.

Competition-led pricing method

Price followership is the pricing strategy based on competition-orientated objectives so prices do not change until the competitor makes the first move. The manager then responds to maintain the price differential, which may be set in currency or percentage terms. The bed-and-breakfast houses located adjacent to each other on the Victorian terraced streets of English seaside towns like Blackpool watch each other's prices closely. If one reduces its price, the others will quickly reduce their prices to ensure they do not lose customers. The bed-and-breakfast house owners will also be reluctant to increase the prices, but if a market leader is able to raise its prices, the other owners will increase their prices too.

Marketing-led pricing methods

Yield management

Hospitality companies have learnt from the computerized reservation systems developed by the airline industry, and seek to maximize their potential revenue by using price as a demand management tool. Known as yield management, this is a complex form of price discrimination used in larger properties to help maximize REVPAR (revenue per available room). Because of the focus on sales, yield management is also known as revenue management. Room yield is the ratio, given as a percentage, between the actual room sales revenues and the total potential room sales revenues during a given period.

The formula to calculate yield is:

$$\frac{\text{Revenue raised}}{\text{Revenue potential}} \times 100$$

To calculate a property's yield ratio, the following information is required:

- Period of time (day, number of days, week, month, quarter, year)
- Number of rooms, room types and room rates
- Potential room revenue
- Rooms sold
- Achieved room rate.

The revenue realized is the number of rooms sold, multiplied by the achieved room rate. The potential room revenue is:

All room types × number of rooms in each room type × each room type's rack rate

Table 7.3 Simple Yield Management Calculation

Period	One day
Rooms sold	200 rooms × 95% occupancy = 190 rooms sold
Revenue realized	Rooms sold × achieved room rate
	= 190 × £90 = £17,100

Room type	Number of rooms	Rate (£)	Potential room rate (£)
Executive suites	20	200	4,000
Executive doubles	40	150	6,000
Standard doubles	40	120	4,800
Standard singles	100	100	10,000
Total potential revenue			24,800

Yield	(Revenue realized/revenue potential) × 100
	= (17,100/24,800) × 100
	= 68.95%

The example in Table 7.3, using a 200-bedroom hotel operating at 95 percent occupancy with an achieved room rate of £90, for one day, will help to illustrate the method.

If the hotel illustrated in Table 7.3 decided to improve its yield by sacrificing 5 percent of its occupancy in order to increase the achieved room rate to £110, the yield calculations would be:

Period	One day
Rooms sold	200 rooms × 90% occupancy = 180 rooms sold
Revenue realized	Rooms sold × achieved room rate
	= 180 ×£110 = £19,800
Yield	(Revenue realized/revenue potential) × 100
	= (19,800/24,800) × 100
	= 79.84%

Yield management systems are normally found in hotels with at least 75 bedrooms and which have computerized reservation systems (CRS) and/or computerized property management systems (PMS). Sophisticated software programs have been developed to calculate the complex data, which compute the recommended prices quoted to customers. A minimum of three years' historic information needs to be inputted into the program to obtain an accurate projection. Table 7.4 demonstrates an example of the booking pattern in a hotel during the five months prior to 10 March. The historic room occupancy range, current state of reservations at the beginning of each month, and the yield management system's recommended rates are recorded. Table 7.5 provides details of the booking lead times and price-sensitivity of key hotel market segments.

Advantages of yield management Yield management is a marketing tool designed to tackle the problems caused by the special characteristics of service industries. Hoteliers have always recognized that it is better to sell a room at a low

Table 7.4 Example of a Yield Management System

Time prior to booking date	Historic room occupancy range (%)	Current reservations (%)	Recommended rate (£)
1 November	20–30	22	90
1 December	35	29	85
1 January	55	60	95
1 February	75	72	98
1 March	85	86	110
9 March	94	98	115
10 March	96	97	110

Table 7.5 Price Characteristics of Hotel Market Segments

Market segment	Booking lead time	Price sensitivity
International conference	5+ years	Low
National conference	2–3 years	Low
Major company conference	6 months–1 year	Low/medium
Leisure tour group	3–18 months	High
Individual leisure (FIT)	1 week–12 months	High
Small business meeting	1–12 weeks	Low/medium
Domestic business traveler	1–7 days	Low
International business traveler	1 day–12 weeks	Low

price tonight rather than have an empty room, because of the low marginal cost to service another room. Each room sold above marginal cost, even at lower prices, helps to contribute towards the fixed costs of operating a hotel property. A yield management system prevents reservation clerks from making critical decisions for themselves, since the computer will not accept a reservation with an incorrectly quoted price. Although there is an over-ride facility to allow some discretion by the reservations supervisor, any excessive use of the over-ride facility has to be justified to the management. In some chain-owned hotels, the management of properties that use the over-ride facility more than three times per month will be asked to explain why.

Disadvantages of yield management Like all data retrieval systems, the effectiveness of yield management is dependent upon the accuracy and completeness of the information originally entered into the computer. The number of customer, property, competitor and other environmental variables that need to be recorded and then processed is very large. Mistakes in the manual data entry process can easily be made, given the amount of historic data that has to be entered to make the system work.

Another difficulty concerns the nature of a typical hotel and its room stock. Many hotels have a wide range of room types, in different parts of the premises and often with their own idiosyncrasies. Some rooms are quieter while others are noisier;

some have been recently redecorated and others have tired décor; some have a sea-view and others overlook the air-conditioning units. This can present difficulties when reviewing the room inventory for yield management purposes.

However, the most critical aspect of yield management is the customers' aware-ness and perception of the variation in prices quoted to them. Whilst airlines have trained their customers to accept price fluctuations, hospitality customers may be more resistant. If prices to transient business travelers vary too much from a perceived rack rate, then vital customer loyalty may be eroded.

Price-sensitivity measurement

Lewis and Chambers (2000) suggest a pricing method that measures consumers' price sensitivity before a company sets its prices. This model uses consumer market research techniques to establish the range of prices acceptable to customers within a product category. Consumers are asked questions that will test the lower and upper acceptable price points, and the prices at which the service would not be pur-chased because it is considered either too cheap or too expensive.

Since price-sensitivity measurement (PSM) is based upon consumer perceptions of value, the model embraces the marketing concept; however, it could be argued that consumer perceptions are also shaped by competitors' product/price offers and that the range of prices solicited by PSM research could be determined by analyzing competitors' price brackets. Given the cost of consumer market research, hospitality companies are reluctant to commission PSM.

Price promotions

The impact of price promotions needs to be carefully evaluated in the planning stage to protect core revenue business and brand image. City hotels offering low season price promotions to leisure travelers ring-fence the promotion to prevent business travelers from taking advantage of it, by insisting on pre-booking conditions. Price-led promotions must also make a realistic contribution towards the overheads and justify the cost and effort that goes in to their development and promotion.

One tactic is to use loss leaders to attract customers. Bars typically have a special drinks offer – perhaps half-price on quiet evenings, or 'doubles' at a single price during a happy hour promotion. Joint marketing initiatives between hotel chains and newspapers make use of other promotions – one example is 'free accommoda-tion' at selected hotels, which is offered exclusively to the readers of a newspaper providing the customer pays a minimum price for meals whilst staying in the hotel. 'Two for the price of one' or BOGOF (buy one, get one free) promotions are popular and effective in promoting hotel and restaurant products.

These price-led promotions help to boost sales in quiet periods, but they do have limitations and drawbacks. Theoretically the promotion should attract new cus-tomers who, having enjoyed the hospitality experience, are expected to return at other times and pay the normal prices. In practice, many (even most) of the cus-tomers who enjoy a promotional price do not book at the 'normal' price once the promotion has finished. There is also the danger of cannibalizing customers. This means that loyal customers may take advantage of the price promotion, changing their booking and purchasing habits, and consequently the hotel or restaurant loses prime rate business and suffers a reduction in sales and profits.

Product price bundles

All sectors of the industry bundle a package of benefits at an all-inclusive price. Examples include foreign package holidays, activity leisure breaks, 24-hour conference delegate packages, wedding receptions, and fast-food and drink combinations. The advantages of product price benefit bundles for the consumer include the perception of added value (indeed, really effective packages *do* provide customers with added value), and the ease of booking all the features of the bundle at one price in one transaction.

Price cuts

There is considerable research into the effects on company and industry profitability of price cuts and price wars. Although individual companies who initiate price cuts may gain market share, eventually competitors are forced to respond. If a price war ensues, customers begin to expect a lower price point, reacting unfavorably when companies attempt to increase prices later.

The evidence suggests that all companies in an industry involved in a price war lose profitability. Price cuts in hospitality are a natural reaction to excess capacity, but the consequences can be damaging if maintained for a long period. The dangers of price-cutting can be explained by Figure 7.2. This chart illustrates the additional occupancy a hotel needs to generate for a price reduction to maintain the same room revenue. If a hotel has a current occupancy of 60 percent and initiates a price cut of 10 percent, then an increase in occupancy of 7 percent will be required to keep accommodation revenue at the previous level. In the real world, to achieve a 7 percent increase in room occupancy is not a simple task. This increase in occupancy will also incur additional laundry, housekeeping, maintenance, energy and front desk costs,

Current occupancy	Occupancy required to maintain sales revenue, following rate cuts of:				
	5%	10%	15%	20%	25%
50	53	56	59	63	67
52	55	58	62	65	69
54	57	60	64	68	72
56	59	62	66	70	75
58	61	64	68	73	77
60	63	67	71	75	80
62	65	69	73	78	83
64	67	71	75	80	85
66	69	73	78	83	88
68	72	76	80	85	91
70	74	78	82	88	93
72	76	80	85	90	96
74	78	82	87	93	99
76	80	84	89	95	101
80	84	89	94	100	107
88	93	98	104	110	117
90	95	100	106	113	120

Figure 7.2 The cost of cutting prices (source: Buttle, F., 1986, *Hotel and Food Service Marketing*, Cassell, p. 266, reproduced by kind permission)

as well as possible marketing communication costs involved in the promotion of the new pricing policy. A similar situation occurs in restaurant operations. If a company is able to introduce an innovative process that significantly reduces its cost base – for example, eliminating an intermediary in the channel – and then passes some of that saving to the consumer, then its 'price cut' is a new pricing policy, which is sustainable.

International pricing

The difficulties in setting a pricing policy for companies operating in more than one country are compounded by:

- The different currency and cost structures between countries
- The different types of competitors – global, regional, national branded chains, and local independents
- The different stages of the market/product life cycle in each country
- Different inflation rates and fluctuations in the currencies
- The ability to repatriate profits, which again varies significantly from country to country.

For companies aiming to promote and protect their hospitality brands by standardizing the product offer, a uniform price position presents particular problems. The response in countries like Egypt and India is to charge a lower price for domestic customers and a higher price for international customers. The Paradise Sun Hotel (see Case study 7.1) illustrates the difficulties which hospitality businesses, dependent upon international markets, have to address when setting pricing policies.

Case study

7.1 Pricing at the Paradise Sun Hotel, Seychelles

The Paradise Sun Hotel, Praslin, Seychelles, is an 80-bedroom four-star resort hotel owned by Southern Sun Hotels. The hotel is dependent upon international leisure business from a mix of European countries, Southern Africa and the Middle East. The hotel segments its markets on a geographic country-by-country basis. Seven- and fourteen-day holiday packages are organized by tour operators in each target country for the hotel, and are generally booked through travel agents. The Paradise Sun management negotiates different prices with each of the different country tour operators, based on the historic prices from last season and the projected volume of guests that the operator is planning to book in to the Paradise Sun. Prices are agreed in the local Seychellois currency. The contract is negotiated up to eighteen months in advance of the booking, due to brochure publication deadlines.

Exchange rate fluctuations in the period between agreeing the contract and potential customers booking their holiday affect the relative price of the Seychelles compared to alternative island sun destinations. The volume of bookings from different countries changes according to the relative low/high exchange rate, which is governed by the prevailing economic conditions in each country.

Conclusion

In the final analysis, customers decide whether the company is charging the right price. However, given the hospitality industry's reluctance to carry out marketing research, and the dominance of financial concerns in budget planning, most pricing decisions will continue to be governed by cost and other financial objectives. Companies only find out if they are charging the wrong prices when customers desert their offer. Although pricing decisions are the easiest element of the marketing mix to change, they remain the most complex of decisions to pitch accurately.

In this chapter, we have explained:

- That pricing is the tool that matches supply and demand
- That price is the only element of marketing mix that is not a cost, because price generates revenue
- That price, in the absence of other cues, is an indicator of quality and sets customer expectations
- That price is the summation of all sacrifices made by a consumer in order to experience the benefits of the product
- Why companies have little control over the *external* factors that influence pricing decisions, but considerable control over the *internal* factors that influence pricing decisions
- Why the majority of for-profit hospitality organizations focus on financial objectives, rather than marketing objectives, when making pricing decisions
- Why pricing decisions should reflect quality strategies
- That larger hotels utilize computerized yield management systems to maximize occupancy and achieved room rate to improve profitability
- Price promotions, linked to product benefit bundles, which are extensively used to grow revenue in low season periods
- International pricing decisions, which are subject to local country environmental factors.

Review questions

Now check your understanding of this chapter by answering the following questions:

1 Why is pricing significant in the pre-encounter hospitality marketing mix?
2 Discuss the external and internal factors that influence pricing decisions. Provide examples from the hospitality industry to illustrate your answer.
3 Evaluate pricing and product quality strategies in three hotel markets.
4 Discuss the advantages and disadvantages of the following pricing methods:
   - cost-led
   - profit-led
   - competitor-led
   - market-led.
5 Evaluate the role of price promotions in the hospitality industry.
6 Discuss the pricing issues for a standardized international hotel brand.

References and further reading

Doyle, P. (2002). *Marketing Management and Strategy*. Prentice Hall.

Harris, P. J. and James, P. (1999). *Profit Planning*. Butterworth-Heinemann.

Kotler, P. (2000). *Marketing Management*. Prentice Hall.

Lewis, R. C. and Chambers, R. E. (2000). *Marketing Leadership in Hospitality: Foundations and Practice*. J. Wiley, pp. 419–422.

Lovelock, C. H. (2002). *Principles of Service Marketing and Management*. Prentice Hall.

McDonald, M. (1999). *Marketing Plans*. Butterworth-Heinemann.

Chapter 8
Distributing the offer

Chapter Objectives

After working through this chapter, you should be able to:

- Understand the role of distribution in hospitality markets
- Explain the function of travel and tourism intermediaries from a hospitality perspective
- Understand how computer reservation systems (CRS), global distribution systems (GDS) and Internet technology impact on the hospitality distribution network
- Evaluate channel relationships between principals and intermediaries.

Introduction

In this chapter we will explain the channel options available to hospitality operators, define the role of intermediaries, and review how technology is changing hospitality and tourism distribution systems.

The concept of a distribution channel is relatively simple, but in practice can be extremely complicated, especially for large organizations. The role of distribution is to help customers find information about products and to make purchasing easy. Intermediaries, for example travel agents and tour operators, help customers to choose hospitality and travel products. They are normally paid by charging a commission to the hotel that receives the booking. Since hospitality products are perishable, it is crucial to generate advance bookings. Major hotel companies with thousands of bedrooms to fill in hundreds of locations need to use a wide range of distribution channels to reach all their potential customers. The relationship between channel players is complex, especially if a hospitality organization becomes dependent upon high volume sales generated by intermediaries.

You will obviously be aware of the information communications technology (ICT) revolution, with the growth of the Internet and the development of powerful computerized systems. This revolution is changing the mechanics and tools of the distribution channel. However, the principles of distribution remain the same, regardless of the technology.

Channels of distribution

When we discuss the theory of distribution, we describe airlines, hospitality organizations, car hire firms and leisure attractions as principals. These principals can be distributed via a number of different channels (see Figure 8.1), some of which are described below. Principals provide the core product, which customers consume. Without principals there is no product. However, principals, especially in leisure travel markets, need intermediaries to package a combination of travel products and sell the total package to consumers.

Channel 1: Direct-to-customer

In the first channel, hospitality organizations and customers communicate directly with no intermediaries. This is called direct marketing. Principals use a combination of direct distribution methods, primarily online reservations, and marketing communications activity to reach potential customers. Direct marketing is particularly effective when targeting repeat customers. Since there are no intermediaries taking a commission, this channel can be the most cost-effective for principals.

Channel 2: Referral network

Branded hotel and restaurant chains, whether corporate-owned, franchised or members of voluntary associations, use each individual retail outlet to market the other properties in the chain. No intermediaries are involved and, providing customers are satisfied with the hospitality offer, the 'referral network' is another

Channel	Distribution system				Number of intermediaries
1. Direct marketing	Hospitality unit	→		Customer	0
2. Referral network	Individual hospitality unit	→	Branded outlets and C.R.S →	Customer	0
3. Retail networks	Individual hospitality units	→	Travel agent →	Customer	1
4. Wholesale network	Individual hospitality unit	→	Tour operator →	Customer	1
5. Wholesale network with travel agent as retailer	Individual hospitality unit	→ Tour operator →	Travel agent →	Customer	2

Figure 8.1 Sample of hospitality and tourism distribution channels

cost-effective distribution channel. Hospitality chains provide brochure racks, often close to reception, and place hotel directories, which describe other hotels in the group, in the bedrooms. Customers can book directly for themselves, or at reception desks, via the hotel chain's computerized reservation system (CRS).

Channel 3: Travel agent as intermediary

In tourism distribution, travel agents perform the role of a retailer stocking a range of hospitality and travel products. Information about principals' products and prices is stored in databases and manual directories, and is provided via brochures. The travel agent advises customers on all aspects of travel. Agents make bookings, collect payments, provide tickets and accommodation vouchers, and over time develop a close relationship with regular customers. The travel agent works on the customers' behalf, and will take up customer complaints with the principals. In leisure and most business markets, the travel agent does not charge the customer for this service; instead, the principal pays the travel agent commission.

Channel 4: Tour operator as intermediary

Tour operators are wholesalers in the travel and tourism industry. A tour operator negotiates bulk allocations of seats from charter airlines and bulk accommodation from hotels, and then develops a packaged product, which is marketed to consumers directly. The tour operator does not charge principals a commission; instead it agrees discounted prices with the different principals involved, and makes a profit by charging the customer an inclusive price for the package holiday.

Channel 5: Tour operator and travel agent as intermediaries

This channel is similar to channel 4, with one major exception: tour operators often use travel agents to promote their all-inclusive travel products. In this situation, the tour operator has to pay the travel agent a commission for any bookings. If there are more intermediaries in a channel there can be a problem for the principals, because each intermediary needs to make a profit for the service provided. This means that there are greater pressures on the principal to keep prices low.

Benefits and disadvantages of distribution channels

From a hospitality perspective, the benefits of distribution channels include:

- More effective demand management for perishable products
- Convenient global/local access points for customers away from the hospitality location
- The provision of relevant information and guidance to potential customers by knowledgeable travel experts
- The bundling of hospitality products into combined travel packages
- An advance reservation and payments system
- The opportunity to work with specialist intermediaries who understand the dynamics of their own markets.

The disadvantages for hospitality organizations using intermediaries include:

- The loss of margin paid to agents through commission
- The loss of margin caused by charging tour operators low accommodation rates for volume business
- The loss of control of a key element in the marketing mix (the distribution channel), which can lead to an unhealthy dependence upon intermediaries (for example, large travel agency chains will not allow principals to promote their own products at point-of-sale)
- Intermediaries can be closer to the end user, taking 'ownership of the customer' away from the hospitality organization.

Activity 8.1

Think about booking a package holiday in a hotel in a foreign country.

- List all the organizations, intermediaries, principals and any others who might be involved in making, paying and delivering the packaged travel product.
- Note what each organization provides in the delivery of the holiday.

Intermediaries

The structure of the travel and tourism industry is continually evolving. In Europe, change drivers include the deregulation of air travel and the growth of Internet technologies, which can deliver economies of scale and cost savings to the larger tourism organizations. Whilst the vast majority of intermediaries are small, independent bodies, major international companies have emerged, which dominate the package holiday market.

Intermediaries can be categorized under the following broad headings:

- Travel agent
- Tour operator
- Conference and meeting planner
- Corporate business travel agent
- Incentive travel house
- Representative agent
- Internet web portal and virtual travel agent.

Small-scale intermediaries normally focus on a specific leisure or business sector, whilst the large-scale organizations provide both leisure and business services. Table 8.1 provides current examples of intermediaries operating in specific sectors. We will discuss each category in more detail from a hospitality perspective.

Travel agents

Bricks-and-mortar travel agents are involved in booking individual and group travel for both business and leisure markets. Travel agents primarily rely on computer systems to make bookings, either directly to the hotel chain or through tour operators. Agents are dependent upon hotels paying commission, and obviously

Table 8.1 Examples of Intermediaries

Intermediary	Specialist sector
Leisure travel agent	Thomas Cook, Going Places, Lunn Poly, Flight Centre, STA Travel
Corporate/business travel agent	American Express, Carlson Wagon Lits, Travelforce, Corporate Traveler
Tour operator	Club 18–30, Saga, Kiwi Experience, Kuoni, Ski World
Conference/meetings organizer	Banks Sadler, BI Worldwide, Concept Meetings and Incentive Travel
Incentive travel house	P&MM Travel, Universal Conference and Incentive Travel, World Event Management
Representative agent	Utell
Internet web portal and virtual travel agent	Travelocity, Expedia, lastminute.com, laterooms.com

prefer prompt payment. The lowest hotel commission paid is 8 percent and the norm is 10 percent, with certain hotels paying up to 30 percent commission on specific products available during the low season. Hotel groups use the following tactics to target travel agents:

- Advertising in the travel trade press – e.g. the *Travel Trade Gazette* in the UK
- Hotel newsletters and direct mail promotions
- Sales visits to head office and individual retail outlets
- Incentive promotions, with rewards for the most successful staff
- Familiarization trips to the group's hotels (although the effectiveness of 'fam' visits by travel agent staff is debatable).

The sales team of the hotel chain negotiates with the head office of the retail travel agent chain on a regular basis. They review sales figures, discuss customers' complaints and guest satisfaction surveys, and negotiate commission rates and the racking of brochures on shelves. Individual hotels rarely target travel agents, since their product offer is too narrow and localized to be of interest.

Tour operators

Tour operators devise inclusive holidays, combining the travel and accommodation elements with varying degrees of food, beverage, activities, entertainment and sightseeing. Some tour operators specialize in particular products (ski packages) or destinations (South-East Asia); others offer a wide range of tours. Tour operators generally work on volume sales, offering attractive, all-inclusive prices to generate high sales, with low margins. This formula implies a high break-even point, which makes tour operators financially vulnerable. Hotels wanting to target tour operators must be prepared to offer low rates, and accept that the additional spend in the bar and other areas can be low. To protect themselves hospitality operators need to transact business with tour operators who are covered by recognized trade indemnity policies, and make sure they are paid on a regular basis.

A driver and/or tour guide/tour leader/rep acts as a representative for the tour operator throughout the holiday, and plays a key role in supporting the relationship between tour customers and the hotel. Much tour operator business is booked into hotels for a set number of nights – five, seven, ten or fourteen nights are popular blocks – to coincide with working consumers' holiday patterns. However, the senior citizens' market can book for months during the low season in large holiday hotels. Another option is booking on a series basis. An example of a series schedule is a weekly coach tour of Scotland, departing every Saturday with approximately 40 customers, on an agreed itinerary staying at the same hotels each day of the week for a sixteen-week season. This type of group travel appeals to older people.

Marketing insight

Competitor Research in the Tour Group Market

The enterprising manager of one Welsh resort hotel, the Deganwy Castle near Conwy, decided to target coach business. The manager visited the car parks of competitor hotels, took the names and addresses of the coach companies from the coaches, personally contacted the coach companies/tour operators, and negotiated a number of successful contracts for the next year.

Conference and meeting planners

These specialist agencies provide venue search and selection services and expert advice in event management. The meeting planner does not normally charge the client a venue-finding fee; instead, the venue will pay the meeting planner a commission on the business booked. Meeting planners justify their role by:

- Providing impartial advice as to the suitability of the venue
- Negotiating the contract between the client and the venue
- Ensuring that the venue delivers what the organizer is looking for.

Meeting planners adopt a professional approach to the business, especially since their customers can be high-spend, frequent users. They will often personally inspect alternative venues, and develop considerable expertise about the conference and meetings market. All the major hotel groups regard conference and meeting agencies as a priority target market.

Corporate or business travel agents

Business travel agents focus on service quality, in addition to price, in dealings with corporate customers. They arrange air travel and car hire as well as hotel bookings. The globalization of business has increased the demand for corporate travel, but at the same time the cost of traveling and staying in hotels has become a significant cost item. An American Express survey revealed that travel-for-business is the third highest item of controllable costs for companies.

Whilst smaller business travel agents still rely on commission payments, the largest have reinvented themselves to provide their clients with cost-effective travel advice. These business travel agents are not interested in collecting commission from hotels; instead, they charge their clients a management fee for providing a travel management service – just like any other professional organization charges for a service. Business travel agents are keenly interested in negotiating competitive rates with the hotels that their clients want to use, to demonstrate that they are delivering better value to their clients.

Incentive travel houses

Companies often use travel as a reward to motivate customers, dealers, distributors, salespeople, staff and managers. This concept has developed into a major sub-sector of the tourism business, and is called 'incentive travel'. The demand for incentive travel has increased dramatically during the past twenty years, and specialist incentive houses have developed expertise in this market. To be a successful motivator and 'incentivize' the target audience, the reward mechanism should be highly desirable, often foreign, frequently unusual and especially exotic. This specialized market is not suitable for all hotels; however, exclusive hotels in idyllic locations can seriously target the incentive travel market.

Incentive houses carefully check the facilities and quality of service of hotels in appropriate destinations. Since the promoters of incentive schemes are always looking for unusual themes, quality venues can help incentive travel houses by packaging distinctive, interesting programs that are suitable for well-traveled, sophisticated consumers. Some incentive packages involve large numbers of winners all traveling in one party at the same time; others are designed for couples, and can be booked on an individual basis as and when it suits the winners.

Representative agents

Representative agents are another type of intermediary who link hotels, travel agencies and customers. These are independent companies with their own sales teams. The largest representative agency in the world is Utell, which books millions of room nights each year into the hotels they represent. Utell connects 5000 hotels, including many of the leading brands and independents, to 450,000 reservation terminals in travel agencies everywhere using the Global Distribution System (GDS). Utell also has its own sales force, which negotiates competitive rates for corporate clients and provides incentives to travel agents to book via Utell.

Virtual travel agents

Virtual travel agents are travel agents who only take bookings on the world-wide web. Unlike high street bricks-and-mortar travel agents, a virtual travel agent does not have any travel shops for customers to visit; all transactions are conducted on the Internet (see Case study 8.1). Major corporations own some of the largest virtual travel agents. Expedia is owned by Microsoft and Travelocity is owned by Sabre, one of the four Global Distribution System companies.

Case study

8.1 Lastminute.com

Lastminute.com is Europe's leading online retailer selling a wide range of travel and hospitality products. The concept is based on principals, such as hotels and restaurants, discounting inventory to fill rooms and seats at the last minute. Lastminute.com has over seven million subscribers in Europe, Australia/New Zealand, South Africa and Japan, who receive weekly newsletters about last minute offers. There is both an on-line and an automated telephone booking system.

Horizontal and vertical integration

Today's major travel organizations have evolved first by taking over or merging with competitors in the same sector (horizontal integration), and then by taking over or merging with principals and/or intermediaries in different sectors of the travel industry (vertical integration).

Figure 8.2 provides a diagram demonstrating how a major player takes over or merges with competitors in the hotel sector, using Hilton Hotels as an example of horizontal integration. Hilton's rapid expansion in the UK was based on the acquisition of competitor hotel chains like Stakis. Their international expansion included the purchase of the Scandinavian hotel chain Scandic. The acquired hotels are carefully

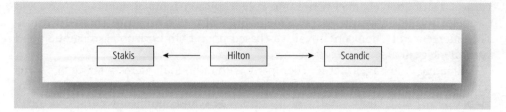

Figure 8.2 Horizontal integration

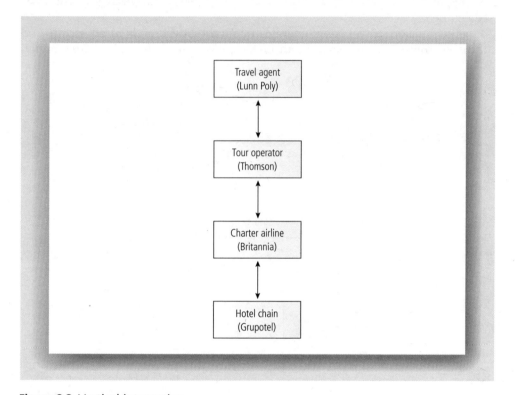

Figure 8.3 Vertical integration

evaluated to see whether their property profile fits with the requirements of the Hilton brand standards. Hotels that conform to brand standards are re-badged as Hilton Hotels; hotels that do not are sold.

Larger organizations enjoy economies of scale, which contribute to improved profit margins. Examples include:

● The ability to negotiate better terms with suppliers, through bulk purchasing
● The opportunity to leverage higher brand awareness and drive volume sales, by owning more retail outlets and spending more on marketing communications
● The opportunity to expand operations more efficiently and quickly, by gaining access to capital markets
● The development of managerial economies of experience.

Eventually, expansion-minded travel organizations will seek to acquire both customers and suppliers in their own distribution channel. Figure 8.3 illustrates a conventional vertical distribution channel with Lunn Poly, Thomson Tours, Britannia Airways and Grupotel, which all became part of a major British travel company – Thomson Travel. The emergence of Thomson Travel was based upon both horizontal integration and vertical integration.

Ultimately Preussag, a German company with industrial interests, shifted its focus to travel and acquired German, British and French tourism companies like TUI, Hapag-Lloyd and Thomson Travel to form a new and significant European travel organization. At the time of writing the company is called TUI, and it owns 3700 travel agencies, 81 tour operators, 88 aircraft flown by their airlines, 32 inbound agencies, and 285 hotels with approximately 150,000 bedrooms in over 70 countries (see Figure 8.4).

Emergent leisure travel conglomerates retain the best brands in all sectors and effectively control, by ownership, all of the players in their vertical distribution

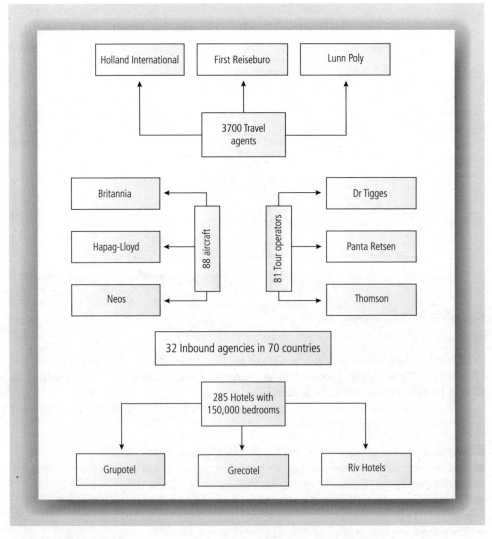

Figure 8.4 A vertically integrated marketing channel – the World of TUI (source: www.tui.com)

channel. The advantages of a VIMC for the company include:

- Coordination of all operational and marketing activity across all channel members
- Improved communication between channel members
- Reduction of channel conflict between the channel members, who are all working for the same company
- Cost savings through economies of scale
- Potentially superior customer service
- The opportunity to respond quickly to changes in the PESTE environment.

The main disadvantage for a dominant travel conglomerate is the threat from regulatory authorities (for example, the EU Commission and the UK Mergers and Monopolies Commission) over possible monopoly concerns and the lack of consumer choice. For customers, there are potential benefits in terms of a better coordinated holiday experience; however, there is a major concern about 'switch-selling' by travel agents. Since the travel conglomerates own a range of travel agents, tour operators, charter airlines and hotel operations, customers do not always realize this common ownership. Travel agents can clearly influence the choice of holiday and push their own parent company's travel products, which inhibits competition and may not be in the best interests of the customer. Whilst this is an ethical issue for travel agents, it is interesting to note from a hospitality perspective that conglomerates like TUI have become major owner-operators of hotels in the Mediterranean.

Global distribution systems and CRS

A global distribution system is a network of large-scale computer reservation systems, which link principals to intermediaries anywhere in the world. Global distribution systems (GDS) are described as 'global travel supermarkets', and provide travel agents with rapid search, booking and confirmation facilities for airline, hotel and car-hire products. In hospitality, GDS are dependent upon modern hotel computer reservation systems (CRS), which provide full details of properties, locations, room types, availability, prices and booking conditions.

Development of GDS and CRS

The origins of electronic distribution stemmed from the airlines' internal inventory systems developed in the 1950s and 1960s. The airline companies recognized that the installation of booking terminals in travel agents, with instant access, real-time availability, prices and reservations, would give their customers a better service. The system was cost-effective and efficient, and gradually more and more bookings for the airlines were sourced through travel agents. In the late 1970s airlines further developed their systems, increasing the capacity of the network. In 1976 SABRE established the first GDS, followed by Amadeus, Galileo and later Worldspan (see Figure 8.5). However, the high cost of developing and operating these systems, which had excess capacity, meant that the airlines encouraged travel agents to cross-sell complementary

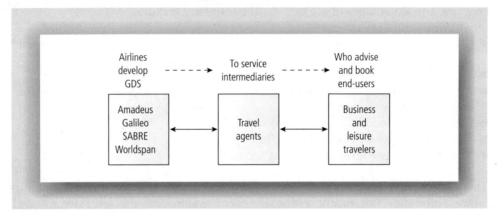

Figure 8.5 The growth of GDS

travel products, and in particular hotels and car hire. These GDS, founded by airline partnerships, are now independent corporations, with connections throughout the world; Galileo has 40,000 installations in travel agents on every continent.

Accommodation products are core complementary products to travel. Originally, hotels recognized the advantages of distributing their product and price details through the GDS because of the opportunities to increase volume sales via travel agents. However, there were technological problems caused by the inherent differences between airline and hospitality products. An airline seat is a relatively simple, homogenous product, whilst most hotels offer a heterogeneous product with a wide range of room types, a more complex rate structure and different property characteristics. The data architecture of the airline system was not compatible with the needs of the hotel chains, so hotel chains developed their own CRS systems with enhanced capabilities, which were suitable for internal company reservations. To resolve the problem of connecting several different hotel companies' CRS to the four GDS, the leading hotel brands worked together to develop a 'universal switch' mechanism. The switch enables each hotel CRS to connect with each of the GDS using a single interface. This enables all the travel agent intermediaries who are linked into the GDS to book hotels in seconds. There are two switch companies, called THISCO and WIZCOM (see Figure 8.6).

We have already mentioned the problems of compatibility between different databases. From a GDS reservations perspective, these problems are increased if there is a time lag between updating the hotel unit's reservations from their Property Management System (PMS) to the hotel chain's CRS, or between updating the hotel chain CRS and the GDS (see Figure 8.7).

The concept of single image inventory, which simply means that all the different computer systems 'see' the same reservations inventory in real time, is designed to overcome this problem (see Figure 8.8). However, this solution is not easy to implement unless all the IT systems are connected seamlessly (see Case study 8.2). Seamless connectivity enables *all* the screens in the travel agents, the hotel chains telesales reservations center, and the individual hotel PMS to search, book and confirm reservations *in real time*.

The Marriott Hotel Corporation has developed the technology to another level. It invested $70 million in new information systems that include a sales force automation

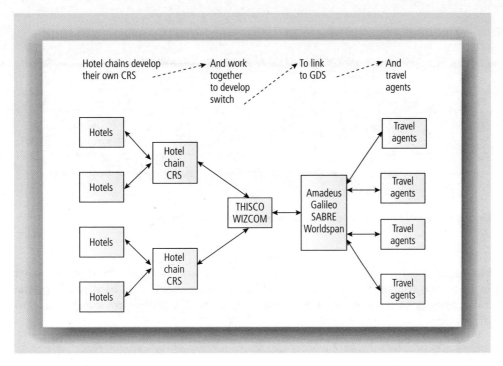

Figure 8.6 The development of switch companies

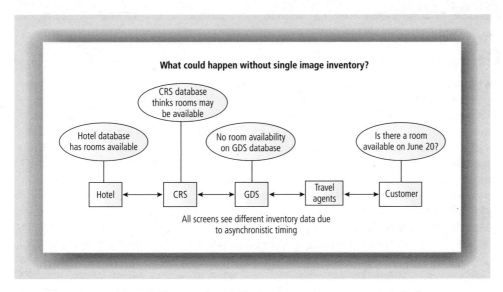

Figure 8.7 The problem with asynchronistic databases (source: Ian Mitchell and HEDNA)

database to link sales people with accommodation and meeting room availability in properties across *all* the Marriott hotel brands. If a customer wants to book a bedroom at the Marriott Marquis Hotel in Peachtree Center, Atlanta, and the hotel is full, the integrated sales system allows the salesperson to say 'sorry, the Marquis is filled up,

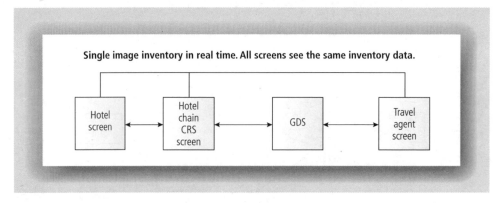

Figure 8.8 Single image inventory (source: Ian Mitchell and HEDNA)

but for the same rate we can get you into the Renaissance, which is two blocks away'. In one year, Marriott captured $55 million in cross-chain sales as a result of the automation software system, and enhanced customer loyalty by providing an accommodation solution conveniently.

Case study

8.2 The hotel manager's view on controlling inventory: the problem with single image inventory

The Belmont House Hotel in Leicester, England, is a Best Western hotel with a PMS for reservations and a separate terminal that links to the Best Western CRS Lynx system, which connects to THISCO and on through the GDS to travel agents worldwide. The Belmont House Hotel provides a small allocation of rooms (less than 10 percent of stock) on free sale to the Lynx CRS, and manually transfers any bookings to its own PMS. The hotel management is reluctant to lose control of their reservations system. The reasons include the fear of losing the ability to manage the inventory and customer mix – for example, too many single-night bookings on a busy midweek night could prevent the hotel accepting more lucrative, higher yield, multiple bookings for several nights during the same week. There is also the issue of intermediaries reserving block bookings during high season periods at the lowest rates. Hotel managers are keen to retain control of their inventory, regardless of future developments in technology.

A more recent development, using modern distribution technology, is the Destination Management System, which helps destination tourism organizations to coordinate a wide variety of tourism products. This is especially useful for the smaller, independent operators. Some DMS are state supported, and they may become more important in the future.

The costs of distribution

Each organization involved in the GDS needs to cover its costs and make a profit. The organizations include the travel agent, GDS, switch company, hotel chain CRS, credit card company (since most reservations are confirmed using credit cards), and the hotel property. From a hotel property's perspective, all these charges are deducted from the rate charged to the customer who is actually staying in the hotel. Assuming a $100 per night room rate, the total deductions can be as much as $26.55 (Middleton, 2000), which only leaves $73.45 for the hotel (although this does include an internal company charge of $9 for the hotel chain's CRS).

It has been argued that distribution is the highest marketing cost for hotels. Principals have only recently tried to reduce travel agent commission costs – most notably the airlines in the USA, who capped commission payments to travel agents and managed to halve commission rates. However, few hotel companies have challenged the commission rates charged by travel agents, apart from some budget chains who are able to generate high occupancy without needing intermediaries and differential pricing. The high cost of distribution forces principals to investigate more cost-effective distribution channels, like the Internet.

The Internet and hospitality distribution

Since the GDS is a closed network, information is only available to the users – the principals and the intermediaries. End-user customers do not have access to the system. The emergence of the Internet now allows end-user customers direct access to principals' booking engines. This enables hotel companies to communicate with and sell directly to their customers. The advantages for accommodation providers include:

- The elimination of intermediaries' commission, the GDS booking fee, and switch costs
- The relatively limited capital investment needed to develop Internet websites, compared to the high cost of intermediary charges
- Control over the information content that is communicated to customers
- The opportunity to provide high quality contemporary information on the website directly to customers, for example virtual room tours
- A search, book and confirmation capability 24 hours a day, 7 days a week, 365 days a year
- Opportunities to sell distressed inventory cost effectively directly to the consumer without incurring intermediary costs.

Whilst the Internet is an open network, which anyone can access, an intranet is a closed network for people working within the company. Extranets, which utilize Internet technology, provide a dedicated link between suppliers and customers. Increasingly, hotel chains are enabling corporate account customers to access their website via a dedicated extranet link. This allows a hotel group to give key account clients the opportunity to book online using privately negotiated, confidential prices.

Effective Internet marketing

From an accommodation provider's perspective, effective Internet marketing is based upon an understanding of how search engines work, recognizing the importance of destination links, developing accessible and easy-to-use websites, developing effective booking engines, and the transparency of pricing. We will explore these issues in more detail now, and will discuss how the Internet is influencing channel relationships later.

Search engines

Numerous surveys confirm that Internet users depend upon search engines and directories when looking for information on the Internet. Search engines such as Google and AltaVista provide an indexed guide to websites. Directories or web catalogues such as Yahoo! provide a structured hierarchical listing of websites, grouped into categories such as business, entertainment and sport. To capture the widest possible Internet audience, a website needs to ensure that the domain name, destination, text copy, page titles, description tag and meta tags are designed to ensure that search engines and directories find the web pages. Optimizing easy accessibility for Internet searchers is clearly important for the hospitality brand.

Destination links

Hotel properties and other types of accommodation need to ensure that their Internet websites are linked to the destination, since most consumers use location as a primary search tool. Innovative hoteliers like David and Chris Grant, who own the Corisande Manor Hotel in Cornwall, England, launched their own website called 'cornwall-calling' in 1997. Consumers searching the web for information about tourism attractions in Cornwall are directed to the cornwall-calling website. Because of the website name and meta-tag descriptors, searchers also find details about the Corisande Manor Hotel. The home page of this website provides over 30 items of travel and tourist information about Cornwall, including details about the history, culture, attractions, sporting activities, the weather and travel directions. As a result of the hotel's successful website, Corisande Manor does not pay intermediaries commission, does not advertise and no longer produces a printed brochure. All telephone and postal enquiries are directed to the website for further information. David Grant has been so successful in developing his own website that he now designs websites for other hotels, including Pride of Britain.

Internet website design

Marketers need to understand how web users search websites. Hospitality websites should be user-friendly in terms of:

- Navigation (moving around the site)
- Visual design (which appeals to the target market)
- Range of language options (based upon country target markets)
- Secure easy-to-use booking technology (the number of clicks to book and type of information required)
- Easily accessible customer support.

Activity 8.2

- Log on to the following websites:
  www.cornwall-calling.co.uk (The Corisande Manor Hotel, Cornwall)
  www.ihgplc.com (The InterContinental Hotels Group)
  www.ianschragerhotels.com (Ian Schrager Hotels)

- Compare and contrast the navigation, visual design, language options
  and booking processes of each website from a user's point of view.

Transparent pricing

Consumers searching hospitality and tourism Internet sites can easily compare
the products offered and the published prices, making Internet prices transparent.
The transparency of Internet prices presents hotels that are dependent upon tour
operator and travel agent business with a dilemma. Consumers can and do compare
prices listed on a hotel website with prices for the same hotel on the websites of
intermediaries. The intermediaries' prices can be lower than those published by the
hotel on its own website, and this can create confusion for consumers and a loss of
revenue for the hotel company if consumers choose to book a lower, commissionable
price via an intermediary. Holiday Inn Hotels has recognized this problem, and
promises that customers will not find their hotels priced lower on an intermediaries'
website.

Channel relationships and management

The Internet has changed channel relationships between some types of customers,
principals and intermediaries, and this process is continuing to evolve. For hospitality providers, there is a constant imperative to drive down distribution costs.
We have already discussed the high costs of intermediary commission, and the
costs of GDS, which hospitality companies wish to reduce or eliminate. Hospitality
companies see the Internet as a means of reducing distribution costs and enabling
direct communication with consumers and customers. However, using the Internet
for marketing applications is not without costs. There can be significant hardware,
software and human resource costs attached to developing and operating a direct-
to-customer distribution strategy. The process of cutting out the intermediary is
called disintermediation, and accommodation providers clearly favor this
approach. However, the role of the intermediary is well established; the major tour
operators and travel agents organize travel and accommodation for millions of
tourists every year. Intermediaries are obviously aware of the threat posed by the
Internet, but they also embrace the Internet as a tool for communicating with their
own customers.

Conclusion

Innovations in information communications technology continue to drive the development of distribution channels in hospitality and tourism. Depending upon the size of the business and the market segment targeted, accommodation providers need to use intermediaries to obtain advance bookings to generate occupancy, but the high cost of distribution forces hospitality companies to look for alternatives. The Internet has become an important tool in the tourism distribution channel, and helps hotels to reduce their distribution costs. However, travel agents and tour operators remain important intermediaries for most hotel brands and many hotels.

In this chapter, we have explained:

● The different channels of distribution in hospitality and tourism
● The benefits and disadvantages of distribution channels from a hospitality perspective
● The role of major travel and tourism intermediaries
● The expansion of companies using horizontal and vertical integration
● The role of the GDS in facilitating accommodation bookings
● The high costs of intermediary commissions and GDS charges for hotel companies
● The impact of the Internet on the hospitality and tourism distribution system.

Acknowledgements

The authors acknowledge the help of Ian Mitchell and Alex Paraskevas from the Department of Hospitality, Leisure and Tourism Management, Oxford Brookes University, in preparing this chapter.

Review questions

Now check your understanding by answering the following questions:

1 Discuss the role of distribution in the hospitality and tourism industry from a hotel company's perspective
2 Evaluate the relationship between hotel organizations and intermediaries
3 Discuss the similarities and differences between a GDS and the Internet from the perspective of:
   ● the customer
   ● the accommodation provider
   ● the travel agent
4 How can a hotel be marketed effectively on the Internet?
5 Who, if anyone, owns the customer – the hotel where the customer stays, or the intermediary who makes the booking for the customer?

References and further reading

Buhalis, D. and Laws, E. (2001). *Tourism Distribution Channels: Practices, Issues and Transformations*. Continuum.

Buhalis, D. (2003). *Etourism*. Prentice Hall.

Middleton, V. T. C. and Clark, J. (2000). *Marketing in Travel and Tourism*. Butterworth-Heinemann.

O'Connor, P. and Galvin, E. (2001). *Marketing in the Digital Age*. Prentice Hall.

O'Connor, P. and Frew, A. J. (2002). The future of hotel e-distribution; expert and industry perspectives. *Cornell Hotel & Restaurant Administration Quarterly*, June.

Porter, M. E. (2001). Strategy and the Internet. *Harvard Business Review*, **79(3),** 62–79.

Reichheld, F. F. and Schefer, P. (2000). E-loyalty: your secret weapon on the web. *Harvard Business Review*, **78,** 105–14.

Strauss, J., El-Ansary, A. J. and Frost, R. (2003). *E-Marketing*, 3rd edn. Prentice Hall.

Chapter 9
Communicating the offer

Chapter Objectives

After working through this chapter, you should be able to:

■ Understand the primary role of marketing communication in communicating the hospitality offer
■ Explain the marketing communication process
■ Evaluate each of the elements of the hospitality communication mix
■ Understand how to plan a marketing communication campaign.

Introduction

In the marketing mix, communicating the offer is variously known as promotion, the promotion(al) mix, communication, the communication mix or marketing communication (which is sometimes abbreviated to Marcom). The public knows it as advertising and selling. We mentioned in Chapter 1 that there is much more to marketing than simply advertising and selling. By now you should be aware of the importance of each of the other elements of the marketing mix, and that effective marketing is dependent upon marketing research, segmenting markets, understanding customers, designing hospitality products at the right price for appropriate target markets, finding the most suitable location(s), and using the distribution network to reach target markets.

Providing the pre-encounter marketing mix has been designed to provide an attractive offer, then communicating that offer should raise awareness, influence expectations and ultimately increase sales and profits. However, sometimes companies think that marketing communication campaigns can compensate for deficiencies in other elements of the marketing mix. If the offer does not satisfy customers, then investing in marketing communications is a waste of resources, which can lead to serious problems with unhappy customers, and negative word of mouth.

Companies used to consider promotion as a tool to communicate with customers, but today they realize that communication with customers should be a two-way dialogue. Companies are interested in feedback from customers, and modern marketing communication strategies recognize this. For example, companies can use contact centers and websites to interact with customers. We will now discuss the role of marketing communication and review the different elements of the marketing communication mix.

The role of marketing communication

The end goal of most marketing communications is to influence demand and generate sales. To influence demand and generate sales successfully, Marcom needs to raise the target audience's awareness of the hospitality brand and help form their expectations of the hospitality experience. Marcom's end goal can be achieved in different ways, depending upon the characteristics of the target audience and their knowledge of hospitality companies' brands and products. There are three main communication strategies – to inform, to persuade, and to build relationships with target audiences.

Inform communication strategies

Companies need to ensure that potential customers are aware of their marketing offer. This is partly about building brand awareness and partly about developing product knowledge – both of these help the prospective customer to form expectations. Brand awareness for the major hospitality brands is continually researched in company marketing research and omnibus surveys. For companies with low brand awareness, a typical marketing communication objective is to raise brand awareness so that more potential customers actually recognize and learn the brand name. Companies also need to ensure that target audiences understand what the marketing offer represents. Companies who have successfully communicated their marketing offer to target audiences develop stronger reputations. A company with a weaker reputation has not conveyed an appropriate message in the marketing communication activities; however, trying to change consumers' beliefs about, and attitudes towards, a brand is a very complex task, particularly when these beliefs and attitudes are deeply held.

Persuade communication strategies

Consumers who are brand aware and have a favorable perception of the brand still need to be persuaded to buy the company's hospitality product. We have already discussed how consumers have choice, and that there are many types of different competitors competing for consumers' disposable income. Hospitality marketers therefore need to persuade target audiences to buy their product instead of the competitors' offer. Marketers stimulate buyer behavior by offering attractive inducements and incentives to book now rather than later – or never at all.

Relationship communication strategies

We mentioned in the introduction that, increasingly, hospitality companies want to build long-term relationships with target audiences. Generating repeat and referral sales is crucial in most hospitality markets. Major hospitality companies use computerized databases, which hold relevant customer information (including membership details of loyalty clubs), to communicate with customers. When this is linked to automated marketing processes, for example within a customer relationship management software suite, this is known as *campaign management*. Smaller hotel companies compile mailing lists of their customers to send out mail shots. Both approaches can be effective in building closer relationships with customers.

   Throughout this discussion, we have been using the expression 'target audience'. The starting point for any communications activity is to establish who the target audience is. In hospitality, the target audience might be end users, intermediaries, or key people in the decision-making unit. Each of these different target audiences has different characteristics, and therefore different types of communication activities need to be used to communicate effectively with each audience. By stimulating demand and creating consumer awareness, marketing communications is also establishing customer expectations. This creates a dilemma in the planning of marketing communication campaigns. Companies' marketing communication activity must attract the target audiences' attention, stimulate interest and, most importantly, persuade them to buy, without over-promising what can really be delivered. Unfortunately, because of competitive pressures some hospitality marketing communication campaigns exaggerate the quality of the promised service and raise customers' expectations beyond what can be delivered. Customers who book in good faith, believing the promise, end up being disappointed when they actually experience the hospitality service. Many ordinary restaurants make exaggerated claims about the quality of their cooking, which then disappoints discerning customers.

The marketing communication process

Typical communication tasks in hospitality include:

- Raising awareness about the launch of a new product
- Promoting a low season price offer
- Creating publicity as part of a repositioning campaign
- Sending out a newsletter to regular customers.

Ultimately, the goal of most Marcom is to persuade target markets to purchase the hospitality product. However, this goal is not as simple as it sounds, because consumers in modern societies are bombarded with thousands of competing messages from hundreds of different organizations every day. We call this interference 'noise', and noise disrupts a company's communication with potential customers. Figure 9.1 provides a simple model of the communication process. The model comprises a sender, a target audience (or receiver), noise in the communication environment, message, medium and feedback process.

- The *sender* is the hospitality organization that wants to communicate with target audiences.
- The *target audience* (receiver) consists of the end users, influencers, decision-makers, gatekeepers, or intermediaries. The target audience must be precisely defined to ensure that the marketing communication campaign reaches the right people cost-effectively.

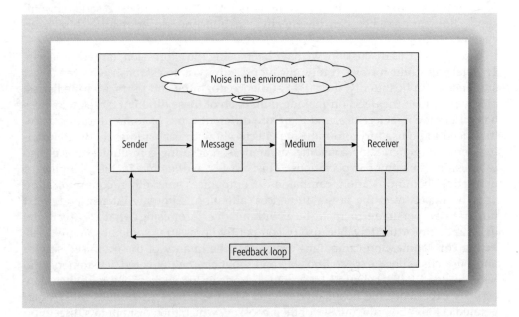

Figure 9.1 The communication process

- *Noise* comprises all the communications from other sources, including both people and organizations, which compete for the target audience's attention and interfere with the sender's message.
- The *message* is the content that the sender wants to communicate to the target audience.
- The *media* are the various communication tools that senders can use to communicate with target audiences. Media include personal communication (such as sales visits) and non-personal communication (printing brochures, placing adverts in newspapers, and public relations activity).
- *Feedback* from the audience tells the sender whether the communication objectives have been achieved.

A crucial stage in the communication process is to develop an effective message to communicate the marketing offer. Some marketers use a framework called AIDA to ensure that the message and media choices lead to an effective outcome. AIDA stands for:

- Attention – the message should grab the target audience's attention
- Interest – the message should arouse the target audience's interest
- Desire – the message should stimulate desire so that the target audience wants to experience the product
- Action – the message should encourage the target audience actually to buy the product now.

Different communication tools may be needed at each stage of AIDA – for example, advertising can stimulate attention and sales promotions can generate action. Before constructing messages and choosing communication media, marketers need to be clear about their communication objectives. Generally these can be split into three categories. Communicators want their targeted receivers to learn, feel or do something. Examples include:

- Learn: raise awareness of a new product launch; recall the brand name; recognize the company logo
- Feel: develop a positive attitude to the company; prefer the brand to competitors
- Do: telephone the contact center; ask for a brochure; make a booking; pay in advance.

Messages need to be constructed so that they achieve the specified communication objectives. In devising the message, marketers have to decide what to say (message content) and how to say it (message format).

Message content

The message content depends first upon the objectives of the campaign and then on the characteristics of the target audience and their knowledge and understanding of the hospitality product. A campaign for a new brand will most likely stress information that builds awareness and influences expectations – for example, the brand name, location and a description of the customer experience. For an established brand aiming to fill rooms in the low season, the focus will be on price and availability. Audiences who are already aware ('Attention' in the

AIDA model) are at an advanced stage of readiness to buy. Message content for them can be more attuned to interest, desire and action outcomes. Different members of the decision-making unit may be at different AIDA stages, and therefore need different messages.

The marketer then needs to decide what type of appeal to use in the message – rational, emotional or moral.

- *Rational messages* appeal to the target audience's practical mindset. This approach is effective in markets where the end user has a set of tangible requirements. A rational message can provide the factual answers, which reassures the audience. 'Just 50 meters from the beach' and 'Close to the airport, but quiet' reassure leisure and corporate markets.
- *Emotional messages* are explicitly designed to arouse consumers' passions, interests and activity. This approach is effective in dining out and leisure markets. Appeals to book a table for two in a restaurant on Valentine's Day, or to take a relaxing weekend leisure break, are popular examples of emotional messages in hospitality. Restaurants that promote non-genetically modified or organic food appeal to consumers' core emotive values.
- *Moral messages* are linked to consumers' belief and value systems. There are a number of religious organizations that arrange holidays for members of their faith, and some faiths have even bought their own hotels to cater for their members. These organizations, which provide dedicated facilities for their fellow believers, still need to carry out marketing communication activities, and their moral message is essentially a spiritual one.

Message format

Messages are communicated using one or more of our five senses – sight, sound, smell, taste and touch. Message format depends upon the choice of communication channels, and refers to the actual design of the advertisements, brochure, public relations activity, and/or sales visits. Examples include the layout, copy and illustrations in an advertisement or brochure; the gimmick and storyline to create interest in a public relations campaign; food samples from the restaurant; and the design of the hotel's conference laptop presentation. Attention to detail in designing the appropriate message format is time-consuming, relatively expensive, and crucial.

Activity 9.1

Review the advertisements for hotels and restaurants in one local newspaper, one national newspaper and one magazine.

- Who is the target audience for these adverts?
- How emotional and how factual are the adverts?
- Is there a difference between adverts placed by well-known brands and by independent operators?

Communication channels

There are two main classes of communication channels; personal and non-personal. Personal communication refers to people who are directly talking to each other, face-to-face in a meeting, or on the telephone, or via video-conferencing. It can also include personal correspondence by mail, fax or email. The advantages of personal communication are primarily the 'personal contact' that such communication allows. By directly talking with customers and influencers the hospitality organization creates the opportunity for a dialogue, so that the customer can ask questions about the hospitality company's brands and products. The customer is also able to give feedback on the company's performance.

Non-personal communication channels refer to mediated and publicity events, and include all print, broadcast and display tools. The main differences between using personal communication and mass media/publicity channels is that the latter do not provide a personalized message, and so they are not guaranteed to capture the attention and respond to the specific concerns of the target audience. The design and production of mediated communications requires support from specialist suppliers like design companies, advertising agencies, print companies and public relations agencies. These agencies develop expertise in visual imagery, copywriting, photography, radio and television advertising, and nurture useful contacts in the media for publicity purposes. They provide important advice and a professional service in delivering a marketing communication campaign.

The hospitality communications mix

Figure 9.2 presents the key communication tools used by hospitality companies, and each of these marketing communication tools is discussed here in detail. In small

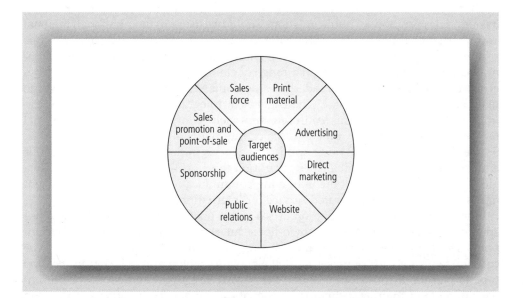

Figure 9.2 The hospitality communication mix

hospitality businesses, the owner/manager will typically be very involved with the planning and implementation of all marketing communication activity. The owner's control over these activities should ensure that the promotional campaigns are coordinated and integrated. This is important, to ensure that a consistent message is always communicated to the target audience. In this sense, smaller hospitality companies do have an advantage over their larger rivals.

Integrated marketing communications (IMC)

The global hospitality giants, like McDonald's, Burger King, Accor, Hilton, Marriott and ICHG, invest billions of dollars, pounds, euros and yen in promoting their products and brands to millions of customers in different target audiences around the world. This creates enormous marketing communication and organizational difficulties.

Cultural differences and regulation in different countries are the major barriers to effective marketing communication. First, there is the issue of language. Some languages need more copy space than other languages – for example, written French and Italian need up to 25 percent more space than written English, whilst written German and Scandinavian languages need up to 30 percent more. This creates different page layout requirements from a visual design perspective. When translating the meaning of a phrase from one language to another, for example an advertising message, it is very difficult to convey an accurate interpretation, especially if humor is involved. Humor often involves a play on words, which does not have the same meaning in a second language. Secondly, there is the issue of cultural symbolism, where different colors and different traditions mean that consumers have different interpretations of the same communication. Finally, there is the problem of different governmental approaches to regulating marketing communication activity. Even a relatively simple pan-European sales promotional campaign targeting families with children can be difficult to implement because of the different national government restrictions on promotions to young people (see Table 9.1).

Major hospitality organizations employ their own marketing specialists working in sales, sales promotion, public relations and advertising in their national, regional and international offices. They also have to work with external advertising, public relations and design agencies in several countries. With so many marketing communication specialists working on a range of campaigns, but all involved in delivering the global company's branded message, it is easy to see how it is difficult to maintain a consistent message. The concept of integrated marketing communications is the response to this confused approach to organizing the international marketing communication function. Major international advertising agencies like Saatchi & Saatchi acquired other specialist agencies in the fields of public relations and self-promotion, in capital cities all around the world. Their aim was to create a global one-stop shop for all the marketing communication activities a global client needs, and provide an integrated service for international campaigns.

Whether a hospitality corporation uses a global one-stop shop or continues to use specialist agencies and their own in-house marketing specialists, the important point is that effective international marketing communication campaigns need to be coordinated across all countries, and all elements of the marketing communication mix, to provide a consistent branded message to the target audiences. The recent development of Internet technology has enabled the hospitality chains to develop intranet solutions to the problem of delivering brand-consistent Marcom collateral

Table 9.1 The Legality of Sales Promotion in Europe (Source: Yeshin, 1998)

	UK	Irish Republic	Spain	Germany	France	Denmark	Belgium	Netherlands	Portugal	Italy	Greece	Luxembourg	Austria	Finland	Norway	Sweden	Switzerland	Russia	Hungary	Czech Republic
On-pack price reductions	Y	Y	Y	Y	Y	Y	Y	Y	Y	Y	Y	Y	Y	Y	C	Y	Y	Y	Y	Y
Banded offers	Y	Y	Y	C	Y	C	N	Y	Y	Y	Y	N	C	C	C	C	N	Y	Y	Y
In-pack premiums	Y	Y	Y	C	C	C	Y	C	Y	Y	Y	N	C	Y	N	C	N	Y	Y	Y
Multiple purchase offers	Y	Y	Y	C	Y	C	C	Y	Y	Y	Y	N	C	C	Y	C	N	C	Y	Y
Extra product	Y	Y	C	C	Y	Y	C	C	Y	Y	Y	Y	C	Y	C	C	C	Y	Y	Y
Free product	Y	Y	Y	Y	Y	Y	C	Y	Y	Y	Y	Y	Y	Y	Y	Y	Y	Y	Y	Y
Re-usable pack	Y	Y	Y	Y	Y	Y	Y	Y	Y	Y	Y	Y	C	Y	Y	N	Y	Y	Y	Y
Free mail-ins	Y	Y	Y	N	Y	C	Y	Y	Y	Y	Y	C	N	Y	Y	N	N	Y	Y	Y
With-purchase premiums	Y	Y	Y	C	Y	C	C	C	Y	Y	Y	N	C	Y	C	C	N	Y	Y	Y
Cross-product offers	Y	Y	Y	C	Y	C	N	C	Y	Y	Y	N	C	C	N	C	N	Y	Y	Y
Collector devices	Y	Y	Y	C	C	C	C	C	Y	Y	Y	N	N	C	N	N	N	Y	Y	Y
Competitions	Y	Y	Y	C	C	C	Y	C	Y	Y	Y	C	C	Y	C	Y	Y	Y	Y	Y
Self-liquidating premiums	Y	Y	Y	Y	Y	Y	Y	C	Y	Y	Y	N	Y	Y	C	Y	N	Y	Y	Y
Free draws	Y	Y	Y	N	Y	N	N	N	Y	C	Y	N	N	Y	N	N	N	Y	C	Y
Share-outs	Y	Y	Y	N	C	N	N	N	Y	C	C	N	N	C	C	N	N	Y	Y	C
Sweepstake/ lottery	C	C	C	C	C	N	C	C	C	C	C	N	C	Y	N	C	N	Y	U	C
Money-off vouchers	Y	Y	Y	N	Y	C	Y	Y	Y	C	Y	C	C	C	N	C	N	Y	Y	Y
Money off next purchase	Y	Y	Y	N	Y	N	Y	Y	Y	Y	Y	N	N	C	N	N	N	Y	Y	Y
Cash-backs	Y	Y	Y	C	Y	Y	Y	Y	Y	N	Y	N	C	C	C	Y	N	Y	Y	Y
In-store demos	Y	Y	Y	Y	Y	Y	Y	Y	Y	Y	Y	Y	Y	Y	Y	Y	Y	Y	C	Y

Y, permitted; N, not permitted; C, may be permitted with certain conditions.

across all the units in the company. The brand manual and brand standards are provided on the intranet in a digitalized format, with standardized layouts for adverts, print material and signage, a photographic library, and a history of successful marketing campaigns and press releases to help support marketing activity. Links are provided to external suppliers such as advertising agencies, designers and printers like Kall Kwik, which has local printing shops in many key locations. A unit planning to develop a Marcom campaign can access the intranet and customize the promotional material, inputting the menus, prices, dates and address/contact details on its PC. The artwork is sent on-line to the corporate head office for approval, which is much quicker than relying on snail-mail. Once approved, the artwork can then be sent to the commercial printers on-line. This use of technology is cost-effective, and allows the corporate head office much greater control in delivering consistent brand standards in Marcom materials.

Print material

Hospitality units need a wide range of print material, which is also described as collateral. The Hospitality Marketing Association carried out research into the marketing practice of major British hotel brands, and found that significantly more of the marketing budget is currently spent on producing print material such as brochures and leaflets than on any other form of marketing communication activity. Print material for individual hospitality units includes:

- Stationery
- Hotel brochures, tariff and price lists
- Restaurant menus and wine lists
- Conference brochures
- Wedding brochures
- Function menus
- Promotional material for the sales team
- In-room information (hotel facilities and in room service menus)
- Special product brochures (for example, murder mystery weekends)
- Special price promotional flyers
- Newsletters.

Print material produced for branded chains includes:

- Corporate directory listing all branded hotels in the country, region or world
- Corporate leisure breaks brochure
- Corporate conference brochure
- Group business brochure targeting tour operators
- Corporate sales team promotional material
- Corporate newsletters
- Loyalty club leaflets, application forms and newsletters
- Special promotions.

Printed material combines a number of roles, including projecting the brand image, providing information, and supporting other elements of the marketing communication mix. We will now explore each of these roles in more detail.

Projecting the brand image

The quality and design of printed material communicates impressions to target audiences. The use of color, photographs and graphics, the style of copywriting, and the quality of paper all influence consumers' perception of the hospitality brand.

Providing information

Different types of print material provide different types of information and have different lengths of shelf life. Shelf life is the period of time for which the collateral material performs its communicative function. The design and production costs of a new full-color brochure will be relatively high and, with reprints, will be expected to have a shelf life of many years. A leaflet promoting a single restaurant event for dinner on Valentine's Day night this year will have a finite shelf life of a few months, and be relatively cheap to produce. Only general information should be provided in the long-life pieces of print, whilst price details, which can change more frequently, need to be produced separately.

Specialist collateral needs to provide all the essential information a customer wants to know. For example, the conference organizer needs:

- Accurate location maps
- Information regarding the availability of car parking
- Conference/meeting room layout details, including the number of delegates who can be accommodated in boardroom, horseshoe and theatre-style layout; the width, length and height of meeting rooms; the location of light fittings and power points
- Information regarding ventilation and air-conditioning facilities
- Details of the number of bedrooms and bedroom types available
- Menus
- 24-hour delegate rates.

Linking print material with other elements of the marketing communication mix

Print material is used to support a number of other marketing communication activities. The hotel or corporate sales team need print material when they are discussing potential client needs in sales visits away from the hotel premises. Although the major companies have computerized presentations available on CD-ROMs and via the Internet, many clients still want to be provided with print collateral to look at when the sales person has left the meeting. There should be a mutual relationship between print material and hospitality websites. Collateral can promote the website address and direct information seekers to the site, whilst the brochure can be downloaded from the website.

Advertisements in local and national print media are often restricted in space terms, and are mainly used to stimulate consumer interest and encourage a telephone call for further information or a visit to the website. The brochure, tariff and accompanying sales letter are designed to convert the inquiry into the booking. Another use of print material is in direct mail campaigns, often to members of the loyalty club and/or guests who have stayed before. The letter, newsletter and special promotion mailing are all pieces of print material that form the core of direct mail activity.

Future developments in print material

Unfortunately, recipients throw a large number of brochures and leaflets away. There is also the problem for companies of the disposal of boxes of dated print material, as removal can be expensive in terms of freight haulage costs. The combined environmental costs in terms of destroyed trees and waste disposal are significant. The wastage and high costs of producing quality hospitality brochures, coupled with inaccurate target marketing, means that companies are always searching for more cost-effective solutions. Whilst the Internet revolution is clearly changing marketing communication techniques, the prediction that promotion via the Internet will completely take over from print material is premature for all but a small number of independent operators.

Sales force (personal selling)

Personal selling uses direct communication techniques to present information about the hospitality company to target markets. Although personal selling includes correspondence and telesales, the main focus in hospitality is face-to-face contact with potential clients by the sales force. Employing a sales person is very expensive, with major costs including salary, commission and bonuses; travel and accommodation costs; professional presentation equipment; laptop computers with intranet access to demonstrate the company's products, locations and prices; CD-ROMs to leave with the client after the presentation; and administrative support. Indeed, personal selling is the most expensive marketing communication activity available to hospitality companies, and for this reason most small hospitality companies do not employ sales people. However, the owner/manager can adopt the sales role and go out and actively promote the company to prospective clients.

From a customer's perspective, low-risk and low involvement hospitality products do not really need a detailed personalized explanation via a face-to-face meeting. Budget hotels are simple product purchases, and budget brands do not need to employ a sales force. However, more complicated hospitality products – for example, major conference bookings from key corporate accounts, and intermediaries who can produce volume bookings – require more detailed discussions in face-to-face meetings. Prospective clients, who are often knowledgeable about the hospitality industry and are aware of the value of their booking, expect a sales person to pitch for their business; and because of the high sales value, the competition will almost certainly want to talk to prospective clients as well. Face-to-face selling is appropriate when:

- The product is complex or risky and needs detailed explanation
- The product specification can be adapted to suit the needs of the client
- The potential value of the sale is relatively high
- The price is negotiable
- The prospective clients, or intermediaries, can influence or make the decision to book business
- The prospective clients expect a sales visit
- Competitors are likely to pitch for the business.

In larger hospitality companies, responsibility for unit sales can rest with either the corporate sales organization or the unit. In the latter case, proactive general managers will join their hotel sales executives when meeting key accounts. Indeed, most medium and large hotels will employ at least one sales executive, unless this function is entirely managed by the head office.

The corporate sales team

We have frequently mentioned that the hospitality industry is extremely competitive, and all the major hospitality organizations use personal selling as an important competitive tool in servicing clients. Important clients are called 'key accounts', and potential clients are called 'prospects'. Selling is a professional art. Effective sales executives follow systematic procedures when organizing sales visits. The sales process includes:

- *Prospecting*. This refers to the search for prospective customers. It includes searching for new leads from local organizations and local companies, and finding existing and lapsed customers from the hotel's database. Prospects need to be qualified, which means checking that the contact has the authority and budget to buy. Salespeople can also check that the prospect is a good fit with existing customer segments.
- *Sales calls*. Hotel sales executives will occasionally turn up at a prospect's office unannounced, hoping to arrange a meeting by chance. This tactic is called 'cold calling', and can occasionally be effective. However, the most effective sales approach is to pre-book an appointment by telephone or email. This ensures that both the prospect and the sales executive do not waste valuable time. Often a sales executive will have to meet a client several times and gradually build up a personal relationship before actually signing any business. Arranging sales meetings with existing clients is also an important function of the sales executive, in order to continue building a close relationship with the customer.

Occasionally a sales force will organize a 'sales blitz'. This is a coordinated sales campaign using a large number of sales executives who work together to saturate a target geographic area, combining cold calling, telesales, and pre-booked meetings with prospects and key accounts. Although a sales blitz is an effective tool, it requires a considerable amount of organization.

Finally, prospective customers who want to book business will often contact hotels directly and arrange to visit them. The hotel sales executives, the conference and banqueting manager or the duty manager will host the meeting, show the prospect the hotel's facilities, and explain the services available. These visits are key opportunities to impress potential customers.

Personal selling is an important part of the marketing communication mix. The salesperson represents the unit and the brand, and can be regarded as the human face of the company.

Advertising

Advertising is any paid-for mass communication activity. Although advertising reaches a wide audience, the proportion of readers, listeners and viewers who are potential customers can be relatively small. For this reason, advertising is relatively expensive and it is notoriously difficult to measure its effectiveness. Although the advertiser does have control over the message content, message format and message source, there are legal, voluntary and social constraints that advertisers need to recognize. Most countries have legal restrictions on advertising, ranging from tight censorship controls in countries like Saudi Arabia to voluntary agreements like the British Code of Advertising Practice. These regulations are designed to ensure that adverts do not mislead consumers with inaccurate or dishonest claims. Finally, advertisers need to recognize that inappropriate adverts that offend people's religious or cultural values can be extremely damaging to their product and company.

Most hospitality advertising is aimed at customer and business markets, but occasionally a major company will communicate with other audiences (such as financial and political stakeholders) by advertising in the mass media. When there is a contested takeover battle, both companies will invest in advertising to influence the outcome. The bitter acquisition in the UK of the Forte Group by Granada was accompanied by major advertising campaigns by both companies to try to influence shareholders.

The following media can be used for advertising campaigns:

- Newspapers
- Magazines
- Tourist board publications
- Broadcast media (radio, cinema and television, including teletext)
- Banners or pop-ups on search engines, directories and websites
- Billboards and posters
- Ambient media (buses, taxis, overground and underground trains, gas and petrol stations).

The decision as to which media are selected depends upon the campaign's marketing communication objectives and the available budget. We will now discuss the advantages and disadvantages of the main advertising media.

Newspapers

Newspaper advertising varies in cost according to:

- Circulation and readership – the number of copies sold and the number of readers per copy
- Geographic coverage – local, regional, national
- Audience profile – social grade, income and lifestyle
- Size of advert – bigger adverts cost more; display adverts can use graphics such as line drawings or photographs, whilst classified advertising is copy only
- Location of advert – where an advert is actually placed in the newspaper (front page, back page and requests for a specific spot are more expensive)
- Timing – Sunday is one of the most popular days to read the newspapers, and so it is more expensive
- Number of adverts placed – a series of adverts booked at the same time can qualify for volume discounts.

The key point about newspaper advertising is the short shelf life. This means that yesterday's newspaper has old news; readers quickly throw out old newspapers and the adverts in them.

Magazines

Magazines have similar cost variables to newspapers, with two important differences. First, whilst newspapers have a broad readership, magazines are often highly specialist in their subject areas and attract discrete, distinct readership profiles – so country hotels targeting leisure break consumers can advertise in specialist bird, gardening and walking magazines. Secondly, magazines have a longer shelf life; this means they can continue to generate enquiries many months after the publication date. Magazines generally have higher quality paper and encourage full-page color adverts to emphasize lifestyle advertising (see Figure 9.3).

Tourist board publications

Destination marketing organizations produce tourist board publications, which carry advertisements for and listings of accommodation, attractions, bars and restaurants, and events taking place in the area. Potential visitors to the area contact the destination marketing organization to request information, and are sent these brochures. For smaller accommodation businesses, for example a farmhouse with bed and breakfast, Tourist Board publications provide one of the most effective promotional tools.

Television

Television reaches mass audiences, and is consequently the most expensive advertising medium. However, costs vary enormously depending upon the length of a television commercial (regular 'spots' can vary from ten seconds to one minute) and the time it is broadcast. The norm for a TVC (television commercial) is 30 seconds, though night owls have the opportunity to view 30-minute infomercials in the middle of the night when there is no other programming. A prime spot during the evening news or in the middle of one of the most popular national programs costs a significant sum of money, because these programs attract peak audiences. An advert running during the 'graveyard shift' in the middle of the night on a local television channel is much cheaper because the audiences are so much smaller. The impact of television advertising can be diminished because viewers channel hop or leave the room during the commercial break. Effective television advertising requires significant budgets to afford the slots and frequency to generate brand name or message recall. Television advertising is appropriate for mass marketing products, and for this reason the most significant hospitality advertisers on major television channels are the fast-food brands like McDonald's, Burger King, KFC and Wendy's.

The introduction of satellite television shopping channels has created new opportunities for companies to promote hospitality, travel and tourism products. Travel agents like Thomas Cook have developed their own dedicated interactive television channels, which promote package holidays, cruises and destinations that can be booked by viewers as they watch the programs.

Teletext advertising is a more controversial medium; its advocates believe teletext provides effective low-cost television advertising, whilst its critics suggest that the audience is small and the adverts have limited impact.

Cinema

Cinema advertising has many similarities to TV advertising but is not as expensive. Generally cinemas attract a younger audience, typically aged between 18 and 30. The main hospitality advertisers on cinema are the fast-food chains and local restaurants.

Radio

In recent years radio has become a more popular advertising medium because the target audiences have become much more tightly defined. Different stations have

Figure 9.3 Best Western magazine advert (source: Best Western Hotels)

clearly identified target audiences and formats such as Top 40, Classical Music, Talk, Sport, 60s to 80s music, and because of this programs hold the attention of the audience better than television. Radio advertising is not as expensive as television, and the cost of making radio commercials is considerably lower. Most stations offer simple advertising production facilities for advertisers.

Sales promotion and point-of-sale

The primary role of sales promotion and point-of-sale material is to stimulate short-term or immediate sales. Virtually all hospitality organizations utilize these tools at new product launches (to attract trial purchase), during low and shoulder periods (to boost demand), or at obvious customer contact points (to promote in-house offers). Effective sales promotions are designed well in advance. However, on occasions, when there is a sudden collapse in demand, the marketing department needs to respond quickly with a sales promotion campaign. Sales promotions are often packaged into product/price bundles, which offer enhanced value for the customer. The design and pricing of a hospitality packaged sales promotion must be:

- Carefully targeted and conform with current marketing objectives – in particular, a sales promotion must be targeted at compatible target markets that will fit in with the existing customer mix
- Competitive, since competitors will probably have a similar demand pattern and will be planning their own sales promotion
- Properly costed – both the level of the discount and the promotional costs (print material, advertising and mailing) must be calculated during the planning stage of the campaign; bookings from sales promotions are generally stimulated by an attractive discounted price, but the price must cover the costs of the campaign
- Consistent with the current market position and brand image
- Creative! The promotion needs to grab the interest and imagination of the target audience and encourage potential customers to respond quickly, so creativity in designing and publicizing the offer is essential to ensure that the sales promotion stands out from competitors
- Of a fixed time period that is long enough for the target audience to learn about the promotion and have time to book the offer, but not so long that there is little urgency for the customer to book.

Sales promotions that become the principle long-term marketing communication activity eventually become ineffective. Sales promotions lose their vitality, and over a longer period of time repeated price discounting can damage the brand image.

There are a number of issues to consider when planning a sales promotion. First, the price of a sales promotion can be particularly complicated. If two restaurants in the same product class are competing and one restaurant has a sales promotion offering 'Two meals for the price of one' (the equivalent of a 50 percent discount), then the other restaurant cannot compete effectively with a 25 percent discount voucher. Secondly, sales promotions do not necessarily generate customer loyalty. Indeed, bargain hunting customers are unlikely to remain loyal, as they will always be looking to patronize competitors with similar or better sales promotions. Finally, the sales promotion should not be too attractive, because the company has to be able to satisfactorily service the increased demand generated by a creative promotion.

Examples of typical sales promotions include:

● Price discounts on accommodation, food, drink and leisure activities
● Added value promotions – bundling a range of hospitality products into a single price and package
● Discount vouchers and coupons.

Pauline and David Baldwin created Sheffield's most successful banqueting operation at Baldwin's Omega. In the summer season, a 'Salmon and strawberries' sales promotion is publicized in-house and sent out to party organizers to stimulate sales on quiet nights. The literature is designed to make it easy for organizers to book, and this cost-effective promotion has been working successfully for more than twenty years.

Point-of-sale material

Hospitality businesses use a variety of point-of-sale material to promote in-house products. Examples of point-of-sale material include menus, leaflets, coupons and posters at the reception desk and in the lift, bedrooms, bars and restaurants, and at leisure outlets. Point-of-sale material is usually a tangible piece of collateral that projects the image of the business and is noticed by customers. Many hospitality brands produce excellent point-of-sale material, but there are also many units with dated, tired collateral, and this sends out negative signals to customers. The Belmont House Hotel in Leicester, England, organizes a series of events throughout the year, which combine opportunities for communicating with loyal customers along with public relations activity and sales promotions. The point-of-sale leaflet is placed in bedrooms, bars and restaurants to maximize interest in the events (see Figure 9.4).

Public relations

The focus of public relations is to generate positive publicity for the company in the media. Such publicity is generally regarded as 'free', since space and time is not bought as in advertising, although the design, effort, creativity and networking required to generate media coverage is not cheap. Public relations (PR) is a profession with a structured career pathway, and specialized education with formal examinations. Many countries have professional bodies representing their PR industry.

The major hospitality corporations employee PR managers in their national and international head offices. The corporate public relations role includes managing publicity aimed at financial stakeholders and political bodies, as well as promoting the parent company image and specific brands. Although the management of media relations at national and international level is clearly a role for the professional PR executive, individual hospitality owners and general managers can become adept at generating publicity for their own properties. The principles of effective public relations are the same regardless of the scale of business. Public relations activity should:

● Ensure that the proposition, or the publicity idea, is consistent with the brand's positioning and the current brand image. Some hoteliers are so keen to be in the news they forget the purpose of PR activity, which is to generate positive publicity for the business. Inappropriate stunts can generate significant amounts of irrelevant or even negative publicity, which undermines the brand's position in the marketplace.
● Develop a creative concept that stimulates the media's imagination. Media journalists and their editors are well informed, very aware and frequently cynical.

Figure 9.4 Point-of-sale collateral; the Belmont House Hotel calendar of events

To capture their imagination, the publicity concept needs to be different, interesting and therefore newsworthy.

- Make sure that press information is professionally presented and made available at the right time. Old news is not interesting. The tools that PR executives use include press releases, a press pack with all the relevant company information, photographs, and arranging familiarization visits for journalists.
- PR activity needs 'stories' around which a publicity campaign can be created. Suitable stories include company news (for example, new hotel/restaurant openings, new product launches), events, new menus and special offers, winning accolades and awards from hotel and restaurant guides, and human interest stories about customers and employees.

Effective public relations activity uses a wide range of different activities, events, and human interest stories that generate brand awareness and raise brand image. Success is measured by print column inches and air time minutes, but the level of sales generated by PR is more difficult to calculate. Premier Hotels, a British company that held franchises for Days Inn, Holiday Inn Express and Howard Johnson, developed a PR campaign for opening a new hotel using the theme 'Be a Star for the Day!' Working with local schools, children entered the competition and the winner (along with his or her family) was given VIP treatment for the day. The family was collected from home in a limousine and driven to the new hotel; the winner 'cut the tape' to open the hotel formally, with several journalists and photographers present. The family was then dined and looked after before being driven home again in the limousine. Local media found the human interest angle newsworthy; it generated significant media coverage and was relatively inexpensive to organize – and, of course, the winner loved the glamour of being a star for the day!

PR and crisis management

Public relations is especially important when a company experiences a newsworthy crisis. Unfortunately, events such as food-poisoning incidents, hotel fires and high-profile court cases involving customers or employees generate media interest, even though the company does not want this type of publicity. The role of PR during the crisis is to present the hospitality company's version of events as favorably as possible. Journalists are more likely to portray the crisis sympathetically if their questions are taken seriously. When a senior figure in the company acts as the spokesperson and answers the media's questions with open, honest and helpful information, the media are more likely to be supportive. However, investigative journalists and those working for certain tabloid newspapers may be more difficult to handle. The major hospitality organizations develop crisis management planning to be prepared for such a crisis; but when an incident occurs it is easy for unit employees and managers to panic in the glare of the publicity and make inappropriate statements. Companies that respond effectively to a crisis can actually improve their image as a result of positive media publicity.

PR and destination marketing

A relatively new dimension in tourism public relations activity is the active promotion of destinations, by destination marketing organizations, to film and television companies. The popularity of destinations that have been featured in successful films and television programs has increased the number of visitors to these locations. The American entertainment industry has been a key attraction for tourists visiting Hollywood, Los Angeles and Orlando in Florida. Films like *The Beach* and *Lord of the Rings* have helped to promote tourism in Thailand and New Zealand. Today, destinations actively promote themselves as ideal locations for film and television productions in the hope that positive exposure will generate an increase in tourism.

Activity 9.2

Log onto the following hospitality companies, find the site map and look for press, press releases or press room:

- www.ritzcarlton.com
- www.sandals.com
- www.mcdonalds.com

> Review the latest press information – these are actual press releases sent out by companies to the media to generate publicity. Evaluate the approach different companies take to creating stories, and the content, interest and writing style.

Sponsorship

Sponsorship is often used in conjunction with PR to maximize publicity. It is a major component in the financing of sports/arts/cultural activities and events. Football teams, tennis stars, golf tournaments, music festivals, art exhibitions and literary events all depend upon other organizations for financial support. Hospitality companies can either provide financial donations or complimentary services such as accommodation as part of a sponsorship arrangement in return for publicity. Sponsored activities promote the name of the sponsor on clothes, equipment, posters and vehicles during the event. The sponsorship can also become the focus of a marketing communications campaign. Indeed, key customers can be invited to the sponsored event and provided with VIP status and exclusive hospitality.

The cost of sponsorship is closely linked to the amount of media coverage generated. Obviously, the higher the sport's profile and the higher the profile of the celebrities, the more it costs. Whilst major hospitality companies can afford to sponsor popular national and international events (see Case study 9.1), small hospitality businesses can, with a modest amount of money, sponsor local community activities just as effectively. The pub sponsoring a local children's football team by buying their strip can generate huge goodwill and a positive brand image.

Case study

9.1 De Vere's effective sponsorship of the Ryder Golf Cup

De Vere Hotels hosted the Ryder Cup Golf match between the USA and Europe at the Belfry Hotel – its prestigious conference and golfing hotel complex. De Vere took the opportunity to sponsor the event, which attracted 180,000 visitors and a television audience of over one billion viewers. De Vere raised brand awareness more than any other UK hotel group that year, and at the same time increased its REVPAR premium compared to competitors to 21 percent. The Annual Accounts recognized the success of the sponsorship in supporting De Vere's marketing objectives.

(Source: www.devereonline.co.uk)

Direct marketing

Direct marketing (DM) is any form of direct-to-consumer communication, such as direct mail, door drops, SMS (text messaging) and email promotions. Usually DM aims to inform and persuade customers to respond to a particular offer. A key benefit of direct marketing is that it cuts out the intermediaries and the commissions paid to them. Originally, direct marketing comprised direct mailings to customers, door-to-door leaflets in the neighborhood, and making sure that advertisements had a response mechanism. This type of marketing communication activity remains popular with smaller hospitality businesses. Newsletters and Christmas cards from small hotels, bed-and-breakfast houses and local restaurants are cost-effective and help build customer relationships. The communications can be highly personalized, if somewhat quirky at times.

We have already mentioned how the cost of computers has fallen whilst the capacity and interconnectivity of computer systems has risen, and the impact of this ICT revolution has enabled major hospitality organizations to capture customer transaction data. The technology enables customer information and geo-demographic details from lifestyle databases to be analyzed to improve targeted direct marketing.

The process of direct marketing in hotels starts with the computer reservation systems. Customer details from the front office are linked to customer transactions and accounts in the back office, to provide a database of customer activity. Companies with a sales force will enter existing accounts and potential prospects into their customer relationship management system, which is a separate software package. Hospitality brands with thousands of customers enrolled as members of their loyalty club normally outsource the management of this service to a specialist service provider, and this database will be located on another site. These different computer systems should all be interconnected, but for various reasons might not be. The process of computerizing hotels has evolved over a number of years, and different hardware and software packages have been brought at different times; even linking front and back office took a long time for some companies to manage. The hotel groups that have grown through major acquisitions have also inherited different property management systems (PMS), different CRS and even different technological hardware platforms, such as Internet booking systems. The cost of installing new complementary systems is high, but such installation is essential if the company is going to have an effective direct marketing system.

Hotel groups store information in secure data warehouses, or data marts, away from the operational units. These store information about customers, including geo-demographic data, number of visits, purpose of visits, time of visits, average spend, and personal comments – for example, birthdays, wedding anniversaries, or the number and age of children. Sophisticated data mining software can analyze the data to identify current customer usage patterns and clusters of customer segments. The software can then identify customers who are most likely to be interested in booking specific hospitality products, at specific times. This information can then be used as part of a more accurately targeted direct marketing campaign, assuming the customers have actually given their permission to be contacted.

In hospitality, direct marketing generates better results in leisure markets where the products have low involvement characteristics and prices are relatively modest – for example, leisure weekends. Direct marketing is frequently used in hospitality new product launches, such as new restaurants. It can also be used when targeting specific business markets, like the conference market. However, if the products have high involvement characteristics, then direct marketing often needs to include a follow-up by the sales force.

Indeed, direct marketing activities can work effectively with all the other elements of marketing communication mix in an integrated campaign. Direct marketing is a powerful marketing communication tool for the following reasons:

- The company has complete control of the message and medium
- Customers and prospective customers are precisely targeted – this solves the traditional criticism of direct mail, which is that many recipients do not want to receive unsolicited mail

- The message can be more easily personalized
- The impact of the direct marketing campaign has immediate results, and the costs and return from a direct marketing campaign can be measured.

Finally, over time people's geo-demographic characteristics alter and their lifestyle patterns change. The major criticism of direct marketing is that contact lists become dated. One estimate suggests that on average people move home at least once every eight years, and many people move much more frequently. This means that computer databases needed to be 'cleaned' on a regular basis to ensure that people who have died or moved house are removed from them.

Internet website

We discussed the role of hospitality company websites in Chapter 8. Whilst the Internet is usually regarded as a distribution channel to facilitate convenient booking, especially for last minute deals, the website should also be considered as a Marcom tool.

The role of marketing communication agencies

The marketing communication industry is a global one comprising a small number of global players, a large number of regional and national companies, and many small local businesses – some with only one employee. Advertising agencies emerged as salespeople who worked for the newspapers and magazines on a commission basis, turned into professional advisers for customers, and created, designed and planned campaigns for them. Today there is a wide range of specialist companies working in each of the different elements of the marketing communication mix. These include specialists in public relations, copywriting, media buying, merchandising, direct marketing, photography and collateral. There are also agencies that monitor and measure the effectiveness of marketing communication campaigns.

Whilst specialist agencies focus on one specific service, full service agencies provide:

- *Creative services* – the design and production of advertising, publicity material, public relations concepts and ideas. Creative planning is needed to make sure the message stands out from all the noise and is heard and seen by the target audience. A creative brief summarizes the task, and the creative team will first brainstorm ideas and then develop those ideas into a storyboard that presents a visual interpretation of the message execution. Storyboards can be used to pre-test the effectiveness of the creative concept, by obtaining feedback from focus groups representing the target audience. Their response indicates whether changes in the message execution are needed. While an agency will be responsible for the creative planning, the client needs to be involved and has to give approval at key stages in this process.
- *Media planning* – selecting appropriate media, negotiating and buying the media space and time. Agencies have experience regarding which media are more effective

to accomplish the task, and can obtain better prices for clients because of their bulk buying power.
● *Research* – including research into audience characteristics, campaign effectiveness and new media forms.

Agencies employ account executives, who are responsible for looking after individual clients and coordinating the agency's services to them. Traditionally, there are three ways in which agencies charge for their work:

1 *Commission*. Here, media owners pay agencies a commission for placing the client's business. The commission is approximately 15 percent, but this is subject to negotiation. However, the system has been criticized because unscrupulous agents can place business with the media that pay the highest commission, which is not always in the client's best interest, or spend more money buying media than is strictly necessary to achieve the campaign's objectives.
2 *Fee basis*. Here, the client pays the agency a fee for the work. This can be on a project basis, or, in the case of PR agencies, clients may pay a regular monthly/annual retainer to ensure that any publicity opportunities are captured as they happen.
3 *Payment by results*. Cost control and a quest for greater cost-effectiveness has produced a third alternative, payment by results. However this is not as simple as it sounds, since measuring the outcomes of marketing communication campaigns and attributing the sales to specific activities is notoriously difficult.

Although all three systems are possible, most agencies use a combination of commission and clients paying on a fee basis.

Planning the marketing communication campaign

The steps in developing a marketing communication campaign include setting objectives, setting the budget, defining the target audience, agreeing Marcom strategies and tactics, implementation, and measuring the results of the campaign. We will now discuss each of these in turn.

Marketing communication objectives

As mentioned earlier, communication objectives can be classified into 'learn', 'feel' and 'do' categories. Marketing communication campaigns for most small hospitality companies are short-term, tactical responses to difficult trading conditions. The marketing communication campaigns for the major hospitality companies such as fast-food chains are part of a long-term, coordinated, planned and professional activity to support the company's marketing objectives. The starting point in planning a marketing communication campaign is setting objectives that support and are consistent with long-term marketing objectives. Most long-term communication objectives focus on the brand, rather than on particular products or experiences. Typically, brand owners want to get customers to understand what the brand means and to develop favorable attitudes towards the brand. These are 'learn' and 'feel' objectives respectively. We will discuss objectives in more detail in Chapter 15, but all objectives should be specific, measurable, achievable, realistic and set to a timetable. Examples of Marcom objectives include:

- *Learn* – a new product launch objective for a restaurant opening in September could be: 'to generate 15 percent awareness of the restaurant among the target market of ABC1 men and women, within a 15-minute drive-time radius of the site, by the end of October'.
- *Feel* – an objective for a conference hotel in an Adriatic tourism destination could be: 'to become the destination's conference hotel of first choice for Italian small and medium-sized professional associations within two years'.
- *Do* – an objective for a leisure hotel could be: 'to generate a 25 percent increase in domestic leisure break Internet bookings in the next twelve-month period'.

Short-term marketing objectives employ tactical activities like sales promotions to drive bookings and sales.

Setting the marketing communication budget

There are four recognized ways of setting a marketing communication budget: affordable, percentage of sales, competitive parity, and objective and task. The approach taken really depends upon the size and ownership of the hospitality business; and which sector a company operates in. Generally speaking, budgeting methods become more systematic as the business grows in complexity.

Affordable   Small hospitality operators, like the independent takeaway sandwich shop, the farmhouse bed and breakfast and the wine bar, make promotional decisions on the basis of what is affordable. These entrepreneurial owners may respond opportunistically to media offers, and make judgments on a trial and error basis. Financial forward planning is rarely a strength of such businesses, but prudent calculations and 'gut instinct' should keep the marketing communication budget within the bounds of common sense.

Percentage of sales   Historically, most hospitality businesses set their marketing budgets as a percentage of last year's or future projected sales. Over time, industries establish norms for marketing costs and expenditure patterns. In hospitality, this process is complicated by a lack of consensus about which budget line items count as Marcom expenses. For example, the sales force can be budgeted as a payroll item or included in the marketing communication budget. Dues paid to a consortium group and which are ultimately used for marketing purposes might appear as a general administrative item in the budget. However, the major hotel companies, which use the Uniform System of Accounts for the Lodging Industry (USALI), have adopted an accounting standard for marketing that includes payroll costs. The following are typical UK hospitality industry norms for marketing communication budgets, stated as a percentage of total sales (TRI, 2003):

Chain hotels	2.8–3.5% (including 0.6% for marketing payroll costs)
Independent hotels	2–6%, depending upon the location and business mix

For example, an independent leisure-orientated hotel with a turnover of $2 million, using 5 percent as the percentage of sales method, would allocate $100,000 to marketing communication activity. Franchised hospitality businesses have developed complex formulae, which include fees, to pay for national Marcom activity as well as local promotions. However, independent restaurants typically spend 2–3 percent on their Marcom activity.

The problem with percentage of sales calculations is that the budget is not linked to the needs of the business. In some years the budget may be too much, because of economic prosperity, whilst during difficult trading periods the budget will not be enough. It also does not take into account each company's cost/profit structure, the different locations or potential opportunities that might require an investment in additional marketing communication expenditure. However, the percentage of sales method remains the preferred choice of most hospitality organizations.

Competitive parity Major hospitality brands competing in mature markets fight for market share and brand loyalty. These companies already invest heavily in marketing communication activity and are very aware of one another's marketing communication campaigns. The competitive parity budget concept recognizes the importance of investing similar amounts of money on marketing communication activity as competitors. If one competitor tries to increase its share of voice (SOV) in this competitive market by substantially increasing its marketing communication expenditure, then competitors may be forced to match the increase in spending in order to maintain their SOV. *Share of voice* is a measure of the amount of money invested in promotion, and particularly in advertising, in comparison to competitors. If total sector spend on advertising is $10 million and your company spends $2 million, your SOV is 20 percent.

Objective and task The objective and task approach adopts a systematic method to budgeting. Specific objectives are set, and the marketing communication tasks to deliver those objectives are determined. The costs are then calculated and the marketing communication budget is agreed. For smaller companies, this is seen as a complicated and time-consuming approach. For larger organizations, especially the more bureaucratic ones, the objective and task method is favored. However, this approach can be problematic if the costs are higher than predicted, and expected sales do not materialize.

Costs

Whilst each budgeting approach has advantages and disadvantages, the important point is that setting a budget is essential when planning the marketing communication campaign. The costs of a campaign include:

- Agency fees for advice and creative design.
- Production costs – a black and white leaflet or a local radio station advert is a relatively low-cost item to produce, compared to printing a high quality, full-color glossy brochure or making a one-minute cinema/television commercial on location with celebrities as part of an international campaign.
- Media costs – this refers to the actual cost of buying the space in a publication or the time on TV or radio stations.
- Buying or renting mailing lists.

Budgeting often becomes an iterative process, as the costs of different media are evaluated and campaign decisions are changed to fit the allocated budget.

Above and below the line

When discussing marketing communications, marketers distinguish between 'above' and 'below' the line to describe different types of activity. *Above the line* is used to describe advertising activities where the space (the page in print, or the time slot in broadcasting) has to be paid for. *Below the line'* is used for any other non-personal marketing communication activity. This terminology originates with the agencies, and refers to commission-earning activity (above the line) and fee-earning activity (below the line).

Target markets

In marketing communications, the target market is described as the target audience, and the key is to match the audience characteristics of the available media with the hospitality organization's target market profile. There are two alternative strategies in prioritizing target audiences for hospitality companies who use intermediaries: push and pull (see Figure 9.5).

A *push strategy* prioritizes intermediaries as the main target audience. Marketing communication activities focus on intermediaries, who should then influence the end user to choose the company's products instead of competitors. Hospitality marketing communication campaigns targeting intermediaries use all the elements of the marketing communication mix, but competitors are also targeting intermediaries – so it is difficult to gain competitive advantage.

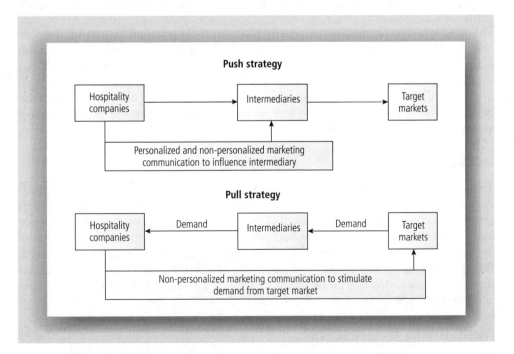

Figure 9.5 Push and pull strategies

A *pull strategy* prioritizes marketing communication activity on the end user, aiming to make the hospitality product the customer's first choice when discussing requirements with an intermediary. Because the intermediary should acknowledge the customer's wishes, the intermediary should then make the appropriate booking.

The major hospitality players use both strategies to influence intermediaries and end users. Accurately defining and prioritizing the target markets helps in the selection of which media to use.

Marcom strategies and tactics

We will now explain the links between marketing objectives, Marcom strategies and budgeting, using hotel accommodation as an example. Marketing objectives for accommodation generally focus on increasing room occupancy, improving achieved room rate and REVPAR; these are formed using percentages, value or volume as a performance indicator. A marketing objective for a hotel that is too dependent upon tour operator sales might be 'to increase higher rate rack, corporate and conference business and reduce the volume of tour group sales next year'. The Marcom strategy and tactics to support the objective could be:

To drive higher rate accommodation sales through:

● Active selling by sales executives to key corporate accounts and conference placement agents (Sales, Sponsorship)
● Sales executives renegotiating higher rates and reduce room allocations for midweek business with selected tour operators; but maintaining weekend rates and allocations (Sales)
● Launching a new state-of-the-art conference package targeting the financial services and IT industries (Print, Sales, PR, Direct Marketing, Sponsorship)
● Developing a new Sunday night promotion (Sales promotion and Point-of-sale).

This example demonstrates how several Marcom tools are used to support a single objective. A typical budget for a 200 bedroom independent hotel in a prime location is provided in Figure 9.6, and a monthly planner for key activities in Table 9.2. For each of these activities a detailed tactical marketing action plan needs to be drawn up, listing the schedule, timing and who is responsible. The PR activity to launch the new conference product will therefore require its own brief to the agency, budget and implementation plan.

Implementation

The major hospitality players have continuous marketing communication activity, and are adept at managing implementation. Smaller hospitality companies run campaigns during specific periods. During the campaign period, target audience responses must be monitored. Occasionally, a campaign can be adapted to improve the message execution or even 'pulled' if a serious error of judgment has occurred. Regular customers and employees can enjoy the 'buzz' and excitement when an innovative marketing communication campaign generates lots of interest – especially if real employees are actually featured in the campaign.

Measuring the results

Effective measurement of results is based on setting measurable marketing communication objectives in terms of what you want the audience to learn, feel or do, and

Table 9.2 Annual Marcom Activities Schedule Planner

Year	Jan	Feb	Mar	Apr	May	Jun	Jul	Aug	Sep	Oct	Nov	Dec
Sales												
Sales visits		New York		Paris		Hong Kong, Shanghai						
Conference sales blitz			X	X	X				X	X		
Exhibitions			Berlin			Tokyo					World Trade Market, London	
Print												
New design and production	X	X	X									
PR		X	X	X	X			X	X	X	X	
Adverts												
Leisure breaks	X	X	X			X	X	X		X	X	
Conference	X	X	X	X					X	X	X	
Direct marketing												
Loyalty club newsletter		X			X			X			X	
Sponsorship												
Golf events				X			X	X				

establishing tracking systems to monitor audience responses. There are two main methods of measuring the results of a marketing communication campaign: one is to use marketing research to measure the effectiveness of marketing communication activity, while the other is to measure the audience responses in terms of enquiries and bookings generated.

Marketing research measurement

A company wishing to raise brand awareness and brand image ('learn' objectives) first needs to employ an agency to establish the levels of awareness and image before the campaign starts. This provides a comparison standard for setting a measurable objective. During and after the campaign, the agency – using the same research methods – can establish whether there have been any changes in the levels of brand awareness and brand image. Similar research tracks the target audience's recall of recent advertising heard or seen, which is another 'learning' measure of the campaign's effectiveness.

Response measurement

Most hospitality companies want a measurable behavioral response to their Marcom campaigns – enquiries or bookings, for example. The reservations department, or the telesales bureau, notes the number of enquiries generated by each of the different elements of the communications plan. Many advertisements ask consumers to quote a code when they call for more information, and this allows the responses for each advert to be separately monitored. However, some campaigns stimulate lots of interest and enquiries, but little in the way of sales. This is why the conversion ratio

A hotel with an accomodation sales target of
£10 million and a 5% marketing budget might
allocate the £500,000 like this:

Sales		£,000
	Salaries	150
	Overseas travel	30
	Exhibitions	20
	Entertaining/FAM visits	10
		210
Marketing agency fees		
	Redesign corporate identity	50
Advertising		
	Directories	25
	GDS adverts	10
	Tactical support	25
		60
Print		
	Hotel brochure	15
	Corporate market	10
	Tour operator	5
	Leisure breaks	5
	Conference	5
	Loyalty scheme	5
		45
Sales promotion		
	In-house point-of-sale	10
PR		
	Agency fees	20
Sponsorship		
	Golf events	20
Direct marketing		
	Loyalty club	20
Other		
	Consortia/Utell	25
	Internet	15
	Contingency	25
		65

Figure 9.6 Marcom budget for hotel accommodation

of turning enquiries into bookings is important. This allows companies to track the actual number and value of bookings generated by each advert in each medium, which in turn allows the marketing team to evaluate the effectiveness of each medium and of different adverts, to learn what works and to improve the campaign for next time. We have already mentioned vouchers and coupons, which are distributed as part of sales promotions and direct marketing activity. The number of customers using the vouchers also provides a simple tracking system to measure the effectiveness of voucher campaigns.

Conclusion

Marketers are primarily responsible for communicating the hospitality offer, and this is the most visible part of the marketing job. When designing a campaign the hospitality marketer has to choose from a wide range of options, and the decision is dependent upon the budget available and the campaign's objectives. Ensuring that a consistent message is delivered across the range of communication tools used in a campaign is essential. Creativity can increase the impact of a campaign. Hospitality marketers work with agencies that provide professional, specialist marketing communication services. All marketing communication activity should have a mechanism for measuring the response to a campaign, or the investment in marketing communication is wasted.

In this chapter, we have explained:

- The role of marketing communication, which is to inform, persuade and build relationships with target audiences
- The communication process, which involves a sender, a target audience, noise in the environment, the message, media and feedback
- Personal communication channels in hospitality, which usually involve sales people directly talking with, or writing to, customers on an individual basis
- Non-personal communication channels, including all print, broadcast and display tools aimed at target audiences
- The hospitality communication mix, which includes print material, the sales force, advertising, sales promotion and point-of-sale material, public relations, sponsorship, direct marketing and the Internet
- That setting marketing communication objectives is a prerequisite for successful marketing communication planning
- Marketing communication campaigns, which comprises a budget, prioritization of target audiences, creative planning, media selection, implementation and a mechanism for measuring the results of the campaign.

Review questions

Now check your understanding by answering the following questions:

1 Discuss the role of marketing communications in communicating the hospitality offer.
2 Evaluate the communication process from a hospitality company's perspective.
3 Discuss the hospitality marketing communication mix and explain the role of each tool.
4 Explain the stages in developing and implementing a marketing communication campaign for a hospitality product.

References and further reading

Kotler, P., Bowen, J. and Makens, J. (2003). *Marketing for Hospitality and Tourism*, 3rd edn. Prentice Hall.
Lewis, R. C. and Chambers, R. E. (2000). *Marketing Leadership in Hospitality: Foundations and Practice*. John Wiley.

Middleton, V. T. C. and Clark, J. (2000). *Marketing in Travel and Tourism*. Butterworth-Heinemann.

Morgan, N. and Pritchard, A. (2000). *Advertising in Tourism and Leisure*. Butterworth-Heinemann.

Reich, A. Z. (1997). *Marketing Management for the Hospitality Industry*. John Wiley.

Smith, P. R. (1995). *Marketing Communication: An Integrated Approach*. Kogan Page.

TRI (2003). *TRI Hospitality Consulting*. TRI, London.

Usunier, J. C. (2000). *Marketing Across Cultures*. Prentice Hall.

Yeshin, T. (1998). *Integrated Marketing Communications*. Butterworth-Heinemann, p. 324.

Zeithaml, V. A. and Bitner, M. J. (2003). *Services Marketing*, 3rd edn. McGraw-Hill.

Part C
Encounter marketing

Chapter 10
Managing the physical environment

Chapter Objectives

After working through this chapter, you should be able to:

- Understand the role of the physical environment in marketing a hospitality business
- Have an awareness of the design principles used in the development of the hospitality product
- Identify the external and internal elements of the hospitality physical environment
- Recognize the importance of maintenance and refurbishment programs in delivering customer satisfaction in hospitality properties.

Introduction

The physical environment sends important signals to all of the hospitality organization's stakeholders, but most importantly to customers. Customers intuitively respond to the signals that the external appearance and internal atmosphere project. If the physical environment is appropriate, then target markets are more likely to find the offer attractive and want to buy; at the same time, potential customers who do not 'fit' into the target market profile can be deterred. In this sense, the physical evidence in the hospitality product helps 'tangibilize the intangible' aspects of hospitality services. At the same time, the physical environment influences customer expectations in the pre-encounter marketing stage, and customer experiences during the encounter.

In this chapter we will explore how environmental psychology helps hospitality companies to understand consumers' responses to the physical environment. We will then introduce key principles in design, and discuss the various elements of the physical environment. Finally, we will focus on the crucial issue of maintenance and refurbishment. The physical environment in hospitality is closely linked to the product, and product design decisions are interconnected with the physical environment.

Environmental psychology and customers' response to the physical environment

This discussion is largely based upon the research carried out by Zeithaml and Bitner (2003), who put forward a framework for understanding the impact of physical surroundings on customers and employees. Figure 10.1 summarizes these influences, and helps us to understand customers' psychological and social behavior within the physical environment. There are four elements, which we will now discuss – individual behavior, social interaction, customer responses, and the characteristics of the physical environment. Although most of this discussion refers to the 'built environment', the principles apply equally to the natural environment.

Individual behavior

Research by environmental psychologists suggests that people respond to the physical environment with one of two diametrically opposed types of behavior. People are, to varying degrees, comfortable in a physical environment or they are uncomfortable. When people are comfortable, this creates *approach behavior*. Customers who demonstrate approach behavior are more likely to enter the hospitality outlet, stay and spend money; they may return and/or recommend the experience to others. When people are uncomfortable with a physical environment, this causes *avoidance behavior*. Consumers who demonstrate avoidance behavior will probably walk or drive past the hospitality unit; if they do enter the premises, they may walk out without purchasing anything. Indeed, consumers with an extremely negative attitude to the physical environment can even become hostile towards that hospitality brand.

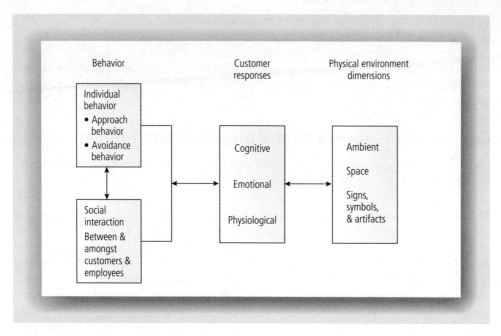

Figure 10.1 Customer behavior and responses to the physical environment (source: Zeithaml and Bitner, 2003)

When designing the physical environment, it is important both to create positive responses from the target markets to attract them into the premises, and to create an environment in which it is appealing to work. At the same time, environments can be designed deliberately to deter people who do not fit into the target market profile.

Social interaction

Research also suggests that the physical environment influences how customers and employees relate to each other. The design of the physical environment can actually encourage or discourage social interactions.

Different types of hospitality product need to generate different types of social interaction. Hospitality business products and quality restaurants are designed to create more formal social interactions. Customers who do not know each other will be polite, but they will not normally engage in any other type of conversations. Customers will also adopt formal, polite behavior with employees, and similar behavior from the employees will be expected. However, many hospitality leisure products are designed to encourage customers to interact with each other, and with employees, in a much more informal manner. Indeed, social interactions form a significant element of some hospitality product concepts. In some environments, such as dance clubs, social interaction is the core product that customers buy. If the social aspect of the consumption experience is disappointing, this will adversely influence customer satisfaction. Therefore, the character of social interactions needs to be incorporated into the product concept and the design brief. Designers should consider:

- The use of space
- The design of seating arrangements – the distance between the seating can encourage or discourage conversation between customers

- The décor – the choice of colors, fabrics and furniture
- Lighting and background music.

Ultimately the physical environment sends signals to consumers about how to conduct social interaction, by defining what is acceptable and appropriate behavior and what is not.

Consumer responses to the physical environment

There are three types of human responses to the physical environment: cognitive, emotional and physiological.

The physical environment and cognition Cognition in this context means knowledge and perception. The physical environment influences people's beliefs about places, which in turn creates preconceptions about the characteristics of the product and the behavior of people in that environment. Therefore, the physical appearance and layout of hospitality premises, the décor and employees' dress, reinforces or challenges people's prior beliefs about the hospitality offer. Consumers recognize different combinations of the physical environment, and these differentiate different product categories from other product categories. In this sense, the physical environment acts as a tangible clue for consumers and helps them to categorize the firm's marketing offer accordingly.

Activity 10.1

Compare the physical environment of two restaurants you know; one can be a fast food restaurant and the other a fine dining restaurant. What signals does the physical environment send to potential consumers?

Physical evidence	Fast-food branded restaurant	Fine dining restaurant
Surrounding environment		
External building appearance		
Signage		
Décor		
Table setting		
Staff appearance		

The physical environment and emotion As human beings, we are all aware of our own emotional responses to the physical environment. Research suggests that the physical environment can, subconsciously or overtly, generate two types of emotional response: pleasure and arousal. Figure 10.2 illustrates four emotional responses based on the pleasure/arousal continuum. Of course, different consumers will respond to the same physical environment differently – some people will feel

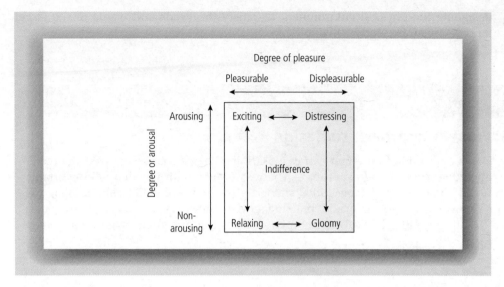

Figure 10.2 Emotional responses to the physical environment (source: Zeithaml and Bitner, 2003)

excited by the sounds, visual and video effects generated in a younger contemporary music scene, whilst other people will be distressed by them. In the same way, some people will be excited and others distressed by an outdoors action-adventure holiday environment. Research suggests that there is a U-shaped relationship between pleasure and arousal; too little or too much arousal is unpleasant, and the optimal level of arousal lies between these two extremes. Consumers' emotional responses to the physical environment influence their behavior, and therefore an understanding of peoples' emotional responses is important when designing the physical environment.

The physical environment and physiological response People have different physiological responses to environmental stimuli. Environmental stimuli can be sensed through one of the following, or any combination:

● Visual stimuli (brightness/darkness; colours; shapes)
● Aural stimuli (the volume, pitch and character of sounds)
● Olfactory stimuli (fresh or foul scents and smells)
● Oral stimuli (bitter/sweet tastes, and hot/cold ingredients)
● Tactile stimuli (the texture in food products, the softness in furnishings, and the level of comfort with the temperature).

Extreme stimulation can cause consumers varying degrees of physical discomfort, ranging from the mildly aggravating to the medically threatening. Clearly these types of physiological factors influence both consumers' and employees' response to the physical environment, and consumers' initial attraction, enjoyment and propensity to return or reject the hospitality offer.

As consumers have become more sophisticated and markets more fragmented, hospitality operators have recognized the importance of physiological stimuli in designing the physical environment to satisfy the needs and wants of the target markets (see Case study 10.1).

Case study

10.1 TGI Friday's approach to design

TGI Friday's was one of the first American casual dining chains that recognized that consumers were looking for a dining experience. The restaurants, with wooden floors, Tiffany lamps, bentwood chairs, striped tablecloths, stained glass and authentic memorabilia, are designed to provide a comfortable and relaxing environment. TGI Friday's has always emphasized the design of the physical environment as a key component in its marketing offer.

(Source: TGI Friday's website)

Variations in consumer responses to the physical environment

Throughout this discussion, we have mentioned the differences in consumer responses to the same physical environment. Consumer behavior research into personality traits can explain why certain types of personality might respond to certain types of physical environment differently. Each of us can also respond to the same physical environment differently according to changes in our disposition (good mood/bad mood). Variations in peoples' responses can be linked to different lifestyles and different cultural backgrounds. In hospitality markets, we have already discussed how the 'purpose of visit' influences consumers. The same customer may show different responses to the same physical environment, depending on whether the purpose of the visit is business or leisure.

Dimensions in the physical environment

Companies can control the built environment and create atmosphere through design. Three environmental dimensions – ambience, spatial layout and functionality, and signs, symbols and artifacts – influence the cognitive, emotional and physiological response behavior.

The *ambient dimension* refers to the sensory elements we have just discussed – features such as color and lighting (which impact on consumers' visual senses) and temperature (which impacts on consumers' sense of physical comfort) can be linked to consumers' zones of tolerance (see Chapter 3). Relatively minor irritations can be a source of amusement for some consumers, while more extreme ambient conditions can be a genuinely serious issue and create highly distressed customers.

Spatial layout refers to the way in which space is used (the actual layout of the lobby and front desk, and access to public rooms and bedrooms), and where furniture and equipment is placed in rooms. The scale and size of a hospitality property influences the spatial layout. Functionality refers to the effectiveness of the spatial layout to facilitate efficient service and deliver customer satisfaction. Spatial layout achieves an optimal balance between operational requirements and customer expectations. Employees such as kitchen crew and waiting staff need to be able to perform their jobs effectively and efficiently, but the needs of the customer must also be considered.

Signs, symbols and artifacts refers to the range of tools that companies can use to communicate either directly or indirectly with consumers.

Each of these three dimensions needs to be coordinated effectively to ensure that a consistent and appealing physical environment is achieved.

Design and the physical environment

During the development stage of a new hospitality product, factors such as ownership, the site's characteristics and planning permissions/conditions will influence the type of development built. Multi-brand operators will evaluate the market potential for their different branded concepts before selecting the most appropriate brand for a specific site. Hospitality brands vary from the formulaic, standardized concepts, where the design component is replicated in each unit, to eclectic collections of units that have no common design theme at all. From a design perspective, ownership is also closely linked to the budget available. Occasionally, wealthy individuals can afford to be extravagant when investing in an ancillary interest like a hospitality development, but usually the independent sector is characterized by restricted funds. However, the major operators have access to more significant financial resources and can invest in design. When the product concept and funding has been agreed, the architects, interior designers and management team need to draw up detailed plans for the site. Architects are not hoteliers or restaurateurs, and many new-build hospitality units have problems because marketing objectives are not included as part of the design brief. Effective marketing is based on the design concept satisfying the needs of target markets and ensuring the service process is efficient. Marketers and operations personnel should be involved in developing the design brief and providing input into the planning stage.

The physical environment has also been described as a 'servicescape' (Zeithaml and Bitner, 2003), paralleling the landscape of the natural environment. Servicescapes have two dimensions, servicescape usage and service space complexity, that can be used to identify different classes of physical environment. We will now discuss three elements that need to be considered when designing the physical environment.

1 Servicescape usage – how each area in the site plan will be used
2 Service space complexity – the level of complexity in the operation;
3 Aesthetics – the creation of the design style.

Servicescape usage

Different hospitality product concepts have different servicescape characteristics, according to the level of service that is offered and the amount of interaction between customers and employees in the operation. Three categories of servicescape are self-service, interpersonal service, and remote service (see Table 10.1).

Table 10.1 Typology of the Physical Environment for Hospitality and Leisure (adapted from Zeithaml and Bitner, 2003, Services Marketing, p. 285, reproduced with permission of The McGraw-Hill Companies)

Servicescape usage	*Complexity of the servicescape*	
	Elaborate	*Lean*
Self-service (customer focus)	Self-service restaurant	Vending machine dispensing food
Interpersonal services (customer and employees)	Cruise ship	Coffee shop
Remote service (employee focus)	Contract catering for airlines	Pizza home delivery

A *self-service operation* relies on customers serving themselves. There are few (if any) employees, and the design of the physical environment focuses on ensuring that customers can conveniently and cost-effectively look after themselves.

An *interpersonal service operation* involves both customers and employees using the same physical environment at the same time. The design of the servicescape needs to ensure that customers are comfortable within the physical environment, and at the same that employees can perform their job efficiently. Sometimes poor design of the servicescape creates conflict between customers and employees.

Remote service, in this context, means a physical environment where there are no customers. The key design issues focuses on employee needs and efficient production. Since customers never visit the servicescape, there is limited if any customer/employee interaction.

Service space complexity

Obviously there is a wide variety of different types of hospitality operations, ranging from small-scale, simple, single product units to large-scale, complex, multi-product units. The scale and complexity of the operation will influence the servicescape needs. Simple servicescapes are described as lean, and complex servicescapes as elaborate.

Lean servicescapes have a limited number of variables, products, equipment and employees to control, and only require a limited amount of space. The key focus in design is the effective use of this limited space.

Elaborate servicescapes have many variables, and are much more complex. There can be different floor levels, different types of room usage, and more equipment – which can be technologically very sophisticated. Elaborate servicescapes need more space, and the design issues can be complicated and intricate.

Aesthetics

Aesthetics is the study of form and beauty. In design, aesthetics is concerned with the tastefulness of the décor. The interior designer is given a design brief and the budget, as part of the hospitality product concept, to create the décor scheme. The scheme should include floor and wall coverings, lighting, fabrics and furniture, and artifacts. It is the interior design that provides the tangible elements of the atmospherics in the hospitality product – look at the Case study 10.2, which presents details of Sweden's atmospheric Icehotel.

Case study

10.2 Sweden's Icehotel

In November each year, building starts on the new Icehotel in Swedish Lapland, just 200 km south of the Arctic Circle. The hotel is entirely constructed of ice – some 30,000 tons of snow and 4000 tons of ice are used to build the 60-bedroom resort complete with restaurant, an Iceart Exhibition, Absolut Icebar (drinks are served from iceglasses sculptured from the River Torne), Icehotel cinema, an Icechurch for weddings, and conference facilities. There is a wide range of winter sports activities available for customers. In the winter season, more than 14,000 guests spend the night and 37,000 day visitors walk in through the 'reindeer-skin covered doors'. A different hotel is designed every year by architects Ake Larsson and Arne Bergh, because by the end of April or early May the hotel slowly melts away back into the River Torne. The 'ice' theme obviously dominates this unusual and very successful hospitality design concept.

(Source: www.icehotel.com)

Design and designers are in the fashion business. At one time, hotels were considered to be boring, functional places with unimaginative décor. However, in recent years hotels and restaurants have engaged with the fashion industry and designers have been allowed to use their flair to create visually striking exteriors and interiors for hospitality product concepts in a wide range of different types of hospitality buildings. Visionary hospitality entrepreneurs, like Ian Schrager and Terence Conran, have championed this design revolution, and global hospitality chains have been influenced by the independents. The 'W' brand, Sheraton's boutique hotel chain, is a chain-hotel response to competition from independent boutique hotels. Table 10.2 provides examples of innovative hospitality design concepts.

Table 10.2 Innovative Design Concepts (Riewoldt, 1998)

Hotels	Examples
Contemporary designer hotels	The Mondrian, Los Angeles, USA, designed by Philip Starck
Art hotels	Art'Otel, Dresden, Germany, designed by Rolf and Jan Rave and Dennis Santachiara
New business hotels	Sheraton Paris Airport Hotel, Roissy, France
New grand hotels	Park Hyatt, Tokyo, Japan, and the Four Seasons Hotel, Istanbul, Turkey
Resort and theme hotels	The Palace of the Lost City, Sun City, South Africa, and Kingfisher Bay Resort and Village, Fraser Island, Australia

Elements of the physical environment

The physical environment for hospitality products comprises external features, the internal design, employees and customers. Table 10.3 provides a summary of the key components of the physical environment.

External

The external environment for hospitality products is the equivalent of a shop window in retailing. The visual display in a shop window sends powerful messages about product and service quality, and price. The shop window reinforces the positioning and brand image. The surrounding environment, the external appearance of the building, landscaping, access routes, car parking facilities, signage and logos, and lighting are the shop window for the hospitality business.

We discussed the surrounding environment in Chapter 6, within the context of site selection criteria, and emphasized that the surrounding area must be compatible with the product concept. When the surrounding environment does match the hospitality product, potential customers will be attracted to the physical environment. However, through no fault of the hospitality operator, the surrounding area can change over time; neighboring properties can be sold, and the new owners might change the use of buildings in a way that changes the character of the area. When the surrounding environment becomes incompatible with the existing hospitality product, then the operator will have to make a strategic decision whether to sell the property or reformulate the product concept.

The external appearance of the hospitality premises – the building, its size, age, architecture and, in particular, the quality of maintenance – sends cues to customers. Attractive, well-maintained properties inspire confidence, but buildings that appear neglected can actually deter potential customers. Effective landscaping can transform the visual appearance of a property. Well-maintained grounds, attractive

Table 10.3 The Physical Environment in Hospitality Premises

External	*Internal*	*Employees*	*Customers*
Surrounding environment	Internal spatial layout	Appearance	Appearance
External appearance of the building	Décor, furnishings and furniture	Dress (uniform)	Dress
Access	Equipment	Attitude	Attitude
Landscaping	Signage and point-of-sale material	Behavior	Behavior
Parking	Temperature and air quality		
Signage and logos	Music		
Lighting	Smell		

lawns and gardens, pretty flower boxes and elegant outdoor swimming pools all contribute towards a positive image of a hospitality property. The availability of sufficient secure car parking, close to the property, is important for all hospitality businesses that depend upon customers traveling by motorcar. Well-maintained attractive signage, including brand logos, and effective external lighting send out positive signals to customers, whilst tired and damaged signage and poor lighting send out negative signals. Investment in the external physical environment can help to attract customers into the premises.

Internal

Whilst the external environment creates the first impression for potential customers, it is the internal environment that is most significant in determining whether customers are going to enjoy consuming the hospitality product. Internal factors include the layout, décor, furniture and furnishings, equipment, internal signage, temperature and air-quality, music and smells, which, combined together, convey the all-important atmosphere of the premises.

The internal layout refers to floor plans of the lobby area, front desk, lifts, bedrooms and bathrooms, restaurant, bar, conference, function and leisure areas. Although an architect is responsible for drawing the room layouts and making sure all the services (electrics, heating, ventilation and air-conditioning, communication systems, water supplies and drainage) comply with local building and safety regulations, it is essential for the hospitality management team to ensure that the layout actually functions effectively to meet the requirements of employees and customers. Numerous new-build hotels and restaurants have design faults caused by inexperienced architects and management who have failed to understand key operational details.

Décor is really a matter of personal taste; but in hospitality it is a crucial ingredient in creating the 'feel' in a property. Décor translates the product concept into a reality, determining the mood and style of the hospitality experience. Creating a décor scheme is a job for a professional interior designer. Every element of the hospitality product that is visible to the customer should be designed professionally. The interior designer ensures that the floor and wall coverings, the curtains and lighting, the seating, beds, desks and tables, and the pictures, bric-à-brac and ornaments deliver a consistent style. For the product concept, décor is another tangible cue.

Equipment, in this context, refers to equipment that customers actually use – for example, the air-conditioning system in the bedroom, or the shower in the bathroom. It also includes equipment which employees use in front of customers. Customers expect equipment to work. Faulty or dirty equipment, especially in the bedrooms and bathroom, is a serious problem for customers and a major source of complaints.

Customers also expect the internal signage to provide clear directions throughout the property. Getting lost in a large hotel complex is embarrassing and frustrating for customers. The quality of the signage is another indicator of image.

We discussed the role of point-of-sale material in Chapter 9. From a physical environment perspective, point-of-sale material should be current, professionally presented and relevant. Unfortunately many hospitality businesses suffer from dated and tired point-of-sale material, which is counterproductive in generating a positive image.

Air quality and temperature in hotels, clubs and restaurants are governed by local responses to climate and cultural conventions. In guest bedrooms, customers need to be able to control air-conditioning and heating systems for themselves. Customers who experience extremes of heat in bedrooms and restaurants, compared to their normal environment, can be very uncomfortable. If the management cannot respond quickly to solve the problem, customers may even check out and find a competitor with a more comfortable temperature.

Background music, live music or no music is another matter of personal taste. However, when designing the hospitality product, music plays a key role in complementing the décor and creating atmosphere in public areas. In particular, bar and restaurants use music to attract target markets and to generate atmosphere.

Smell in hospitality is mainly associated with food and beverage outlets. Attractive cooking smells can stimulate the taste buds and attract customers. Foul bar and cooking smells – the combination of stale beer, cigarettes and fried food sometimes found in bars – are a powerful disincentive to many customers.

The combination of all these internal factors creates an overall atmosphere that should, if properly designed, appeal to the target market. However, if some of the key internal environmental factors fail, or do not fit with, the customer's expectations, then customers can be dissatisfied.

Employees

The appearance, attitude and behavior of employees should complement the positioning, product concept and physical environment. Employees' cleanliness, deportment and dress should reinforce the design theme and send a consistent message to customers. In formal, business-orientated hospitality operations, the staff uniforms reflect the business environment – professional attire in conservative colors and fabrics is the norm. In leisure and themed hospitality concepts, casual uniforms designed as part of the theme or no uniforms are appropriate. Contemporary boutique establishments often have contemporary designer-style dress for the employees' uniforms. Customers need hardly notice employees' dress and behavior, when it matches the brand image and other elements of physical environment. However, if the employee's appearance, attitude and behavior are inconsistent with the design concept, then customers will probably notice the inconsistency because it sends out a mixed message and confuses them.

Customers

We discussed inseparability in Chapter 1. The customers' appearance and behavior when consuming the hospitality product also contribute hugely to the atmosphere in the physical environment. Potential customers see and hear other customers. If what they see and hear conforms with their expectations, then potential customers will feel comfortable. If other customers' dress seems inappropriate and their behavior in terms of language, loudness, politeness and sobriety is inconsistent with the expectations of potential customers, then again an inconsistent message causes confusion. We have already discussed the problems caused by mixing incompatible target markets. In today's social environment, conventions regarding dress and behavior are more informal than for previous generations. This makes it more difficult for hospitality management to control the dress and behavior of customers. A number of exclusive clubs, restaurants and hotels (such as the Ritz, in London) still insist on a dress and behavior code for customers.

Activity 10.2

If you can, visit the two hospitality units that you identified in Activity 10.1. Evaluate the external appearance of the units before entering, and then go into the units and evaluate the internal décor, employees and customers.

- Does the external environment match the internal environment?

- Do you think the physical environment is appropriate for the target markets?

- Does it match your expectations of a fast-food restaurant and a fine dining experience?

Maintenance and refurbishment

In our discussion of the external and internal physical evidence, we referred to the problems caused by damaged furniture, faulty equipment and tired décor. The role of maintenance and refurbishment is to maintain the hospitality product at an acceptable level to ensure customer satisfaction and efficient operation. Unfortunately, the nature of the hospitality business means that both customers and employees accidentally, and occasionally deliberately, cause damage to the property. In particular, bathrooms and toilets suffer from abuse and accidental water damage. The costs of not maintaining a property correctly include (Lawson, 1996):

- The loss of future revenue streams from potentially loyal customers who choose to patronize a competitor with a better-maintained product
- Loss of revenue caused by current customers walking out
- Loss of revenue caused by the inability to sell rooms that are out of operation because of maintenance problems
- Inefficient performance caused by faulty equipment and a loss in employee productivity
- Liability for safety and legal infringements.

Although the responsibility for maintenance and refurbishment is an operational issue, marketing tired brands and tired properties is extremely difficult.

The maintenance and refurbishment life cycle

Effective maintenance should be planned into a new property as part of the design brief. The financial planning of a hospitality business will include a depreciation charge to cover the costs of wear and tear, and this depreciation charge is calculated by estimating the reasonable life expectancy of the décor, fittings, furniture and equipment. The life expectancy will be dependent upon the quality standards of the original décor scheme, and the desired market position. Whilst the depreciation charge is a book-keeping transaction, companies will also provide a maintenance budget of approximately 2–4 percent of sales to cover repairs and redecoration. Older inns and hotels that have been converted from other uses can have difficult and costly maintenance issues. New-build properties should have fewer maintenance problems during the first years of operation.

Maintenance and refurbishment planning can be categorized under four headings (Lawson, 1996):

1 *Preventative maintenance* comprises the regular servicing of equipment, such as elevators, kitchen equipment and air-conditioning plant, to ensure they do not break down.
2 *Breakdown maintenance* includes all the minor damage caused during the normal daily operations of the business.
3 *Corrective maintenance* includes regular redecoration according to a planned schedule; when the hospitality product becomes tired, a major refurbishment program is needed.
4 *Designing out faults* is necessary when design faults emerge during the operation of the facility, and can improve guest comfort, operational efficiency, or both.

The refurbishment of public rooms, bars and restaurants varies according to usage and product concept. A popular venue with a short product life cycle might be refurbished every three years; and an established product might need new carpets and furniture as part of a major refurbishment scheme between every five and ten years. Hotel bedrooms should have a planned life cycle for maintenance as follows (Lawson, 1996):

Décor and fabrics	2–4 years
Carpets and electrics	5–8 years
Furniture	7–10 years
Bathrooms	Renovated or replaced every 10–15 years

The implementation of a refurbishment program can create problems for the hospitality business. Bedrooms and food and beverage outlets need to be closed whilst the work is undertaken, resulting in a loss of sales. Customers can suffer from the noise and mess, and possibly a reduced service level. Seasonal hospitality businesses can carry out routine maintenance and major refurbishment when the property is closed or during the low season. However, managers of properties in prime locations that enjoy high revenue throughout the year have to plan redecoration programs carefully to minimize the disruption to the business. Unfortunately, financial constraints during economic downturns often mean that the maintenance and refurbishment budgets are cut first, when in fact this is an ideal time for investment because there is less likelihood of losing revenue and upsetting customers.

Conclusion

In this chapter we have discussed the importance of the physical environment in attracting customers into the premises and in contributing to the customer experience during the service encounter. Hospitality businesses that continually invest in refurbishment are more likely to enjoy high repeat and recommended sales and nurture customer loyalty. Hospitality businesses that fail to maintain the physical environment of their premises will eventually become tired and have to compete on the basis of lower prices to attract customers; and this will result in lower profitability.

In this chapter, we have explained:

- The science of environmental psychology and customers' response to the physical environment
- How individual behavior, social interaction, customer responses and the characteristics of the physical environment influence customers and employees
- The importance of design in the hospitality servicescape
- The role of servicescape usage, servicespace complexity and aesthetics in designing the physical environment
- The characteristics of the external and internal environments in hospitality units
- The maintenance and refurbishment cycle (preventive maintenance, routine maintenance, corrective maintenance, and designing out faults).

Now check your understanding of this chapter by answering the following questions:

Review questions

1 Discuss environmental psychology and customers' response to the physical environment in a hospitality context
2 Evaluate servicescape usage and servicescape complexity when designing a new hospitality premises for:
   - a self-service concept
   - an interpersonal concept
   - a remote service concept.
3 Why is the physical environment important to a hospitality premises?
4 Discuss the role of maintenance and refurbishment in the life cycle of a bar or restaurant.

References and further reading

Kotler, P., Bowen, J. and Makens, J. (2003). *Marketing for Hospitality and Tourism*, 3rd edn. Prentice Hall.

Lashely, C. (2001). *Employing Human Resource Strategies for Service Excellence.* Butterworth-Heinemann.

Lawson, F. (1996). *Hotels and Resorts: Planning, Design and Refurbishment.* Butterworth-Heinemann.

Lewis, R. C. and Chambers, R. E. (2000). *Marketing Leadership in Hospitality: Foundations and Practice.* John Wiley.

Riewoldt, O. (1998). *Hotel Design.* Lawrence King Publishing.

Zeithaml, V. A. and Bitner, M. J. (2003). *Services Marketing*, 3rd edn. McGraw-Hill.

Chapter 11
Managing service processes

Chapter Objectives

After working through this chapter, you should be able to:

- Understand the importance of managing service processes from a hospitality marketing perspective
- Evaluate dimensions of service quality in a hospitality context
- Identify the principal reasons for service failure
- Use service blueprinting to map a hospitality service process
- Understand why, when and how customers complain about their hospitality experiences
- Explain service recovery strategies for hospitality companies.

Introduction

Although managing the service process is the responsibility of operations management, marketing managers need to understand the principles of service processes. Customer satisfaction is dependent upon the hospitality operation delivering the promise that pre-encounter marketing has communicated. The key marketing role of managing demand is made significantly easier when the service process consistently delivers the experience and quality customers expect. However, when the service process fails to deliver, marketing the hospitality property and the hospitality brand becomes much more difficult.

In this chapter we will discuss the importance of managing service processes effectively, and then introduce the concept of service blueprinting, which is a customer-focused tool for specifying service standards, and the SERVQUAL 'gaps' model of service quality. We will also review the crucial role of service recovery when a customer complains about the service received.

The importance of managing service processes

In Chapter 1 we discussed the special characteristics of services (SIPIVISH) that present challenges in marketing the hospitality business and managing the service process. To recap, some of the key issues include:

- Intangibility – since the hospitality product is intangible, customers cannot be certain about the quality of the service they will receive until it has been consumed.
- Inseparability – in virtually all hospitality services, customers are present whilst the product is produced. More importantly, customers are themselves an essential component of the product and the physical environment. Customers are therefore part of the product/service, and help to shape the experience of other customers.
- Seasonality – all hospitality services have busy and quiet periods. The service process can be stressed, and fail, during extreme periods of demand. When the operation has too many customers, the service process can fail to cope with the demand, resulting in customer dissatisfaction. When the operation has too few customers, a vital ingredient of the hospitality product – atmosphere – can be missing, resulting in customer disappointment.
- Variability – the intangibility, inseparability and seasonality contribute to the variability that customers experience when consuming the hospitality product. Variability – the lack of standardization in service outputs – is endemic in hospitality services; it confuses customers and creates uncertainty.

A crucial issue for hospitality businesses is to try and deliver a consistent service quality through managing service process effectively. The culmination of these factors presents challenges for hospitality service operations.

Understanding processes

Processes can be classified in a number of ways that help you to understand their importance from a customer perspective: vertical and horizontal; front-office and back-office; primary and secondary.

- *Vertical processes* are those that are located entirely within a function or department. For example, the food production process resides totally within the operations department. *Horizontal processes* are cross-functional. The new service development process might involve sales, marketing, operations and general management.
- *Front-office processes* are those that customers encounter. The check-in/check-out and complaints management processes are examples. Back-office processes are hidden from customers, as in, for example, the procurement process. Some processes straddle both front and back offices.
- A distinction can be made between primary and secondary processes. *Primary processes* have major cost or revenue implications for companies. For example, the human resource management process in hospitality companies contributes significantly to the cost base of the business. *Secondary processes* have minor cost or revenue implications. Customers may also have a different perspective on what is important: they typically do not care about back-office processes, but about the processes they touch. In hospitality, these include the reservation process, the processes encountered during the meal experience, and the billing process.

It is important to identify the important processes from a customer perspective, and design these processes so that they contribute to customer satisfaction and customer retention. It is not just front-office processes that have an impact on customer experience; the same is true of back-office processes. If procurement people do not know the quality requirements of the marketing offer to customers, they may source inputs of too high or too low a quality. Similarly, if operations people are not aware of the quality expectations of customers, they may create service encounters that are unacceptable. Clearly a major concern for hospitality marketers is that front-office and back-office processes should work together to create service experiences that meet or exceed customers' expectations, especially in terms of quality.

Case study 11.1 illustrates an unusual way of making the service process transparent to customers in a luxury restaurant.

Case study

11.1 A table for two in the kitchen!

Whilst many hospitality managers are nervous about customers seeing what goes on behind the scenes – and especially what goes on in the kitchens – one of England's most innovative hoteliers, Eric Marsh, actually encourages customers to dine in the kitchen! Since a 1980 refit, there has been a table for two customers in a corner of the main kitchen at the Cavendish Hotel. Eric believes that if customers want to see the back of house operation, they can.

Originally the chefs were apprehensive at the thought of customers watching every aspect of the food production process in an award-winning hotel restaurant, whilst the customers, who still dressed up for dinner, were not quite sure what to expect. However, the truth is that the chefs enjoy the opportunity to perform, and the customers enjoy the excitement of watching the fine cuisine being cooked along with the frisson at the service encounter when the kitchen is busy. Today the table is booked a couple of times each week. This novel approach sends a powerful signal to customers about the high quality of the kitchen management service processes at the Cavendish. It has also generated an enormous amount of media publicity, and is an interesting example of tangibilizing the intangible.

Service quality

People can view service quality from a variety of different perspectives, according to the context of the situation.

- Transcendental quality implies innate excellence, which consumers know or sense but cannot always define. It is normally associated with artistic experiences of the highest quality; in hospitality, when the service experience exceeds the consumers' highest expectations, it is a perfect occasion. Since transcendental quality is an ephemeral concept, it cannot be measured and is difficult to incorporate into service quality specifications.
- Production- (or operations-) based quality focuses on delivering service quality standards as defined in the Standard Operating Procedure manuals typical of chain hotel organizations. Operational quality is regarded as high when service outputs comply with the defined service standards. However, a production focus can sacrifice crucial customer needs and wants in the goal to be more efficient.
- Product-based quality views quality from an objective and measurable perspective. It takes a narrow product-based focus. For example, fillet steak is assumed to be better quality than sirloin, according to technical product specifications. Because product-based quality fails to consider additional perspectives (for example, the customer's), it is not helpful to the marketer.
- User-based quality does take a consumer perspective, and in particular recognizes that different consumers will have different approaches to evaluating service quality standards.
- Value-based quality takes the customer's perspective, and recognizes the relationship between quality, price and value.

A budget hotel can deliver poor value for money if the perceived quality is below expectations for the price charged, while a luxury hotel can deliver excellent value for money if the perceived quality is above expectations for the price charged.

Dimensions of service quality

Delivering service quality has become a topic of major importance for both academia and industry. Measuring service quality is complicated, because service performance

Table 11.1 The Five Dimensions of Service (Source: Parasuraman *et al.*, 1985, reproduced by kind permission of the American Marketing Association)

Dimension	Definition
Reliability	The ability to perform the promised service dependably and accurately
Empathy	The caring, individual attention given to the customer
Tangibles	The appearance of physical facilities, equipment, employees and communication materials
Responsiveness	The willingness to help customers and provide prompt service
Assurance	The knowledge and courtesy employees, and their ability to convey confidence and inspire trust

is not easily defined. Consumers judge service quality on many different factors, and their own disposition can significantly influence their evaluation of the service process. Parasuraman *et al.* (1985) suggested that customers evaluate service quality across five dimensions: reliability, empathy, tangibles, responsiveness and assurance (see Table 11.1).

Reliability

Pre-encounter marketing makes a promise to the customer, and customers therefore expect the hospitality business to deliver on the promise. Customers expect the product, service quality and price to match the promise. When companies deliver on the promise, they are considered to be reliable; when they do not, consumers consider them unreliable. Sometimes promises are specific to individual customers; sometimes they are segment-specific.

Empathy

In this context, empathy means treating customers as individuals and providing them with personalized service. Companies that are able to make customers feel important score highly on service quality. In hospitality, a smaller, independent operator can generally empathize with a customer more easily than a branded chain operation.

Tangibles

In Chapter 10 we discussed the physical environment and its impact on customers. Tangibles represent the physical environment in this model of service quality.

Responsiveness

Responsiveness refers to how efficiently companies respond to customers. During the hospitality service process customers will naturally ask lots of questions (how is the dish on a menu prepared? where are the washrooms? what time is check-out?), perhaps mention minor problems, and possibly even complain. How the service process system (and in particular the customer-contact employees) demonstrates willingness to help customers influences the customer's perception of service quality.

Assurance

This dimension refers to employees' courtesy and product knowledge. In hospitality, customers expect the employees to be polite and to know what job they are meant to be doing. When employees are polite and knowledgeable, customers have more confidence that the company can deliver its marketing promise. Assurance is all about employees inspiring customers to trust the company. Of course when employees are rude customers are offended, and when the employees clearly do not know how to deliver the hospitality service, customers understandably lose confidence in the company's ability to deliver.

Although this approach has been criticized for having either too few or too many service dimensions, consumers clearly judge service quality using a variety of process criteria as well as outcomes criteria. Process criteria are concerned with *how* a service is delivered; outcome criteria are concerned with *what* is delivered. For example, a meal that is exquisitely prepared and badly served would be high on outcome and low on process quality.

The 'gaps' model of service quality

Parasuraman *et al.* (1992) also proposed an integrated model of service quality that explains why companies can fail to deliver the service customers expect. The model identifies four 'gaps', which are the principal reasons for service failure.

Gap 1: Management not knowing what customers expect

Hospitality managers often think they know what customers want, and develop the marketing offer on the basis of their own interpretation of customer service expectations. For example, some independent hoteliers have aspirations for their restaurant operations that are considerably higher than the needs and wants of their customers. Poor (or no) marketing research into customer expectations can cause this misunderstanding. Effective marketing research, which should include both customer and employee perspectives, will identify the service expectations of the target market. When managers actually know what customers expect, they can then start to formulate an appropriate offer to match customer expectations.

Gap 2: Service quality standards do not match customer expectations

Assuming that management actually understands customer expectations, the second service gap focuses on the design of the service quality process. The design of service quality standards should match the customers' expectations; however, less professional hospitality companies do not set formal service standards, and can have ambiguous, reactive approaches to service systems design. More professional hospitality companies can create formal service specifications that have been developed from an operations perspective, and fail to take into account the customers' perspective. Sometimes the service system becomes internalized, and customer focus can be lost. Management needs to think creatively to overcome these service design problems and ensure that service quality matches customer expectations.

Gap 3: Service-performance gap

Even when management has designed an effective service process system that is capable of delivering an offer that matches customer expectations, the actual service delivery can still fail. This type of service failure can be attributed to the human resource function in the hospitality business (poor recruitment, poor training, and poor reward policies); technology problems (reservation system down, faulty TV); the special characteristics of services (SIPIVISH); and the customer's own mood. The role of customer-contact employees in delivering a quality service is discussed in Chapter 12.

Gap 4: Delivering the service promise

Gap 4 is the gap between what the service system (both people and technology) delivers, and the promises made in advertising, PR and sales communications to customers. In Chapter 9 we discussed the importance of pitching promotional messages appropriately. If the hospitality marketer makes undeliverable promises, the customer will be disappointed. From a customer's perspective, it is crucial for the company and employees to keep promises. This includes customer-contact employees during the service encounter, who in their many dealings with customers inevitably make promises. Breaking a promise to a customer leads to customer disappointment.

Closing the gaps

When gaps 1–4 are closed, the company will be promising and producing service experiences that are based on meeting clearly understood customer expectations. Service quality gaps can be a major cause of customer dissatisfaction. Hospitality managers who want to close the service quality gaps and improve customer satisfaction need to analyze the actual service delivery against customer expectations for each gap.

Service blueprinting

A key concern is to design the service processes that deliver the desired quality performance. Shostack (1981) developed a pictorial method for designing service processes, called service blueprinting, which helps to analyze the performance of the service process. Borrowing flowcharting techniques from manufacturing industries, a service blueprint is a map that provides a specification of how a service is (or should be) delivered.

In hospitality new-product development, a service blueprint is used to establish all the various elements involved during the customer's visits to the premises whilst consuming the hospitality product. From the moment the customer arrives to the moment he or she leaves, all the actions that the customer and/or employees carry out are mapped on a diagram (see Figure 11.1). The actions are listed under the following headings:

Physical evidence	Represents the facilities and equipment used in delivering the service
Customer	All the activities/actions taken by the customer.
Contact employees	Visible front of house employee actions and invisible front of house employee actions
Support processes	The back-of-house service support systems that help the front-of-house employees deliver the service

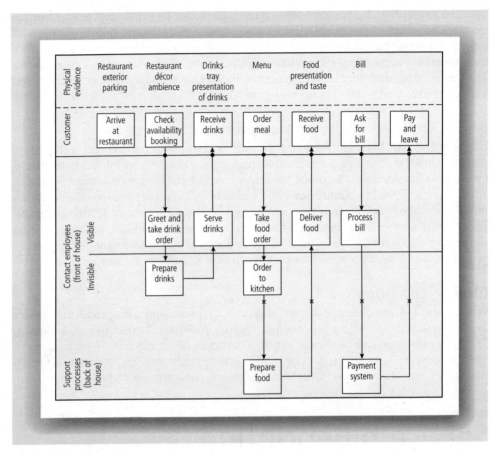

Figure 11.1 Mapping a restaurant service, customer service encounter; x internal service encounter

The service blueprint map has three horizontal lines, which separate the various types of activities. The first horizontal line divides customers and front-of-house employees, and is called the *line of interaction*. Where a vertical line crosses this horizontal line (for example, when the customer checks a restaurant booking with the greeter), then a service encounter between the customer and a front-of-house employee has taken place.

The second horizontal line is called the *line of visibility*; this separates those front-of-house employee activities that the customer can see from those that can't be seen. For example, the restaurant order-taker walks out of the customer's sight and into the kitchen with the order. In the kitchen, the front-of-house employees are invisible to the customer.

The third horizontal line is called the *line of internal interaction*. Where the vertical line crosses the line of internal interaction, these are internal service encounters.

By actually mapping the service process from a customer's perspective, management can strive to match service performance to the customers' expectations. Indeed, the crucial point about a service blueprint map is that although the service process is analyzed from the customer's perspective, both the employees' role and the service process can be evaluated at the same time. If you study Figure 11.1 and read this simplified version of a blueprint map from left to right, you follow the service delivery from the customer's perspective. To look at the service from the customer-contact employees' perspective, read the horizontal lines above and below the line of visibility. In this way, the front-of-house employees' role can be evaluated and employees' job descriptions can be devised. The blueprint can also be used in training to show employees how their role links to other employees and functions in the organization. To review key elements of the overall service process, the blueprint map can be analyzed vertically. For example, the efficiency of the kitchen (back-of-house) service system is crucial in delivering a quality restaurant service. By critically examining the service encounters at the line of internal interaction, potential fail-points or bottlenecks in the system can be identified and eliminated. Sometimes the fault can be attributed to kitchen production problems, and sometimes the fault is the front-of-house service staff efficiency. The blueprint map enables management to understand why the failure or bottleneck has occurred, which helps with establishing strategies to correct the problem.

A blueprint map can also be used to redesign an existing service. The first step is to map the current service process, and the second stage is to establish the desired service performance. The next stage involves comparing what actually happens with what the company wants to deliver, and identifying discrepancies. Finally, a solution will be proposed and mapped out on a new blueprint.

The benefits of blueprints can be summarized as follows (Gummesson and Kingman-Brundage, 1991):

- Service process weaknesses are identified and can be the focus of improvement schemes
- The interdepartmental linkages are made transparent
- They help employees to understand their own role within the entire service process
- They help to facilitate internal marketing.

Complexity and divergence in hospitality services

The service process can also be defined in terms of its complexity and its diversity (Zeithaml and Bitner, 2003). The level of service complexity refers to the number of steps and sequences that need to be carried out to perform the service – the fewer steps, the lower the service complexity. A person working on a hotdog stand has a very small number of actions to perform to serve a hot dog, so a hotdog stand has a lower level of complexity. Conversely, a full-service hotel has a very large number of activities and processes involved in catering for many different customers, and therefore has a higher level of complexity.

The level of diversity refers to the degree of tolerance allowed in delivering the service process. Some service processes are highly standardized and consequently have a very low degree of diversity; the service process for making a hot dog has a lower degree of diversity because it is a relatively standardized process. Some services can be considered as unique performances because of the artistic skills required to deliver the service; for example, live entertainment in pubs and restaurants, where each time the musicians perform, is a unique event. This type of service process has a higher degree of diversity.

Every service process can be analyzed on both its level of complexity and its level of divergency. Figure 11.2 provides an example of a customer using a hotdog stand, a full-service hotel, live entertainment and a gourmet restaurant. A gourmet restaurant has a complex service process because of the wide range of ingredients

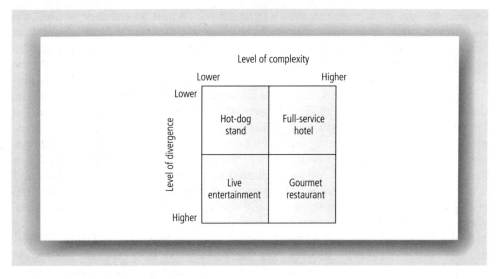

Figure 11.2 Complexity and divergence in hospitality services (source: adapted from Zeithaml and Bitner, 2003)

and cooking skills required to produce a gourmet meal. There is also a higher degree of divergence, as each meal created can be considered an individual performance by highly skilled chefs.

Service process strategies

By mapping the service process using blueprinting, a company can establish the levels of complexity and divergence in its service operations. The service process can be changed either to increase or decrease the levels of complexity and divergence. There are four alternative strategies:

1 *Complexity reduction strategy.* To reduce the complexity of a service process, the number of steps and sequences used to produce the service are reduced. This might mean specializing in specific customer segments and narrowing the marketing offer. The reduction in complexity should improve consistency and cost control. However, such a strategy risks alienating customers who enjoyed the service standards of a more complex operation, and they might transfer their loyalty and patronage to a competitive establishment.
2 *Increased complexity strategy.* Increasing the complexity of the service process means adding more activities to the existing service and providing customers with an enhanced marketing offer. By providing customers with additional services, the company should be able to generate additional revenue and/or enhance customer satisfaction. However, increased complexity might create service quality problems and increase costs, and some customers may not be interested in paying more for the new offer. McDonald's has recently introduced a raft of new products, making the offer much more complex and introducing a level of operational complexity that franchisees have found challenging.
3 *Divergence reduction strategy.* Reducing the level of divergence in the service process implies a greater standardization of the services. With a higher level of standardization, there should be increased productivity and cost reductions

through economies of scale. This type of service process strategy is linked to a volume orientation and mass-marketing approach. From a customer perspective, the advantages include greater consistency and reliability in the service quality. However, some customers may resent the changes and react negatively to the standardized service offer.

4 *Increased divergence strategy*. Increasing divergence allows for greater customization in the service offer. This is a niche positioning strategy, which in hospitality could be linked to a human resource empowerment strategy where employees are encouraged to respond to customers' individual needs and wants. However, increasing divergence can mean less control and could be linked to greater fluctuations in service quality. A customization strategy implies higher prices to cover the additional costs of an increased divergence strategy.

Reasons for service failure

Service failures occur when the service provided does not match the customer's expectation of the service promised in the pre-encounter marketing mix. Typical hospitality service failures include the following:

- Facilities and services that have been promoted in Marcom collateral are not available
- The physical environment is disappointing (damaged furniture, tired décor, poor hygiene standards, inappropriate music, atmosphere not welcoming)
- The service is slower than expected
- The standard of cooking is poor (overcooked/undercooked food, too much/too little seasoning, food served at the wrong temperature)
- Employees who do not care or, even worse, are rude to customers.

Obviously some service failures are relatively minor for the customer, whilst others are very important. Dissatisfied customers, with serious complaints, can litigate against hospitality companies. The characteristics of the product, the type of occasion, the price charged, the nature and seriousness of complaints, and the personality of the customer all influence how customers complain. Consumers have been categorized into passives, voicers, irates, activists and terrorists, depending upon their propensity to complain (Singh, 1990).

Passives
Not all customers complain about the service, even when they have justifiable reasons for doing so. Some customers believe that it is simply not worth the trouble to complain, and that perhaps the employees (and the company) do not really care about their service problems. Other customers do not know how to complain; this can be a problem for international visitors, who might not be familiar with the cultural norms when traveling in a foreign country. Passive customers are unlikely to tell others about their experience.

Voicers
Unlike passive people, some consumers believe that actually complaining is a positive action for both the customer and the company. They think that complaining helps

the company to improve its service, and they give the company the opportunity to recover from the service failure. Voicers can develop a positive attitude to the company, if it responds appropriately to the complaint.

Irates

Irate customers will tell their friends and relatives about the service failure and spread negative word-of-mouth. They may have complained to the company, but not necessarily. They are likely to switch to a competitor.

Activists

Some people like to complain, and even enjoy the confrontation either with service employees at the time of the incident, or later by correspondence. Activists are more likely to complain to third parties, and they may become unreasonable in their demands for compensation. They are vociferous, telling as many people as they can about their poor treatment.

Terrorists

A tiny minority of customers who complain can become obsessed with what they believe to be the company's inadequate response to their complaint. These alienated individuals publicize the service company's failings in newspaper advertisements. They encourage other unhappy customers to complain, and by generating considerable amounts of negative publicity in the media, can damage the company significantly. Companies like McDonald's and Starbucks have suffered from this type of publicity. Today the Internet provides low-cost opportunities for terrorist customers to set up anti-company websites to publicize their complaints to others.

Activity 11.1 Starbucks and the coffee terrorist

Read the following account of an incident, and then answer the question.

A customer bought a defective cappuccino-maker from Starbucks and, whilst returning to obtain a replacement, decided to buy another one as a gift for a friend. During the second service encounter, the customer claimed that the employee was rude and forgot to give him half-a-pound of free coffee, which he was promised. Then the cappuccino-maker that was purchased as a present for a friend also turned out to be faulty.

The customer demanded that Starbucks replace the gift with the most expensive cappuccino-maker, which costs $2000 more than the original. Although the customer threatened to publicize his complaint, Starbucks refused his request – so the customer took out a full-page advert in the *Wall Street Journal* explaining his complaint and encouraging other customers also to complain. The media took up the story, which generated a huge amount of negative publicity for Starbucks.

● What should the company have done to avoid this minor incident becoming a major public relations disaster?

(source: Zeithaml and Bitner, 2003, p. 192)

When and how customers complain

Customers can complain to the company and third parties using a variety of approaches.

Concurrently

When a customer complains at the same time as the service failure occurs, this allows the customer-contact employees to respond and attempt to rectify the problem. From both the company's and the customer's perspective, this is the most opportune moment to solve the service failure. It allows the customer to explain the nature of the complaint in more detail. In hospitality services, this can include customers pointing out the defects in the quality of food, or the lack of cleanliness in a bathroom. It also allows management and the customer-contact employees the opportunity to apologize to the customer immediately and to take appropriate corrective action. If the remedial action works the customer's initial disappointment can be turned into a positive incident, and customer loyalty can even be enhanced.

Subsequently

Customers can telephone, email, text or write letters of complaint. With the passage of time, even a few days, a customer can feel more strongly about the service failure. The details of the critical incidents can be magnified, especially if the complainer enjoys embellishing the description of the events. However, since the customer has contacted the company and provided details of the complaint, there is still the opportunity for the company to retrieve the situation and win back the customer.

Third-party complaints

Finally, the unhappy customer can contact other organizations, typically consumer affairs bodies or legal entities. Local or national governments, consumer protection bodies, tourist boards, motoring organizations, hotel and restaurant guide books all respond to customers' complaints by discussing the problems with the management of the hospitality business concerned. Normally a hospitality company will agree a course of action with the third party, and respond to the complaint satisfactorily.

Unhappy customers can also record the evidence of their dissatisfaction by taking photographs, or filming the situation on a camcorder. In extreme cases the customers can give the evidence to the media, which ensures extensive negative publicity about the complaint for the company. There are also examples of customers suing hospitality companies for damages caused by unsatisfactory service. This type of negative publicity is extremely damaging to the business' reputation, and could even lead to a collapse in customer confidence, with disastrous consequences for the company (see Case study 11.2).

Case study

11.2 Restaurant failure due to negative publicity and word-of-mouth

An Oxford restaurant, the Gousse d'Ail, went into receivership, and the owner blamed the bad publicity from a food critic's negative review (Gill, 2001). Jonathan Wright bought a popular restaurant called The Lemon Tree, invested in a major refurbishment program, and turned it into a quality French-style operation. Bookings were slow during the opening phase, partly because of the high prices and partly because of the location. However, when a highly critical article in the *Sunday Times* by a well-known food critic, A. A. Gill, received a lot of local comment, fewer and fewer customers patronized the restaurant. The poor reputation spread, and a few months later the business collapsed.

Negative word-of-mouth

Unfortunately there will always be customers who do not enjoy the service and who will not communicate their dissatisfaction to the hospitality company. This means that the company does not have the opportunity to apologize and is not able to respond to the problem. These customers tell their family, friends and acquaintances about the 'poor' service; and create a difficult situation because of the power of negative word-of-mouth criticisms. Hospitality companies do not normally know who spreads negative gossip, and are not really able to respond.

Service recovery strategies

Given the inevitability of service failure, all hospitality companies should have a service recovery strategy. The more professional companies are acutely aware of the importance of handling customer complaints effectively, and have procedures that are included in employees' training programs. Service recovery strategies include the following.

The zero defects strategy (or do it right first time)

The concept of zero defects is borrowed from manufacturing, and is linked to Total Quality Management (TQM). The key principle is to design out every potential problem before it can occur. The special characteristics of services make the adoption of a zero defects strategy difficult to implement for a hospitality company; but the idea of TQM is to create a service culture within the company of 'doing it right first time'. By working to reduce operational service failures, perhaps by service blueprinting, companies can reduce the incidence of customer complaints.

Encourage complaints!!!

This might at first sound strange; but if a company can improve customer service by learning effectively from a complaint, then encouraging customers to complain can improve sales and service quality. Many hospitality companies provide customer comment cards and questionnaires to encourage customer feedback. This helps those customers who want to make comments. Unfortunately, most companies do not respond to the critical comments from customer feedback and lose the opportunity to create a positive dialogue with the unhappy customer. Responsive companies write and thank customers for their observations, and respond appropriately to the comments; such a response can turn a critical customer into a potentially loyal customer. Unfortunately, negative comment cards and questionnaires can be deliberately 'lost' by employees who do not want to be disciplined if they are responsible for the customer complaint. A key issue regarding encouraging customers to complain concerns unit managers who do not want to be seen as having a poor complaints record, even though a positive attitude to encouraging complaints could mean that their unit is actually providing a better service than units with a lower level of complaints.

Treat customers fairly

Customers have a sense of 'fairness'. Following their complaint, customers look for three types of fairness from the company (Tax and Brown, 1998):

1 *Outcome fairness* refers to the tangible result the customer expects to receive after a complaint. Hospitality companies use a range of compensation options when customers complain, including apologies, replacing a menu item, providing a complimentary drink, providing a room upgrade, reducing charges or offering complimentary accommodation/meals, depending upon the type of complaint. Most customers expect fair compensation in respect of the magnitude of the complaint. If the outcome is 'fair', the customer at least feels that the company took the complaint seriously. However, when companies refuse to offer compensation, or the compensation offered is regarded as 'unfair', then the unhappy customer will be disappointed or even angry.
2 *Procedural fairness* refers to the company's policy and procedures for handling complaints. When a problem arises, customers ideally want the first employee they talk to to be able to sort out the problem or find someone who can. Procedural fairness links to the company's policy and processes on responding quickly and efficiently to the complaint. Customer-contact employees and front-of-house management need to find out what the customer's problem is, apologize, and take prompt, courteous and efficient action to provide a solution. This can significantly reduce or eradicate the complaint during the moment of truth.
3 *Interactional fairness* refers to customers expecting employees and management to treat them politely and honestly. Customers want companies genuinely to care about their problem. This might seem to be commonsense, but some hospitality companies do not provide training in customer care and do not allow front-line employees to take decisions. Some employees lie to customers and to management, and do not take customer complaints seriously. When customers feel they are unfairly treated because of the response from the customer-contact employees, they are more likely to defect to competitors.

Learning from customer complaints

Analysis of the pattern of customer complaints provides important clues to sources of service failure. If customers consistently complain about a certain problem, then management can develop solutions to the problem, reduce customer complaints and improve customer satisfaction. By using customer complaint data, the service process and marketing offer can be much improved.

The recovery paradox

It has been shown that customers who experience a service failure, complain, and then are extremely satisfied by the response from the company, can become even more loyal than customers who have enjoyed good service and not had cause for complaint. The recovery paradox demonstrates that an effective service recovery strategy can redeem a potentially disastrous situation, and turn customers with complaints into loyal customers. Excellent service recovery demonstrates two dimensions of service quality – empathy and responsiveness – that are less visible when service is delivered right first time.

Professional complainers

Hospitality companies are aware that some customers like to complain about the service in the hope of obtaining compensation. Companies like Hampton Inns record the details of customers who complain on dubious grounds in the CRS database. If these customers want to book again, they are informed at the time of booking that any complaints may not receive compensation. Tour operators that normally compete will sometimes share data on customers who are serial complainers.

Conclusion

Designing the service process to deliver what customers expect from the hospitality offer is a crucial component of encounter marketing. Companies need to develop a deep understanding of customer expectations to ensure that the service process delivers satisfaction. However, in the hospitality business there will always be some customers who complain, so companies must have a service recovery strategy to respond to complaints. Indeed, managing complaints effectively can turn dissatisfied customers into very loyal customers.

In this chapter, we have explained:

- How processes can be categorized as vertical or horizontal, front-office or back-office, and primary or secondary
- The importance of managing service processes to deliver customer satisfaction
- The five dimensions of service quality – reliability, empathy, tangibles, responsiveness and assurance
- The gaps model of service quality, which can explain the gap between customer expectations and customer perceptions of service quality after the service performance
- How to map a hospitality service using blueprinting
- The complexity and divergence in service process strategies
- The reasons for service failure in a hospitality context

- The characteristics of customers who complain – passives, voicers, irates, activists and terrorists
- When and how customers complain
- The role of service recovery strategies
- The importance of auditing service process strategies to ensure conformance to brand standards.

Now check your understanding by answering the following questions:

Review questions

1 Discuss the role of service process management in hospitality from a marketing perspective
2 Evaluate the gaps model of service quality, using examples from the hospitality industry
3 Map a hospitality service process that you know either as an employee or as a customer, evaluate the service from the view of a customer, and make recommendations to improve service quality
4 Discuss the reasons for service failure in the hospitality business, and suggest what companies should do when a customer complains.

References and further reading

Gill, A. A. (2001). Restaurant review, *Sunday Times*, 5 August.

Gummesson, E. and Kingman-Brundage, J. (1991). Service design and quality: applying service blueprinting and service mapping to railroad services. In P. Kunst and J. Lemmink (eds), *Quality Management in Services*. Van Gorcum.

Parasuraman, A., Zeithaml, V. and Berry, L. L. (1985). A conceptual model of service quality and its implications for future research. *Journal of Marketing*, **49**, 41–50.

Parasuraman, A., Zeithaml, V. and Berry, L. L. (1992). Achieving service quality through gap analysis and a basic statistical approach. *Journal of Services Marketing*, **6(1)**, 5–14.

Shostack, L. (1981). Service positioning through structural change. *Journal of Marketing*, **51**, 34–43.

Singh, J. (1990). A typology of consumer dissatisfaction response styles. *Journal of Retailing*, **66(1)**, 57–99.

Tax, S. S. and Brown, S. W. (1998). Recovering and learning from service failure. *Sloan Management Review*, **40**, 61–75.

Zeithaml, V. A. and Bitner, M. J. (2003). *Services Marketing*. McGraw-Hill.

Chapter 12

Managing customer-contact employees

Chapter Objectives

After working through this chapter, you should be able to:

■ Understand the importance of customer-contact employees in creating the customer experience

■ Identify the sources of conflict for hospitality customer-contact employees

■ Evaluate service-orientated culture in hospitality companies

■ Understand the concept of internal marketing and empowerment in a hospitality context.

Introduction

A defining characteristic of service industries is the crucial role played by employees during the service encounter with customers. It is the behavior of customer-contact employees that creates impressions of high service quality. Furthermore, they are the personification of the brand – a key role in the competitive markets of the hospitality industry. Although recruiting, training and rewarding employees is a human resource management function, marketers need to understand employment strategies to ensure that the brand values and standards are delivered. At the same time, the human resource managers have increasingly adopted marketing strategies in their approach to the labor market. This type of human resource management strategy is called internal marketing.

In this chapter we will discuss the links between the physical environment, the service process and employees in delivering service quality during the hospitality encounter. We will then examine service encounters, the service culture and internal marketing in hospitality organizations.

The importance of customer-contact employees

In Chapters 10 and 11 we repeatedly referred to the key role of employees in delivering service quality. Considerable research has been undertaken in this area, which demonstrates the influence of employees on service quality and customer satisfaction. At the simplest level, W. J. Marriott (Snr)'s famous quotation accurately summarizes the importance of employees – 'it takes happy employees to make happy customers and this results in a good bottom line' (Lashley, 2001). At a more complex level, it is the customer-contact employees who deliver on most aspects of the five dimensions of service quality: reliability, empathy, tangibles (partly), responsiveness and assurance.

The service profit chain (Heskett *et al.*, 1994) is a model that demonstrates the link between employee satisfaction, service quality, customer satisfaction and business performance. When employees are satisfied with their work environment, they are more likely to work productively for the company. These employees know the company's service quality standards, and should therefore be capable of meeting the quality standards that the company and customer expect. Customer satisfaction leads to repeat and recommended sales. The customers like to see familiar faces when they return; and when the same employees greet regular customers by name this helps in the development of loyalty. Loyal customers are more profitable, so the business can increase sales and profits.

If employees are not satisfied in their work environment, the business can suffer from a cycle of poor employee retention, staff shortages, and employees with limited company experience and product/service knowledge who deliver service quality below the customers' expectations. Customers are less likely to return, and if they do return they are unlikely to be recognized. With fluctuating service standards and little continuity of customer-contact employees, the opportunity to develop closer customer relationships is lost, the business does not generate sufficient repeat and recommended sales, and profits can decline.

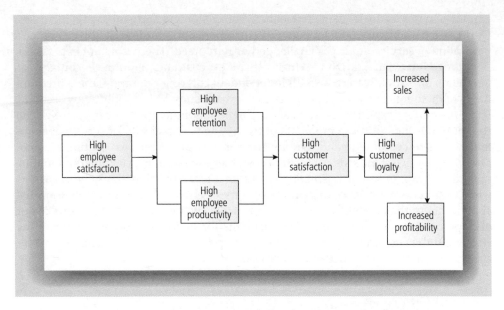

Figure 12.1 The service profit chain (adapted from Heskett *et al.*, 1994)

The service profit chain (Figure 12.1) demonstrates the links between employee satisfaction and customer satisfaction. However, this relationship is complex, and there is no simple causal link. For example, some long service employees may fall into a pattern of poor customer service, especially in a hospitality unit that has changed ownership or management several times. Employees can become cynical and bored with their work environment, leading to indifferent service attitudes and lower standards of service.

Service encounters

There is a wide variety of different types of hospitality service contexts, ranging from low customer-contact services to high customer-contact services (see Figure 12.2 for an example of food service concepts). The importance of customer-contact

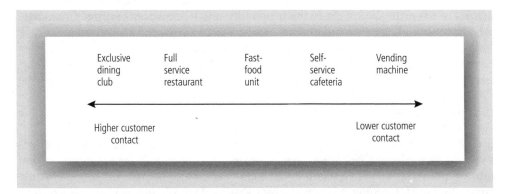

Figure 12.2 Higher and lower customer-contact service contexts – an example from food service

employees rises as the level of contact between customers and employees increases. During each and every contact between customers and employees, the customer's perception of service quality is challenged or reinforced. There is an apt expression, popularized by Jan Carlzon, which describes customer/employee contacts as 'moments of truth'. Even in a small independent catering operation, there are hundreds of moments of truth. These moments of truth may last for only a few seconds. Some hospitality experiences, such as staying in a holiday hotel for two weeks, can contain thousands of these moments of truth. The vast majority of service encounters between customers and employees can be described as routinized and, providing service standards conform to customer expectations, customers should be satisfied. However, in all hospitality operations there will inevitably be occasions when customers experience disappointing service encounters. Many are minor disappointments that do not adversely impact on customer satisfaction, but major disappointments can become critical incidents for hospitality organizations. How effectively the customer-contact employees respond to critical incidents will influence the customer's intention to repurchase.

Critical incidents

When a critical incident occurs, the response and actions of customer-contact employees can either save the situation or turn the incident into a significant source of customer dissatisfaction (Bitner *et al.*, 1990). Research suggests that there are three broad categories of critical incidents in service contexts:

1 The employees' responsiveness to service delivery system failures
2 The employees' responses to customer needs and requests
3 Unprompted and unsolicited employee actions.

Table 12.1 summarizes employees' responses to customer issues, which can result in either customer satisfaction or dissatisfaction.

Customers want service failure problems solved quickly and politely. If the customer-contact employees apologize and provide a satisfactory solution to the problem at the time of the incident, then customers are more likely to forgive the company. If the customer-contact employee fails to apologize or is unable (or even unwilling) to help, then the incident can become a source of a serious complaint.

Inevitably, some customers will have special needs and make special requests that are out of the ordinary sphere of the hospitality unit's operational norms. Customers who have special dietary requirements or who want to arrange a special event will ask for help and advice. By definition these requests are unusual; indeed, they may even be contrary to the company's Standard Operating Procedures. How customer-contact employees respond to these situations sends signals to customers. If employees can be flexible and have the confidence to adapt the service to the needs of the customer, then customers are likely to be highly satisfied. If, however, employees appear inflexible and are unhelpful, this can be a source of customer dissatisfaction.

Customer-contact employees can sometimes give customers delightful surprises by their unexpected behavior, which exceeds customers' expectations. These unprompted and unsolicited employee actions are major sources of customer satisfaction. However, employees who demonstrate a lack of courtesy or use bad language in front of customers can be responsible for major customer dissatisfaction.

Table 12.1 Positive and Negative Responses to Critical Incidents (Source: Lashley, 2000)

Critical incident	Customer satisfaction	Customer dissatisfaction
Employee response to service delivery failure	Could be turned into incidents that employees use to advantage and generate customer satisfaction: an employee reacts quickly to service failure by responding sensitively to customers – by compensating the customer or upgrading the customer to a higher status service	More frequently, however, staff responses are likely to be a source of dissatisfaction – where an employee fails to provide an apology or an explanation, or argues with the customer
Employee response to customer needs and requests	Employee responsiveness, flexibility, and confidence that he or she can match whatever is required by the customer are important sources of positive customer responses	Employee intransigence, inflexibility and perceived incompetence are all likely sources of customer dissatisfaction
Unprompted and unsolicited employee action	This might involve employee behaviors that made the customer feel special, or where an act of unexpected generosity takes the customer by surprise	Customer dissatisfaction could be the result of a failure to give the level of attention expected or inadequate information, or might involve inappropriate behavior, such as the use of bad language

Of course, unreasonable customers, who can be aggressive, insulting and even threatening, sometimes confront customer-contact employees, especially when customers are inebriated. Good employers do not tolerate bad customer behavior, and airlines like British Airways have a 'zero tolerance policy' to protect cabin crew from abusive customers.

Sources of conflict

Customer-contact employees are confronted by both interpersonal and interorganizational conflicts whilst working for hospitality organizations (Lashley, 2000). Conflict at work can be a source and a symptom of employee dissatisfaction. Continuous excessive conflict creates powerful emotional responses, including unacceptable levels of stress for employees. Understanding the sources of conflict can help managers to reduce stress in the work environment.

Personal/role conflict

Employees have to perform roles at work that may sometimes conflict with their own values and belief systems. Young people may resent a strict dress and grooming code; vegetarians might have an ethical issue preparing meat dishes; people with a strong religious faith may have moral issues with the service and consumption of alcohol; and the behavior of customers (for example, female near-nudity at resort hotels in some Muslim countries) can be offensive to social conventions. In these situations, the employee's values are challenged by the workplace. This is a personal conflict that individual employees need to resolve, or they may have to choose to leave the company.

Organizational/customer conflict

Organizations have policies, processes and procedures that regulate the boundaries of employee conduct. Many of these rules are designed to deliver the brand promise and to help customer-contact employees. Occasionally customers will make what appears to be a reasonable request of customer-contact employees, but which unfortunately breaks the house rules. For example, mid-market hotels with food and beverage facilities normally have opening and closing hours for their restaurant and bar; when customers want to eat or drink and the facilities are closed, customer-contact employees face a dilemma. Do they maintain the house rules and not serve the customer, which results in customer dissatisfaction, or do they break the house rules, serve the customer, and deliver customer satisfaction? This type of organizational conflict with customers puts the customer-contact employee in a difficult situation. However, if a customer makes an unreasonable request, for example asking the customer-contact employee to help in an illegal activity, then the employee should maintain the company's regulations and not help the customer.

Intercustomer conflict

Some of the most difficult situations for customer-contact employees arise from disputes between customers. In most hospitality services customers are in contact with each other in a myriad of different ways, which can cause problems at times. Customers park their own cars in hotel and restaurant car parks; queue for service; drink with each other in bars; and dance with each other in nightclubs. Customer contact is normally an essential and positive element in the product concept and atmosphere, but occasionally, especially when customers are waiting for service, there can be conflict. Long queuing times are a major source of customer conflict, but again it is the conduct of the customer-contact employees that can help to resolve the conflict or exacerbate it.

Developing a service-orientated culture

In this discussion, we have already mentioned how a hospitality company's formal Standard Operating Procedures can help or hinder an employee's relationship with customers. A company's culture has a powerful influence on how employees look after customers. There is a limit to the management's ability to monitor and control service encounters; so customer-contact employees have enormous scope to interpret the company's rules. What guides customer-contact employees in choosing their behavior towards a customer is the organization's service culture.

Each hospitality organization has its own culture. In everyday language, culture is what an employee describes when responding to the question: 'what's it like working here?'. Culture, in this context, means the shared core values, beliefs and assumptions that underpin how the organization treats its employees. These cultural components are often deeply rooted in the organization's founding, history and recent development. Entrepreneurs like Bill Marriott, whose strong Mormon faith provided the ethical foundation for treating employees in a positive, caring manner, still influences the Marriott Corporation's approach to human resource management. Companies that have been created through a series of mergers and acquisitions and regard shareholders as the key stakeholders can have a culture that values financial performance above all else. This can be less attractive to employees.

Case study 12.1 provides an illustration of a service culture.

Case study

12.1 Service culture at the Hard Rock Café

Founded in London in 1972 by two American entrepreneurs, the Hard Rock Café (HRC) has developed a loyal customer base throughout the world because of its strong service culture. Although the HRC has been owned by a major corporation (the Rank Group) since 1990, the central theme in the restaurants is fun! The success story is based upon core values of treating every individual with respect, and all stakeholders equally.

There is a 'bill of rights' for guests and employees, which provides a focus for training and inculcates HRC values at the start of an employee's induction. Guests' rights include the right to: 'a unique and pleasant greeting; great food and friendly, attentive service; fair pricing; a spotlessly clean restaurant; and the right to sit at any table they want'. Employees rights include the right to: 'work in a safe, healthy and fun environment; be trained in a consistent and thorough manner; immediate feedback on performance; ask questions and get answers without fear; and have opportunities for personal development'.

The HRC practices the philosophy of empowerment and promote employees from within. Keith Errington, a Regional Manager from Colorado, states that 'employee retention is not an issue at HRC; we know how to treat our employees and they stay'.

(Source: www.hardrock.com, and *Customer Management*, 2000)

Employees learn the organizational culture through the routine behavior and messages sent out by head and regional offices, and through the unit's general manager – who represents and personifies the corporate culture. Employees' shared perceptions of the organizational culture, the visible manifestations of the surface layer of the company, are described as the 'climate' (Schneider and Bowen, 1995). Although the climate and culture in a company is not normally written down for an employee to read, it influences both service culture and how customer-contact employees interact with customers. Sometimes a company's senior management will draft a statement reflecting its vision, mission and values. This can encapsulate the culture of the organization.

In small and medium-sized owner-managed hospitality businesses, the 'family' culture will be more visible to employees (see Case study 12.2).

Case study

12.2 The Blunsdon House Hotel, Swindon, England

Over the past 45 years, the Clifford family has turned a farmhouse bed-and-breakfast business into a major four-star conference and leisure hotel, The Blunsdon House Hotel. Founders Zan and Peter Clifford have always been customer orientated, and their son John continues the tradition, stating: 'we are obsessive in our ambition to provide excellent service'. The founders live on the premises, and still take a passionate interest in customers' welfare – demonstrating their commitment and leading by example. They also recognized the need for developing and looking after their employees as the business grew. Key employees, and members of their families, have worked with the Clifford family for generations. Most heads of department have long service awards, and the general manager was also appointed a director.

The service culture in a family business is often highly personalized, and provides guests with a genuinely local hospitality experience.

In larger organizations, employees individually and collectively evaluate the true meaning of the many and varied messages. Nearly all major hospitality organizations claim to be good employers, and suggest 'Our employees are our most important assets'. Employees might not believe these messages when the company's actual human resource practices are poor. Where employees hear company messages that imply a certain kind of behavior but witness contradictory actions and behaviors by management, then the organization suffers from cultural schizophrenia. Like a split personality disorder, such inconsistency undermines the organization's aim to deliver service quality. Clearly, culture and climate reflect the philosophy of the senior management team, which must be consistent with the organization's strategies and behavior. In some organizations the senior management team may have a genuine ambition to provide high quality service, but middle managers, who are responsible for controlling costs, may thwart the company's intentions.

The general manager as a role model

Different units within the same hospitality brand can have different cultures and climates. Whilst the characteristics of a successful hospitality general manager will vary, the personality, behavior and actions of the general manager send powerful signals to the employees, and help to shape the culture and climate of the unit. Employee morale and motivation are a reflection of the general manager; employees respond to the leadership provided – and follow the example and direction set – by the general manager.

Service myths, heroes and villains

Those hospitality companies aspiring to provide excellent service often use examples of extraordinary customer-contact employee actions in their advertising.

By publicizing these events, the company is explicitly informing both customers and employees about the service expectations that the company wishes to provide. Occasionally, because of legal actions or investigative journalism, the media may highlight examples of poor behavior in a hospitality organization. Over time, if repeated, these events can become part of the dominant service culture. In the extra-ordinary service company, heroes become the personification of what is best about the company. However, some maverick companies employ characters (notably chefs/managers) who become 'villains' through negative publicity, and enjoy their controversial reputation.

Support systems

Customer-contact employees are dependent upon support systems, both human and technological, to help them deliver quality service. In hospitality, there has tradition-ally been tension and conflict between front-of-house employees and back-of-house employees, especially between the restaurant and kitchen. If the organization wants to foster a service culture throughout the company, then back-of-house employees should think of front-of-house employees as internal customers.

We have already discussed how the company's policies can either nurture or inhibit customer-contact employee's responses to customers. Companies set boundaries for employees in terms of the authority they are allowed when dealing with customers. Some companies restrict the authority of customer-contact employees, who have to follow rules and regulations and report to the more senior managers who take deci-sions. A different perspective, which we will discuss in more detail later, is the notion of empowerment. Empowerment gives customer-contact employees the responsibility, authority and tools for solving customers' problems. Technological support systems include the computer systems, equipment and infrastructure within a property or across a network. Obviously it is difficult for customer-contact employees to provide quality service if the computer systems are slow and not capable of handling the data inputs efficiently, or if food and beverage equipment does not function properly. No matter how pleasant customer-contact employees are, if the support systems do not work, the organization's claim to have a service orientation will appear inconsistent to the customers and the employees. Finally, in a genuine service culture, all employees – regardless of their role and status – should be customer focused. Indeed, some experts, like Gummesson (2002), contend that all employees in service companies are involved in marketing.

Activity 12.1

If you have worked in a hospitality organization, think about the service culture you observed whilst working.

- Evaluate the culture and climate of the company, the role adopted by the general manager, the service myths and company heroes, and the adequacy of the support systems.

- What do you think the company did well? What could be improved?

Internal marketing

The services marketing triangle (Zeithaml and Bitner, 2003; see Figure 12.3) links pre-encounter marketing (also called external marketing) with internal marketing and marketing during the encounter (also called interactive marketing). The promises made to customers during the pre-encounter marketing strategies have to be delivered during the service encounter. We have already discussed the role of employees, and specifically customer-contact employees, in the service encounter. Increasingly, human resource managers have adopted marketing techniques to recruit, communicate and motivate employees, and this approach is called internal marketing (Varey and Lewis, 2000).

The main driver of internal marketing is the recognition of the competitive labor market for hospitality employees by companies who compete for the best available talent. Since the success of the hospitality offer is dependent upon the quality of service, which is dependent upon employees, hospitality companies need to attract, train, motivate and retain the most appropriate employees for their product concept. Internal marketing involves marketing the organization to current and prospective employees in much the same way as the organization markets its offer to external customers.

Recruitment

Societal perceptions of working in hospitality vary according to the importance of tourism to an economy. In societies where tourism is a key industry, like the Caribbean, or where tourism is rapidly developing, like in China, careers in hospitality are regarded favorably. Potential employees recognize that hospitality jobs are

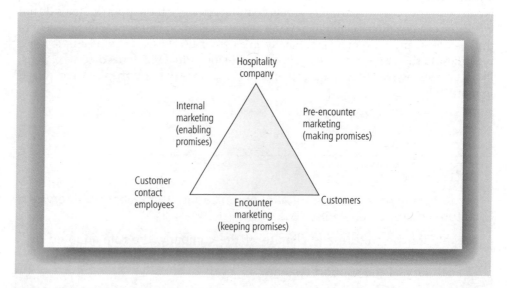

Figure 12.3 The services marketing triangle (adapted from Zeithaml and Bitner, 2003, Services Marketing, p. 319, reproduced with permission of The McGraw-Hill Companies)

relatively well paid and enjoy high status. In these societies, employers can select potential employees from a large pool of available talent.

The InterContinental Hotel, Phnom Penh

Thierry Douin's first appointment as a General Manager was the challenging task of opening a new InterContinental Hotel in Phnom Penh in 1996. Cambodia was just beginning to recover from 30 years of civil war, famine and disease, and employment prospects for local people were poor. The hotel needed to recruit 400 local employees, but over 3800 people applied for the jobs – working in a five-star hotel represented, for many Cambodians, a unique opportunity to earn a good income.

Marketing insight

In societies where service companies are generally regarded as lower status employers, with lower pay and prospects, the recruitment challenge is more difficult. The image and reputation of the company as an employer is key to attracting appropriate employees. Indeed, the most attractive recruitment strategy is to aim to be the 'preferred employer in the area'. An advertisement for a conference sales manager at the Radisson Edwardian Heathrow Hotel stated: 'we aspire to be one of the top ten best employers in London'. The copy continued with a discussion of the company's business philosophy, including their commitment to 100 percent customer satisfaction: 'to achieve this we need team members who are 100 percent satisfied'.

Service inclination

An essential quality that employers seek in employees is the 'right service attitude'. Some people seem to have a natural aptitude for service; they spontaneously respond to customers and co-workers, and have a cheerful disposition. These characteristics are linked to an individual's personality, interpersonal communication skills and initiative. As such, attitude cannot really be taught. Unfortunately, one of the problems for hospitality employers in competitive labor markets is the lack of potential employees with the right service attitude. This means that unsuitable employees, who do not have an aptitude for service, are recruited and, these employees can undermine management's attempts to deliver a quality service. Another important element in hospitality employment is teamwork – the ability to fit into a team and play a role. Some people enjoy working in a team, they are good team players and are supportive to those around them; however, other people are awkward in teams and are not good team players, which can be demotivating for co-workers.

Service competencies

Employees need to have skills and knowledge to be able to perform their job effectively. Skills and knowledge in service industries are called service competencies. Historically, most hospitality managers had limited education and learnt service competencies whilst working in the industry. Today there is a well-established system of hospitality and tourism education in many parts of the world. Colleges offer craft training and diplomas, universities offer Bachelors, Masters and PhD programs, and there is a range of study-mode options. The best institutions have very close links to the hospitality industry – for example, in Thailand the Dusit Hotel Chain set up the Dusit Thani College to provide training and higher education for hotel, kitchen and restaurant, and tourism management students. These educational institutions prepare students for the industry and provide them with core competencies in the field of hospitality study.

Training

Each hospitality company has its own service culture, operating systems and service standards. New customer-contact employees need induction training to become familiar with the product (product knowledge training) and customer care philosophy, and to meet co-employees working in the same team. Induction training in the large organizations is formal and structured, whilst in the smaller hospitality firms it is likely to be less formal. Continuous training and career development is a hallmark of the most successful hospitality companies. Companies with seasonal operations, like Ski Olympic, have particular challenges when inducting their employees (see Case study 12.3).

Case study

12.3 The training challenge for Ski Olympic

Ski Olympic recruits over 150 employees each year to work in its Alpine chalets and chalet hotels for a five-month season. Approximately one-third of last year's employees return for the new season. Other employees are mostly recruited by 'word-of-mouth' from the friends of recent employees and the families of customers. The challenge each year is to train up to 100 new employees how to deliver the Ski Olympic experience, in less than two weeks. The training is conducted at the Ski Olympic chalet-hotel Les Avals. As soon as the employees arrive they are greeted and treated like guests, following exactly the same schedule with breakfast, afternoon tea and dinner. The new employees adopt different roles, taking it in turns to be customers and then employees, and teams of chefs prepare the same meals that customers will eat on their holidays (the real challenge is cooking at Alpine heights – it takes much longer to boil an egg!). Each employee learns his or her role during this intensive period, and departments have written job lists to help ensure that Ski Olympic's operating standards, even in an informal, fun environment, are maintained. Gary Yates, an Area Manager, explained that treating the employees as customers was the most effective way to show them the customer experience. The success of Ski Olympic is built upon customer satisfaction – 72 percent of sales are repeat business.

(Source: Gary Yates, Ski Olympic)

Empowerment

Customer-contact employees work within the boundaries of authority given to them by their companies. We have discussed how some hospitality companies set limits to what customer-contact employees can do in responding to customer requests. An alternative approach is to empower employees to take responsibility for ensuring customers are satisfied with the service encounter. This responsibility needs to be matched with delegated authority and supported by appropriate resources such as technology, training and budgets. It is claimed that this approach, championed in hospitality by Marriott and their luxury brand Ritz Carlton, is more

Table 12.2 Forms of Empowerment in Hospitality (source: Lashley, 2001, p. 6)

Form of empowerment	Organization
Quality circles	Accor Group
Suggestion schemes	McDonald's Restaurants
'Whatever it takes' training	Marriott Hotels
Autonomous work groups	Harvester Restaurants
De-layering the organization	Bass Taverns

customer focused and motivates employees, involving them, to a greater or lesser extent, in self-management in the workplace.

Table 12.2 illustrates various forms of empowerment in hospitality.

The concept that any customer-contact employee will take ownership if the customer has a problem, and actually responds to customers' need and wants, is attractive. Customers want speedy solutions, especially when complaining, and resent having to repeat their complaint to several different employees. However, customer-contact employees do not necessarily want to take the responsibility for customer satisfaction because:

- Employees may not be given genuine authority by the company to solve the problem
- Hospitality companies are traditionally bureaucratic and hierarchical organizations, where the middle managers may resent customer-contact employees assuming their authority
- Employees may not receive the appropriate training and resources to make correct decisions
- Employees may feel that they are not paid enough to take this responsibility
- Some employees may not like the idea of taking responsibility at all, and prefer to follow the orders of managers.

Though many companies talk about empowering employees, few have genuinely developed the organizational strategies and culture to support empowered employees. However, Marriott's training is recognized as a leader in the hotel industry. Its 'Whatever it takes' program has customer service as the core theme, with empowerment as the strategy to encourage employees to be empathetic towards customers needs and wants (Lashley, 2001). The training involves 40–60 hours, and looks at the guest experience by encouraging employees to act out role-plays. Employees learn that guests need to be acknowledged whilst waiting; want to be treated as individuals; want to see employees who they know and who like their job; and, most importantly, do not want 'hassle' when they are staying in a hotel or dining in a restaurant. Marriott continues to search for new ways to deliver the basic brand values through their associates (all Marriott employees are called associates).

Reward systems

Reward systems for employees include tangible and intangible benefits. Tangible benefits are pay, bonuses, tips, meals provided free of charge, and discounted accommodation for live-in employees. The perceived 'fairness' of the distribution of the tips in hospitality businesses can be a controversial topic. Many of the intangible benefits of working in hospitality environment compensate for the antisocial hours and lower pay. Intangible benefits can include the excitement, fun and teamwork that many hospitality employees enjoy. There can be a sense of pride when customers make favorable comments about the hospitality service, and when family and friends respect the company where employees work.

Communication

One important lesson that human resource management has learnt from marketing is the value of regularly informing employees about the company's current situation and future plans. As well as formal communications about company policy, most hospitality company employee magazines include career development opportunities; articles about social activities, fun events, competitions and long service awards; and interesting anecdotes about individual employees. Important achievements are highlighted, and employees are meant to feel more involved with the company. From a marketing perspective, it is essential for customer-contact employees to be aware of new openings, new-product development and new marketing programs, so they can inform customers during service encounters.

Criticisms of internal marketing

Critics of internal marketing challenge the theory and practice on a number of grounds (Mudie, 2000). For example, it is claimed that the champions of internal marketing (and in particular empowerment) have relied on rhetoric to promote an idealized workplace. The reality is that many hospitality premises are unpleasant, or even hostile, places of work. There are often staff shortages, which increase the workload for the remaining employees and create stress. Unfortunately, hospitality employees can suffer from sexual abuse and violence from customers and co-workers. Because managers are primarily interested in cost efficiency and profits, they can be accused of poor communication with employees and of not genuinely caring for them. Indeed many employees feel cynical about management and are suspicious of internal marketing innovations, such as de-layering, which appear to be more a cost-cutting exercise than genuine empowerment. Whilst there are poor employers in the hospitality industry, internal marketing theory incorporates the best practice and demonstrates the advantages of adopting a positive approach to managing employees.

Emotional labor

Customer-contact employees work long hours, at all times of the day and night, dealing constantly with customers. Working with people can be emotionally tiring, especially if there are staff shortages or if customers complain. Whilst working in hospitality can be great fun, it can also be very stressful. However, companies expect customer-contact employees to suppress their own feelings and their own identity to ensure that customers are satisfied. Some hospitality organizations even provide cues and scripts to help customer-contact employees say the right words to customers. In particular, empowerment means that customer-contact employees are expected to take on more responsibility, which can lead to more stress. The term *emotional labor* has been used to describe these emotional characteristics of work in service industries. Both hospitality managers and customer-contact employees can suffer from the long-term effects of emotional labor, resulting in minor illness, anxiety, depression and fatigue, which can lead to alcoholism, nicotine dependence, eating disorders and, ultimately, cancer, heart disease and nervous breakdowns.

Activity 12.2

If you have worked in a hospitality organization, think about the service culture you learnt whilst working.

- Evaluate the company's recruitment and training policies, the service inclination and competencies of the other employees. Did the company 'empower' employees?

- How valid are the criticisms of internal marketing in a hospitality company compared to your own experience?

Conclusion

Hospitality companies must develop effective employee communications strategies to succeed in managing customer-contact employees and delivering customer satisfaction. This process is called internal marketing. Hospitality companies claim to be good employers. However, the industry does suffer from high employee turnover rates, and examples of poor treatment of employees are publicized in the media and spread by negative word-of-mouth.

In this chapter we have explained:

- The link between employee satisfaction, service quality, customer satisfaction and business performance (the service-profit chain)
- That during the hospitality encounter, moments of truth reinforce the customer's perception of service quality
- That when there is a critical service incident, such as service failure or unusual customer requests, the responses and unprompted actions of customer-contact employees influence customer satisfaction/dissatisfaction
- That customer-contact employees who experience role conflict, organizational/ customer conflict and intercustomer conflict can suffer from work-related stress
- How each hospitality company has its own culture and climate, which guides customer-contact employees in choosing their behavior towards customers
- The three components of the services marketing triangle, which are pre-encounter marketing, marketing during the encounter, and internal marketing
- How human resource departments that use marketing techniques to communicate with employees are adopting an internal marketing strategy
- That empowerment gives customer-contact employees the responsibility for solving customer problems
- That critics of human resource management in service industries, and especially of empowerment, suggest that empathetic employees can suffer from emotional labor, resulting in stress and illness.

**Review
questions**

Now check your understanding of this chapter by answering the following questions:

1 Discuss the role of customer-contact employees in delivering the brand offer
2 Discuss the sources of conflict for customer-contact employees whilst working in hospitality organizations. Provide examples to illustrate your answer
3 Evaluate the role of culture and climate in hospitality companies
4 Analyze the theory and practice of internal marketing in the hospitality industry
5 What are the advantages of using 'empowerment' as a human resource strategy in a hospitality business, from each of the following perspectives:
 ● the customer
 ● the employee
 ● the business.

References and further reading

Bitner, M. J., Booms, B. H. and Tetreault, M. S. (1990). The service encounter: diagnosing favourable and unfavourable incidents. *Journal of Marketing*, **54**, 71–84.

Customer Management (2000). Towards best practice. *Customer Management*, Jul/Aug, 6–11.

Gummesson, E. (2002). *Total Relationship Marketing*. Butterworth-Heinemann.

Heskett, J. L., Jones, T. O., Loveman, G. W. *et al.* (1994). Putting the service profit chain to work. *Harvard Business Review*, **72**, 164–70.

Lashley, C. (2000). *Hospitality Retail Management*. Butterworth-Heinemann.

Lashley, C. (2001). *Employing Human Resource Strategies for Service Excellence*. Butterworth-Heinemann.

Mudie, P. (2000). Internal marketing: a step too far. In R. J. Varey and B. R. Lewis (eds), *Internal Marketing; Directions for Management*. Routledge, Chapter 15.

Schneider, B. and Bowen, D. E. (1995). *Winning the Service Game*. HBS Press.

Varey, R. J. and Lewis, B. R. (2000). *Internal Marketing: Directions for Management*. Routledge.

Zeithaml, V. A. and Bitner, M. J. (2003). *Services Marketing*. McGraw-Hill.

Part D

Post-encounter marketing

Chapter 13
Managing customer satisfaction

Chapter Objectives

After working through this chapter, you should be able to:

- Define customer satisfaction
- Understand the importance of satisfying customers
- Evaluate customer satisfaction guarantees in hospitality
- Describe tools for measuring customer satisfaction in the hospitality industry.

Introduction

The concept of satisfying customers is rooted deep in the philosophy of marketing and is a key element in most marketing definitions. Academics and practitioners agree that customer satisfaction is a crucial concept. In this chapter we will explain why customer satisfaction is important; we will then discuss customer satisfaction guarantees in hospitality and explain how companies choose between investing in improvements in customer satisfaction and investing in returns to the stakeholders. Finally, we will review measures for capturing customer satisfaction data and customer complaint processes.

Measuring and understanding customer satisfaction are important elements in the post-encounter marketing mix. Satisfaction has a significant influence on customer attitude and behavioral intention. Customers generally have pre-encounter expectations of hospitality experiences and after the encounter they evaluate the experience against those expectations, effectively asking: 'Did that experience meet my expectations?' If expectations are underperformed, dissatisfaction is likely to result. Dissatisfied customers are at risk of defecting to competitors. Satisfied customers, whose expectations are met or exceeded, however, hold out the promise of further business. Consequently it is important for marketers to measure and understand the major influences upon customer satisfaction.

Defining customer satisfaction

Satisfaction is a complex phenomenon (Zeithaml and Bitner, 2003; Figure 13.1). In Chapter 3 we discussed consumer expectations, which are formed prior to purchase.

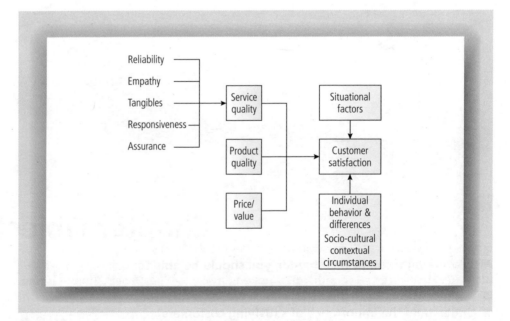

Figure 13.1 Customer satisfaction (adapted from Zeithaml and Bitner, 2003, Services Marketing, reproduced with permission of The McGraw-Hill Companies)

Expectations are important comparison standards that help consumers to evaluate the perceived performance of the hospitality offer throughout and at the end of the service encounter. At the simplest level, customers are satisfied if the experience matches or exceeds their expectations, and dissatisfied if the service performance fails to match their expectations. Customer satisfaction can therefore be defined as a positive attitude towards a supplier that is achieved when the customer's expectations are met. One situation that does not fit this definition is when customers expect that a service experience will be poor, and those expectations are met! Meeting these low expectations does not generate satisfaction. However, when expectations are positive, this definition of satisfaction is perfectly adequate. Since customers needs and wants change over time, consumer expectations of the hospitality offer also change over time.

Customers can enjoy a range of different types of satisfaction, including:

- Contentment, when a routine service is delivered satisfactorily
- Pleasure, when a service makes the consumer feel happy
- Delight, when a service surprises the consumer and exceeds expectations
- Relief, when a service overcomes a potentially difficult situation and delivers satisfaction.

Activity 13.1

Can you identify a number of hospitality experiences that have given you the following feelings:

- Contentment

- Pleasure

- Delight

- Relief.

Can you explain why you felt the way you did?

Why customer satisfaction is important

Customer satisfaction is important to the success of hospitality businesses. Few hotels and restaurants can manage to survive if they consistently deliver unsatisfactory experiences. When customers have alternative providers, they may choose to reduce the amount of business done, or even not to return at all. They may also utter negative word-of-mouth, discouraging potential customers from visiting. Commonsense tells us that satisfied customers must be good for business. Research into a number of conditions supports this commonsense notion – the cost of acquiring new customers; the benefits of repeat purchases by satisfied customers; and the impact of positive word-of-mouth recommendations.

Marketing insight

An Example where Customer Satisfaction is Less Important

Hospitality units in prime tourist locations with transient visitors sometimes take advantage of tourists and can remain profitable despite delivering customer dissatisfaction. A restaurant close to the Rialto Bridge in Venice attracts tourists with a low-priced tourist menu, and then encourages customers to eat local fish specialities at high prices. The dissatisfied tourists will never return, and the restaurant continues to trade profitably because of its prime location.

The cost of acquiring new customers

Throughout this book we have emphasized the competitive marketplace in which hospitality companies operate. Attracting customers carries significant marketing costs – primarily selling, advertising and sales promotion costs. Indeed, research suggests that the cost of attracting a new customer is five or six times greater than the costs of retaining an existing customer. At the same time, competitors are also striving to attract the same customers. Therefore, when a customer is initially attracted to your marketing offer your company is given a unique opportunity to make a sale and perhaps develop a longer-term relationship with the customer. Customer retention strategies are predicated upon delivering customer satisfaction the first time a customer experiences the hospitality offer; customers who are not satisfied may never return, and the investment in the pre-encounter marketing activities will have been wasted.

Repeat customers

For the vast majority of hospitality businesses, repeat customers are an essential element of the customer mix. The cost of attracting repeat customers – providing they are satisfied – is significantly lower than and in many situations minimal compared to the costs of acquiring new customers (Reichheld, 1996). There are also non-economic benefits derived from repeat customers, including the following:

● Repeat customers know where and how to book, what to expect, and how to find the premises
● Customers who return have expectations that can be met – they already know what the hospitality offer represents, and this indicates that they were relatively satisfied with their first experience
● Customer-contact employees greeting regular customers provides reassurance to first-time visitors regarding product quality and customer satisfaction
● Regular customers are less costly to look after because they know how the service operation works.

Indeed, repeat customers can become powerful advocates for the business, encouraging others to patronize the establishment.

Positive word-of-mouth recommendation

A word-of-mouth recommendation from a satisfied customer is simply the most cost-effective form of customer acquisition. When friends or relatives tell us that a restaurant served really good quality food at reasonable prices, or that the atmosphere, company, drinks and music at a nightclub were excellent, then the next time we book a meal or go clubbing we will seriously consider following that word-of-mouth recommendation. Word-of-mouth has a positive influence on customers because the source of the message (our friends and relatives) is highly trusted. They have no reason to lie to us, and we know them so well that we are likely to believe their advice. Customers who give positive word-of-mouth are also more likely to be retained for the longer term.

Word-of-mouth recommendations are dependent upon all the elements of the hospitality marketing mix working effectively. Helpful, smiling staff cannot win over customers when the prices are too high; a good product in the wrong location will suffer; and wonderful food served by rude staff is normally counterproductive. Ultimately, it is marketing during the hospitality encounter that delivers customer satisfaction and generates word-of-mouth referrals.

Basic principles of customer satisfaction

Effective management of customer satisfaction is based on several principles:

1 Identify which customers you are trying to satisfy. Not all customers or prospects are equally important.
2 Identify what is important to those chosen customers. Not all customers value the same components of the hospitality offer, and not all elements are equally important. For example, some customers value food quantity, while others value food quality. The same customers' expectations may change over time: customers generally want faster service at lunch, but more leisurely service in the evenings.
3 Get it right first time. Customers' expectations, once understood, should be satisfied at the first opportunity. You should try to eliminate the causes of customer dissatisfaction, such as slow service, ill-informed contact staff and malfunctioning equipment.
4 Excellent recovery. Accepting that occasionally a hospitality company will fail to meet customer expectations, you need to have in place recovery processes to mitigate customer dissatisfaction, pre-empt negative word-of-mouth and promote retention.

Customer satisfaction guarantees

When consumers buy manufactured products, the manufacturer provides a guarantee and will normally repair or replace the product if the customer is not satisfied.

Both consumers and manufacturers understand the concept of satisfaction guarantees, which plays an important role in marketing manufactured products. However, most hospitality managers are intuitively opposed to the idea of customer satisfaction guarantees. They believe that too many guests will be dishonest and make bogus complaints, even when they have enjoyed their stay or meal. It is interesting to note that virtually all hospitality providers do compensate customers when they have a genuine complaint, and this compensation implies that companies do actually have some sort of customer satisfaction guarantee, even if they do not inform customers about it. This controversial topic can be better understood if we explain the different type of service guarantees that companies can adopt (Zeithaml and Bitner, 2003).

Implicit satisfaction guarantee

When customers book into a hotel or restaurant, they assume that they will receive a satisfactory outcome for the price they will pay, even though the hospitality outlet has not given the customer any guarantee. There is an implicit understanding, grounded in experience, education and consumer protection legislation, that the hospitality provider will compensate a customer with a genuine complaint. Whilst there is no formal contract with the customer, most hospitality companies do compensate customers who complain. The problem with this informal type of customer satisfaction guarantee is that neither the customers nor the company know what an implicit guarantee covers. There are no guidelines setting out what the company offers and how customers will be compensated if something goes wrong.

Explicit satisfaction guarantee

An explicit satisfaction guarantee is based upon a specific, measurable performance factor. Time based services, like room service delivery or pizza home delivery, are good examples of explicit satisfaction guarantees. The length of time to deliver the service can be fixed as part of the service guarantee, and it is then simple to establish whether the service has been delivered on time or not. These guarantees have been used with varying degrees of success. Unfortunately, Domino's Pizza had to withdraw a 30-minute guaranteed delivery time because of problems caused by employees driving dangerously fast whilst trying to deliver pizzas on time. Another example of an explicit guarantee is the conference package offered by Ramada Jarvis Hotels' 'Summit Conferences', which includes a money-back guarantee that the conference equipment will be fully checked well in advance of the meeting, and messages will be delivered promptly. Although Ramada Jarvis suggest they will serve a two-course meal in just 35 minutes as part of a conference package, this service is no longer included in the guarantee.

Marketing insight

Holiday Inn's Guest Charter

Holiday Inn introduced a guest charter and a hospitality promise informing customers that 'making your stay a complete success is our goal'. If customers are not satisfied with any part of their stay, they are invited to inform the front desk or duty manager. The Holiday Inn promise is to solve the customer's problem, and if the problem cannot be solved, then the customer does not pay for that part of their stay. This promise, which has a trademark copyright protection, is mainly promoted in the bedrooms. Although the promise offers a service guarantee, the way it is worded does not have the same impact as an explicit satisfaction guarantee or an unconditional 100 percent complete satisfaction or money-back guarantee.

Unconditional satisfaction guarantee

An unconditional satisfaction guarantee promises customers complete satisfaction or their money back. An unconditional guarantee makes a powerful statement about the confidence a hospitality service provider has in the integrity of the offer. An unconditional guarantee gives consumers:

- Confidence to purchase the service (by reducing risk) in the knowledge that a 100 percent refund is available if they are not satisfied
- Reassurance that the company can deliver on the promise, or it would not provide a service guarantee
- Preference over competitors who do not provide a similar guarantee.

Before a hospitality company can introduce an unconditional guarantee, the following conditions must be fulfilled:

- The target market must be clearly defined
- The company must understand the drivers of customer satisfaction for the products and services offered
- Product or service quality standards must be set to deliver customer satisfaction
- Employees must be aware of the 100 percent satisfaction guarantee, and be capable of fulfilling their role in the service experience.

A hospitality company intending to introduce an unconditional guarantee must be prepared to invest significantly in marketing research to evaluate the drivers of customer satisfaction, competitive standards, and consumer's perceptions of price and value, as well as investment in product quality and training; it must also ensure that there is an effective quality audit process. Most importantly, if a company cannot deliver consistent customer satisfaction then it simply cannot afford to offer an unconditional service guarantee.

The small number of hospitality companies that introduced unconditional service guarantees have:

- Been forced to adopt a customer orientation, and to view customer satisfaction from the consumer's perspective
- Had to review the entire customer experience to eradicate failure points (areas of customer dissatisfaction)
- Effectively used the service guarantee as a differentiator in marketing communication campaigns
- Increased brand awareness and market share
- Been able to monitor the cost of consumer dissatisfaction by the cost of refunds to dissatisfied customers
- Used customer complaints to identify and correct service and maintenance problems

- Given managers and employees measurable customer satisfaction performance goals
- Effectively used the concept of unconditional guarantees in employee team-building exercises
- Achieved significant reductions in employee turnover.

From a quality perspective, unconditional guarantees force companies to 'do it right first time' or the costs of complaints would be unacceptably high. However, despite all these advantages few hospitality companies can seriously entertain the notion of providing a 100 percent satisfaction guarantee. Many hospitality organizations do not have the product/service consistency to be able to offer an unconditional guarantee, and in these cases the costs of compensating customers who complained would be too high. Such companies should not consider introducing an unconditional guarantee policy.

Hampton Inns in the USA pioneered the introduction of unconditional guarantees in hospitality (Case study 13.1), and more recently Travel Inn in the UK has adopted this policy (Case study 13.2). Both operate in the budget accommodation market, with a price-led strategy, a relatively standardized product, simple pricing policies and few employees. This type of brand formula delivers a homogeneous marketing offer, which lends itself to an unconditional guarantee.

Case study

13.1 Hampton Inns

In 1990, Hampton Inns – the US budget hotel brand that was then owned by Holiday Inn – took a calculated gamble and introduced the following customer satisfaction guarantee:

Hampton Inn 100 percent Service Guarantee. We guarantee high-quality accommodations, friendly and efficient service, and clean, comfortable surroundings. If you are not completely satisfied, we don't expect you to pay.

Prior to this innovative strategy, Hampton Inns had carried out a detailed quality audit to eliminate any failure points and to ensure customer satisfaction standards. After a successful trial period the policy was introduced, and any customer who is not satisfied with his or her stay now receives a night's accommodation free. This hassle-free money-back policy has helped Hampton Inns to capture the highest retention rate of customers in the USA.

The problem of customers abusing the unconditional guarantee is solved in the following way. If the customer-contact employee handling a complaint believes the customer does not have a valid reason, a comment is entered on to the database. The customer is not charged on the occasion of making a complaint. If, however, the customer tries to book again, the reservations department informs the customer that he or she is welcome to stay at the Hampton Inn, but in the event of a complaint the unconditional guarantee will not be offered.

Hampton Inns continues to use the 100 percent guarantee as the focus of its marketing activities.

(Source: Zeithaml and Bitner, 2003)

Most mid-market hotels target many market segments. They have a complex range of accommodation, food, beverage and leisure products, with a wide variety of prices and price bundles, and a relatively large number of employees. This type of company delivers a heterogeneous marketing offer, and so it would be difficult to provide an unconditional guarantee, even if the management were interested in offering one.

Luxury hotels and restaurants providing high-quality service and well-maintained facilities do not need to introduce an unconditional guarantee. The reputation of Four Seasons Hotels, or the Savoy Hotel in London, carries an implicit guarantee of complete customer satisfaction.

Case study

13.2 Complaints and customer satisfaction at Travel Inn

Since introducing the 100 percent satisfaction guaranteed or money-back policy, Travel Inn has witnessed an increase in the number of guests complaining (the most common complaints are about noise from other guests, car alarms and delivery lorries), and has consequently paid out 0.5 percent of sales revenue in refunds. However, the company believes the refunds are an investment in customer satisfaction. Travel Inn carried out research with 10,000 customers, and discovered a significant increase in satisfaction with the complaint resolution process. The Managing Director, Carl Leaver, said: 'our research proves that increased customer loyalty drives incremental sales that pay back the cost of the refunds many times over'.

Constraints on customer satisfaction

We have discussed the difficulties that hospitality companies have in delivering 100 percent customer satisfaction guarantees. Whilst most companies could almost certainly improve their level of customer satisfaction, there are constraints that restrict such improvements. Customers want competitive prices, and there are limits to how much customers are prepared to pay for higher levels of satisfaction. Hospitality companies have other stakeholders who compete for the funds that could be invested in delivering higher customer satisfaction – for example, shareholders want an increase in dividends, management and employees want higher wages and bonuses, and suppliers want prompt payment. Therefore, investment in improving customer satisfaction has to be balanced against the needs of other stakeholders. Indeed, financial constraints frequently inhibit investment in the hospitality product and improvements in customer satisfaction.

Activity 13.2

Log on to the following hotel brand websites and evaluate their approaches to providing customer satisfaction guarantees:

- www.holiday-inn.com
- www.hamptoninn.com
- www.travelinn.co.uk
- www.jarvis.co.uk (Summit Conferences)

Measuring customer satisfaction

Hospitality companies use a combination of direct and indirect methods to measure and monitor customer satisfaction. Indirect methods included tracking actual sales and profit figures compared to forecast and previous period performances. Direct methods include customer research, and analysis of complaints and compliments. Although most hotels and restaurants will have customer comment cards or questionnaires in the guest bedrooms and on the tables, the industry does not have a standard approach to measuring customer satisfaction; and companies use a variety of different methods to collect and analyze the data. For example, there is no common scale used in collecting customer satisfaction data – some companies use a numerical scale (1–5), others use word descriptors (poor, fair, good, excellent), and others rely solely on customer's own comments. Each organization will ask customers different types of questions according to their own needs, and will rarely share data on such a confidential topic.

Delivering customer satisfaction consistently is dependent upon listening to customers and customer-contact employees so that performance standards are continually enhanced. A number of different classes of customer can provide insight into the level and causes of customer (dis)satisfaction. Research can be conducted into current customers, lapsed customers, competitors' customers and potential customers. Techniques include the following:

- Analyzing customer complaints and changing service policies and procedures to reduce or eliminate the sources of complaint.
- Post-transaction surveys – customers can be sent postal or email questionnaires when they have returned home, with an incentive to complete and return them. The questionnaires obtain post-experience data about customer satisfaction. Many tour operators give customers a questionnaire to complete on the flight home, and this provides information about the hospitality service during their holiday.
- Key account customers, frequent guests, and members of loyalty clubs understand the level of consistency across a hotel brand better than most employees. Surveying the views of expert customers can identify underperforming units and highlight important brand inconsistencies.
- Employee surveys – encouraging employees to provide feedback on the service operation – provide another technique used by progressive companies. Employees are acutely aware of service problems, and often know the reasons why performance is below the brand standards. Seeking and acting on their views can help to improve customer satisfaction.
- Focus groups of customers and employees allow the coordinator to explore customer satisfaction issues in depth.
- Mystery shopping is a key tool in auditing the service process in hotels and restaurants. Mystery shopping combines a customer-centred approach to monitoring service with measurable performance standards. Researchers pretend to be customers and record their impressions of the service. The mystery shopper survey includes quantitative measures (for example, the length of waiting time for service) and qualitative measures (for example, employee friendliness and courtesy). At the end of the visit, the mystery shopper survey score and report is given to

the unit manager and to head office. Some companies use the results from the mystery shopper survey as part of the manager's bonus scheme, which emphasizes the importance of this auditing tool.

● Internal brand audits – hospitality chains employ their own staff or commission external firms to carry out brand conformance audits to ensure that the unit is delivering customer satisfaction (assuming that the brand standards do actually deliver customer satisfaction!). These inspections are not secret. The general manager and employees know in advance when the audit will take place, and obviously prepare for the inspection. Inspectors have detailed brand performance standards covering all aspects of the operation, and check the unit's performance against the company's benchmarks. In large hotels, several inspectors can stay for three or more days reviewing the service operation. For franchise operations and hotels in consortiums, the brand audit provides the brand owner with evidence to force units performing below the minimum brand standards to improve performance. Ultimately, if the unit continues to underperform, the brand owner can terminate the agreement and withdraw the brand name and support for the property.

Normally, both quantitative and qualitative research methods are used to collect data from customers. Research should be continuous, and over time changes in customer satisfaction can be recorded, with an explanation to account for increases or decreases. Processes for evaluating customer satisfaction include importance/performance analysis, benchmarking and complaints capture.

Importance/performance analysis

Importance/performance analysis (IPA) starts by identifying the elements of the hospitality experience that contribute importantly to customer satisfaction. It then assesses the performance of the firm against those expectations. Many companies conduct qualitative research, such as focus group interviews, in order to identify the important elements of the experience. There are clearly dangers in using standardized instruments (such as SERVQUAL; Parasuraman *et al.*, 1988) that do not account for variance in customer expectations. Questionnaires can then be constructed that assess customer expectations of those elements as well as their perceptions of performance. The normal format is to ask customers to rate, on a seven-point scale, their expectations of an excellent hospitality company and their perceptions of the researched hospitality company's performance (see Table 13.1).

Table 13.1 Importance/Performance Questions

Item	Strongly disagree						Strongly agree
Expectation: Excellent budget hotels provide quiet sleeping accommodation	1	2	3	4	5	6	7
Perception: Hotel XYX provides quiet sleeping accommodation	1	2	3	4	5	6	7

Analysis can then focus on identifying where the company falls short of meeting customer expectations. For example, if a customer were to rate the expectation item above at 7 and the perception item at 4, this would mean a 3-point negative gap (perception score (4) less expectation score (7) = −3). Customers are invited to identify the relative importance of each element or a group of similar elements, such as those relating to responsiveness of contact staff. It is a mistake to believe that every negative gap is equally important to customers. For example, a (−3) gap may also be found for illumination of the car park. For most customers, a noisy bedroom is a much more important issue than a poorly lit car park. For this reason, many satisfaction questionnaires invite customers to identify not only expectations and perceptions, but also the importance of each element. Typically this is done by asking customers to distribute 100 points between the elements or groups of elements in a way that reflects their relative importance.

This information can be used to guide customer satisfaction strategies. For example, where customers have identified a particular attribute as important and the company is not meeting expectations, there is a potential source of customer dissatisfaction and the gap should be closed. However, where the company is exceeding customer expectations on some attribute that is unimportant to customers, there may be a case for reducing expenditure on that attribute.

Results from this sort of analysis can be mapped onto an IPA matrix, as in Figure 13.2.

In the matrix, cell I of the matrix represents a competitive strength – an area where the customer is satisfied with the company's performance on important attributes. Cell II is a threat – the company is failing to satisfy customers on important attributes. Cell III describes the situation where the company is meeting and perhaps exceeding customer expectations on attributes that customers think are unimportant. The options here are to educate the customer as to the attribute's importance or to reduce investment in that attribute. In cell IV, the customer is dissatisfied, but the attribute is not important. It would make sense to monitor the importance of

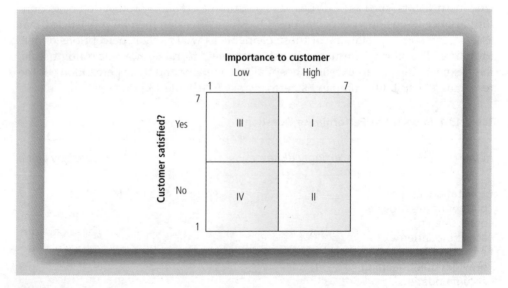

Figure 13.2 Importance/performance matrix

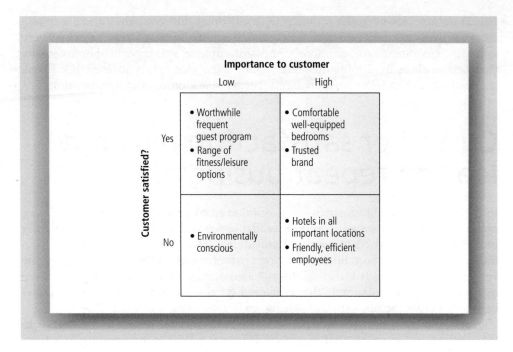

Figure 13.3 Importance/performance matrix, hotel example

that attribute, because if customers come to regard it as important in the future it will become a threat. Figure 13.3 provides an example of seven IPA attributes, for an upscale full-service hotel brand, mapped on an importance/performance matrix.

Benchmarking

Consultancies and marketing research agencies provide hospitality organizations with benchmarking services, which enable companies to compare their own brand's performance on a wide range of indicators against their competitor set and best practice in the industry. BDRC provides the leading hotel companies in Europe with confidential, customized research, benchmarking each brand's performance on key attributes relevant to customers in their market sector. The benchmarking process enables the marketing team to identify and correct important weaknesses compared to the competitor set, and ultimately to improve customer satisfaction.

Complaint capture and analysis

In Chapter 11 we explained that encouraging customers to complain and then responding effectively to the complaint helps to improve customer satisfaction. Companies who take complaints seriously need to develop a management system to capture and analyze the volume and characteristics of complaints. These data can then be used to identify and correct failure points. In hospitality, one source of complaint data is the questionnaires customers complete in hotels and restaurants. Another source is complaint letters, which often describe a catalogue of critical incidents. Both these sources provided management with important information about failure points. However, the problem with customer questionnaires and complaint letters is that they only represent a very small sample of either very happy or very unhappy customers. An effective complaint capture system will employ many channels, such as questionnaires, emails, fax, telephone calls and websites. It will also include a channel to facilitate employee feedback on customer complaints.

Customer satisfaction may not lead to repeat business

In highly competitive industries with commoditized products, low differentiation, many competitive or substitute offers available, low switching costs, and consumer indifference, satisfied customers will still defect. Hospitality markets suffer from these characteristics; so whilst delivering customer satisfaction is essential for the success of the hospitality business, it is not a guarantee for success. Indeed, there are many examples of restaurants that delivered good customer satisfaction but failed because of other factors – such as setting up in the wrong location.

In hospitality, completely satisfied customers may never return to the unit or to the destination for a variety of reasons. For leisure products, many of today's travelers want to explore the world and visit new destinations rather than returning to the same tourist resort. They are variety-seeking customers. Given the industry's over-capacity, price-led consumers can choose from a wide range of competitively priced deals anywhere in the world. Customers attending unique events, like wedding receptions, sports matches and exhibitions, will stay at or near the venue, and may never have another reason to visit the area. However, this does not mean that customer satisfaction is unimportant to these customers. Hospitality businesses that take customer satisfaction seriously will not lower their service standards because of the transient characteristics of customers.

Conclusion

Customer satisfaction is a complex topic, which will continue to be the focus of research because of its important role in generating repeat sales, word-of-mouth recommendation and enhancing profitability. Although most hospitality companies have difficulty in offering 100 percent unconditional guarantees of customer satisfaction, virtually all of them provide implicit service guarantees. The cost of improving customer satisfaction has to be balanced against the willingness of customers to pay more for enhanced satisfaction, and the needs of other stakeholders. Customer satisfaction is the foundation of a successful hospitality business, but satisfied customers may never return.

In this chapter, we have explained:

- A definition of customer satisfaction
- Four different types of satisfaction – contentment, pleasurable, delight and relief

- Why customer satisfaction is important – because of the high costs of acquiring new customers and the economic and non-economic benefits of repeat customers
- The characteristics of an implicit satisfaction guarantee, an explicit satisfaction guarantee and an unconditional 100 percent satisfaction guarantee
- The constraints on improving customer satisfaction due to the needs of other stakeholders
- Various tools for measuring customer satisfaction, including importance/performance analysis, complaint capture and benchmarking
- That some satisfied hospitality customers may never return.

Now check your understanding by answering the following questions:

Review questions

1 Discuss the importance of customer satisfaction to a hospitality business
2 Evaluate the concept of service guarantees in the following hospitality market sectors:
   - budget
   - mid-market
   - luxury.
3 Discuss the role of customer satisfaction measures in improving customer satisfaction for a hospitality brand.

References and further reading

Kotler, P., Bowen, J. and Makens, J. (2003). *Marketing for Hospitality and Tourism*, 3rd edn. Prentice Hall.

Lewis, R. C. and Chambers, R. E. (2000). *Marketing Leadership in Hospitality: Foundations and Practice*. John Wiley.

Parasuraman, A., Zeithaml, V. A. and Berry, L. L. (1988). SERVQUAL: a multiple-item scale for measuring consumer perceptions of service quality. *Journal of Retailing*, **64(1),** 5–7.

Reichheld, F. F. (1996). *The Loyalty Effect: The Hidden Force behind Growth, Profits and Lasting Value*. Baie and Company.

Zeithaml, V. A. and Bitner, M. J. (2003). *Services Marketing*. McGraw-Hill.

Chapter 14
Relationship marketing

Chapter Objectives

After working through this chapter, you should be able to:

■ Understand the differences between a relationship marketing strategy and a transactional marketing strategy
■ Identify the components of a relationship marketing strategy
■ Evaluate the concept of loyalty in the context of hospitality
■ Analyze the role of frequent guest programs in hotel branded chains.

Introduction

The usual focus of marketing activities has been on the acquisition of new customers. This traditional approach to marketing is described as transactional marketing. Once a customer has bought the product there is no attempt to develop the relationship further; the transaction is complete from both the customer's and the company's perspective. This approach to marketing used to be the dominant approach to marketing practice.

The concept of relationship marketing takes a different perspective, and looks at key customers as a business asset that should be nurtured. This approach recognizes that some customers have the potential to generate significant value for companies over a long time period. The focus of relationship marketing is therefore to attract, maintain and enhance customer relationships. In hospitality businesses, 'regular customers' have always been recognized as important customers. The owners and managers of hotels, pubs and restaurants naturally develop a close rapport with regular customers, giving them a special welcome, knowing their preferences, and making sure they are looked after well. However, for branded hospitality chains this recognition of key customers at the unit level was not easily transferred across all the other units in a chain until the ICT revolution provided the computer systems to construct and distribute guest histories. Whilst independently owned and managed units can build upon their traditions of hospitality and develop relationship marketing strategies for the unit, most of the theoretical discussions in this chapter have evolved from research into multiple-unit branded chains.

In this chapter we will explain what relationship marketing is, and discuss the economics of customer retention, the characteristics of relationship marketing, and what multi-unit hospitality companies need to do to implement a relationship marketing strategy. Finally, we will consider the role of loyalty and frequent guest programs in hospitality.

What is relationship marketing?

Relationship marketing is both a philosophy that puts customer retention at the heart of the business process and a marketing strategy, with a set of tools and practices, which a company uses to implement relationship marketing objectives successfully. Table 14.1 contrasts the traditional transactional approach to marketing with relationship marketing.

Gronroos (1994) defines relationship marketing as:

{to}identify and establish, maintain and enhance, and where necessary, terminate relationships with customers and other stakeholders, at a profit so that the objectives of all parties involved are met; and this is done by mutual exchange and fulfillment of promises.

The key point about relationship marketing is the recognition that customers who make repeat purchases have a high lifetime value. Lifetime value (LTV) is the present-day value of all historic and future profit margins earned from sales to a particular

Table 14.1 Relationship and Transactional Marketing

Transactional marketing	Relationship marketing
Single sale focus	Customer retention focus
Focus on product features	Focus on customer value
Short-term promotions	Long-term relational marketing
Customers tend to be price-sensitive	communication
Short timescale	Customers tend not to be price-sensitive
Discontinuous customer contact	Long timescale
Token commitment to customers	Continuous customer contact
Quality is an operations issue	High commitment to customers
	Quality is an issue for all employees

customer or segment. Building close relationships with key customers should be mutually rewarding for both the customer and the company.

However, a relationship marketing strategy should be targeted at selected hospitality customer segments. Not all customers want a relationship, and not all customers merit a relationship. We have already mentioned in Chapter 13 that hotels and restaurants have a large number of customers who are unlikely to return, and therefore trying to build a long-term relationship with these customers is not cost-effective. There are two other customer segments that are unlikely or unwilling to want to develop relationships with a hospitality company. Some customers are aware of the wide choice of competitor products in hospitality markets, do not want to limit their options by developing a relationship with a single brand, and prefer to switch their custom accordingly. Other customers are not interested in any type of relationship with any company, and simply look at the most appropriate quality, value and convenience available at the time of purchase.

There are several circumstances when a business customer may want a long-term relationship with a hospitality supplier. These include:

- When the hospitality product is strategically important or mission-critical – for example, as a component of a bundled offer of a tour operator.
- When financial risk is high – for example, when a company's sales team is large and spends a lot of time on the road, and hotel accommodation becomes a major expense.
- To avoid switching costs – switching costs are incurred when changing to another hospitality provider, and are primarily search and negotiation costs. For corporate clients who arrange major conferences and hospitality events, and intermediaries who handle large volumes of bed-nights, the costs of switching supplier can be significant. Provided the hospitality organization is delivering customer satisfaction at a competitive price, then it is more convenient and cost-effective for the corporate clients and intermediaries to continue to purchase from their existing supplier
- When reciprocity is expected. A food service company may want a close relationship with a hotel company. In return for guaranteed accommodation for its sales team, the food company offers the hotel chain cheaper produce and processed food inputs for its restaurants.

In a consumer context, relationships may be sought when the customer values benefits over and above those directly derived from the hospitality experience. For example:

- Recognition – a customer may feel more valued when recognized and addressed by name
- Personalization – for example, over time a restaurateur may come to understand a customer's particular preferences or expectations
- Risk reduction – a relationship can reduce, or perhaps even eliminate, perceived risk. For example, a customer may develop a relationship with a branded restaurant chain to reduce the perceived performance and physical risk attached to eating when away from home
- Status – customers may feel that their status is enhanced by a relationship with an organization, such as an elite health club in a hotel.

The economics of customer retention

Hospitality companies lose customers each year, for natural and competitive reasons. Consumer customers grow older and move through the family life cycle, changing their employment, home, lifestyle, and consumption habits. Corporate customers and intermediaries go through similar changes, with growth, mergers, takeovers, relocation, downsizing and demise. In addition to this natural loss of customers, competitors lure customers away with new-product initiatives, new openings, price deals, and attractive marketing communication campaigns. For these reasons, hospitality companies traditionally have relatively high customer defection rates. Companies therefore need continually to attract new customers to replace lost ones.

The fundamental reason for companies wanting to build relationships with customers is economic. Companies generate better results when they manage their customer base in order to identify, satisfy and retain their most profitable customers. This is the core goal of relationship marketing strategies. Improving customer retention rates has the effect of increasing the size of the customer base. If competitors lose customers at the rate of 20 percent each year and you lose customers at 10 percent each year, in a few years, other things being equal, you will have a significantly larger customer base. However, there is little merit in growing the customer base aimlessly. The goal must be to retain existing customers who have future profit potential, or are important for other strategic purposes. Not all customers are of equal importance. Some customers may not be worth recruiting or retaining at all – for example, those who have a high cost-to-serve, are debtors or late payers, or are promiscuous in the sense that they switch frequently between suppliers.

Other things being equal, a larger customer base delivers better business performance. Similarly, as customer retention rates rise (or defection rates fall), so does the average tenure of a customer. Tenure is the term used to describe the length of time a customer remains a customer. The impacts of small improvements in customer retention are hugely magnified at the higher levels of retention. For example, improving the customer retention rate from 75 percent to 80 percent grows average customer tenure from 10 years to 12.5 years. Managing tenure by reducing defection rates can be critical for business performance. Research suggests that an increase in customer retention of 5 percent could increase profits from between 35 percent and 95 percent for some service firms (Buttle, 1995). One of the reasons why service firms (including hospitality companies) can increase the profitability significantly by reducing customer defection rates is due to the high fixed and semi-fixed cost structure of the industry. This means that the marginal costs of servicing a repeat customer are relatively small.

Managing customer retention and tenure intelligently generates two key benefits:

1 Marketing costs are reduced. Less needs to be spent replacing lost customers. In addition to reducing the costs of customer recruitment, costs-to-serve existing customers also tend to fall over time
2 As tenure grows, companies better understand customer requirements. Customers also come to understand what a company can do for them. Consequently, suppliers become better placed to identify and satisfy customer requirements profitably. Over time, as relationships deepen, trust and commitment between the parties is likely to grow. Under these circumstances, revenue and profit streams from customers become more secure.

Characteristics of relationship marketing

Hospitality companies who want to implement a relationship marketing strategy successfully need a strong service culture, including a commitment to internal marketing, an effective segmentation strategy, an interactive relational database in all properties, trust from their customers, and to develop customer recognition and reward strategies. We will discuss each of these factors in more detail.

Service culture

The starting point for a successful relationship marketing strategy is the company's service culture. The company needs to invest in a genuine customer-orientated service philosophy that delivers the service quality customers expect. This investment includes a financial commitment to maintain and improve the quality standards and physical product, and to provide systems and procedures, that facilitate quality service. If the company cannot deliver the service experience customers expect, it cannot hope to develop long-term relationships with them.

Internal marketing is considered to be an essential component of an effective relationship marketing strategy. In Chapter 12 we discussed the crucial role of customer-contact employees in delivering customer satisfaction, and the importance of internal marketing programs to communicate with and empower employees. A service culture that fosters employee involvement and encourages employees to build close relationships with customers provides a strong foundation for a successful relationship marketing strategy.

Segmentation

The segmentation strategy should focus on customers who have a potentially high lifetime value, or are strategically significant in other ways. For example, they might be reference customers (customers that other customers copy), or customers that initially enable a hospitality company to enter a market segment. The Pareto Principle (sometimes called the 80/20 rule) can provide an effective criterion for identifying customers that are strategically significant. This principle suggests that the top 20 percent of customers generate 80 percent of sales and profits. In hospitality, these customers include frequent travelers, corporations, and intermediaries. The branded chains are aware that frequent business travelers, who have a high lifetime value, are important customers and highly sought after. National and international corporations and key intermediaries also generate substantial volumes of hotel bed-nights. Hospitality chains use their customer relationship marketing executives to liaise regularly with these key accounts, nurturing the relationship and trying to protect the business from competitors. Hospitality companies need to be careful in applying the 80/20 rule, as the biggest customers may not be the most profitable. Big customers may require costly pre-, during and post-encounter service as well as deeply discounted rates, thereby reducing their profitability.

Customers who have a relatively low spend per transaction but a high frequency of visits can generate a high spend over the lifetime of their patronage. In family restaurants, the average sale is considerably lower than staying in a hotel. However, research discovered that a loyal 'pizza' customer had a lifetime value of $8000.

A transactional marketing approach is appropriate when the potential lifetime value of a customer is low, and where customers choose not to engage in a long-term relationship with companies.

Figure 14.1 illustrates marketing strategies for frequent and lifetime value customers.

Database

Sophisticated information communications technology is a prerequisite for multi-unit companies interested in developing a relationship marketing strategy. The role

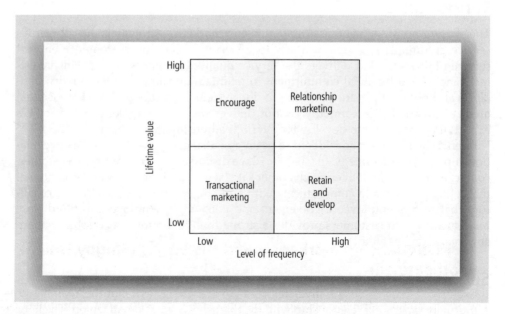

Figure 14.1 Marketing strategies for frequent and lifetime value customers

of the database is to record customer information, monitor consumption activity and facilitate marketing communication activity to relational target markets.

Recording customer information

Regular customers mention their preferences to the customer-contact employees during their stay in a hotel. These preferences might include personal factors, such as a favorite newspaper or type of pillow, or a food allergy. For customers who stay in several hotels belonging to the same hotel chain, these preferences can be recorded in customer information files on the database. This enables all the hotels in the chain to access the information easily, and provide regular customers with enhanced service.

Monitoring consumption

Hospitality companies need to track the sales pattern of key accounts and record the characteristics of key customer transactions in all the chain's properties. Monitoring consumption activity enables the company to identify potential new key accounts, reward those customers who maintain current high value sales, and track accounts that are declining in sales volume.

Marketing communication campaigns

In Chapter 9 we discussed the role of the database in personalizing communications with key customers. The database is crucial in identifying key customers to target with specific promotions, and in providing accurate contact information.

Trust and commitment

Trust and commitment are core concepts in relationship marketing. Customers must have confidence in the company's competence and integrity. In this sense, it helps for the customer and the company to have shared values. It is less attractive for customers to develop a relationship with a company whose activities conflict with the customers' value set. Trust is built up over time, and depends upon the company being competent in delivering on its promises, and not exploiting the customer. The long-term relationship provides opportunities for the company to demonstrate its values and fairness to the customer. By trusting the company, the customer feels secure in the relationship and the company earns the customer's commitment.

As part of a long-term relationship, there is an implication that both parties are prepared to make short-term sacrifices for longer-term benefits. From a hotel company's perspective, this means that opportunistic behaviors to make short-term profits should be avoided – for example, the company may maintain a price commitment to key customers during high season periods.

Case study 14.1 provides an illustration of successful relationship marketing.

Case study

14.1 Relationship marketing and the English Rugby Union Football team

Exclusive Hotels, owner of five-star Pennyhill Park, AA Hotel of the Year, has entered into a mutually rewarding relationship with the English Rugby Football Union. The hotel became the official England Rugby's pre-match venue and training facility in Surrey – partly because Exclusive Hotels willingly spent £150,000 on a good-quality rugby training pitch. General manager David Broadhead said: 'They use the hotel approximately sixteen weeks of the year, and international sport is at such a level now that people are used to this level of comfort. A lot of the gym equipment in our new spa has been bought in consultation with the RFU and designed for players. It's really more of a partnership than a client–customer relationship'.

(Source Hayward, 2003)

Clearly, delivering consistent customer satisfaction is an essential condition for implementing a relationship marketing strategy. Customers who suffer from inconsistent service standards cannot give their trust to a company that is incompetent.

Recognition and reward

Customers who have entered into a relationship with a company generally expect recognition. The customer information file on the database enables key customers to be identified before checking in to the hotel. Bedrooms on executive floors and individually named suites easily identify key customers to all of the customer-contact employees, who should be trained to recognize, greet and look after them appropriately.

A mutually beneficial relationship implies that there are rewards for both parties. We have already discussed how the company gains in additional sales and profits by cultivating long-term relationships with key customers. Loyal customers should also be rewarded for their patronage. Whilst recognition plays an important role in rewarding customers, tangible reward systems can help to build customer loyalty.

Loyalty

We will now discuss the concept of loyalty, the relationship marketing ladder of loyalty, frequent guest programs in hospitality, and customer disloyalty.

The concept of loyalty

We have established that virtually all hospitality companies are interested in encouraging customers to repeat purchase and generate positive word-of-mouth. However, there is a distinction between a frequent customer and a loyal customer. Frequency is not an indicator of loyalty – for example, a frequent business traveler might be compelled to stay at a particular brand because of his company's expenses policy. Other frequent customers may regularly patronize the establishment because there are no effective competitors in the area, and these customers could easily defect if serious competition emerged in the neighborhood. Indeed, some frequent customers might even be extremely dissatisfied with the offer, and complain, but still have to stay because of the lack of alternatives. Just because a customer visits a hospitality premises on a regular basis, it does not mean they are loyal!

A loyal customer is true, faithful and constant. A loyal customer is completely satisfied with the marketing offer, emotionally committed, and does not seriously consider competitor alternatives. There is also evidence to suggest that totally satisfied customers are six times more likely to repurchase, and probably have a greater propensity for loyalty than partially satisfied customers. Loyal customers take ownership of the relationship and refers to the brand in first person terms (for example, loyal pub customers often refer to 'my local pub'), they tune into the marketing communication messages sent out by the brand, and shut out the messages from competitors. If there is a service problem, loyal customers are more likely to report it because they genuinely want to help. Price is less of an issue, and is considered as part of an equitable brand value proposition. Most importantly, loyalty creates a major barrier to switching behavior and is closely linked to relationship marketing. True loyalty can transcend rational behavior, and customers who are truly loyal to their hospitality brand have become emotionally involved with the brand, its persona and its values. Customer loyalty is therefore a powerful concept in marketing.

However, customer loyalty is a complex phenomenon. A key issue is to aim to build loyalty with customers who belong to the target market profile; attracting loyalty from the 'wrong customers' can be dangerous and embarrassing. Building customer loyalty to the brand, and to the unit, is important for the hospitality marketer. In hospitality, customers can be both brand-loyal and loyal to specific units from several brands. There is evidence to suggest that harder, more standardized brands generate customer loyalty to the brand, whilst softer, less standardized brands tend to generate loyalty towards individual units. What is certain is that frequent travelers who visit many destinations on a regular basis become hotel-loyal and not only brand-loyal. An international frequent traveler might therefore stay at first-choice hotels from a range of brands depending upon the location, choosing the Hilton in New York, the Holiday Inn at Birmingham, the Marriott in Athens, the Novotel in Sydney, and the Shangri-La at Kowloon, Hong Kong.

Activity 14.1

Think about your relationships with hospitality brands.

- Can you identify brands (or units), where you have a transactional relationship?
- Are there any brands (units) to which you are especially loyal?
- Can you explain your feelings as a customer towards these brands?
- If you work for a hospitality brand, has your relationship with the brand changed because of your experience as an employee?

It is a common misconception that all companies should adopt a relationship marketing strategy. However, there is a role for transactional marketing in commodity mass markets – for example, in the contract-catering sector. Building frequency is a legitimate marketing objective and strategy, just as building loyalty is an appropriate objective and strategy for companies seeking to develop a relational approach to marketing. Table 14.2 presents the different marketing approaches that can be adopted when developing a frequent or a loyal customer base.

Table 14.2 Marketing Strategies Targeting Frequent versus Loyal Customers
(Adapted from Lewis and Chambers, 2000, reproduced by kind permission of R. C. Lewis)

Marketing activities	Frequent customer base	Loyal customer base
Objective	Build traffic, sales and profitability	Build brand desirability, sales and profit
Strategy	Incentivize repeat transactions	Build personal brand relationships
Focus	Segment behavior	Individual emotional and rational needs
Tactics	Sales promotions, focus on free offers/discounts/rewards; frequent guest program with incentives	Customized communications, preferred status, emotional rewards, added value upgrades; loyalty guest programs with recognition and rewards
Measurement	Transactions, sales growth	Individual lifetime value, emotional responses, attitudinal change

The relationship marketing ladder of loyalty

Research into consumer buyer behavior has categorized customers into six different types according to their usage and loyalty, and different marketing strategies are required for these different types of customers. The bottom of the ladder of loyalty starts with 'prospects', who need to be persuaded to make a first purchase and experience the offer. Once consumers have actually become 'purchasers', then the task is to encourage them to become regular 'clients', and then to turn clients into 'supporters' and supporters into 'advocates'. Finally, 'advocates' become 'partners' in the ultimate, mutually rewarding relationship (Figure 14.2). The idea of the loyalty ladder is to progress appropriate customers further up the ladder. However, customers can of course also move down or off the ladder; and some customers will choose not to move at all. The loyalty ladder recognizes the need for segmenting customers in terms of the propensity for loyalty and their lifetime value. Whilst LTV can be calculated using the customer retention rate, achieved spend and variable costs, it is much more difficult to determine a customer's propensity to be loyal.

Frequent and loyalty guest program

In our discussion earlier in this chapter, we explained the crucial difference between frequency and loyalty. This distinction should also apply to any discussion of frequent guest programs (FGP) and loyalty guest programs (LGP). However, in everyday language these expressions are virtually interchangeable, and hospitality companies use the term FGP to apply to any loyalty program.

'Partner': someone who has the relationship of a partner with you

'Advocate': someone who actively recommends you to others, who does your marketing for you

'Supporter': someone who likes your organization, but only supports you passively

'Client': someone who has done business with you on a repeat basis but may be negative, or at best neutral, towards your organization

'Purchaser': someone who has done business with your organization

'Prospect': someone whom you believe may be persuaded to do business with you

Figure 14.2 The relationship marketing ladder of loyalty (Peck *et al.*, 1999)

The origin of rewarding customers for their patronage in tourism dates from the 1970s, when American Airlines introduced a successful frequent flyer program (FFP) that was quickly imitated by competitors. The airlines' system of managing their FFP provided hotel companies with a template that they copied, and today's FGP enable frequent travelers to receive points and/or air miles whenever they stay at a hotel in the scheme. Although a number of chain restaurants have tried to launch frequent diner programs, few have been successful apart from the Hard Rock Café. The following discussion relates to hotel brands.

A frequent guest program that adopts a transactional approach to marketing aims to build traffic by offering rewards from a wide range of services, including hotels and travel, retail and financial products. In contrast, companies that adopt a relational approach encourage regular customers to join a club to receive recognition as a privileged guest, and focus rewards on added benefits during the stay at the hotel.

Each of the major hospitality brands recognizes the importance of offering a guest program to reward regular customers (see Table 14.3), and the customers are very

Table 14.3 The Frequent Guest Programs
of International Hotel Brands

Brand	Program
Accor Hotels	Compliments
Best Western	Gold Crown Club
Hilton	HHonors
Holiday Inn	Priority Club
Hyatt	Gold Passport
Marriott	Rewards
Shangri-La	Golden Circle
Six Continents	Six Continents Club
Starwood	Preferred Guest

aware of their importance to the hotels. All of these programs provide different levels of membership, which are determined according to the number of nights a customer stays in the hotels. The higher the number of stays, the more generous the benefits become as a customer graduates to the top tier of VIP membership. Some programs allow customers to 'double dip' – this means that a customer who has an airline FFP membership can earn air miles whilst staying at the hotel, and at the same time earn points from the hotel, which are credited to their FGP. We will review two different programs here: Hilton's HHonors and Shangri-La's Golden Circle.

Hilton HHonors

The Hilton program is open to customers staying in any of their current lodging brands, ranging from the budget properties to luxury hotels. However, customers who are on discounted rates booked via channels such as wholesalers, tour operators, aircrew, and Internet auction sites are excluded from the scheme. There are four levels of membership:

1 Blue – there is no minimum qualifying number of stays; benefits include expedited check-in, free newspaper, spouse stays free, and express checkout.
2 Silver VIP – to qualify a customer has to have a minimum of four qualifying stays or ten qualifying nights. The benefits include 15 percent bonus points, and complimentary access to the hotel's health club.
3 Gold VIP – to qualify a customer has to have a minimum of 16 qualifying stays or 36 qualifying nights. The benefits include 25 percent bonus points, and upgraded accommodation when available, depending upon the type of hotel/brand.
4 Diamond VIP – to qualify a customer has to have a minimum of 28 qualifying stays or 60 qualifying nights. The benefits include 50 percent bonus points, guaranteed reservations availability up to 48 hours before booking, and a reward 'planner' service to help arrange all the customer's travel needs.

Hilton has agreements with more than 60 airlines, and encourages double dipping. The rewards for staying in the budget brands are considerably lower in value than those in the mid- and upscale brands. Hilton has negotiated an extensive network of partners to provide customers with the opportunity to either earn HHH points when using their services, or redeem points. The partners include AT&T Wireless for telephone services, Chase and CITIMortgages for real estate finance, Critics Choice Video for DVD and VHS films, FTD.com for flowers, GMAC Insurance, and several car hire firms including National Car Rental.

Although Hilton promotes its guest program as a world of 'recognition and rewards', the scale of the program, with many millions of members from a wide range of hospitality target markets staying at 2,400 hotels and able to redeem their points from a variety of products and services, suggests that this is really a transaction-orientated FGP.

Shangri-La Golden Circle

Shangri-La's Golden Circle is for privileged guests who stay at Shangri-La or Traders Hotels. The focus is on guest recognition and individual personal preferences. There are three tiers of membership: Classic, Executive and Elite. Each hotel has an exclusive Golden Circle members' floor, and other benefits include private check-in and check-out, complimentary breakfast, spouse stays free, free access to the fitness center and swimming pool, and a suite upgrade if available at an extra charge of US$25. Executive and Elite members enjoy additional welcome amenities, guaranteed reservations availability (72/48 hours prior to arrival), and early check-in. The only Golden Circle benefit that is not linked to hotel services is the air miles offered to customers, from approximately 25 airlines.

The Shangri-La program focuses on recognition and provides rewards linked to the hospitality offered by the hotel. With less than 50 hotels, two complementary brands, and narrow target markets, the Golden Circle is a genuine relational marketing program aimed at generating guest loyalty.

Activity 14.2

Log on to Hilton Hotels (www.hiltonworldwide.com) and Shangri-La Hotels (www.shangri-la.com). Both the Hilton HHonors FGP and the Golden Circle FGP are accessible from the home page.

- Compare the language used by Hilton and Shangri-La to describe their FGP

- Review the rewards offered and the conditions in both schemes

- What differences can you identify between these hotel companies' approach to marketing their FGP?

Disadvantages of frequent guest programs

The main disadvantages of FGP include the following:

- Benefits are awarded to individual guests, and the most frequent guests are those staying on business – so their companies pay for the hotel accommodation but do not gain the rewards
- There is the issue of who is liable for paying the tax on the benefits accrued from a FGP
- There is the potential liability of unredeemed rewards eventually being claimed

- Customers who stay in hotels frequently join the FGP of several hotel companies, which erodes competitive advantage and encourages customer switching behavior
- Costs are incurred setting up and administering the scheme.

Problems with relationship marketing

Relationship marketing has been criticized for a number of reasons. First, there is a limit to the number of relationships a customer can sustain with companies. Customers cannot have a one-to-one relationship with every hospitality company they patronize. Whilst companies build unrealistic expectations about their customers' willingness to give them trust, loyalty and commitment, consumers are bombarded with too many competing messages. In reality, consumers can only give their loyalty to a small number of brands. Consumers are also concerned about organizations' use of personal information, which has to be disclosed when staying in a hotel. Unsolicited communication in the form of direct mailings and email messages, which are trying to build a relationship with customers, can actually be counterproductive and turn customers away. Other criticisms include the following:

- Hospitality companies want customers to be loyal, but often fail to deliver the services that customers expect
- The special introductory offers to attract 'new' loyal customers mean that existing loyal customers, who are not offered the same terms, are not treated fairly
- Customers can change their preferences, and do not always want the same newspaper or drink every time they check in
- The treatment given to customers in the FGP can be upsetting, or even offensive, to other customers.

Indeed, some critics suggest that relationship marketing is not really about a genuine relationship but is in fact a one-way communication from company to the customer, and that when a customer tries to communicate with the company it does not seem to listen.

Conclusion

Despite the legitimate criticisms of relationship marketing, loyalty is a powerful concept. Those hospitality companies that can develop meaningful relationships with customers do gain a competitive advantage. However, a relationship marketing strategy is not appropriate for all branded hospitality chains; companies aiming to develop a relationship marketing strategy must have a strong service culture that delivers high customer satisfaction, effective service recovery strategies, and relevant recognition and reward policies, in order to create customer trust, commitment and loyalty.

In this chapter, we have explained:

- How relationship marketing strategies focus on customer retention and recognize the long-term value of loyal customers
- That transactional marketing strategies focus on customer acquisition and short-term, discontinuous customer contact
- That the lifetime value of regular customers is relatively high, and increases in customer retention can enhance profitability significantly
- That all hotel companies are aware of the importance of repeat guests, and have developed FGP to attract and reward frequent guests
- Why frequency is not an indicator of loyalty
- That loyal customers are less price conscious and are unlikely to consider competitors' offers
- That frequent guests are loyal to individual hotels, as well as to hotel brands
- That there are limits to the number of relationships customers can have with companies.

Now check your understanding of this chapter by answering the following questions:

Review questions

1 Analyze the differences between a relationship marketing strategy and a transactional marketing strategy within the context of hospitality
2 A hotel company is planning to develop a relationship marketing strategy. Explain what is required to implement an effective relationship marketing strategy successfully
3 Discuss the concept of customer loyalty in the hospitality industry
4 Evaluate the role of frequent guest programs in the international hotel industry.

References and further reading

Buttle, F. (1995). *Relationship Marketing Theory and Practice*. Paul Chapman.
Grönroos, C. (1994). From marketing mix to relationship marketing: towards a paradigm shift in marketing. *Management Decision*, **32(2)**, 4–20.
Hayward, P. (2003). Back Finds Himself in England Set-up. *Daily Telegraph*, 13 February.
Lewis, R. C. and Chambers, R. E. (2000). *Marketing Leadership in Hospitality, Foundations and Practice*. John Wiley, p. 64.
Peck, H., Payne, A., Christopher, M. and Clark, M. (1999). *Relationship Marketing for Competitive Advantage: Winning and Keeping Customers*. Butterworth-Heinemann.
Reichheld, F. (1993). Loyalty based management. *Harvard Business Review*, Mar/Apr, 64–73.

Part E
The marketing plan

Chapter 15
Marketing planning

Chapter Objectives

After working through this chapter, you should be able to:

- Understand the contexts and types of marketing planning in hospitality organizations
- Describe a generic process for marketing planning
- Carry out the research needed to develop a strategic marketing plan
- Explain how analytical tools are used to evaluate a hospitality business's current and potential situation
- Recognize the limitations of marketing planning, and the importance of contingency planning.

Introduction

Planning is widespread in business of all sizes. Larger companies have more formalized planning processes, but smaller companies also perform planning essentials. A plan can be thought of as a set of decisions about what a company wants to achieve and how it is going to achieve it. The essence of a plan is, therefore, a goal with accompanying strategy and tactics. The goal defines what the company wants to achieve, while the strategy and tactics set out how the goal will be achieved. A marketing plan sets out the marketing objectives that a company wants to achieve and the strategy and tactics that will be used to meet the objectives.

In this chapter we will build on your learning from the pre-encounter, encounter and post-encounter hospitality marketing activities discussed in previous chapters. You will see how marketing plans in operational units consist of objectives, strategies and tactics across the three stages of a customer relationship: pre-encounter, encounter and post-encounter.

Contexts of marketing planning

Although unit-level marketing plans are the major focus of this chapter, it is important to acknowledge that marketing planning is carried out at many levels in more complex hospitality organizations.

Corporate marketing planning

Complex hospitality organizations such as the Marriott Corporation produce strategic marketing plans at the highest corporate level. These are concerned with major strategic decisions, such as which geographic markets to enter, which hospitality formats to offer in those markets, and strategies for market entry – joint venture, acquisition or organic development, for example. Decisions are also made on how to allocate resources to support the marketing activities of member divisions.

Divisional marketing planning

A divisional marketing plan focuses on the goals of a major division of a hospitality company. A division is a profit center comprised of one or more core businesses, run by a dedicated chief executive and management team. For example, a major hospitality group may produce marketing plans for its contract catering division, its resort hotels division and its budget hotels division. Each division will sets its own goals, often in terms of market share, and develop strategies for goal achievement. These strategies will consist of plans to open (or close) operational units, to focus on particular market segments, to position against named competitors and to compete by employing a particular set of competitive advantages.

Unit marketing planning

An operational unit may be a hotel or a restaurant that competes in a particular market. Strategies focus on issues such as targeting, positioning, and developing strong pre-encounter, encounter and post-encounter marketing mixes. Goals can be developed for pre-encounter marketing (raise awareness, develop expectations, develop preference), encounter marketing (achieve revenue and average spend targets) or post-encounter marketing (satisfaction, intention to do repeat business, share of customer spend). Overarching marketing goals are also employed at unit level – for example, occupancy levels, yield, and average room rate.

Departmental marketing plan

Within a hotel, different departments (such as the rooms division, or food and beverages) may produce their own marketing plans. The focus at departmental level is generally much more tactical. The core strategic marketing decisions of segmentation, targeting and positioning will have been made at unit or even divisional level, and departments operate within the parameters of those strategic decisions. For example, the rooms division manager may need to find a solution for an unexpected loss of business. If a tour group suddenly cancels, the manager needs to develop a rapid tactical response to win additional business from targeted customer groups, such as airlines, transients or meetings and conventions.

Types of marketing plan

In general, a distinction can be made between strategic and tactical marketing plans (McDonald, 1999). As the focus of marketing plans shifts from corporate through division to unit and department, plans become much more tactical. Tactical marketing plans are focused on the short term, and generally are developed for a one-year maximum timeframe.

Strategic marketing plans

Strategic marketing plans (SMP) are generally established for a minimum three- to five-year term. They focus on longer-term goals, such as developing market share, building yield, and growing revenues. Core marketing decisions are made about market segmentation, target markets and market positioning, and these decisions establish the foundations on which tactical plans can be built. A company's decision to target, say, aircrew and meetings and conventions, and to position against certain named competitors in each of these segments, will influence the level of investment in developing offers to appeal to these markets, communication strategies to send messages to them, and channels to sell to them. SMP decisions have major cost consequences, and are not easy to reverse. A company that changes its strategic position in the marketplace too frequently runs the risk of confusing customers and alienating investors.

There are two major theories that have identified major alternative strategies: those of Porter, and of Treacey and Wiersema.

Porter

Porter (1980) claims that there are three core strategies for success, whatever the industry. If firms do not adopt any one of these strategies, Porter suggests that they will be 'stuck in the middle', losing cost-sensitive business to low-cost leaders and high-margin business to firms adopting an added-value, differentiated strategy. Firms stuck in the middle are not as profitable as firms that have adopted one of Porter's generic strategies.

Porter's three generic strategies are overall cost leadership, differentiation, and focus.

Overall cost leadership Firms adopting a low-cost position relative to competitors need to pursue a strategy of cost control in every aspect of the business. In hospitality firms, this means that food and beverage costs, payroll costs, energy, maintenance, administration, marketing and distribution overheads, décor, fabrics and furniture costs, are all designed to give the lowest possible running costs; the choice of location should be at the lowest possible land cost, and all these factors are critically examined to achieve and maintain the lowest cost position in the market.

The cost-leadership strategy is most suited to new-build hospitality premises, where the construction of the operation can be designed for maximum efficiency – for example, Formula 1. Companies adopting a cost-leadership strategy need to generate high economies of scale in marketing and purchasing, which implies that the company should be seeking to obtain a high market share. This strategy is most suitable for commodity markets like the accommodation budget sector, where the nature of the product is hard to differentiate.

Differentiation Porter's second generic strategy recommends that firms adopt a product–service differentiation policy that is perceived by customers as significantly different from competitors. In hospitality, differentiation is closely linked to branding and offer formulation. Firms adopting a differentiation strategy strive to deliver a clearly defined experience that differs from competitors'. We have already discussed the role of differentiation in Chapter 4, and provided examples from the hospitality industry.

Focus The focus strategy, Porter's third generic strategy, suggests that firms should concentrate on one narrow market segment, or one geographic area, or one primary product. The benefits of a focus strategy are derived from serving one target segment very well, and more effectively than differentiated or low-cost firms. A focused firm may adopt a differentiated or low-cost strategy aimed at the chosen market segment. We discussed a focus (or niche) marketing strategy in Chapter 4.

Treacey and Wiersema

Treacey and Wiersema (1995) have also identified three major approaches to marketing strategy that companies can adopt: operational excellence, product leadership, and customer intimacy. They call these market disciplines.

Operational excellence This core marketing discipline calls for doing a limited number of things extremely well. It implies the development of a well-defined value proposition based on clearly understood customer expectations, and the repeated production and delivery of the product-service that complies with exact specifications of a Standard Operating Procedure Manual. Companies like McDonald's, Taco Bell and Pizza Hut fit this model.

Product leadership The product leadership discipline is founded on the belief that relevant, customer-focused innovation will win buyer preference. Companies that stress product leadership nurture ideas, translate them into product–service concepts, and market them successfully. These companies experiment and think 'out-of-the-box'. The fully automated hotel cannot be far away. Some hotels have already done away with check-in, check-out and room-keys.

Customer intimacy   The third marketing discipline, customer intimacy, is based upon the provision of solutions that are customized for individual buyers. In these companies, empowerment is pushed to the front line and the company is flexible, doing what it takes to produce satisfied customers. Ritz-Carlton Hotels prides itself on being such an organization.

Tactical marketing plans

Tactical marketing plans differ from strategic plans in both their timeframe and their content. The typical tactical marketing plan (TMP) operates within a short timeframe, normally no longer than one year. The TMP is subordinate to the SMP, and therefore operates within the segmentation, targeting and positioning parameters established by the SMP. TMP consist primarily of campaigns and events, which may be unit- or department-specific.

A campaign is a promotion that runs for a short period of time. Campaigns are generally expressed in carefully targeted and timed customer or prospect communications. A campaign might be a sales promotion designed to fill rooms during the shoulder period, or it might be a sales blitz designed to generated prospects for a salesperson to follow up. Typically, a campaign is designed to produce specific behaviors in the targeted audience – for example, making a reservation, or contacting a call center – in the immediate term.

Event-based marketing is the term used to describe the creation and communication of offers to customers at particular points in time. The event which triggers an offer is typically something that occurs in the customer's personal or business life. For example, an engagement, announced in a local newspaper, might trigger a hotel to offer to host the couple's wedding reception. The scheduling of a 'watch and clock industry' trade show by a city convention center might trigger a timely offer by a hotel chain to house visitors from exhibiting companies. Event-based marketers put together offers that are unique to the event, set the price and promote to a tightly defined target market. The success of an event can only be measured when all the costs and revenues have been compared.

A generic marketing plan structure

In this section we present a generic framework for marketing planning. This offers a structured methodology for establishing marketing objectives, strategies and tactics. Not all of the components of the framework appear in every marketing plan – for example, departmental plans may not incorporate a segmentation, targeting and positioning component. The framework consists of nine major elements:

1 Vision, mission, values
2 Situation audit
3 Objectives

4 Segmentation, targeting and positioning
5 Marketing mix
6 Budgeting
7 Implementation
8 Controls
9 Evaluation

This framework presents an analysis of where the company is now, and provides direction for where the company wants to be at some predetermined future point. It focuses the development of marketing mix strategies and tactics, and addresses the questions of cost, implementation and control.

Vision, mission, values

Many leading hospitality companies have developed vision statements, mission statements, or sets of values. These are enduring statements about what the organization is *en route* to becoming in ten years or more (the vision statement), why the organization exists (the mission statement), and how the organization shall act in relationships with its stakeholders, such as shareholders, customers, employees and local community (the values statement). Many organizations do have policies like these, but merge them into a single generic mission statement that contains elements of all three. These statements serve as both a guide and constraint on marketing planning. If the vision is to be the world's leading themed restaurant chain in ten years' time, then a marketing plan to develop a budget hotel chain, no matter how profitable it might seem, will be ruled out. Corporate values such as respect for the environment might rule out the development of a hotel resort close to an endangered reef. The pursuit of diversity in employment might favor the recruitment of indigenous populations to serve in front-office roles, interacting with Western business guests.

Business mission statements are succinct 'philosophical' statements, at most a page in length. The mission defines the purpose of a business, and the desired benefits that all the stakeholders should enjoy from the business.

Mission statements can be published in annual reports and displayed in prominent places for customers to view – for example, in reception and lobby areas. Mission statements are also given to new employees as part of their induction process. Smaller independent hospitality organizations are less likely to have a formal mission statement, although owners and managers may have a very clear vision of what they want their business to achieve.

The purpose of a mission statement is to enable top management to provide:

● A focus for the future direction of the company
● A link with the company's short- and medium-term objectives, and the long-term goals of the organization
● A tool for communicating top management's perception of the company's future with its various stakeholders.

A mission statement can include the following elements:

1 A definition of the broad scope of the business, the markets served, the products and services offered, and the distinctive benefits provided by the organization to its customers

Figure 15.1 Prêt à Manger's mission statement (source: Prêt à Manger)

2 A summary of the distinctive competencies the business has developed – for example, a service ethos (Marriott), quality (Savoy), product consistency (McDonald's)
3 A description of the desired market position *vis-à-vis* competitors
4 A clear statement about the company's values.

The Prêt à Manger mission statement emphasizes the company's environmental ethics and passion for fresh, healthy and natural food compared to their fast-food competitors (see Figure 15.1). Prêt à Manger's packaging emphasizes the natural ingredients provided by named suppliers, and their good environmental practices. This concise mission statement establishes the company's competitive position and clearly provides a strategic direction for future planning.

Activity 15.1

Log onto the following hotel websites and evaluate their mission statements using the criteria outlined above:

● www.ritzcarlton.com

● www.shangri-la.com

The proliferation of corporate mission statements, some of which are bland, lack originality and appear unconvincing, has prompted considerable criticism. Certainly, the development of a mission statement that does not reflect the company's historic values or its distinctive competencies, and which the employees clearly do not endorse, can be legitimately criticized. Meaningless 'motherhood' statements, providing solemn assurances of service and quality, are really faulty exercises in public relations, and do not convince employees or customers.

Situation audit – 'where are we now?'

An early step in writing a marketing plan for a hospitality company is to carry out research into the company, and its environment, to answer the question 'where are we now?' Hospitality managers must try to be objective and rational about their company when evaluating the business's strengths and weaknesses. Too often an emotional attachment to the business can influence owners and managers, who see the weaknesses identified by customers as being minor, irrelevant or even attractive, rather than the negative attributes they really are. Although managers normally prepare their own marketing plans, the use of outside consultants can bring impartiality to the marketing planning process. Ideally, the situation audit for a property should be written up as brief factual statements covering all the key aspects of the hospitality business. The two sections of the situation audit are the internal audit and the external audit, and the key issues are summarized in a SWOT (Strengths, Weaknesses, Opportunities, Threats) analysis.

Internal audit

The internal audit assesses all aspects of the hospitality unit's operations, with the aim of establishing what the business is doing well – the strengths – and which parts of the business are performing poorly – the weaknesses. Managers can usually identify their business's strengths and, more often than not, know their weaknesses; but the difficulty is recognizing the difference between the symptoms of a problem (for example, low food sales) and the cause of the problem (in this case, unpopular menu items, high prices, poor service, unappealing décor, or a combination of all of these factors). By identifying the causes of the problem, managers can plan action to correct the reasons for the poor performance and improve the offer to customers. Strengths and weakness can be identified in a rigorous way, first by vertical analysis (within business functions – finance, operations, marketing, human resources, for example) and then horizontally, by looking at cross-functional processes and issues such as leadership and culture.

Most medium and larger hospitality companies are composed of a number of strategic business units (SBUs), some of which will be in the early stages of development and some of which will be mature. Some will be heavy users of cash to build market share, others will be powerful generators of cash surpluses. A healthy, well-managed company will have a balanced portfolio of SBUs, and the internal audit should assess the health of the product-service portfolio. One tool that has been developed to help in this assessment is the Boston Consulting Group (BCG) matrix.

The BCG matrix is an analytical model based on a SBU's relative market share and the industry's market growth. The rate of market growth indicates the attractiveness of a market – higher-growth markets are usually more attractive than low-growth markets. Relative market share indicates the degree of dominance a SBU holds in its marketplace, and is the share of the company in comparison to the market leader.

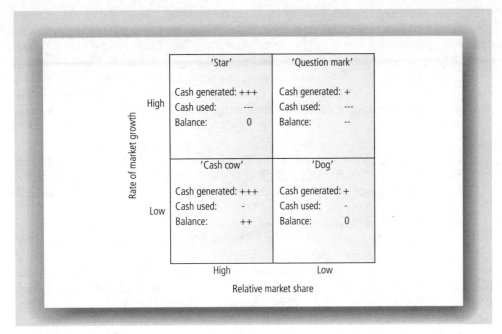

Figure 15.2 BCG portfolio analysis – cash generated and cash used (source: McDonald, 1999, p. 185)

For example, if Company X (the market leader) has a 20 percent market share and Company Y has 5 percent, then Y's relative market share is 0.25. The combination of these factors provides companies with a tool to evaluate possible strategic directions and, most importantly from a marketing planning perspective, to calculate the cash generation and cash usage of each SBU. This model's four quadrants have been labeled as follows, according to the characteristics of the SBU's performance (see Figure 15.2):

1 *Star* (high market growth/high relative market share). A star is a hospitality brand that has a relatively high share of a high-growth market. The company will need to reinvest the cash generated from this SBU in order to roll out the brand by acquiring/building additional outlets and to maintain its position. All the cash generated by this SBU is used within it.
2 *Cash cow* (low market growth/high relative market share). Cash cows operate in mature markets with low growth rates and high relative market share. They generate cash and high profits, because of their economies of scale and low marketing costs. The profits generated are reinvested by the parent company to fund the development of the next category – question marks.
3 *Question mark* (high market growth/low relative market share). Question marks operate in high growth markets, but suffer from a relatively low market share. Most new products start out as question marks. They have a low relative share of a growing market. Companies may develop many new product ideas, and those that are retained require significant marketing support and therefore use more cash than they generate. If they succeed, they can eventually turn into stars and ultimately into cash cows, to support additional innovation.

4 *Dog* (low market growth/low relative market share). Dogs operate in mature markets and have low relative market share. These businesses have to be tightly managed to ensure that they do not become a liability. Dogs can be cash-neutral; but if they start to make a loss they need to be disposed of quickly. Dogs are rarely able to generate the profits and growth expected by major companies. Whilst it does not generate sufficient return for its current owners, in the hands of new owners (who might have different performance measures) a dog may make a satisfactory return.

Marketing planners strive to achieve a balanced portfolio of SBUs with sufficient cash cows to generate profits to satisfy shareholders and fund investment in question marks. The disposal of dogs is essential to avoid them becoming a financial and time-consuming drain on the resources of the company.

The BCG model has been criticized because of its narrow focus in only using two factors to assess cash generation and use. The fragmented nature of the hospitality industry also creates market definition problems, and trying to establish the rates of market growth and accurate market share figures is not always easy. Although the BCG has limited practical use, the language of question marks, stars, cash cows and dogs is used in business, and the principles of cash generation and cash usage are helpful in understanding a multi-product portfolio.

Marketers writing a group or divisional plan also have to compile information on strengths and weaknesses, based on collecting data from the group's operational units. A key issue for head office marketers is delivering a consistent quality standard across hotels marketed under the same brand. A particular difficulty is when hotels under a single brand are a mix of owned, contracted and franchised units. The group marketing plan will also need to address the effectiveness of group sales and marketing activities in creating brand image and raising brand awareness, as well as building long-term relationships with key account customers and intermediaries.

External audit

Remember, the external environment includes all the factors over which the company has no control. The purpose of an external audit is to identify potential opportunities that might be exploited by the firm, and any threats that might damage the business. The external factors are applicable to all companies operating in the same competitor set. The external influences impacting on a company can be classified under two headings: the macro-environment and the micro-environment.

The macro-environment   The macro-environment includes major regional, national and global trends influencing business and society in broad general terms. Earlier in this book reference was made to these PESTE factors, which obviously influence the demand and supply of hospitality services. The macro-environment analysis evaluates current and future PESTE factors to enable the hospitality business to adapt its operations to changes in the needs and wants of customers, and changes in trading conditions.

The micro-environment   Broad trends in the micro-environment influence all the players. A hospitality company's micro-environment includes external stakeholders and, most importantly, customers, competitors and suppliers. There is no doubt that local or regional influences in the micro-environment can seriously impact upon a firm's trading situation.

Summary

Although the situational audit requires considerable in-depth research and the accumulation of extensive data about the company, only a summary of the audit needs to be presented in the marketing plan. The situational audit, with commentary, focuses on the key factors influencing the current and future performance of the company. Appendices containing more detailed analysis – for example, the customer analysis, changes in consumer behavior, competitor analysis – can be included. A thorough understanding of 'where we are now' forms the basis of effective marketing planning, and this is the function of the situational audit. Table 15.1

Table 15.1 Extract from Hotel SWOT Analysis

	Strengths (internal)	Weaknesses (internal)
Positioning	Brand image rating increased by 3% over key competitor according to independent research	Brand image suffers due to lack of consistency, caused by wide variety of standards in group's units
Location	Most convenient access to motorway network	Problems of noise from passing traffic
Product	Recently refurbished bedroom décor is superior to competitors	Standard bedrooms are smaller than those of two newly-built competitors
Price	Customer questionnaires suggest very high 'value for money' ratings	Leisure-break family inclusive price 10% higher than competitors
Distribution	Continued investment in CRS has ensured quicker response times to enquiries	Conference agents' high commission levels eroding profitability on conference bookings
Marketing communication	Recent advertising and public relations campaign has raised brand awareness by 5% compared to competitor set	Standard hotel brochure format dated compared to new competitors' brochures
People	Key heads of department have worked at the unit for 15+ years	High turnover of housekeeping staff is preventing effective staff training
Processes	Improved check-in/check-out at front desk, according to mystery shopper analysis	Banqueting suite does not have adequate hot food storage facilities
Physical evidence	Excellent landscaping and lighting, and prominent signage on major road	Kitchen waste storage and bin area always untidy
Customer satisfaction	High (and increased) level of repeat business travelers staying compared to two years ago	Customer questionnaires identify problems of inconsistent standards of housekeeping

Table 15.1 (Continued)

	Strengths (*internal*)	Weaknesses (*internal*)
Key relationships	Sales manager has successfully built close relationships with three key intermediaries in the conference market	Lost one key account due to inconsistent housekeeping standards, and not price-competitive
	Opportunities (*external*)	Threats (*external*)
Political	Changes in licensing law will increase family market for Sunday eating out	Changes in health and safety legislation means that kitchen equipment specifications will have to be adapted
Economic	Increased consumer disposable income will generate more demand for leisure breaks	High exchange rate makes cost of foreign holidays relatively cheaper and negatively influences demand for domestic holidays
Socio-cultural	Demand for vegetarian meals is growing due to increased public concern about animal rights	Sophisticated consumers are bored with hotel restaurants
Technological	Growth of Internet and e-commerce provides opportunity to promote leisure breaks on the Internet	Business travel agents directing web links to corporate client's intranet is eroding customer loyalty to hotels
Environmental	Concern for environmental issues means consumers will value biodegradable packaging for takeaway food	Concern about air pollution might discourage tourists from staying in city center locations

illustrates some of the key SWOT data that can emerge from a situation analysis. In this illustration, the internal audit data reflect only the strengths and weaknesses of the marketing function.

The situation audit helps to identify *critical success factors* (also called *key factors for success*), which are company-specific (see Chapter 4).

Objectives – 'where do we want to go?'

Having conducted the 'where are we now?' audit, the next step in this generic marketing planning process is to set objectives. Objectives are statements that translate the hospitality company's mission into easily understood goals regarding markets and products, sales, occupancy, and the marketing mix.

Table 15.2 SMART Marketing Objectives

SMART strategic objectives (3–5 years)	SMART tactical objectives (within 1 year)
To increase sales from Eu165 million in the current year to Eu280 million in Year 3	To increase room occupancy from 69% to 70% within 12 months
To acquire 20 upscale, 100-bedroom properties in target European city center locations within 4 years	To acquire 4 upscale properties, with bedrooms ranging from 80 to 130, in Barcelona, Manchester, Prague and Stuttgart within 12 months
To develop a new food and beverage lifestyle concept suitable for residents and non-residents within 2 years	To test-market a new food and beverage lifestyle concept in Sydney between March and September next year
To introduce a 100 percent satisfaction guarantee or money back policy within 5 years	To increase bookings generated through the website by 25% in the next 12 months
To increase brand awareness amongst European conference agents from a current level of 55% to 60%, in the BDRC European Business Travel survey, within 3 years	

Objectives provide answers to the question 'where do we want to go?' Objective setting is an essential step in the marketing planning process. Companies that do not have objectives fail to provide managers and employees with a clear direction. Objectives should be Specific, Measurable, Achievable, Realistic, and carried out within a set Timetable (SMART). SMART objectives provide managers with operational targets that measure the performance of the business and act as a control mechanism in determining whether management is effective. Examples of strategic and tactical hospitality marketing objectives are provided in Table 15.2.

SMART objectives are formed using quantifiable measures like money, percentages, and numbers. The timetable can either refer to the time period during which the target should be achieved ('to achieve £1m sales within the next twelve-month trading period') or to the date by which a target should be achieved ('to achieve a Michelin star for the restaurant by June 2005').

Marketing objectives will vary across the customer relationship from pre-encounter, through encounter to post-encounter. Managers need to think carefully about what is relevant for each stage.

- Pre-encounter objectives focus on achievements such as: raising awareness, generating understanding and knowledge, creating expectations, building interest, and stimulating first purchase
- Encounter objectives focus on generating customer satisfaction, influencing the level of spending, cross-selling, and up-selling
- Post-encounter objectives focus on building repeat purchase intention, growing share of spend, and promoting positive word-of-mouth.

Marketing planning in lifestyle and growth businesses

Marketing objectives will also vary according to whether the business is a lifestyle business that has no wish to grow, or a business with ambitious owners or investors who want to see the value of their investment increase. Lifestyle entrepreneurs are content to see their restaurants busy with regular customers, their staff happy and secure, and enough money coming in to pay the mortgage. Growth-oriented business people are more likely to set ambitious 'stretch' targets that, if achieved, will see the market value or capitalization of their business improve. Two tools enable the growth-oriented business to develop clear objectives and strategies: gap analysis and the Ansoff matrix.

Gap analysis

Gap analysis is an extension of the 'where are we now?' investigation. Company records should tell the marketer the level of sales achieved in the past and those currently being achieved. An examination of the SWOT conditions should give a good idea of what will happen to sales in the future if the identified threats and opportunities do actually impact on the business, and if the company continues to pursue the same strategies. Very often companies finds there is a 'gap' between where they want to be in terms of sales objectives, and where a forecast based on the SWOT analysis tells them they will be. Gap analysis is the art and science of computing the size of the gap. For example, a parent company of a budget lodging company could set a divisional objective of increasing room revenues from $175m to $300m within three years. The forecast shows that in three years' time sales will be $200m if the present marketing strategy is pursued. There is therefore a gap of $100m ($300m objective less $200m forecast) that has to be filled through additional revenue generation activity (see Figure 15.3). The four alternative strategies for filling the 'gap' were developed into a matrix by H. Igor Ansoff.

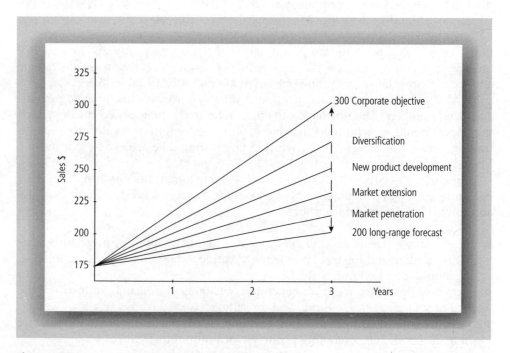

Figure 15.3 Gap analysis (source: McDonald, 1999)

The Ansoff matrix

Ansoff's four strategic options to bridge the revenue gap are:

1 Market penetration
2 Market extension
3 Product development
4 Diversification.

Using each of the Ansoff strategies, where appropriate, a company might be able to bridge the sales gaps, but still not reach the objective. If this were to happen then the company would have to re-evaluate the objectives and perhaps set a revised, lower objective.

A similar approach to sales gap analysis can be used to bridge 'profit' gaps. This approach includes an additional 'operational' strategy, improving productivity. The operations gap includes strategies to reduce costs, improve the sales mix, increase prices, and improve profitability by improving productivity.

Ansoff's four growth options are discussed here.

Market penetration strategy – existing markets/existing products   This strategy is based on the premise that the target markets are satisfied with the existing offer. A market penetration strategy aims to grow the business by increasing sales of the current offer(s) to current target markets. There are three ways to increase sales to existing markets. The first is to increase the frequency with which customers patronize the establishment (i.e. increasing repeat visits), increase customers' spend (i.e. increasing achieved room and meal rates) or, ideally, both. Another method is to attract your competitors' customers. The third route is to grow the market by convincing non-users to buy the product (Figure 15.4). Examples of strategies and tactics used for market penetration include:

- Brand loyalty and frequent stay programs
- Staff training to 'sell up'
- Sales promotions
- In-house marketing activity
- Advertising and direct mail campaigns targeting ex-customers
- PR events for regular customers.

Providing that the market is not changing rapidly and the company is satisfied with profitability, a market penetration strategy is the safest and least risky strategy to adopt.

The danger of relying on a market penetration strategy stems from the problems caused by dynamic changing market conditions, which can change customers' needs and wants and influence competitor activity, thus eroding a company's position.

Market extension or development – new markets/existing products   A market extension strategy features the roll out of existing product-service offers in new markets. In hospitality there are different approaches to market extension, depending upon whether the strategy is focused on growth within existing units or on expanding the number of premises in the group. In existing units, market extension refers to promoting the existing property to new target markets. Most hospitality businesses will target the same primary markets each year, but secondary target markets can change in line with changing market trends. These secondary target markets represent

		Products	
		Existing	New
Markets	Existing	Market penetration or concentration (same markets/same products) Increase market share by: (a) Increase frequency and spend from existing customers (improve internal marketing; brand loyalty programs; frequent-stay promotions; in-house product/price bundles) (b) Attract competitors' customers (promote special offers, raise brand image/brand awareness) (c) Convince non-users to buy products (educate market by informing non-users of the product benefits)	Product development (same markets/new products) Introduce product improvement programs by: (a) Replacement and refurbishment of rooms, food and beverage, and leisure facilities – targeting existing customers (b) Introduction of new technology to improve service quality Introduce product extensions by: (a) Development of new menu items aimed at existing customers
	New	Market extension or development (new market/same product) (a) Target new customers: Identify new target markets and develop marketing communication program to promote existing product, e.g. early-bird diners (b) Target similar customers in different geographic areas: Identify geographic areas with similar demographic profile and roll out existing product (c) Use new distribution channels to reach new markets: e.g. work with intermediaries on joint-marketing initiatives	Diversification and innovation (new market/new product) (a) Intensive (inside the existing firm) Innovative, new bar and food concepts aimed at new target markets, e.g. new leisure center at hotel targeting new local customers (b) Extensive diversification (outside existing firm) Vertical integration (i) Forward (ii) Backward Diversification (i) Horizontal (ii) Concentrated (related) (iii) Conglomerate (non-related)

Figure 15.4 Ansoff or market/product mix

new markets for which the existing product is suitable. Imaginative product/benefit bundles targeting new market segments can highlight the benefits of the company's products. A typical restaurant example is a competitively priced, all-inclusive meal promotion aimed at attracting 'early-bird' diners.

Another approach to market development that is particular relevant to retail hospitality chains is geographic expansion using existing product concepts. There are numerous examples in hospitality of hotel and restaurant brands seeking to expand by rolling out new-build units. Since the product concept is proven, the key issue in expanding geographically is to ensure that the characteristics of the new target market are similar to those of existing successful markets. Hospitality companies also expand geographically by acquisition, which can be riskier, since the newly acquired properties may not conform to the requirements of the branded hospitality chain.

Yet another approach to market development is to reach new markets via extensions of the distribution channel. Joint marketing initiatives with intermediaries who have access to new markets can be effective. For example, an independent hotel can participate in an established leisure break program, like Superbreaks in the UK, and attract new markets by distribution through the travel trade.

Product development – existing markets/new products   Ansoff's product development strategy features enhancement of the product–service offers made to existing customers. Managers in hospitality operations are constantly looking for ways to increase customer satisfaction by improving the product offer. Product development strategies and tactics for existing customer markets include:

- Refurbishment programs to existing operations
- Introduction of new menus
- Introduction of new technology to improve the service operations
- New bar/food concepts aimed at existing customer markets.

Most 'new' product developments in hospitality operations are evolutionary rather than revolutionary. They are product improvements and product modifications, rather than radical new product–service concepts. Many new products are actually line extensions. For example, a new menu item may have been copied from a competitor, because it supplements a company's existing menu. The launch of new products primarily aimed at existing customer markets might also attract new customer groups. Providing the existing markets are profitable markets, product development is a proven strategy to retain customer loyalty.

Diversification – new markets/new products   The diversification strategy focuses on creating new product–service offers for new target customers. This is the riskiest growth strategy, since the company has no existing customer or product knowledge to exploit. Diversification within hospitality units is described as intensive diversification, meaning that new products are offered inside the existing unit. For example, intensive diversification might involve the building of a new facility on the premises, designed to attract new markets. Examples of intensive diversification in an existing hotel might include:

- A new restaurant concept aimed at new target markets (e.g. non-resident customers)
- A new bar targeting new markets (e.g. non-resident customers)
- A new leisure complex aimed at people living in the local neighborhood
- New banqueting/conference and exhibition facilities aimed at new target markets.

Diversification outside the scope of the existing firm is described as extensive, and can take many different forms:

- *Vertical backward integration* means acquiring suppliers – for example, a contract catering firm taking over food distributors
- *Vertical forward integration* involves acquiring intermediaries who have a direct relationship with customers – for example, hotel companies acquiring tour operators, and tour operators acquiring travel agents
- *Horizontal diversification* is the acquisition of a competitor operating in the same market – for example, a mid-market hotel chain taking over another mid-market hotel chain
- *Concentric diversification* is the acquisition or start-up of companies that exploit the hospitality company's core competencies – for example, Haley's Hotel & Restaurant in Leeds started up a delicatessen using its kitchen brigade's skills
- *Conglomerate diversification* is diversification into an unrelated area – for example, builders buying hotels.

The Ansoff matrix enables marketers to evaluate systematically the growth options facing the company. When management has decided which market/product options to pursue, then detailed marketing mix strategies have to be developed to achieve the market/product objectives. For example, in competitive hospitality sectors companies strive to obtain competitive advantage by constantly investing in product development and continually improving the offer to customers. Once this strategy has been decided, the detail of the new product development strategies needs to be considered.

Segmentation, targeting and positioning (STP)

Having set objectives, the next step of this generic marketing planning process is to make the core strategic decisions about how to segment the market, which customer segments to target, and how to position effectively against competitors in the same market. These issues have been addressed in earlier chapters, but it is worth stressing a few points here:

- Market segmentation involves dividing up the market into homogeneous subsets so that marketing strategies and tactics can be developed for one or more segments
- Companies that are innovative in the way they segment a market can enjoy first-mover advantage as they exploit opportunities that have not been recognized by competitors
- Companies can choose to focus on one or more market segments, depending upon the attractiveness of the opportunities and the competencies of the company
- Market positioning is concerned with selecting a competitive position in the market and determining how to compete effectively in that position; for most hospitality sectors, this means choosing a competitive group and identifying how to generate sales to customers.

Until the STP decisions are made, companies cannot begin to develop strategies and tactics. Segmentation and targeting strategies are based upon the findings from the situation audit, whilst the positioning strategy provides the core theme for integrating all the elements of the marketing mix to provide a consistent offer.

Activity 15.2

Log on to the Whitbread website (www.whitbread.co.uk), and at the home page click on 'For Students'. Whitbread provides general information for students about its company history, corporate vision, corporate objectives and strategies.

● Review the data within the context of marketing planning activities, corporate vision and core growth strategies, and markets targeted, as discussed in this chapter.

Marketing mix – 'how do we get there?'

Marketing strategies and marketing tactics are marketing mix decisions made by managers to achieve agreed marketing objectives. Strategies and tactics are deployed to ensure that the company wins sales from the targeted customers (target market segments) against the identified competitors (market positioning).

Marketing mixes for both strategies and tactics will vary according to the stage of the customer relationship – pre-encounter, encounter or post-encounter. Table 15.3 provides a useful framework that can be used to construct appropriate marketing mixes. The eight elements of the hospitality marketing mix are listed vertically and the three relationship stages are listed horizontally. The check marks within the cells indicate the marketing mix elements that are more widely deployed at each stage of the relationship.

Throughout this text we have explained what the responsibility of the marketing team is, and how marketing needs to work with other departments to ensure the marketing offer is consistent and effective. The marketing team plays a major role in pre-encounter marketing to manage demand for the hospitality offer; and in post-encounter marketing to build customer relationships and generate repeat and recommended sales. During the encounter, although marketing should provide input into the physical environment, service process and internal marketing, the primary responsibilities lie with operations and the human resource functions.

Table 15.3 The Hospitality Marketing Mix Matrix

	Pre-encounter marketing mix	Encounter marketing mix	Post-encounter marketing mix
Product/service offer	✓	✓	
Location	✓	✓	
Price	✓	✓	
Distribution	✓		
Marketing communications	✓	✓	✓
Physical environment	✓	✓	
Process	✓	✓	✓
People		✓	

Table 15.4 Accommodation Strategies

Strategy 1 – Lower occupancy/higher achieved room rate	Strategy 2 – higher occupancy/lower achieved room rate
200 rooms at 50% annual room occupancy and an achieved room rate of £273.90 = £10 million	200 rooms at 80% annual room occupancy and an achieved room rate of £172.23 = £10 million

There are two different approaches to constructing the marketing mix part of a marketing plan. In one approach the strategy for each element of the marketing mix in the unit is discussed in turn – for example, the product strategy, the price strategy, the distribution strategy, the marketing communications strategy. In another approach the marketing mix for each functional area of the unit is considered – for example, the marketing mix for the accommodation, the marketing mix for the restaurant operations, the marketing mix for the conference facilities. Either approach is acceptable.

Strategies and tactics need to be developed for each element of the marketing mix, but marketers must ensure that each strategy complements the other marketing mix strategies – inconsistencies between marketing mix strategies will send the target markets mixed messages, and will inevitably be self-defeating.

Just as there is a choice of different marketing *objectives*, so there can also be a choice of different marketing *strategies* that can achieve the same objective. For example, if an annual accommodation sales objective of £10 million has been set for a 200-bedroom hotel, there are different room occupancy strategies and different achieved room rate strategies that can achieve that sales objective (see Table 15.4).

Unit and departmental marketing plans will normally include the detailed tactics that support the broad strategy. These will include events and campaigns that are scheduled for the year ahead. Sales and marketing personnel implement these tactical plans, which typically include answers to the following questions:

- What action is going to be undertaken? (detailed list of events and campaigns)
- What is the event or campaign designed to achieve? (SMART objectives)
- Where will the actions take place? (locations, units, departments)
- When will the action take place? (timetable)
- How much will it cost? (budget)
- Who will run the events and campaigns? (responsibility and authority).

Table 15.5 illustrates the chart for a tactical marketing plan.

Budgeting

Marketing is not free, and companies need to create a budget for the implementation of their strategic and tactical marketing plans. Budgets include two classes of data: forecast revenues and costs. Revenues are generated by departmental sales (rooms division, food and beverage, entertainment, shops and so on), and these appear as forecasts on the top line of an income statement. The marketing plan needs to identify and quantify the cost elements that will be incurred in reaching the revenue targets. Not all cost elements are regarded as marketing costs – for example, food and

Table 15.5 Tactical Marketing Plan

Objectives (SMART)

- Target market(s)
- Positioning
- Financial
- Marketing

Actions	Timetable	Budget	Who is responsible?

beverage input costs are reported as operational department costs. The costs that are attributable to the marketing function, are:

- Market research expenses
- Distribution (commissions to intermediaries)
- Marketing communication activities
- Sales team (salaries, travel costs, support materials and training)
- Customer database management.

In Chapter 9 we provided a detailed discussion of Marcom budgeting. Budgeting in the marketing plan is closely linked to limits set by the corporate financial plan, and marketers have to work within industry norms of 2–6 percent of sales.

Implementation

There are three main aspects to the implementation of any marketing plan:

1 Assigning the roles and responsibilities for resourcing and executing the plan to individuals and organizations
2 Engaging and obtaining the commitment of those people and organizations to ensure that the plan is successfully implemented
3 Designing a process to track the performance of the plan against revenue targets and costs assumptions.

Marketing plans do not simply involve marketing people. Operational units (such as food and beverage) and service departments (such as engineering or front-office) influence customer experience, and need to understand their roles in delivering customer satisfaction and creating customer retention. Marketing plans also need the support of those who control the allocation of resources. A unit marketing plan might need to be endorsed by the division; a divisional marketing plan might need to go the corporate level for funding.

All the hard work in researching and compiling a marketing plan can be wasted if a company fails to communicate with employees. Customer-contact employees are often unaware of the marketing plan's goals, strategies and tactics, and of their role in it. Chapter 12 emphasized the importance of effective employee/management communications. Involving employees in the preparation of the marketing plan provides a good opportunity to facilitate that communication process. Hospitality employees can – indeed they should – be involved in the situation audit. The employees can provide useful insights into how customers view the facilities and service, and often know the strengths and weaknesses of an operation better than management. Also, employees are very aware of competitors. They may have worked for the competition or have friends working in competitor organizations, or even patronize competitors' food and beverage outlets. Finally, customer-contact employees need to be aware of what is happening during the implementation of events and campaigns, in case customers ask them any questions.

Marketing insight	**The Importance of Communicating Marketing Campaigns to Customer-contact Employees**
	Research revealed that front-desk employees in many group-owned British hotels were not aware of the details of their own company's loyalty scheme (Abram Hawkes plc and ICLP plc, 1998). Clearly, a requirement of the successful promotion of an in-house loyalty program is that front-desk staff should know the details of what they are meant to be selling. The same principle applies to food and beverage staff who have to implement marketing action plans in the restaurants and bars.

External persons and organizations may also need to be educated about their role in the plan's execution – for example, intermediaries, consortium partners, franchisees, management contractors, independent sales representatives, and advertising and public relations agencies. Management also needs to communicate their strategic marketing plans effectively to other stakeholders, especially banks and any institutional shareholders.

Controls – 'how do we know we are getting there?'

The penultimate stage of this generic marketing planning process is to design a system to monitor and control the plan's implementation. The key concerns here are to ensure that there is no unacceptable variance between the plan's revenue targets and anticipated costs, and those that are actually achieved. Control mechanisms are therefore mostly concerned with tactical implementations. Unfortunately, there is no such thing as a perfect marketing plan! External events beyond the marketer's control can have a major impact on both revenues and costs – for example, governments may alter their tax regime, resulting in lower consumer disposable income and reduced expenditure on leisure products; suppliers may increase prices, resulting in higher costs. Internal conditions can also influence performance against plan: key employees might leave the company, or there might be publicity about a company's failure of a kitchen hygiene inspection. Controls are necessary to detect, correct and prevent unacceptable variances from the plan's objectives and cost profile. The key to control is setting SMART objectives. Without SMART objectives, managers have nothing against which to compare performance. There are five stages in the control process:

1 Set SMART objectives
2 Establish a reporting process to keep management informed of progress against targets
3 Monitor performance
4 Identify significant variations from target
5 Take corrective action.

Control measures can include financial performance – sales, achieved room rate, occupancy and yield; customer mix ratios; changes in market share; changes in brand awareness and brand image; number of enquiries generated and number of hits on the website; number of bookings (the conversion ratio from enquiries to bookings); changes in the customer satisfaction index.

Providing the objectives are SMART, then variance from the plan can easily be detected when it occurs. Marketing managers need to establish whether variance is minor or major, and whether it affects one market segment or all markets. If the variance is a minor underperformance for a short period in one market segment – say weekend leisure breaks in the North, in January and February, due to poor weather – then it might be tolerated. If it is significant and affects all markets, then urgent action needs to be taken. Appropriate actions might include adapting the tactics, revisiting the strategy or, in extreme circumstances, changing the SMART objectives if they are no longer realistic. Overperformance against plan can also be problematic. This happens when there is too much demand on a property. For example, a hotel might have a commitment to a tour operator for a season of bookings, but changes in the exchange rate have made the location more popular than forecast. This could result in an overbooking situation on a regular basis, and lead to difficulties.

Figure 15.5 summarizes the marketing plan.

Contingency planning

Although the generic marketing planning process described above is founded upon a rigorous SWOT analysis, many companies also develop contingency plans. Contingency planning recognizes that the key assumptions upon which the marketing plan is formulated may be incorrect, and contingency plans are formulated on 'what if?' scenarios – for example, what if our major intermediary is acquired by a competitor? What if a major tour operator customer that has booked a block of rooms ceases trading? Only the major risks are considered in contingency planning.

Contingency planning has become more important as a result of dramatic events that have had a serious impact on hospitality companies. Health scares caused by epidemics such as SARS and foot and mouth, and terrorist activities like the attacks on American cities on 11 September 2001, temporarily destroy demand for hospitality and tourism in all markets (see Case study 15.1). In these circumstances, public health and safety are the most important issues, and price does not influence demand. Hospitality companies respond to these crises by reducing costs as far as possible – especially pay-roll costs. As consumer confidence gradually returns, companies re-ignite their marketing activity to encourage customers to return, often using price-led promotions. The strategic marketing plan should always include a budget item for contingencies. This provides funds to enable the company to take advantage of an unforeseen opportunity, or to respond to a downturn in demand by increasing marketing activity.

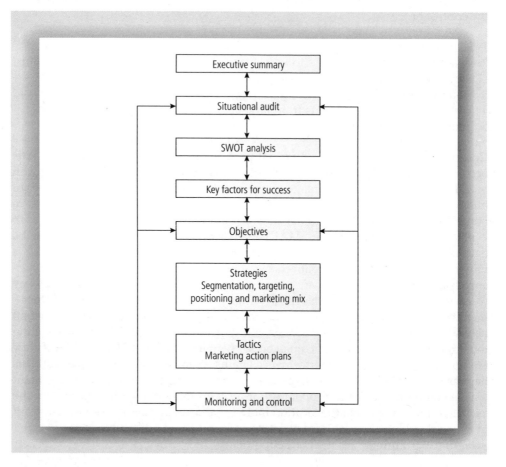

Figure 15.5 The marketing plan (source: McDonald, 1999)

Case study

15.1 Kowloon Shangri-La, Hong Kong

The war in Iraq and the outbreak of SARS caused the high-tariff hotels in Hong Kong to experience a drop in occupancy to 14 percent in April 2003 as travelers avoided flying in the region (Chan, 2003). Restaurants suffered a similar fall in business, as local people were unwilling to meet in crowded places. The Kowloon Shangri-La responded to the crisis by accelerating its refurbishment program whilst the bedrooms and public areas were not busy. The redecorating and 're-imaging' program was brought forward and completed by September. A letter was sent to regular customers explaining the situation, providing reassurance about the stringent hygiene precautions in the hotel (nobody connected to the Kowloon Shangri-La contracted SARS), and looking forward to welcoming them back soon.

Evaluation – 'how do we know we have arrived?'

This is the final step of the generic marketing planning process. Shortly after the conclusion of a planning period, event or campaign, the marketing team needs to evaluate results. The comparison of actual performance with the SMART objectives across all the areas of the business, with a commentary explaining the reasons why, provides useful information for the preparation of the next marketing plan. Companies repeat the successfully tried and tested tactics of previous years, and aim to learn from less-effective activities. Indeed, marketing is a continuous activity. The cycle of forward-planning the next campaign whilst implementing the current marketing action plan and evaluating recent activity is carried out simultaneously.

Criticisms of marketing planning

Critics of marketing planning claim that the uncertainty of the future makes long-term planning unreliable and costly, and that marketing strategies should emerge as a management reaction to changes in the environment. Clearly, a strategic marketing plan can be completely undermined when disease, terrorism or war suddenly break out. However, the planning methods and tools we cite here can be helpful because they provide a framework for organizing marketing activity on a regular basis. Other critics of formalized marketing planning portray examples of successful entrepreneurs (such as Richard Branson, of the Virgin Group) who use their flair, intuition and vision in building dynamic businesses, and suggest that marketing is all about spontaneous ideas. However, companies cannot rely upon spontaneous thinking to solve all their problems, and the marketing planning process can allow opportunities for creativity and flexibility, via contingency planning, within a systematic framework. A valid criticism of organizational planning is the focus on financial matters. Although companies pay lip service to the concept of a customer orientation, the reality is that budgeting, with its emphasis on sales generation, cost control and profit engineering, is dominant in the hospitality industry – and the influence of marketing always seems to be subordinate to financial imperatives.

Conclusion

Marketing planning provides hospitality companies with a structured approach to planning for the future. Although the future is uncertain, environmental trends can be identified and their impact on the hospitality company can be consequently evaluated. Although marketing planning has its critics, primarily because it can be a costly, time-consuming, bureaucratic process, there is little doubt that such planning in any organization improves the chances of survival and success. However, marketing planning alone cannot be a guarantee of success.

In this chapter, we have explained:

- The contexts within which marketing plans are constructed – corporate, division, unit and department
- Two different types of marketing plan – strategic and tactical; strategic marketing planning typically takes a three- to five-year timeframe; whilst tactical planning covers a twelve-month period or less
- A generic marketing planning process comprising nine stages – setting vision, mission, values; situational analysis; establishing objectives; performing market segmentation, targeting and positioning; developing marketing mixes; creating a budget; organizing the plan's implementation; setting controls; and evaluation of the plan's performance
- That objectives should be *S*pecific, *M*easurable, *A*chievable, *R*ealistic, and carried out within a set *T*imetable (SMART)
- That contingency planning provides an alternative in the event of a major deviation from plan
- The key tools in strategic marketing planning, which include the BCG matrix, SWOT analysis, PESTE analysis, gap analysis and the Ansoff matrix
- Why marketing planning has been criticized as being bureaucratic and pointless, given the unpredictability of the future
- That marketing planning provides a structured approach to organizing marketing activity.

Review questions

Now check your understanding by answering the following questions:

1 Discuss the role of marketing planning in hospitality organizations
2 Explain the strategic marketing plan process, illustrating your answer with examples from the hospitality industry
3 Explain why control is important in marketing planning.

References and further reading

Abram Hawkes plc and ICLP plc (1998). *Review of UK Hotel Loyalty Programmes.* Abram Hawkes and ICLP.

Chan, B. (2003). Sharing the experience. *Hospitality Magazine (HCIMA)*, 18–19.

Kotler, P., Bowen, J. and Makens, J. (2003). *Marketing for Hospitality and Tourism*, 3rd edn. Prentice Hall.

Lewis, R. C. and Chambers, R. E. (2000). *Marketing Leadership in Hospitality: Foundations and Practice*. John Wiley.

McDonald, M. (1999). *Marketing Plans*. Butterworth-Heinemann.

Porter, M. E. (1980). *Competitive Strategy: Techniques for Analyzing Industries and Competitors*. Free Press.

Reich, A. Z. (1997). *Marketing Management for Hospitality and Industry: A Strategic Approach*. John Wiley & Sons.

Treacy, M. and Wiersema, F. (1995). *The Discipline of Market Leaders*. HarperCollins.

Index